STUDIES IN THE EARLY HISTORY OF BRITAIN

General Editor: Nicholas Brooks

Wales in the Early Middle Ages

Wales

in the Early Middle Ages

Wendy Davies

Leicester University Press   1982

First published in 1982 by Leicester University Press
First published in 1982 in the United States of America by
Humanities Press Inc., Atlantic Highlands, NJ 07716,
and also distributed by them in North America

Designed by Douglas Martin
Set in Compugraphic Trump Mediaeval
by A.B. Printers Limited, 71 Cannock Street, Leicester
Printed and bound in Great Britain by The Pitman Press, Bath

British Library Cataloguing in Publication Data

Davies, Wendy
Wales in the early Middle Ages. — (Studies in the early history of Britain)
1. Wales — History — to 1536
I. Title II. Series
942.9 DA714

ISBN 0-7185-1163-8
ISBN 0-7185-1235-9 Pbk

Contents

Foreword

The aim of the Studies in the Early History of Britain is to promote works of the highest scholarship which open up virgin fields of study or which surmount the barriers of traditional academic disciplines. As interest in the origins of our society and culture grows whilst scholarship yet becomes ever more specialized, inter-disciplinary studies are needed more urgently, not only by scholars but also by students and by laymen. The series will therefore include both research monographs and works of synthesis, and also collaborative studies of important themes by several scholars whose training and expertise has lain in different fields. Our knowledge of the early Middle Ages will always be limited and fragmentary, so progress will only be made if the work of the historian embraces that of the philologist, the archaeologist, the geographer, the numismatist, the art historian and the liturgicist — to name only the most obvious. The need to cross and to remove academic frontiers also explains the extension of the geographical range from that of the previous series of Studies in Early English History to include the whole island of Britain. The change would have been welcomed by the editor of the earlier series, the late Professor H.P.R. Finberg, whose pioneering work helped to inspire, or to provoke, the interest of a new generation of early medievalists in the relations of Britons and Saxons. The approach of the new series is therefore deliberately wide-ranging, and will seek to avoid being unduly insular. Early medieval Britain can only be understood in the context of contemporary developments in Ireland and on the Continent.

Wendy Davies here inaugurates a series of regional volumes covering the country. Leading scholars have each been invited to provide a brief but comprehensive and up-to-date synthesis of the settlement and history of one of the main regions of early medieval Britain. Whatever the particular special interests of the authors, each volume will seek to provide the layman with a well-illustrated and critical introduction to the history of his own region. Wales presents particularly challenging problems to the early medievalist. Archaeology and place-name studies are still in their infancy whilst the historical and legal sources present acute problems of interpretation which are only just beginning to be tackled. No-one can hope to achieve a definitive study for many years to come, but it has been my privilege to allow Dr Davies the space to respond to the urgent need for a critical modern interpretation of early Welsh history that is aware of the dangers of the myths perpetuated by late sources.

University of St Andrews, September 1981   N. P. Brooks

For John and Hilda

Preface

Despite the difficulty of its subject, I have enjoyed writing this book for two principal reasons. Firstly, I found it unexpectedly enjoyable to write with the primary intention of communicating, rather than using writing itself as a means of investigation; I hope, therefore, that the book is intelligible to people who have no knowledge of any medieval history and no knowledge of any Welsh history, though I also hope that it may contain something of interest for the specialist. Secondly, I have particularly enjoyed talking to the people on whose expertise I have leaned and the opportunity to think hard about their work. I owe a debt of gratitude to many, therefore, for their time and patience in answering my questions and for their generosity in informing me of work in progress, and I should especially mention the staff of all the Archaeological Trusts of Wales in this respect. I am also extremely grateful for the conversations and arguments that I have had with two sets of students: those who studied early medieval Wales in the University of Birmingham between 1973 and 1977 and those who listened to my lectures in the University of Cambridge in 1977 and 1978. The stimulus of teaching forced me to confront problems I should have preferred to avoid, and I was fortunate in having students of exceptional vigour and critical ability. Of the many individuals who have helped, I should particularly like to thank Nicholas Brooks for asking me to write this book, and Leicester University Press for undertaking to publish it; Sally Bergin and Nazneen Razwi, at University College, London, for typing and coping so admirably with the torture of my own typescripts; Wyn Evans, Heather James, Morfydd Owen and David Rollason, for commenting generously and constructively on particular chapters; and Tom Davis and Chris Wickham for undertaking the labour of reading and criticizing the whole work. Though I would not wish to associate any of them with the errors and idiosyncracies of my approach, their help has been invaluable. I would finally extend my thanks to John and Hilda Padel for their great generosity and support during the years that I have been writing the work.

Bucknell, September 1980   Wendy Davies

A considerable number of valuable books, articles and reports has been published since this book first went to press in the autumn of 1980. These include some essential source studies: K. Hughes, 'The A text of *Annales Cambriae*', in *idem, Celtic Britain in the Early Middle Ages* (1980), 86-100; J-C. Poulin, 'A propos du diocèse de Dol', *Francia*, VI (1978), 610-15; H. Guillotel, 'Les origines du ressort de l'évêché de Dol', *Mémoires de la Société d'Histoire et d'Archéologie de Bretagne*, LIV (1977), 31-68; A. Peden, 'Science and philosophy in Wales at the time of the Norman Conquest', *Cambridge Medieval Celtic Studies*, II (1981), 47-72. There is an easily available new translation of *Annales Cambriae* in *Nennius*, ed. and trans. John Morris (1980), 45-9. Recent archaeological work in Wales is briefly summarized in *Archaeology in Wales*, xix (1979) and xx (1980): reports on Bayvil, Bryn-y-Castell, Dinorben, Gaerwen (= Cae Capel Eithin), Hen Domen, Llandough, Llanrhos and Rhuddlan are of particular interest. Charles Thomas has also produced *A Provisional List of Imported Pottery in post-Roman western Britain and Ireland* (Institute of Cornish Studies, 1981). There has, as always, been less comment on particular historical problems, but the institutions of the Welsh church are discussed by K. Hughes in 'The Celtic church: is this a valid concept?', *Cambridge Medieval Celtic Studies*, I (1981), 1-15, and many aspects of late Romano-British Christianity and its relationship to the British church of the fifth and sixth centuries are discussed by Charles Thomas in *Christianity in Roman Britain to AD 500* (1981). Finally, although Wales is peripheral to most of the material in D. Hill, *An Atlas of Anglo-Saxon England* (1981), it includes many useful maps of developments on the eastern side of Offa's Dyke, developments which are often pertinent to the course of Welsh history.

List of illustrations

Acknowledgments and conventions

I have used the term 'pre-Conquest' in this book to refer to the period before the first Norman onslaught, and the term 'Conquest' to refer to the period of initial Norman success, that is between c.1070 and 1093. 'Pre-Conquest', therefore, is loosely used of Wales before the Norman impact and not, as it might be, of Wales before it was completely over-run. I have used the term 'early medieval' to refer to the total period covered in the book, that is the fifth to the eleventh centuries, inclusive. Unless otherwise indicated, or noted in the Bibliography, all references to texts are by page number of the edition or translation. The names of places have been spelled in their modern Welsh forms, as listed by the late Professor Richards in *Welsh Administrative and Territorial Units* (1969), except where an English form — like Cardiff or Carmarthen — is so common that to use the Welsh would cause unnecessary confusion to the English reader; name forms quoted from texts, i.e. not modernized, have not been italicized, for ease of reading. The modern county names — Dyfed, Gwynedd, Clwyd, Powys, Glamorgan, Gwent, especially — are sometimes useful, but they cover very large areas and are often not sufficiently precise in defining locations; the pre-1974 English counties are smaller, and familiar to most people, and provide a more immediate means of reference. I have therefore often used these to indicate approximate area, but have sometimes also used the even smaller areas of the Welsh administrative units — commotes and cantrefs — where this appeared to be more helpful. The extent and location of these varying terms of reference are indicated on the maps overleaf.

The author and publishers wish to thank all those who have kindly given permission for illustrations to be reproduced, as cited in the captions; particular thanks are due to the University of Wales Press for assistance in obtaining material for reproduction from V.E. Nash-Williams's *The Early Christian Monuments of Wales*, to A.G. McCormick, who drew the maps and diagrams, and to Terrence James for providing many of the photographs.

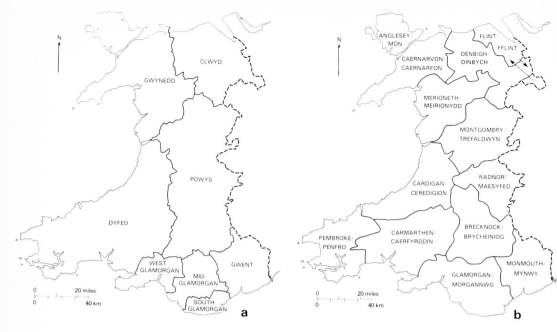

Figure 1. a Wales: post-1974 counties;
b pre-1974 counties;
c cantrefs and commotes
(after D. Thomas, ed., *Wales, A New
Study*, 1977, fig. 2; M. Richards, *Welsh Administrative and
Territorial Units*, 1969,
nos. 1 and 3).

Introduction

It is not possible to write a history of early medieval Wales that will stand up to the requirements of modern scholarship. Interesting though the subject matter is, the available source material is quite inadequate to resolve the simplest problems, and it is no longer acceptable to take material written at a late date and project its implications backwards over several centuries. There is very, very little written material that survives from the pre-Conquest period, and that which does survive is often corrupt and fragmentary; there may well be more physical evidence that is relevant, to be recovered by excavation and by analysis of the landscape, but work on these areas is still in its early stages. Any history, therefore, becomes more of an exercise in speculative imagination than a sober, well-documented analysis, however rigorous the writer might attempt to be. The exercise is, nevertheless, worth undertaking: some questions have to be asked, and even if no-one can be sure of the answers the act of asking them is not without its value. There is, moreover, a point in writing a history that indicates, and even emphasizes, the uncertainties and the lacunae: it is useful to be aware of what we do not know, to pare away accumulated traditions and unquestioned assumptions and to isolate that which may be said with some certainty amidst the mass of suppositions. In writing this book, however, I have also tried to note the content of the later law tracts where thematically relevant. This is not because I consider them acceptable as pre-Conquest evidence but because I think it is valuable to weigh their import against the unelaborated earlier fragments. They are noted, therefore, for essentially comparative reasons: the comparison is often instructive. It is necessary, then, to be vigilant about the source material available, and the use made of it, and in all cases I would ask the reader — by reference to the Appendix — to balance the interpretation I have put upon the surviving fragments against a sober assessment of their nature and limitations. I have for this reason given references to English translations where they are available.

It is a good time to consider old assumptions and ask new questions, although it is probably too soon for any effective synthesis, for in the past generation, and in particular in the past ten years, exceptionally valuable new work has been undertaken in three particular fields, work that is still in progress. Archaeological investigation must provide the greatest opportunity for increasing the corpus of knowledge of the early medieval period, and, with the establishment of the Archaeological Trusts for the new administrative counties in the mid-1970s, alongside those archaeologists already working in Wales, the work of systematic collection and recording has received a considerable stimulus. There is every reason to expect a steady flow of new material in the future, in addition to more sophisticated analysis of the extant corpus. The second field of development lies in the very difficult area of Welsh law already mentioned, in the studies which have been undertaken by a group of scholars working together for the past 20 years or so, often supported by the Board of Celtic Studies. Here the problems are quite different, for they concern the understanding and isolation of different strata within generations of accumulated practice, all recorded relatively late in the Middle Ages. Much of this material must have a relevance for the pre-Conquest period in Wales — and hence my concern to note its essential content — but it has always been difficult to define the appropriate parts. The very close textual studies which are now being undertaken — though they obviously have great relevance for the late medieval period too — may well succeed in defining a corpus of material of considerable significance in understanding the social and political structure of pre-Norman Wales. Lastly, and more miscellaneously, the range of detailed textual and linguistic studies of early medieval sources that has been published during the past ten years is beginning to transform the subject. Such work makes it possible to begin to understand the few sources that do survive; without them, one could not begin — or begin again — the business of interpretation.

This book is about Wales between the termination of Roman political control of Britain in the early fifth century and the beginning of Norman conquest in the late eleventh century. Though a period of quite exceptional obscurity, it would be possible to write much more on and make much more of the political history of this period than I have done, even allowing for the source problems. Questions other than the political are equally important, however, and require equal treatment in a general work. The reader who requires a political framework should therefore turn to chapter 4, but I have preferred to give a different sort of overall framework to the problems here considered.

Such Roman military garrisons as remained in Wales after the second century, which were not many, appear to have been withdrawn by the late fourth century and the formal contacts of central Roman government with the provincial administration of Britain appear to have ended in the first decade of the fifth century. Membership of the Roman Empire left an uneven impression on Wales, however, and by the fourth century the character of the South-East — with its many villas and well-worked estates — was in many respects distinct from the rest of Wales. This Roman background, and in particular the experience of having been part of a wide network of economic relationships, continued to mark the South-East, conditioning development over the next three centuries in particular. By the eleventh century, however, the distinction was much less clear. Indeed, one of the most interesting trends of the early medieval period as a whole is the gradual loss of these distinctive characteristics.

The Normans conquered England in 1066 and the Norman conquest of Wales began within four years of this. Unlike the conquest of England it was an extremely piecemeal affair with no centralized direction, which began from the strongpoints of Chester, Shrewsbury and Hereford in the marches and which was conducted independently by different Norman lords. Although much of Wales appeared to be in Norman hands by the early 1090s, there was a revolt in north Wales in 1094, which spread to the South; as a consequence the Normans effectively withdrew from the North in 1098, thereby ensuring north Welsh independence until the Edwardian conquest of the late thirteenth century. The marches, the South-East and much of the

South-West — all termed the March of Wales — remained largely under Norman political control, however, though it was a control exercised by many lords in many independent lordships. Conflict over the extent of the March and conflict between the immigrants and the Welsh supplied much of the political interest of the twelfth century, for the bounds of the March and the relationships between leaders were by no means fixed by the progress of the initial conquest. The conquest of Wales, therefore, was something which took more than 200 years to complete.

The period between Roman Empire and Norman Conquest is a long one and must contain many of the determinants of the character of Wales — Welsh Wales — in the better-documented struggles of the central and later Middle Ages. I have tried to make clear what hints of this pre-Conquest development are contained in the all too few and fragmentary early medieval sources, and I have tried to make the character of these sources clear in the Appendix. Political and social developments, however, did not happen in a vacuum and were themselves conditioned by the physical shape of Wales. Though it is important that as historians we are always aware of the nature of the available sources, we should also remember the immense influence of land and landscape on society, religion and politics, as well as on economy. It is proper to begin, therefore, with the land itself.

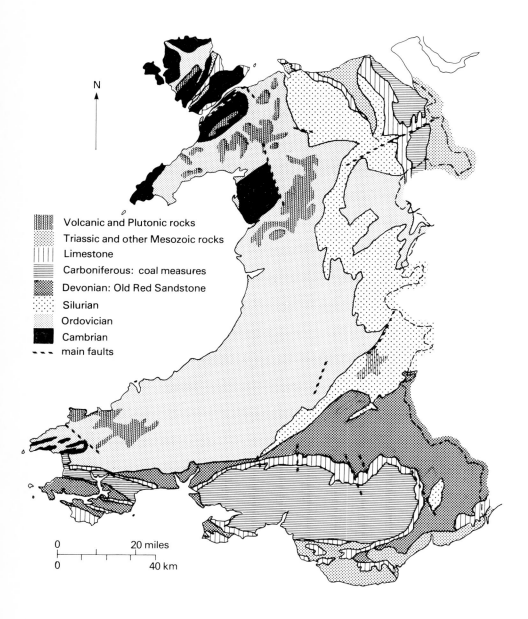

N

Volcanic and Plutonic rocks
Triassic and other Mesozoic rocks
Limestone
Carboniferous: coal measures
Devonian: Old Red Sandstone
Silurian
Ordovician
Cambrian
- - - main faults

0   20 miles
0   40 km

Figure 2. Wales: solid geology (after W. Rees, *An Historical Atlas of Wales*, 1959, pl.2).

1 Land, Landscape and Environment

The land of Wales is dominated by the mountains which form its core; hence, the peaks and the plateaux which delight the modern tourist have conditioned and continue to condition economic exploitation, communications and political development. The good arable lands, the areas which attract most settlement, are largely coastal and are in effect isolated from each other by the mountains. Modern geographers, therefore, conceive of Wales as a central mountainous heartland, surrounded by the coastal regions of the North-West and Anglesey, the West, the South-West, the Vale of Glamorgan and Gower, and also by the borderlands which were always more or less open to English influence — northern, middle and south-eastern.[1] Wales is also a land of old, hard rocks: the oldest — in Anglesey and Llŷn — are now somewhat worn down; the next oldest, Cambrian — in Meirionydd and Arfon — are hard grits which produce rugged outcrops; placed against them are the Ordovician then Silurian strata which cover more than half of Wales, curving round from Denbigh, through Radnor, to Pembroke, with stretches of volcanic rock piled up among them — in the North-West especially, the South-West and round Builth. To the south, in Brecon, lie the newer belts of Old Red Sandstone and then the carboniferous rocks which include the coalfield — sands, grits and limestones. Only in the Vale of Glamorgan and the north-eastern borders do we find the newer Mesozoic sandstones and deposits of limestone (see fig. 2)[2]. The north-east/south-west folding of the old rocks, pushed against the oldest in the North-West, remains a dominant influence on communications.

The land is not merely old. More than a quarter of Wales is over 1,000 feet high and there are no vast stretches of lowland as there are in England. Giraldus Cambrensis, travelling in the late twelfth century, reacted strongly to the peaks of north Wales: 'This territory of Cynan, and especially Meirionydd, is the rudest and roughest of all the Welsh districts. The mountains are very high, with narrow ridges and a great number of very sharp peaks all jumbled together in confusion. If the shepherds who shout to each other and exchange comments from these lofty summits should ever decide to meet, it would take them almost the whole day to climb down and up again'.[3] In fact, it is the series of depositions of the old rocks which has largely determined the variations in the present upland structure. Indeed, though the volcanic rocks do form peaks and protrusions, much of the mountain area consists of high rounded plateaux, punctuated by trough-like valleys carved out by glaciation at a considerable altitude. Other, deeper valleys project into the central massif, however, and their rivers — the Severn, the Wye, the Tywi, the Teifi, the Usk, the Dee — run for long distances to the sea, dropping hundreds of feet from the central watershed. Giraldus, therefore, contrasted with the summits of the Black Mountains 'the deep vale of Ewias, which is shut in on all sides by a circle of lofty

Figure 3. An upland glaciated valley in the Wye valley near Rhayader
(SN 955695) (photograph Terrence James; copyright reserved).

mountains and which is no more than three arrow-shots in width' and went
on to comment on its mild, damp, cloudy aspect.[4]

Rainfall is now high in Wales, which lies across a westerly wind belt. The
heaviest falls on the highest mountains, so that the borderlands lie in a rain
shadow, experiencing an average rainfall — like Anglesey — in the order of 30-
40 ins a year. Snowdonia and the Brecon Beacons, by contrast, get over 90 ins
a year. Modern, English, annual rainfall, popularly regarded as heavy, is
much lower and averages just over 30 ins. Unlike rain over most of the
European landmass, more rain falls in winter in Wales and the spring is therefore relatively dry; rainfall is, nevertheless, fairly evenly distributed throughout the year and this means that the risk of drought is slight. Temperature
range is similarly moderate: the warming influence of the sea on three sides
of Wales prevents extremes of cold in winter; and the relatively large amount
of high land means that temperatures do not rise very high in much of the
country and do not begin to rise until late in the spring. Modern geographers
will stress, however, the great range of climatic variation induced by purely
local features; though parts of the upland have a sub-Arctic climate even
today, the broad distinction between upland and lowland is modified by the
fact that inland valleys are subject to fog and frost and to night-time
temperature inversions while some high valleys do not suffer shading in the
early morning and late evening and do not therefore cool at the rate of the
lowland.[5]

All of this is significant because of its effects upon the range of crops that
can be grown, and on the success with which they can be cultivated. Most

food crops need sufficient warmth for the seed to germinate, sufficient moisture to assist growth, and a long enough growing season to ripen. Professor Le Roy Ladurie, citing Slicher van Bath, has demonstrated how specific is the range of variations that produces ideal wheat-growing conditions: late September — damp; October, November to 20 December — rather dry, not too mild; 21 December to the end of February — rather dry, no strong wind, no frost below − 10°; March — no frost after germination has begun; April — regular rain, sun; May to 15 June — rain, warmth but not too hot; 16 June to 10 July — cool, cloudy, not too much rain; late July, August, early September — dry, warm, sunny but not too hot.[6] He argues that the critical factor in successful production is rainfall: too much means disaster. In some areas of Wales, and certainly at higher altitudes, the summer is too short to provide an adequate growing season while even in the lowlands there is often too much rainfall and too little heat to guarantee an adequate ripening of cereals. All crops do not have the same requirements, however, and oats, barley and rye will grow successfully at much higher altitudes than will wheat.[7] The length of the growing season, moreover, varies not just in relation to altitude and proximity to the sea but also in relation to purely local factors. Maps of first and last frosts, and of the start of the modern growing season, are notable therefore in emphasizing the exceptionally fortunate position of St David's, and the only slightly less fortunate position of Gower, the Vale of Glamorgan, Llŷn and Anglesey (see fig. 4).[8]

We should expect the early medieval climate to be much as that of today, though warming somewhat towards the year A.D. 1000 and noticeably more so in the eleventh and twelfth centuries, the so-called 'little climatic optimum'.[9] The suggestions are that the annual temperature variation may have been slightly greater: winters were a little colder than at present c.850 and not much warmer by the twelfth century. Great frosts are characteristic of European winters between the fifth and tenth centuries, and the skates found in Viking levels in York may give some human meaning to the relative figures.[10] Temperatures had probably dropped at the outset of our period from the more favourable climate of Roman times. These centuries also seem to have seen an increase in rainfall, and floods were particularly noticed by Europeans in the late fifth and sixth centuries.[11] Hence, the climate of early medieval Wales probably experienced two major changes — a drop in temperature and increase in rainfall at the start, to levels below those of the present; and a gradual warming, intensifying at the very end, to levels above the modern.

The temperature changes of the fifth and sixth centuries must have shortened the growing season in some areas and may have provoked some abandonment of mountain arable. Indeed, it has been suggested that the 'serviceable upland' of lowland England lay exhausted by c.600, and we may imagine some comparable deterioration for Wales.[12] At the other end of the period, by contrast, in the twelfth and thirteenth centuries, evidence of cultivation has been noted in upland areas of Wales. It may well be, then, that productive capacity experienced a sharp downward jolt at the opening of our period but that gradually over several centuries conditions became more favourable until, by 1200, they were better than those of today. Indeed, in work which has been carried out at Cefn Graeanog at the north-eastern end of

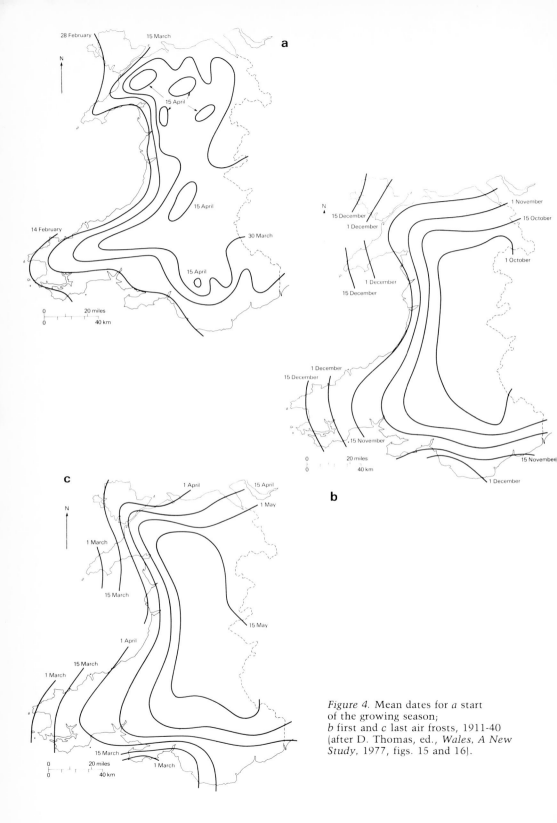

Figure 4. Mean dates for *a* start
of the growing season;
b first and *c* last air frosts, 1911-40
(after D. Thomas, ed., *Wales, A New
Study,* 1977, figs. 15 and 16).

the Llŷn peninsula, changes in the flora and fossil fauna might suggest that we have some evidence from the period of early medieval climatic change in north Wales and of its catastrophic effects.[13] Though the interpretation of the evidence from this site remains controversial, it is clear that occupation ended in the late or post-Roman period and that wheat could no longer be grown (whether or not the period of change may be confined to the seventh century is the matter at issue). We should expect, then, that Wales was as wet in the early medieval period as it is now, or even wetter, that the tendency of the rivers to flood because they drop so far would have been as great, and that the relatively high rainfall would have been similarly contrasted with that of England.

The weather and the seasons cause as much comment as the landscape itself in medieval Welsh authors, comment which largely supports the impression conveyed by the modern evidence discussed above. Growth in May was particularly noted: harvest in autumn, drinking in winter, cuckoos in spring, brown furrows in May and sprouting shoots.[14] The weather might be more than the object of a passing comment:

> Cold the lake-bed from winter's blast;
> Dried reeds, stalks broken;
> Angry wind, woods stripped naked.
>
> Snow is falling, white hoar-frost.
> Shield idle on an old shoulder.
> Wind intense, shoots are frozen.
>
> Snow is falling on the slope.
> Stallion confined; lean cattle.
> No summer day is today.
>
> Storm on the mountain, rivers embroiled,
> Floors of houses flooded:
> To one's sight, the world is a sea.[15]

Snow did come in some areas, but the experience of it lying from the beginning of January till the feast of Patrick (March), as it did in 1047, was clearly unusual.[16] Rain was more of a problem: destructive floods in the lowland; the swollen height of the river Neath; ditches that flowed with streams in a deluge of rain; frequent coastal flooding, in which the sea destroyed buildings. The images are consistent and powerful, though Rhigyfarch noted near St David's — an area distinguished by its mildness — that the winter's torrent became a tiny stream in summer and the land could be 'drained of water'.[17]

The Landscape, Modern and Medieval

The modern landscape changes from the high rounded plateaux of large areas of central Wales, cut by its deeper and shallower valleys, to the rocks and summits of Snowdonia in the North-West and again to the long, steep cuts of the coal valleys in the South-East. Around the mountain the lowland changes

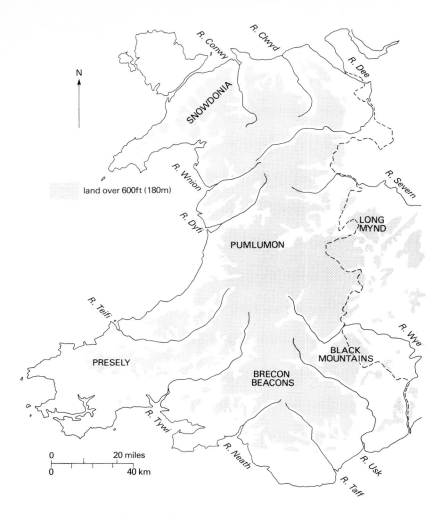

N

land over 600ft (180m)

SNOWDONIA

R. Conwy

R. Clwyd

R. Dee

R. Wnion

R. Dyfi

PUMLUMON

R. Severn

LONG MYND

R. Teifi

R. Wye

PRESELY

BLACK MOUNTAINS

BRECON BEACONS

R. Tywi

R. Neath

R. Usk

R. Taff

0   20 miles
0   40 km

Figure 5. Wales: relief (after W. Rees, *An Historical Atlas of Wales*, 1959, pl.3).

character again and again. The narrow strip along the northern and north-western coasts broadens into the windswept, enclosed pastures of the Llŷn peninsula and extends over much of Anglesey; both Llŷn and Anglesey have their stony outcrops and both have their milder, sheltered parts, but the predominant impression is of a rather bare lowland. South of the Dyfi estuary the coastal strip broadens again to form the western coastlands, an area of more trees, more settlements and more use, and these in their turn extend south into the peninsula of Pembroke and Carmarthen. Here, in the extreme West by St David's, the land is bare and windswept like Llŷn, also largely enclosed, with the Presely Mountains jutting out to the north; over much of the peninsula, however, the land seems lush: woods and trees, undulating hills and mixed farming are characteristic, and the dense network of roads and settlements bears witness to centuries of use by man. Moving east round the coast the mountain nears the Channel again by Swansea and Neath, leaving the long-used lands of Gower projecting into the sea and effectively separating South-West from South-East. The coastal strip gradually broadens into the highly fertile lowlands of the Vale of Glamorgan, again enclosed and given over to mixed farming, while in the East beyond Cardiff a 'westward thrusting tongue of the English lowland' forms the undulating hills and fields of Gwent and Ergyng (south-west Hereford). Here too, as in the South-West, the land is much used and much settled. From Gwent northwards along the marches, the traveller moves through the flatter arable lands of north Hereford into the enclosed, sheltered, hilly, pastoral country of the middle borderlands, and finally into the less extensive lowlands of the North-East, which turn eastwards towards the Cheshire plain, before reaching the coast again.

The modern landscape is both a useful and a misleading pointer to that of the early medieval period. Over much of the mountain heartland, with its few and isolated settlements and its rare enclosures, the modern aspect bears some relationship to that of 1,000 years ago, but the nature and extent of the vegetation would almost certainly have been different. The natural mixed deciduous woodland — birch, alder, oak — may well have extended up to a height of 2,000ft, except on ill-drained or steeply sloping land, and except in the places where neolithic, bronze age and iron age man, and Roman military requirements and forest management, had cleared it. The modern upland landscape, dominated by grass and conifers, has been largely determined by the twin agents of sheep and the Forestry Commission. The planting of conifers has been an essentially twentieth-century development — but it has the virtue of indicating how high trees can grow; extensive grazing by sheep did not begin until the thirteenth century and has caused considerable limitation of the available vegetation. The early medieval upland landscape, therefore, would have had fewer uninterrupted, broad expanses of grass, would have been more mixed in its vegetation, with patches of scrubby woodland, but would have had as comparably few settlements as today.[18] The Domesday surveyor of north Wales accordingly commented that most of Rhos and Rhufoniog was 'wood and moor' and could not be ploughed.[19] The banks and hedges, the roads and buildings of the modern coastlands, on the other hand, are almost invariably the product of man's efforts in the centuries after the Norman Conquest. We should attempt to envisage for the early medieval period a landscape in those areas with fewer roads and settlements, far fewer permanent enclosures, and — of course — more trees.

The closest we can come to sustained description of the early medieval landscape are the comments in the works of Giraldus Cambrensis, a man from Wales and travelling about Wales in the late twelfth century, a century after the first Norman incursion, although much of the earlier poetry of *Canu Llywarch Hen* betrays an intense awareness of landscape and alludes to it frequently. Giraldus will have us believe that 'The island of Anglesey is an arid stony land, rough and unattractive in appearance. It is rather like the cantref of Pebidiog, round St David's, to look at, but in its natural productivity it is quite different. The island produces far more grain than any other part of Wales. In the Welsh language it has always been called ''Mon mam Cymru'', which means ''Mona the Mother of Wales''. When crops have failed in all other regions, this island, from the richness of its soil and its abundant produce, has been able to supply all Wales'. He adds: 'I must not fail to tell you about the mountains which are called Eryri by the Welsh and by the English Snowdon, that is the Snow Mountains. They rise gradually from the land of the sons of Cynan and extend northwards near Degannwy. When looked at from Anglesey, they seem to rear their lofty summits right up to the clouds. They are thought to be so enormous and to extend so far that, as the old saying goes: ''Just as Anglesey can supply all the inhabitants of Wales with corn, so if all the herds were gathered together, Snowdon could afford sufficient pasture'' '.[20] In the South-West, on the other hand, he emphasizes the prominence of the town of Carmarthen, surely one of the significant nucleated settlements of pre-Norman Wales, even before the building of the castle and the English, Norman and Flemish settlement of the twelfth century: 'This ancient town is enclosed by brick walls, parts of which still stand. It is situated on the noble river Tywi, and surrounded by woods and meadowlands. To the east lies Cantref Mawr... a safe refuge for the inhabitants of South Wales, because of its impenetrable forests'.[21] Later he goes on to describe Pembroke as the most attractive part of the most beautiful part of Wales, at once rich in wheat and fish.[22]

Men writing between the fifth and eleventh centuries dwelled much more briefly upon their natural surroundings. The poet of *Armes Prydein* in the early tenth century commented on the contrast between forest and plain, hill and dale, and 400 years earlier Gildas had described the 'wide plains and agreeably set hills and mountains', the 'high hills and dense forests' of the land of Britain.[23] References to the large expanses of mountain are, in fact, rare, apart from the 'white hilltops' and 'gray mountain tops' of Powys in *Canu Llywarch Hen*; this must reflect the fact that most people neither lived in nor travelled through the mountains; they kept to the coastal lowlands.[24] A sense of the forest is much more evident. 'Dense oak tops', 'grass and trees', 'field and forest' are the local images of the poems, and earlier the woods and dense forests of Gildas had been clear enough.[25] The eleventh- and twelfth-century Saints' Lives sustain the picture: a wolf-infested forest was thought to have surrounded St Tatheus at Caerwent; the valley near St David's was woody, like that found by St Illtud; Illtud had come upon a thick wood with wild animals in it, and an 'unfelled' wood near Llantwit Major; St Cadog would send his monks to the woods to fetch timber while the approach of King Rhun was enough to send men of the locality off to the woods to hide.[26] The Cheshire Domesday reveals the incidence of plenty of woodland in Clwyd, and a preponderance of wood and moor in Rhos and Rhufoniog as noted above.[27] Much earlier, St Samson had to make his way through a frightening forest, quite possibly the 'impenetrable forest' of Giraldus's Cantref Mawr.[28] In the South-East the message is specified and localized by the evidence of the Llandaff charter boundaries in the ninth, tenth and eleventh centuries: here the bounds of estates commonly run through small woods and copses, giving the impression of a landscape of partly cleared, patchy woodland rather than dense forest.[29] The Cefn Graeanog pollen evidence from north-west Wales would indicate the same. We must suppose, therefore, large stretches of forest in some areas; and patchy woodland in others. In both cases, a much more wooded landscape than the present.

When Illtud found the ideal spot for his monastic settlement there were 'no mountains or infertile wilderness but a fertile open plain' and a pleasing river. Outside the mountains, however, land without settlements was often seen as bad land. Around the plains were bogs and marshes, thickets of reeds and no dry ground, valleys covered with thorns and thistles.[30] The people who went to hide from their enemies in the woods had 'secret caves... heaths and thorny thickets'.[31]

The flora (and fauna) of early medieval Wales are sometimes specified in poems and narratives. Cuckoos sing from the 'ivy-covered branch', while eagles hover about the estuaries; jays and crows and thrushes appear, if less romantically; stags and wolves were among the wild animals in the unsettled places.[32] Oak and ash, alder and holly, apples and broom and meadowsweet adorn the hills and valleys; there is brown and black heather in winter; reeds cluster in the ill-drained valleys — defeated heroes fell 'like rushes'.[33] Images of growth abound in the invective of Gildas, emphasizing the nearness of the natural world. Apart from the references in literature, some sources are concerned to list and detail available resources. Eleven species of highly valued tree are named in the laws: alder, apple, ash, beech, crab, elm, hazel, oak, thorn, willow and yew, though we know that beech was only common in the South and on the English border. The pine characteristic of the prehistoric period appears to have died out by the time that the laws were recorded, while sycamore, known to have been introduced at some point in the Middle Ages, does not appear yet.[34] In the South-East, charter boundaries again specify ninth-, tenth- and eleventh-century trees and bushes: apple, ash, broom, gorse, hazel, thorn and willow.[35] The excavations at Cefn Graeanog produced evidence of flag iris, foxglove and cow parsley as well as a range of deciduous trees comparable to the modern one.[36] The list seems long and varied, though in fact the native flora of Wales is not generally regarded as a rich one.

The effect of man on the landscape is much less noted than its natural aspects. Cattle do not seem to have wandered freely and were usually in their stalls; ploughing and furrows broke up the view of grass; dykes and ditches were dug; stones and cairns and crosses were erected — sometimes above isolated burials. When Llywri was murdered a standing stone was placed to mark the spot where he was buried, supposes the author of the Life of Cadog; Maen Gwyddog, 'the stone of Gwyddog', was used as a boundary marker in the area of Llandeilo Fawr in the ninth century; other stones, and cairns too, were often used on property boundaries in the South-East, especially in coastal parts.[37] In lowland areas of the South and of the extreme North-West the numbers of inscribed tombstones are high, and they must have formed a distinctive feature of the landscape. Some are monumentally large, and stood alone at the roadside, to be utilized as boundaries, like the 12ft Maen Madog standing on the Roman road Sarn Helen in southern Brecon; or the 6ft Maen Serth standing on a ridge at a height of nearly 1500ft in Radnor.[38] By the tenth and eleventh centuries, it is reasonable to suppose some gathering of these into churchyards, but before that many may well have been freestanding;[39] by that period churches themselves may have been notable here and there, like those occasionally noticed in the bounds of the Llandaff charters.[40] The most striking buildings, however, must have been Roman ruins, for since we now find churches built within and near old Roman forts at Caerhun, Llanbeblig and (?) Caergybi, the source of stone must have survived throughout the early

Middle Ages. Giraldus's comments on the walls of Carmarthen have already been quoted, and he became eloquent on the remains still surviving at Caerleon in the twelfth century:

> Caerleon is the modern name of the City of the Legions.... It was constructed with great care by the Romans, the walls being built of brick. You can still see many vestiges of its one-time splendour. There are immense palaces, which, with the gilded gables of their roofs, once rivalled the magnificence of ancient Rome.... There is a lofty tower, and beside it remarkable hot baths, the remains of temples and an amphitheatre. All this is enclosed within impressive walls, parts of which still remain standing. Wherever you look, both within and without the circuit of these walls, you can see constructions dug deep into the earth, conduits for water, underground passages and airvents. Most remarkable of all to my mind are the stoves, which once transmitted heat through narrow pipes inserted in the side-walls and which are built with extraordinary skill.[41]

Appropriately, recent archaeological work has suggested that the baths remained roofed until the twelfth or thirteenth century. Contemporary settlements, on the other hand, might have an air of impermanency: when Cadog went away from Llancarfan, his first buildings fell down. And the poet of *Canu Llywarch Hen* looked sadly at the deserted and overgrown settlement of Urien: nettles, grass, brown stalks, brambles, thorns and dock leaves thrive; a pig roots in it; a chicken scratches round it.[42]

Travel and Communications

With so much land dominated by mountain, travelling across and about Wales has always been problematic and the north-east/south-west folding to which the old rocks were subjected after their deposition has determined much of the character of the natural communications of the North and the West. Even today it is a standard joke that meetings of representatives of the five colleges of the University of Wales — Bangor, Aberystwyth, Lampeter, Swansea and Cardiff — take place on Shrewsbury station, the easiest place for all to reach, and there is more than a little truth in this. Even by car, the journey from Bangor to Cardiff or Carmarthen remains lengthy for the distances involved. Such problems — essentially the difficulty of crossing the mountain — were undoubtedly felt in the early medieval period and clearly contributed to the relative isolation of different parts of the country, a circumstance which had its own political consequences. The later writers of Saints' Lives made a point of commenting that a journey was 'prosperously accomplished', an implicit recognition of the risk involved, while the earlier writer of the Life of Samson dwelt upon the fatigue of the journey undertaken by Samson's parents when they went to visit Librarius, and the fears provoked by the huge forests through which Samson and his companions had to travel — in the South — to visit his father.[43] The short scenes of daily life by which the compiler of the Colloquy taught his lessons include a number of comments on the problems of travel: 'light a fire ... for us and do it quickly, because I am weak and tired from the labour of the journey or from walking and with the very long and dirty way; marshes and dung abound there, and it is a very difficult and hard journey. ...Rise friends and awaken from your accustomed sleep; put on your belts and in the morning let us go out on the road, for the road is long and the day is short. One person asks you on which road we shall go, and another says: "I am experienced, follow me, because I know the road and its short cuts; there's no need to ask anyone'''. And after more discussion of the need to find the right way and know the short cuts, the talkers move to the problems of the robbers who might be lying in wait. [44] The importance of knowing the way is amusingly illustrated by the tale of the thieves who stole a herd of pigs, but lost their way and kept returning to the point from which they had started. [45] Dirt, direction, robbers, all hampered the traveller, though this did not seem to deter a great many people from

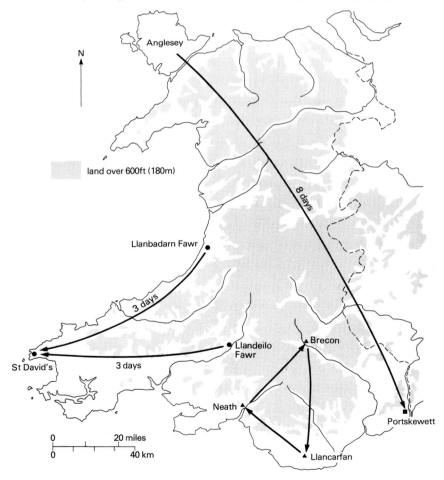

Figure 6. Travelling times in Wales in the early Middle Ages.

undertaking the hazards; Gildas commented on the willingness of clerics to undertake long journeys in the sixth century, even overseas if they failed to purchase office at home.[46] Travelling took time. Teilo and Padarn each took three days to get to St David's, presumably from Llandeilo Fawr and Llan-badarn Fawr respectively; the long journey to the river Usk made by David and Teilo and Docgwin caused Lifris to comment on their fatigue; but some miraculous 'wooden horses' could get to Neath and Brecon and back from Llancarfan in a day — truly a wonder.[47] In the twelfth century Giraldus said it took eight days to travel from Anglesey to Portskewett — north-west to south-east — and his own preaching tour round the perimeter of Wales took nearly two months (see fig. 6).[48]

Long journeys meant that provision for hospitality was essential. The Cadog charters detail the acquisition of lands by the monastery at Llancarfan, and installation of stewards who were to manage them, for the explicit purpose of providing entertainment and hospitality for the community while travelling, and it is reasonable to suppose that similar measures were taken by other major religious houses. When comparable provision had not been made, then the traveller was dependent upon the hospitality offered by the people he met. The travellers of the Colloquy hasten on to the next villa, where they know they will be able to get beer; and the obligation of giving food, drink and more to the pilgrim is made explicit in this text. Germanus and his party, on the other hand, were refused hospitality by the wicked Benlli, and had to accept that of a poor householder who was his servant; the Lives of Illtud and Tatheus both envisage the possible refusal of hospitality to strangers, for they stress that their respective saints were always generous with it.[49] Apart from the hospitality owed to the owners of property and kings there appear to have been no regular institutions of support for others, though the strength of the moral obligation to provide for those who needed it is indicated both by the special consideration afforded to the needy who had stolen because they failed to get alms and by Giraldus's observation that 'no one begs in Wales. Every-one's home is open to all, for the Welsh generosity and hospitality are the greatest of all virtues. They very much enjoy welcoming others to their homes. When you travel there is no question of your asking for accom-modation or of their offering it: you just march into a house and hand over your weapons to the person in charge'.[50]

Means of travel are only briefly indicated. The traveller of the Colloquy above went on foot, and this must have been the normal method for all those of moderate means. Horsemen came to fetch St Samson to attend his father, and he made the journey back by horse and cart; Asser went from Sussex to St David's on horseback, while the kings of the Lives invariably moved about in the same fashion. Ox carts were sometimes used to move goods around.[51] There must have been some roads, and presumably the network of Roman roads remained in use for some period. This was quite clearly so in the South-East, where there are charter references right through until the eleventh century to properties which lay not only on local roads but on the main road, the *fordd mawr*; the properties thus defined are sometimes located beside the course of what we know to have been Roman roads.[52] By the late eleventh and twelfth centuries, however, there were changes: Rhigyfarch's monks of the South-West dug out a road to make access easier; Llancarfan was 'impassable

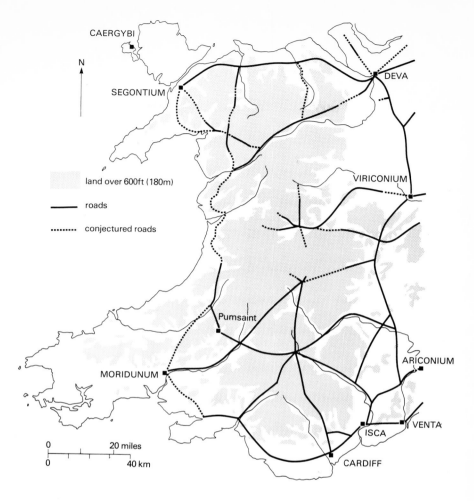

CAERGYBI

N

SEGONTIUM

land over 600ft (180m)

——— roads

········· conjectured roads

DEVA

VIRICONIUM

Pumsaint

ARICONIUM

MORIDUNUM

VENTA

ISCA

CARDIFF

0   20 miles
0   40 km

Figure 7. Roman roads in Wales (after D. Moore, *Caerleon Fortress of the Legion*, 1975, fig.5).

before Cadog cut paths'; while the routes taken by Giraldus in the twelfth century suggest that many Roman roads had lost their value by that time. [53] Crossing rivers was no easy problem: fords were used wherever possible, like the ford over the Usk where the meeting between Arthur, Ligessog and others took place, and like the many fords mentioned in the charter boundaries of the *Liber Landavensis*. [54] But the river Taff could sometimes only be crossed by boat, and even Giraldus went by boat on parts of the western coast, crossing the Dyfi in this way and rowing across the two branches of the river Mawddach. [55] At times, rivers were totally impassable; Cadog's clerk could not contrive to cross the river Neath until the waters had gone down; Giraldus detailed other dangers:

> We set out once more and, not far from Margam, where the twin
> hazards of a sandy shore and an incoming tide begin, we crossed the

ford over the river Avon. . . . As we approached the Neath, which is
the most dangerous and difficult of access of all the rivers of South
Wales, on account of its quicksands, which immediately engulf
anything placed upon them, one of our pack-horses, the only one
possessed by the writer of these lines, was almost sucked down into
the abyss... In the end it was pulled out with some difficulty, thanks
to the efforts made by our servants, who risked their lives in doing
so, and not without some damage done to my books and baggage.

He goes on to tell how they ignored the advice of their guide, so scared were
they that they hurried where caution should have prevailed, and eventually
crossed the river itself by boat, since the fords changed with every monthly
tide and could not be located after a heavy fall of rain.[56] He later mentions the
wicked priest — employed by the bishop of St David's as a guide for crossing
the river — who rushed off through it and refused to return until reinstated in
a lost chaplaincy and financially compensated. Local guides were essential at
problem spots like Neath, and presumably at the quicksands by Coleshill in
the North-East.[57] Bridges *were* known, however: Giraldus occasionally
mentions them — as he does north of the Dyfi — and we apparently have
remains of a pre-Conquest footbridge along the shore at Barmouth; occasionally we find references to bridges in charters, as at Llandenni, Aber-carn and
Llanmelin in the South-East, though fords are much more frequently
mentioned.[58]

Travel by sea, of course, was a different matter, for in many ways the
easiest method of communication was by sea rather than land. Any glance at
a settlement map will indicate the coastal distribution of the greater number
of Welsh settlements both then and now, for settlement itself was easier in
the coastal perimeters than in the mountain heartland. Monastic sites like St
David's, Penally and Clynnog look seawards rather than inland. We often,
therefore, hear of ships: ships that sailed to Ireland and ships that sailed to
Gaul.[59] The routes are regular, unremarkable to the commentators; and
abbots had their harbours.[60] Ships were also associated with enemies,[61] from
the warships of the Saxon enemy who attacked Britain in the fifth century to
the pirate fleets of Vikings that harried the coasts of Wales in the ninth and
tenth centuries, and it was envisaged that the English might one day be driven
back to the sea.[62] We hear of small boats — skiffs stopped with pitch,
coracles, boats constructed of timber and hides.[63] Though small — Illtud's
was rowed by two people — they might nevertheless make the crossing to
Ireland, as we know from quite different contexts: most striking is the famous
case of the three Irishmen who arrived at King Alfred's court in the late ninth
century, having set out from Ireland in a small boat without oars. Giraldus
described a type of coracle commonly in use within Wales, made of withies,
pointed in front but rounded in a sort of triangular shape, left bare inside but
covered outside with untanned animal skins, carried on the man's back when
he went home from the river.[64] Rowing was not the only source of power, for
the masts and sails and canvas of the ships coming into harbour are as
frequently mentioned and the eleventh-century poem of Ieuan ap Sulien uses
an extended image of the ship, its sails and oars.[65] Though the oars might be
used (Cadog's monks rowed from Barry to Holm), saints and sailors would

more usually wait upon the wind before they began any long journey, and were accustomed to the delay that that might impose.[66] These masted ships must have been larger than the skiffs and coracles, though there is nothing local which gives us any useful indication of size.

Settlement

The predominantly coastal nature of Welsh settlement has already been noted, but it is very difficult to make precise and localized comments about the early medieval period. If we are right in assuming that some named religious communities occupied sites somewhere in the vicinity of their still surviving churches — St David's, Llanbadarn, Llandudoch (St Dogmaels), Bangor Fawr, Clynnog, Llanelwy (St Asaph), Welsh Bicknor, Llantwit, Llancarfan, Penally and so on — then it is possible to make some observations about the topographical characteristics of religious settlement sites: they are lowland, within reach of tidal waters, often sheltered from the sea but with access to it, on valley sides or alluvial cones (like Llanbadarn) or river terraces, avoiding damp valley floors.[67] Evidence of a different and more localizable type comes from archaeology, which indicates, firstly, the occupation of hilltops like Dinas Powys and Dinas Emrys at least in the first half of the period, an observation also made by Gildas in the sixth century and a practice presumably conditioned by defensive considerations; secondly, the continued occupation of some Roman sites, like Caerwent and (?)Caernarfon; thirdly, the possible use of some southern cave sites for habitation; and fourthly, the continued occupation of hut groups from the late Roman period until the sixth or seventh centuries. The latter are often to be found at relatively high altitudes, on hill slopes and plateaux, and are especially characteristic of the North-West.[68] However, whereas in the North-West there is much to suggest the continuity of occupation of domestic sites from the late Roman period, with changes occurring in the seventh century, in the much more heavily Romanized South-East there are factors which suggest some shift in settlement sites began already in the late Roman period but was not complete until the eighth century.[69] Climatic change and the consequent break in cultivation of some upland arable may well have occasioned the abandonment of some sites. All of this constitutes useful evidence about the nature and distribution of settlement in Wales in the early Middle Ages, but it does not provide enough to warrant generalizations about it. The distribution of inscribed stones, for example, must to some extent be representative of settlement patterns: it is not unreasonable to suppose that it broadly represents areas that were inhabited, but it is perfectly clear that it is useless as a precise indicator, since many stones have been moved from their original positions, and since the communities of some areas did not adopt the practice of erecting them.

Whether or not settlement was dispersed or nucleated is as important a question as that of density and topography, and almost as difficult to resolve. It is a commonplace fact that modern Welsh rural settlement consists of hamlets and isolated farmsteads rather than the nucleated villages which characterize much of the English countryside. This is certainly true of many

Figure 8. Sites with material suggesting defensive or domestic use in the early Middle Ages.

areas today, and is an observation also made by Giraldus in the twelfth century: 'They do not live in towns, villages or castles, but lead a solitary existence, deep in the woods. It is not their habit to build great palaces, or vast and towering structures of stone and cement. Instead they content themselves with wattled huts on the edges of the forest, put up with little labour or expense, but strong enough to last a year or so'.[70] However, there are several indications to the modern scholar that — though the contrast with England was probably marked, and though there is little in the surviving fabric that would suggest 'towering structures' and large towns in early Wales — the notion that there was no nucleated settlement at all is quite unreasonable. Both royal courts and religious establishments represent specialized but nucleated communities. The royal court with its collection of houses and tents, with other dwellings in view nearby; the huge households attributed to saints Cadog and Illtud, with workers, soldiers, dependent women and children — all of these indicate agglomeration of dwelling units.[71] Moreover, there are suggestions of some increasing tendency towards nucleation in other contexts in the eleventh- (and twelfth-) century lowlands. The settlement 'round the church' recorded in the Life of Gwynllyw, of Newport, has parallels in the south-eastern charter material, which also implies the attraction of settlement to churches at the same time.[72] Of course, as Professor Bowen has pointed out, a high percentage (nearly a half) of churches bearing Celtic dedications still do *not* act as a focus for nucleated settlement, the greater proportion of these lying in lowland Wales, though there is a tendency to nucleation round them in the eastern borders and western and southern coastal fringes.[73] But, apart from nucleation in association with churches, Lifris wrote of an *urbs* and an *oppidum* visited by St Cadog in such a way as to imply that he had nucleated settlements in mind rather than fortifications — a return to the classical usage, in fact.[74] Moreover, if the law tracts are correct in suggesting that the working of some estates was carried out by bond men, living in bond settlements, then the implication is the same, as G.R. Jones has recently argued; changes from this pattern in the late medieval period might explain the isolated of some proportion of the churches.[75] Though we may suppose isolated and unostentatious settlement very common in Wales, it is increasingly likely that there was some nucleation as well.

Some indication of the size of settlements might be gathered from consideration of the 'hut groups' so characteristic of north-west Wales. Arguing on the assumption that each individual needs 100sq.ft. of roofed space, it has been suggested that some hut groups may have housed 5-9 individuals and others between 10 and 20.[76] Nearly 50 years ago, the excavator of the Romano-British site at Rhostryfan suggested there may have been 3 or 4 people per hut there, and the figure of 5 per hut is commonly cited. Attempts to calculate population from these surviving monuments are surely hazardous: since population size and density can itself affect settlement patterns, we surely cannot argue about the size from observation of the pattern without knowing the density.[77] It is pointless to guess at population levels in terms of precise numbers, and even more pointless to speculate whether the smaller hut groups represent the residences of nuclear families, the larger those of extended families. It may have been so, but other explanations are possible — nuclear families with dependants, or associations of nuclear families, or families that could afford more accommodation per person.

Written sources do give some indication of the size of residential groups, although it would be difficult to interpret hut group evidence in the light of it. The indications of household and family size that can be found in the written sources are too few and too fragmentary to resolve the problem, though they are of some interest. Apart from heroic notions of the leader, surrounded by his retinue, dependants and supporters in his hall, the greater number of such references imply that the nuclear family of parents and children represented the normal household unit, as may also be implied by the law tracts when it is specified that the paternal home should be inherited by the youngest son (though, equally, some co-residence of brothers is implied).[78] Hence, the poor householder of the *Historia Brittonum* lived with his nine sons; the richer *satraps* Baia of the Life of David lived with his wife and their household; a steward of the Life of Cadog lived with his daughter.[68] The writers of the prose tales, on the other hand, sometimes envisaged the co-residence of a wider family group: Branwen and her brothers, and Manawydan and his cousin; even Gildas seems to imply the co-residence of a priest with his mother and sisters, and it would be possible to read the Colloquy as implying the same for grandfather, aunt and son.[80] This evidence is interesting but not decisive, except for making the obvious point that the households of rulers would tend to be larger. We cannot therefore make any generalizations about the size of settlements in the pre-Norman period.

However, thanks to the archaeologists of the past generation and to the systematic work being undertaken at the present, it *is* possible to begin to say something about some specific settlements. The written sources are consistent in supposing there to have been forts and fortified places through-out the period, and in associating them with the holders of political power — nobles and rulers. According to the *Historia Brittonum*, both the rulers Benlli and Gwrtheyrn had their citadels, strongly defended, though Gwrtheyrn failed in his attempts to construct a citadel (*arx*) in Snowdon, despite the 'carpenters and stone masons' he imported for the purpose. The context of the description, in both cases, associates the citadel with the seat of political domination.[81] The writer of the Life of Carannog similarly described the *arx* of Cadwy, with its hall and people, while Rhigyfarch made much of the wicked Irishman Baia who came into conflict with St David in west Wales, fulminating amidst the ramparts of his citadel. In 822, moreover, the citadel of Degannwy, at the mouth of the river Conwy — *arx Decantorum* — was destroyed by the Saxons, as a result of which the region of Powys fell into their power; the implication is that the citadel was essential to the main-tenance of the political integrity of Powys, and the symbol of its independence.[82] Precisely what was involved in its destruction is not specified, but the Annals record the burning of it ten years earlier and we may therefore assume some easily fired wooden buildings within and possibly wooden ramparts round the defences. Unfortunately excavation did not reveal any traces of structures that could definitely be associated with this period.[83] The most telling of all written references, however, is the ninth- or tenth-century poem written in praise of the fortress of Tenby, *Dinbych*, that is 'small fort':

> There is a fine fortress on the broad ocean,
> A mighty stronghold, sea-girt....
> There is a fine fortress on the ninth wave,
> Fine are its men when taking their ease.
> They make merry without reviling....
> There is a fine fortress on the promontory,
> Graciously each one there receives his share.
> I know at Dinbych — pure white is the sea-gull —
> The companions of Bleiddudd, lord of its court.
> My custom it was on New Year's Eve
> To sleep beside my prince, the glorious in battle,
> And wear a purple mantle, and enjoy [every] luxury,

founded. The siting of later churches within and very near Roman forts, towns or villas — as at Caerhun, (?) Caergybi (see fig. 10), Llanbeblig outside Caernarfon and possibly Carmarthen and at the Roman villa of Llandough whose walls were actually utilized by the thirteenth-century monastic complex(see fig. 64) [92] — could also indicate some early medieval activity, comparable with the developments at Caerwent. This certainly happened at an early period in England — as at sites like Bradwell in Essex — and also on the Continent.

The other sphere of non-domestic building on which some comment can be made is indeed that of church and monastery. The church was obviously special, although it is now extremely difficult to reconstruct physical characteristics. Where churches survive within the walls of Roman forts, it is

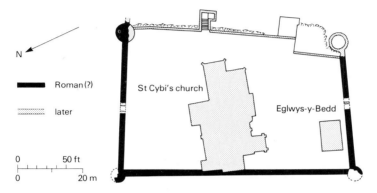

Figure 10. Caergybi (after E.G. Bowen, *The Settlements of the Celtic Saints in Wales*, 2nd edn 1956, fig.33).

a not unreasonable presumption that they have pre-Conquest antecedents and that they were so situated in order to make use of the building materials available, among other reasons. It is quite possible, therefore, that some stone churches were built at an early date and there are occasional references to such structures in written sources. [93] It must be admitted, however, that there are rather more references to timber buildings: Cadog's monks went off to fetch new timber for their monastery; the timber roofs of Llancarfan were visible from a distance; Cadog collected timber to build an oratory on the banks of the river Neath; and the initial construction of Llancarfan involved much earth-moving. [94] The wattle remembered in the name Bangor, applied to at least two foundations in north Wales — Bangor Fawr near Caernarfon and Bangor on Dee — recalls the wattled oratories mentioned by Giraldus; and Eglwysail, the earlier name of Llangadwaladr on Anglesey, contains the element *eilio*, 'to weave', presumably referring to some comparable construction. [95] The surviving fabric of most modern Welsh churches has nothing to suggest pre-Conquest structural features, and only at Presteign, in the English-influenced Marches, is there some good reason to suppose that the Norman church lies on earlier foundations. [96] In most cases it would seem that the existing stone churches have been constructed upon ancient, long-used sites, replacing earlier timber ones. We might expect, then, that most pre-Conquest complexes of religious buildings, though distinctive and physically separate, were essentially composed of timber structures. Such religious complexes would often have been further distinguished by a separating enclosure, like those of pre-Conquest churches in Ireland. The churches of Llanmerewig and Meifod in Powys are still surrounded by near-complete oval enclosures — basically earth banks — and there is some reason to believe that these represent the enclosures of pre-Conquest structures. Llanmerewig is a small church, in a remote upland situation, attached to a small hamlet. Meifod is a much more substantial building in a much larger enclosure in a major lowland site, associated with the royal families of Powys. Here there were several churches within the enclosure in the early modern period, and we know that their disposition was not new at that time; they almost certainly represent a pre-Conquest arrangement. The church at Eglwys Gymyn, near Carmarthen, again an isolated site, is even more impressive (see fig. 11). Here the church is built on a barrow within a *rath-*

Figure 11. The enclosure and church at Eglwys Gymyn (photograph Doug Simpson).

like enclosure; its position on the barrow — a pagan burial place — strongly suggests some continuity of ritual use of the site over a very long period. [97]

Domestic Buildings

We know less of domestic buildings. As late as the twelfth century Giraldus would still comment upon the temporary and flimsy nature of the wattled huts that were the natural residences of the Welsh, and could draw a comparison between these and the stone built castles and towns of Norman England. [98] Reed huts, houses supported by a single roof beam, and houses used as grain stores as well as living quarters are all reported by written sources, but the material is insufficient to allow generalizations; we may suspect, moreover, that Giraldus was drawing an extreme contrast for his own particular purposes. [99] Certainly in north Wales in the earlier centuries of the Middle Ages we know from still surviving physical evidence of the occupation of groups of stone-built huts, of which several hundred remain, mostly on the upland. In many of these cases the buildings are quite solidly constructed and there is no reason at all to visualize them as miserable hovels. Some of them , like the Roman-period Din Lligwy, near Pant-y-saer, look more like a northern equivalent of the Roman villa than any sub-standard 'native' housing. They are of dry-stone or rubble build, comprising circular or sub-rectangular 'huts', often within a stone enclosure. Most of those that have been investigated are clearly associated with iron age or Roman material, but some have produced evidence of the very early medieval period as well: they must therefore be taken into consideration when reviewing medieval settlement types. The size and shape of the hut groups varies considerably and attempts have been made to differentiate between function and social status in accordance with this variation. Hence, it is argued that mixed farming requires a wider range of facilities — storage for fodder and stalls for plough teams, as well as domestic accommodation — while stock-rearing needs great compounds but less permanent accom-modation; and therefore that two functional classes can be distinguished: stock stations and mixed farms. The former are those with a high proportion of open to covered space; the latter are those with round and rectangular huts, for human and animal accommodation respectively. Indeed, excavations at two of them have produced evidence of paved floors with drains and many are associated with terraced (and therefore presumably once-ploughed) fields. The suggestion is attractive, and the further suggestion that the two types form the early equivalent of the later medieval *hendre* (home farm) and *hafoty* (summer pasture settlement) is reasonable and adds to its attraction (cf.fig. 17). [100]

Those with plentiful fourth-century evidence — like Ty Mawr near Holyhead, Din Lligwy, Hafoty-wern-las, Cae'rmynydd — ought especially to be kept in mind in the post-Roman context. [101] The best-evidenced group that was certainly used in the post-Roman period is that at Pant-y-saer, on Anglesey, though Cefn Graeanog, on the upland above Clynnog, has been more recently and thoroughly investigated (see fig. 12). Here, within a rectangular enclosure, some circular huts dominated three of the corners, and

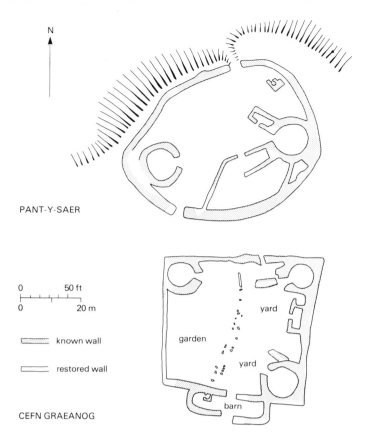

N

PANT-Y-SAER

0   50 ft

0   20 m

known wall

restored wall

yard

garden

yard

barn

CEFN GRAEANOG

Figure 12. Pant-y-saer (after L. Alcock, *Dinas Powys*, 1963, fig.10); and Cefn Graeanog (after R.B. White, in 'Roman Britain in 1977', *Britannia*, ix, 1978, 406f., fig.3.)

evidence of occupation, iron working and farming is plentiful in the third to fifth centuries; the masonry of the buildings was of good quality; a third of the enclosure was made into a garden and a rectangular building at the entrance has been more than plausibly reconstructed as a barn plus byre. The final phase of occupation of this site, dated fifth- to seventh-century by the excavator, involved a decrease in the standard of building and reduction in population: only one building (C) continued in domestic use; another was used for smithing. [102] Another hut group outside the iron age hill-fort of Caer Drewyn, near Corwen on the modern A5, has been supposed to be of post-Roman construction. If, alternatively, caves were used as settlement sites — and finds of imported pottery from Longbury Bank Cave (Pembroke) and miscellanea including jewellery at Radyr (near Cardiff), Minchin Hole, Culver Hole and Bacon Hole (all in Gower) might suggest that they were — we know nothing of the nature of their occupation. [103]

The largest of the investigated sites is not a cave nor a hut group but the settlement on the island of Gateholm, off the coast of Pembroke, west of Milford Haven (see fig. 13 and fig. 56). Here there may have been as many as and shelter all affect the productive capacity of the land. The amount and type of produce can therefore vary immensely, even within a single locality, however comparable the soil structure. Factors like climate, altitude and the length of the growing season further complicate the pattern of variation.[9] So although one should expect Anglesey, the south-western peninsula and the South-East to be the most favoured parts, one must also expect both considerable local variation and the occasional favoured inland pocket.

The less extensive grasslands and more extensive woodlands of the early medieval period provided a more varied habitat and more possibilities for hunting and gathering than are apparent today.[10] Despite the problems presented by the surface of the land, it nevertheless offered means of support, and much of the written comment of the early medieval period suggests that the natural produce of the land was used and highly valued by the inhabitants. Apart from the people of St David's who were accustomed to gather nuts, we hear little of the fruits of the forest except in the law tracts, where fruiting trees bear a particularly high value.[11] The food value of nuts should not be underestimated, however, for it has been calculated that 1.6 square miles of hazel could supply four families with 25 per cent of their diet for four of the winter months.[12] By the eleventh century hunting, unlike such gathering, appears to have been an aristocratic pleasure, and the twelfth-century writer of the Life of Illtud laboured to detail the story of King Meirchion, whose anger had been directed at the saint for occupying the waste where he liked to hunt; an angel rebuked the king for thus preventing cultivation and he eventually gave in and disposed of the land, so that the peasantry could start farming it.[13] Hounds, horns, horsemen and the chase are a recurrent feature of the vernacular prose tales, and in 'Manawydan' hunting for pleasure is explicitly distinguished from hunting for necessity.[14] Earlier references, however, indicate that this had not always been so: Gildas lamented that, in the troubles of the fifth century, the only source of food left had been that which the huntsmen could find; occasionally the charters of the South-East specify hawking rights, while the objects of the chase — hawks, hounds, horses and horns — often featured as the objects of payment in the eighth century.[15] The cradle.song recorded with the poem *The Gododdin*, though it almost certainly refers to north Britain rather than Wales, shows that hunting might have a more essential role for the family:

> When your father would go to hunt, with a spear-shaft on his
> shoulder and a club in his hand, he called to the nimble (?) hounds,
> 'Giff, Gaff, seize, seize, fetch, fetch!'....
> When your father went to the mountain he would bring back a
> roebuck, a wild pig, a stag, a speckled grouse from the mountain, a
> fish from the falls of Derwennydd. Out of all those that your father
> got at with his dart, whether wild pig or fox...none escaped unless it
> had wings.[16]

Fish, particularly river fish, were an important element of diet. Cadog took pains to secure a half share of the fishing rights in the rivers Usk and Neath to supply his communities at Llancarfan and Llan-faes, says his eleventh-century biographer, and the exploitation of the rivers Usk, Wye, Dee, Clwyd and the Severn tributaries was clearly well developed and closely controlled by the time of the Domesday Survey of England and the borders undertaken by the Norman government of England in 1086.[17] Before that, charters from the South-East occasionally specified fishing rights together with rights in property: at Tidenham and Dixton in the early eighth century, at Pwllmeurig and Caerleon in the ninth, near Llandaff in the early eleventh century, and so on.[18] Giraldus was very specific about fishing stocks 150 years later: trout, perch and eels in the lakes of Snowdon and that of Llan-gors (which was also rich in pike and tench), and salmon in the rivers Teifi, Dee, Usk and Wye, while the latter two would also produce trout and grayling.[19]

The other natural source of food that was frequently noted is honey, and an 'abundance of bees' was often a characteristic of descriptions of situations particularly favourable for settlement; of course, some of these were stereotyped descriptions, but such repetition emphasizes the writer's aware- ness of the value of the product. Hence, the Colloquy of Bodleian MS 572 instances corn, wine, milk, oil and honey as the characteristic properties of the fertile land; while the writer of the Life of Illtud in the early twelfth century praised the fertility of Llantwit by stressing not only the good harvests of the area, but the abundance of flowers and of honey.[20] Likewise, Rhigyfarch, in the late eleventh century, made much of the bees of the St David's area and even included anecdotes about them; his point was also echoed in the prose tale 'Manawydan': Dyfed was rich in honey and fish.[21]

More usually, of course, it was the fertility of the land and its agricultural potential which called forth comment upon exceptional places: Britain itself was 'excellently appointed for agriculture'; St Cadog was fortunate in owning 'many fertile lands'; Giraldus noted the corn of Anglesey, of Brecon and of Ewias.[22] Though communities might well make the most of the foods offered by nature — fish, honey, sometimes even game — writers nevertheless assumed that it was normal to clear and dig and plant. The expectation was that settlement would be accompanied by cultivation. Thorns and thickets were cleared when a new settlement was established, not merely to assist habitation, but to prepare the ground for cultivation. Contemporaries, there- fore, contrasted the 'smiling land' of occupation with the waste; they equated a lack of ploughs with desolation; they berated the kings who preferred to leave the land waste with wild beasts rather than allowing cultivation.[23] Con- temporaries also noted that the resource of manpower was necessary for all to be well: the annalist of *Brut y Tywysogyon* noted that the good years around 1022 were the times when there were no empty settlements — the land was peopled — while the poet of *Armes Prydein* bemoaned the fact that many deaths might cause starvation; they left insufficient cultivators. Hence, when Gruffudd left valleys waste in 1063 this was bad for the community as a whole: the land should have been worked.[24]

Some good lands were, of course, more suited to provide pasture, and the expectations of the inhabitants were not confined to arable exploitation. After desolation the land became peopled again with herds as well as dwellings, while it was the mountain pastures of Snowdon and of Brecon that caused Giraldus to comment on their fortunate nature. Ewias and Llanthony, indeed, represented the ideal, for 'those mountain-heights abound in horses and wild game, those woods are richly stocked with pigs, the shady groves with goats, the pasture-lands with sheep, the meadows with cattle, the farms with field systems in other parts of Britain, like Cumbria and Dartmoor, has produced good arguments for the value of upland field systems in relation to herd management.[36]

Outside the North-West, evidence is much more fragmentary, but field systems identified at Llowes and Crickadarn in Powys may belong to the early middle ages.[37] Indeed, irrespective of their period of construction, prehistoric earthworks would have remained to be utilized in the historic period. Hence, the banks and ditches often mentioned in the charter boundaries of the south-

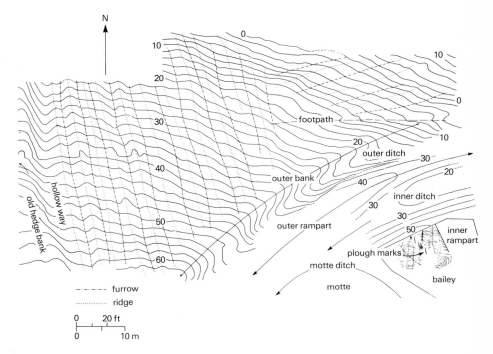

Figure 16. Contoured survey of Field A at Hen Domen, showing a pre-Conquest field system (reproduced from P. Barker, 'A pre-Norman field system at Hen Domen, Montgomery', *Medieval Archaeology*, xv, 1971, fig.16, by kind permission). Contours in feet.

eastern lowlands may well have had a much earlier origin but have retained a functional significance; it should be noted, however, that their function appears to be proprietary rather than agrarian. At Hen Domen in the Marches, however, the most specific of physical evidence is preserved for, beneath the Norman bailey and in the field north of the castle, there are cultivation marks — traces of ridge and furrow with ridges about 13ft apart — left from pre-Norman ploughing (see fig.16).[38] Pollen analysis of these levels produced much weed and bracken, suggestive of arable cultivation and subsequent reversion to scrub.

Overwhelmingly, the object of agriculture was to grow corn, and apart from the few herbs and vegetables noted above the only other crop specified is the flax seed necessary for the making of linen.[39] Most frequently we hear merely of the corn, the cornfields, the seed, the harvest, without specification of the type of grain, although the Colloquy has plenty of distinct proper terms.[40] Many types must have been known and recognized, their different qualities guarded and valued. Wheat — the source of the best, white, wheaten loaves — is specified more frequently than other grain types and at an earlier date: wheat as seed corn due as part of a seventh- or eighth-century render; wheat sown by 'David's' monks.[41] Wheat was also present in the deposits analysed at Cefn Graeanog, as were spelt, emmer and six-rowed barley.[42] Barley and oats were specified by eleventh- and twelfth-century writers — as barley bread and fodder for horses — though Giraldus rather idly (and clearly inaccurately) commented that the whole population lived on oats (and dairy products).[43] We cannot, again, say anything of proportions or of yield except to note that when Rhigyfarch wanted to quantify the bounteous harvest he wrote of those who reaped a hundred fold, and others who reaped sixty fold, and others thirty fold — that is, a crop 30 times the weight of the seed sown. These figures were, doubtless, wildly in excess of anything that might have been expected. In early modern Britain a three-fold yield was not uncommon and a fifteen-fold yield would have been regarded as exceptionally good. Likewise Lifris indicated Cadog's good fortune by arguing that he only had to sow one acre of his many fertile lands in order to get support for the year; presumably he too exaggerated the normal amount necessary for the support of a household.[44] Eleven bushels a year were needed to support a single Roman soldier and that has been calculated as slightly more than the likely product of one acre in Roman Britain.

The year's routine is not as obscure as some other aspects. Ploughing is commonly noted as a metaphor, much more so than cultivation by hand. We hear of monks who dug by hand in the sixth-century 'Preface on Penance' and the eleventh- and twelfth-century Lives of David and Cybi, but such practices are rare.[45] In the Cambridge manuscript of Juvencus, *such*, 'point, tip', glosses *vomis*, 'ploughshare'; and the width of an acre is cited in *Canu Aneirin*, implying some standard practice.[46] Not only ploughing as such, but ploughing with animals is noted: two yoked oxen or even an oxen and an ass, at least in the eleventh and twelfth centuries, and probably, on the evidence of 'Canu Heledd', earlier.[47] Plough teams were noted in Domesday Clwyd, Montgomery and mid-Wales; and even a few in Rhos and Rhufoniog, though their sparsity was noted by the surveyor; a winged ploughshare, suitable for heavy, wet soils, was discovered in late or sub-Roman layers excavated at Dinorben. Gathering the harvest was an autumn task:

> Wooden crook, here's harvest time:
> Red the bracken; yellow the grass.[48]

After reaping, the sheaves were gathered and apparently stored in barns in bundles, for the Old Welsh word for 'barn' means, literally, 'collection of sheaves'. The later, eleventh-century, material speaks more often of threshing and of storing the grain in granaries or storehouses after threshing. This, together with the early ninth-century reference in the *Historia Brittonum* to winnowing the corn, might suggest some development of technique or at least wider practice of threshing in the course of time, though it would be unwise to overemphasize this. The same collection of glosses as provides a vernacular term for 'barn' also provides one for 'threshing floor.'[49] Very occasionally we hear of measures taken to care for the productive capacity of the arable: land left fallow and manuring from scrub that had been burnt;[50] the references are few but at least they betoken some awareness of good husbandry.

The pastoral side of farming involved the rearing of sheep, cattle, pigs and occasionally goats; now and then we are told of chickens scratching around.[51] Oxen were kept for ploughing, and as beasts of burden, as were asses occasionally; while horses more usually appear to have been kept for the transport of persons rather than goods.[52] The distinction sustained between 'best' and other horses in the Llandaff material, however, may suggest that some horses were used for agricultural work.[53] Two yoked oxen were used to fetch timber at St David's, while David himself did not hesitate to take a horse if making an errand on monastic business. The evidence which we have is inadequate to suggest any regional chronological variations in the practice of animal husbandry, but such as there is clearly indicates that cattle were a more significant source of meat and milk products than sheep at all periods. References to cattle are much more common:[54] it is the image of the *cow* in the corn which is so frequently invoked, not the sheep or the pigs; it is cattle disease which has serious consequences; it is in terms of cattle that values are sometimes assessed and payments and/or compensation actually made;[55] the Dunsaete Ordinances are concerned, essentially, with procedures for tracing stolen cattle; it is cattle raiding, not sheep raiding, which forms the stuff of heroic poetry. All of this indicates a standard of reference which underlines the importance of cattle in the total agrarian economy. It is, perhaps, notable that sheep appear as single items in transactions.[56] Pigs were honourably mentioned and the writer of the prose tale 'Math' commented that their flesh actually tasted better than that from cattle.[57] For what it is worth, the Dunsaete Ordinances valued a mature horse at 30s., an ox at 30d., a cow at 24d., a sheep at 12d., a pig at 8d. and a goat at 2d.[58] The analysis of midden material at Dinas Powys provided 61 per cent of pig bones, 20 per cent of cattle and 13 per cent of sheep; these were food bones and the proportions should not therefore be taken as an indication of total stock in the area.[59] The relative proportion of pig to sheep is particularly notable, however.

There is some evidence about the care of animals. The pigs had their swineherds and would feed on acorns in woodland, as in mid-Wales at the time of the Domesday Survey, or indeed on scrub and thorns.[60] Sheep and cattle might also have their proper herdsmen, and their pastures were of prime importance, their separate and specific function identifiable, though the implication of the lowland evidence at least is that they were not permanently enclosed: in the Life of Illtud an evil steward offended the community by enclosing some of the pasture. Ieuan of Llanbadarn noted the suitability of the mountain slopes of Pumlumon in the eleventh century.[61] Sometimes cattle might be pastured at some distance from the settlement, as Ieuan presumably implied, at other times near at hand, to be brought in at night. Both possibilities seem to be envisaged by the cryptic comment of Gildas on the suitability of the mountain for 'alternate' pasturage, for he appears to have had the later attested practice of transhumance in mind. In

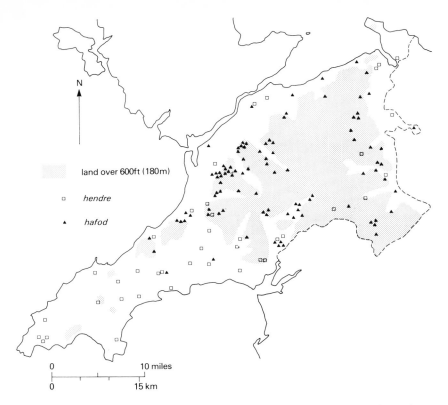

N

land over 600ft (180m)

□   hendre

▲   hafod

0   10 miles
├────┼────┼────┤
0   15 km

Figure 17. Hendre and *hafod* in Caernarfon (after E. Davies, 'Hendre and hafod in Caernarvonshire', *Trans. Caerns. Hist. Soc.*, XL, 1979, fig.5).

Wales the prominence of settlements associated with this practice — lowland *hendre* (principal settlement) and upland *hafoty* (summer pasture house) — indicates that seasonal transhumance was characteristic of the late medieval and modern periods (see fig.17). It has been argued that some of the so-called 'hut groups' of the North-West may have performed a comparable function in iron age, Roman and very early medieval times, with the same implication of transhumance to both long-distance and nearer pastures: some of the hut groups are of such small size that it is difficult to envisage permanent settlement therein.[62] The same practice is implied within the multiple estate, where such were to be found in the early medieval period.[63] Of course, all transhumance pastures were not necessarily on mountain sides, as is clear in Anglesey, and we should not forget the use of lowland riverside grazing in summer as appears to have happened in Somerset and Oxfordshire, on lands that were wet and ill-drained in winter.[64] Seasonal transhumance, therefore, does not only occur in the uplands; and the suggestion that it was common — utilizing upland or lowland — in the early medieval period is a reasonable one and does not conflict with the written indications. It remains true, however, that there *is* a break in the settlement *type* — hut group to platform house — and this points to at least some change in practice; in any case, it remains unlikely that the practice of transhumance was as widespread and as characteristic of the upland mass as it was with the development of sheep-runs in the late medieval period. Some transhumance might be expected in our period, therefore, but not as much as later.

In winter the cattle got thin, says the poet of *Canu Llywarch Hen*, and these were presumably the cattle that stood waiting in their stalls.[65] If they got thin, they were clearly not slaughtered; and even if the ages of most of the animals eaten at Dinas Powys were young, they still imply *some* overwintering.[66] In winter they were sustained, presumably, on hay, the product of the meadow lands that are occasionally if infrequently mentioned, the *guertland*, 'green enclosure', of the glosses.[67]

Storage of food for the long nights of winter was obviously essential for survival. The stuffs that are most commonly specified as renders due to landlord or king are beer, bread, flesh and honey — both beer and bread being grain products — and very occasionally milk products like cheese or butter. Salt is notably absent, and was noted amongst the wonders of the *Historia Brittonum*.[68] It is to be presumed that these represented the easily storable as well as the easily transportable products. The use of honey in the making of beer and bragget and mead — the beverages of poets and heroes[69] — was probably as significant, if not more so, than as a general sweetener and it was hence regarded as a very valuable commodity. Honey, therefore, is a constant element in many specified renders; jars of it were stored and guarded in monastic enclaves; the law tracts note the value of swarms, hives and wax.[70] The tending of hives indicates that honey was not merely gathered from the woods and that bee keeping was therefore a further aspect of early medieval animal husbandry.

Subsistence and Surplus

If most people lived on the land and from the land they did not do so in the same ways. Some worked it, some merely ate its products or distributed the fruits of their properties to their supporters. The basis — and almost the entire nature — of the economy may have been agrarian, but this does not mean that it worked equally for all men or that the allocation of resources was anything other than uneven. The very existence of rents and renders — the beer and bread and flesh and honey that had to be returned once or twice a year — indicates that some of the land was worked as estates by tenants who gave their labour for the benefit of 'owners'. Whether or not land, the fundamental resource, was in short supply is difficult to tell; the story of King Meirchion preserving waste for hunting when it would have been better turned over to cultivation suggests that by the twelfth century there may have been some land shortage.[71] There is little in previous periods which might argue for the same; and the possibility is high that there was no land shortage until the period of the Norman Conquest. Shortage of labour is much more likely to have been the characteristic scarcity. Though it is quite impossible even to make guesses at demographic change nothing suggests that the population of Wales in the early medieval period was anything other than exceptionally small; indeed after the recurrent plagues of the fifth, sixth and seventh centuries the population level is likely to have suffered major crises, and, as in the rest of Europe, to have dropped. What use was land without the hands to work it or the time to tend the cattle? Unenclosed pastures demanded labour that might not have been as arduous as some but was nevertheless as time-consuming. The crucial importance of labour — and contemporary awareness of this — is epitomized in the line of the tenth-century poem *Armes Prydein* cited above: 'many deaths mean want'. [72] If the population was reduced, then someone had to starve. Labour, therefore, and the control of it, was fundamental to the working of the economy and to the institutions devised to sustain it.

Ancillary to the fundamental resource of labour is that of tools — the means by which labour can be saved and effort can be directed more efficiently. The writer of the tenth-century Colloquy had no doubts about the value of tools, which he classified generically as 'benefits', and the very long list of tools which follows — axe, billhook, adze, spade, and so on — includes vernacular equivalents for all items. [73] Rhigyfarch presented his monks setting to with mattock, hoe and saw; and cutting a way for a new road with a two-edged axe. Ploughs, as we have seen, were common and seem to have been drawn by yoked oxen, and the natural resources of iron were certainly being mined in Clwyd by the time of the Domesday Survey. [74] Whether or not there were technological improvements or developments within the period is impossible to say; there are certainly no hints, even, of anything that might qualify as technological revolution. Though one may suppose, then, a good range of iron hand tools, the burden of manual labour remained.

There are many indications that the exploitation of much of the land was organized through a framework of large estates. We know of estates in the South worked by dependent peasants and we know of slaves. This does not exclude the possible existence of the free peasant proprietor, or of smaller units of exploitation than the estate, but the evidence allows no comment. We know from the Llandaff charters that much of the South-East — certainly its cultivable lands — was exploited as estates of some considerable size. The smallest were in the order of 40 acres (and these were exceptionally small); the largest in the order of 6,000 acres (exceptionally big); most sizes fell between 100 and 1,000 acres. Slaves and dependants were sometimes alienated together with an estate when it was granted away to a new owner. A single tenant farmer sometimes had sole responsibility for the return of rent for such an estate; in such cases he performed, presumably, as some sort of managing tenant. The indications are of extreme tenurial complexity, with owner, tenant farmers and workers all being supported from the larger estates at all times between the sixth and eleventh centuries. The charters attached to the *Vita Cadoci* are particularly interesting in that they specify the number of people to whom payments might be made in order to secure a grant or sale; hence, the acquiescence of some tenants as well as owners was necessary before a sale was completed, since tenants might well have hereditary rights in properties as well as hereditary obligations. In all of this it is perfectly clear that these properties were not worked by the single nuclear family; indeed, continental analogy might suggest that the 'average' estate — the commonest, three *modii*, size (in the order of 120 acres) — supported a working population of between 30 and 40 people. Though there was certainly some tendency for the early, very large estates of 1,000 acres or more to split into smaller units after the eighth century the units still remained large, relatively, rarely dropping below the standard size.

We do not know much about slaves beyond the fact of their existence, but their very existence may well explain why we have no evidence of labour service in pre-Conquest Wales; though units of ownership and exploitation were large, work appears to have been done either directly by the slave or indirectly by the tenant who had freedom to choose how he might dispose of his labour from day to day. We know very little of the organization of work on an estate or of the relation of work pattern to settlement, although the implication of changes in terminology in the eighth century would suggest that the new smaller estates depended upon one focal settlement, the *tref* or *villa*. The residence therefore gave its name to the whole unit — Villa Dewi filii Iust, Villa Cynog (Cynog's villa, Dewi ab Iust's villa), and so on — now defined in relation to the settlement.[75]

In recent years much has been written not merely on the early Welsh estate, but on the 'multiple estate', the term used by G.R. Jones to refer to the grouping of estates for the better utilization of available resources. The model of the multiple estate is taken from Welsh law tracts of the twelfth century and later where it has an essentially fiscal and administrative import. Hence, according to the north Welsh tracts, there were four *trefi* (usually translated 'townships') in every *maenor*; twelve *maenolau* plus two *trefi* in every commote; and two commotes in every *cantref* (hundred), which therefore consisted of a hundred *trefi*. The two supplementary *trefi* in every commote were reserved for the use of the king, and in addition he received an annual food-rent (*gwestfa*) from each free *maenol* (eight per commote) and a summer and winter food-gift (*dawnbwyd*) from each servile *maenol*, as well as some more or less onerous services such as building works, carting and hospitality. This is, of course, a highly schematized model (and the numbers of constituent units vary in the tracts from different regions), but it provides for a perfectly rational scheme by which the king not only ensured his own

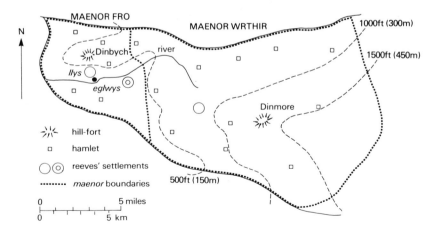

Figure 18. A pair of hypothetical Welsh multiple estates, comprising an upland *maenor* and a lowland *maenor* (after G.R. Jones, 'Multiple estates as a model framework', in *L'Habitat et les paysages ruraux d'Europe*, ed. F. Dussart, Liège, 1971, fig.1).

support but guaranteed for himself some income from every part of the land. Moreover, whereas the *maenol* is the essential fiscal unit — the unit in relation to which food-rents were assessed and paid — the *tref* is the essential working unit (both settlement and land) upon which each *maenol* is constructed (see fig.18).

Now, it is quite clear that this scheme is relevant to royal exploitation in twelfth- and thirteenth-century Wales. The problems lie in its application to the pre-Conquest period. G.R. Jones, in a series of stimulating and valuable papers, has argued that the *maenol* (or its southern variant *maenor*) of the law tracts is but a late manifestation of the multiple estate which had been characteristic of Welsh agrarian organization since at least the seventh century and probably since the Roman period. That is, he suggests that the land was typically exploited in large tracts, of 12 square miles and more, which consisted of a number of component units, *trefi*, which constituted both the focal settlements and the land worked from those settlements, and in relation to which the servile population made their renders. With such relatively large units of exploitation something like self-sufficiency could be achieved: with upland and lowland included within the bounds, there might be summer and winter pastures, as well as the woodland, meadow and arable necessary to a mixed farming economy; each *maenol* would have its central administrative focus (*llys* or court) and its religious focus (*llan* or church); each *maenol* could provide for the protection of its population in a well-known fortifiable place, to which resort could be made in times of need.[76]

G.R. Jones has been able to demonstrate from pre-Conquest evidence that *maenolau* (large estates) existed in the South; that on the evidence of the Lichfield marginalia, no.3 and 4, *trefi* which were the constituents of larger units might be alienated, like Trefwyddog near Pumsaint; that groups of *trefi* might be jointly administered, like the groups of 13 and 14 *uillae* in Domesday Gwent; and that a summer and winter render might be demanded, as instanced once in the Trefwyddog case (see fig.19).[77] The *maenor* of Meddyfnych (which includes modern Llandybie) is mentioned in the sixth of the Lichfield marginalia, in the ninth century; its perambulations indicate that its extent was only slightly less than that of the modern parish of Llandybie, and that it included upland and lowland; and its reference to 'Gwaun Henllan', 'the meadow of the old church', suggests a religious settlement within its bounds (see fig.28). Its size would suggest that there must have been more than one settlement within it, and certainly in the late medieval period the parish included seven *trefi*.[78] G.R. Jones has also made a reasonable case both for the identification of some such estates, like the manor and hundred of Aberffraw and the manors within the commote of Caeo, on the basis of later administrative topography, and also for the identification of their principal secular and religious and defensive foci, on a similar basis. The location of a fourteenth-century lord's court (*llys*) at the farm of Dinorben, coupled with reference to the hearth of Dinorben in the tenth-century 'Stanzas of the Graves' and with possible post-Roman occupation of the nearby hill-fort of Dinorben (Parc-y-meirch), suggests that this neighbourhood may have housed the seat of aristocratic power — the secular focus — for many centuries. It therefore seems quite clear that groups of *trefi*, farms, were sometimes associated, for administrative and/or proprie-

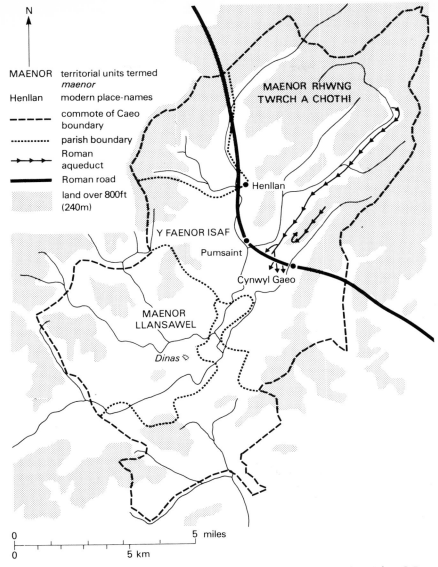

N

MAENOR — territorial units termed *maenor*

Henllan — modern place-names

- - - - commote of Caeo boundary

.... parish boundary

→→→ Roman aqueduct

▬▬▬ Roman road

land over 800ft (240m)

MAENOR RHWNG TWRCH A CHOTHI

Henllan

Y FAENOR ISAF

Pumsaint

Cynwyl Gaeo

MAENOR LLANSAWEL

Dinas

0 ——————— 5 miles
0 ——————— 5 km

Figure 19. The territorial framework of Trefwyddog, Carmarthen (after G.R. Jones, 'Post-Roman Wales', in *The Agrarian History of England and Wales*, I pt 2, ed. H.P.R. Finberg, 1972, fig.44).

tary reasons, and that resources in a neighbourhood were consequently shared. Aberffraw hundred provides a good example, at least of the distribution of royal rights. It is also clear that kings had an interest in these arrangements by the late eleventh century, since the law tracts consistently assign to Bleddyn ap Cynfyn, who died in 1075, responsibility for altering some assessments. What is less clear, since the evidence is so fragmentary, and is highly questionable, is the universal applicability and uniformity of this framework and the invariable inclusion of all its distinctive characteristics. We do not have any evidence of the nature of the association between *trefi*. Indeed, since the model must be essentially a fiscal one, it implies a consistency over many centuries in the machinery of proprietorship which appears extremely unlikely in a period of considerable political change; and a consistency in the units of ownership which seems equally unlikely in a period which saw certain climatic and apparent demographic alteration, and therefore presumably some fundamental agrarian change. Can both land use and political organization have been so static, so unchanging? The effects of inheritance, at least, would have inaugurated some modification. On present evidence, then, the universality of the system is far from proven and it remains an open problem in most areas of Wales. In the South-East, at least, the overwhelming trend of the ninth-century and later evidence is to suggest the fragmentation of larger estates into smaller, independent *trefi*. By the eleventh century any functional relationships between groups of *trefi* were largely lost (though they may still have been grouped for fiscal purposes).[79]

The renders due from the southern estates give some idea, if a hazy one, of productive capacity. Nine measures of beer, with bread, flesh and honey, were due *per annum* from the Villa Conguoret in Pencenli; 3 measures of beer, with unspecified additions, from the half Ager called Idraclis; 9 measures, with additions, from the Ager Pencarn; 12 measures of beer, a sester of honey, and additions, from the Villa Cadroc by the river Thaw; 40 loaves and a wether in summer and 40 loaves and a sow in winter from a *tref* near Llandeilo; 60 loaves, a wether and butter from another nearby; 6 measures of beer with bread, flesh and a sester of honey from the 500 or so acres at Llanfannar each year. These are the renders returned from the tenants of large areas in the eighth and ninth centuries and must represent the surplus relatively easily realizable after workers had been supported. They are in some respects comparable to the renders demanded by the king from 'bond' *trefi* in the later law tracts: a winter food-gift which included a sow, butter, oats, bragget and 26 best loaves, and a summer food-gift of a wether, butter, cheese and 26 loaves. By the late eleventh century many of the eastern estates rendered money as well as goods: five Welshmen with five carucates (ploughlands, maybe 100 acres) in Ergyng rendered five sesters of honey, five sheep with their lambs, and 10d.; sesters of honey, pigs, cows, loaves, beer and pence were rendered from estates in Gwent; in mid-Wales, in Cynllaith and Edeirnion, we hear of a cow-rent and payments in shillings; but at the estate of Bistre in north Wales the render from each ploughteam was 200 *hesthas* (? loaves), a vat of beer and a vessel of butter.[80] The amounts are not enormous — interestingly, they are notably less, for example, than the render per hide from the estate of Hurstbourne Priors in Hampshire[81] — but they make it perfectly clear that some surplus *was* being produced, as does the very fact that the estates existed. Whether or not this was true of the whole of Wales in the pre-Conquest period is hard to tell, though the presence of estates in the more mountainous area around Llandeilo Fawr, the occasional reference to a *praedium* or an *ager* in Ceredigion and to the territory pertaining to monastic settlements in Pembrokeshire, and the assumption of the annalists of the *Brut* that the *tref* represented both settlement and agricultural

unit, would all suggest that it was true of much of it. [82] Whether or not there
was one or more type of estate is equally difficult, but our knowledge of
changes in the South-East must make uniformity unlikely. Indeed, even if the
estate was widespread, we still do not know if there were small independent
peasant proprietors as well. The householder with one cow and calf who gave
hospitality to Germanus behaved with considerable independence, even
though his status was servile. [83]

Apart from this problem, it remains clear that the surplus was not evenly
distributed. Some people had richer clothes; some people had plenty to give
away — mead and lands and gold and gifts — and were celebrated for their
bounty. Indeed, mead, one of the products of good husbandry, became the
symbol of generous bounty in the heroic poetry. Some people had the power
to gather and distribute the products of the land; some could store more than
was essential for survival through the winter: 'though he stored like a miser,
it was shared for his soul's sake'. [84]

Wealth

A social ethic which applauded the distribution of surplus did not prevent its
accumulation and conversion into riches and there is no part of this period in
which wealth — and the proper use of it — goes unnoticed. Wealth was
invariably conceptualized as movable and portable, often as hidable. The
wealth of Stirling was returned after it had been seized; Patrick was able to fill
his ship with treasures; Maelgwn could stuff bags with them; Glamorgan
could be pillaged of the whole of its wealth by William Rufus; the treasures of
the South could be carried off by Rhun. [85] Treasure might, alternatively, be
kept in a special place: 'I sang a famous song about the destruction of your
treasure-house...'. [86] It might be buried: the precious fire carried by the
youthful Cadog was too holy to be used by ordinary men and so was hidden,
buried in the earth like precious treasure. [87] Accordingly, we sometimes
discover hoards of precious goods, buried in the earth: 60 Anglo-Saxon silver
pennies deposited at Laugharne, not far from Carmarthen, round about 975;
18 Anglo-Saxon silver coins of Cnut deposited in the eleventh century at
Drwsdangoed, near Caernarfon; more than 200 coins deposited near
Llandudno on the north coast round about 1025. [88] We may suspect the
particular stimulus of Viking activity in these cases — given the dates and the
coastal locations — but they remain examples of treasure, buried as the
written sources suggest. If they were not buried, then the proper place for
wealth, treasures and riches was often considered to be with kings: the poet of
Canu Taliesin saw wealth in abundance round his king, 'gold-king of the
North'. [89] For some ascetic writers, though this was an unusual view, all
possessions were riches and their accumulation was detestable; wealth was
wickedly alluring, a temptation to be resisted by those who sought to live by
spiritual values; wealth was also transient, an aspect of the riches of this
world which would inevitably be lost, unlike the perpetual riches of
heaven. [90] These views were expressed by Gildas in the sixth century, and by
some of the hagiographers of the eleventh and twelfth centuries, but on the
whole they are remarkably rarely evoked, even by clerical writers; the

bounteous distribution and receiving of rich gifts is the far more prominent ethic.

If wealth was portable, was there a consistency of approach in defining the objects of wealth? The objects that the bounteous kings and leaders of the heroic poetry of the middle period had to distribute included weapons and cattle as well as jewels and clothing:

> Rhun the Wealthy gave me
> A hundred war-bands and a hundred shields;
> And one war-band was better — a great protection.

> Rhun, pleasing prince, gave me
> A hundred dwellings and a hundred bullocks;
> And one that was better than those. [91]

Horses, swords, purple clothing, bracelets and brooches feature as prominently in the lists of poetic gifts. [92] But this bounty included more than mere wealth and other evidence is notable in distinguishing both landed property and men — though both were crucial to survival — from wealth. [93] Land and men — resource and labour — were seen as necessary; they were not seen as wealth in themselves. The Colloquy contained in Bodleian MS 572 includes a splendid list of objects of wealth in its dramatization of the discussion of those possessions that ought to be guarded while the master was away: 'Stay behind and guard my clothes, gold, silver, copper, brass, incense, iron, tin, lead, *pecunia*, *schola* and library of books'. [94] Of these, clothing and gold are the objects most frequently cited as precious in other sources. An inscribed stone records the view that good character and wisdom were even better than gold; Ieuan, on the other hand, saw knowledge as a store of treasure, and described how Sulien returned from Ireland to divide up the gold of his learning; the warriors of Gododdin took gold to the altar; King Maelgwn was distinguished by his wearing of golden clothes; Heledd's brothers had great plumes of gold to adorn them'. [95] Costly clothes might change hands in payment for goods; kings would dress up in costly clothes if they wished to impress both intruders and visitors. [96] Jewels were also a favourite notion of wealth, especially in the later material and in the secular tales, though even *The Gododdin* has amber beads and torques, and the *Historia Brittonum* has a jewel rescued from the mud which is to be added to other treasures. Brooches and rings and precious stones, harness and trappings decorated with gold and jewels, swords with gilded hilts are evoked; and the English Bishop Ahlstan actually lost his gold enamelled ring near Llandrillo-yn-Rhos in the ninth century. [97] Money, as such, is only rarely mentioned but its metal — gold, silver and base metal — sometimes features in lists of the precious, as in the Colloquy list cited above. Hence, the author of the *Historia Brittonum* fantasized that Constantine had sowed seeds of gold and silver and brass in the fort at Caernarfon so that no-one in future should be poor, doubtless a contorted reference to finds of coins made on that Roman site of Segontium. [98] The production and source of wealth is rarely analysed except in such cases as the curious speculation above, but Rhigyfarch, writing in west Wales in the late eleventh century, was at least clear that one's talents could be doubled by dabbling in commerce, for an angel reported that David had done this by commerce and should now take his talent from the earth and see to its increase.[99] So, by the end of the period, it is clear that the notion that wealth might be multiplied was circulating in Welsh ecclesiastical circles at least.

Production and Specialization

A few incidental references indicate that there must have been some sort of production other than the agricultural, though they are exceptionally few. The lists of gifts characteristic of the heroic poetry, gold- and jewel-work especially, should not encourage us to suppose that all these fine and exotic objects were necessarily in circulation; and even if some were they need not necessarily have been produced at home. The naming of metals like iron and tin in the Colloquy's list of precious objects, as also its very long list of tools and implements, would certainly indicate some necessary smithing; and a smith is named as witness in one of the earliest of the Llandaff charters, of the late seventh century.[100] Excavations at Dinas Powys and Dinas Emrys suggest that iron smelting took place at those domestic sites, using ores acquired locally, and that smithing took place at Dinas Powys too in the fifth and sixth centuries and at the late Roman hut groups like Din Lligwy. One hut was used for smithing in the last phase of occupation of Cefn Graeanog.[101] Gildas forged his own bell, according to the Life of Cadog, while swords changed hands as part payments in transactions in the South-East in the eighth century.[102] Such indications as there are suggest that these and necessary agricultural and domestic objects were made locally, possibly under the patronage of landowners lay and clerical; we should therefore expect to find evidence of such work at estate centres, like the smith of the court and the settlement smithy mentioned in the later law tracts.[103] Dinas Powys and Dinas Emrys also produced clear evidence of jewel-working, using gold, glass and enamel, as occurred at contemporary sites in Scotland and Ireland.[104] The images of the poetry may not be entirely wishful thinking, therefore, and Samson's parents had to find silver rods to hand over to Librarius.[105] Beyond this, domestic crafts like spinning and weaving, leatherworking and flint knapping may all be supposed to have taken place, producing goods for home and immediate consumption rather than distribution. All were evidenced at Dinas Powys. Very occasionally there is a hint of more specialized production, such as the stone quarrying mentioned in the late eleventh century in the Life of Cadog.[106]

There is reasonable and quite full evidence of specialization of function, as might be expected if such goods were to be produced, though much less good evidence of specialization of occupation. There is some notice, at the very latest period, of travelling craftsmen, men with skill who moved about to exercise their skills: hence, the Irish masterbuilder who came to Cadog looking for work in Glamorgan or the travelling craftsmen of the prose tale 'Culhwch ac Olwen'. Indeed, it is only in the late prose tales that there is clear evidence of specialized occupations, that is of trades in the modern sense. Saddlers, shieldmakers, shoemakers all appear, but it is notable that the context often suggests that such trades were to be found in England; one must travel in order to patronize such men or work among their number. In

Wales, references to smiths are so rare that we cannot be sure that the men who did such work lived by smithing alone; it may be more likely that it was a skill shared by several and practised together with other necessary crafts. Hence, Gildas forged his bell, but was also a monk, active in the clerical life. Goldsmiths perhaps worked in a more concentrated way and are certainly named as such by the poet of *Canu Aneirin*.[107] There are some slight suggestions of specialization within the building trade, particularly towards the end of the period. Cadog's builder searched for work so that he might exercise his trade. Masons are mentioned elsewhere in the same Life, as they are also in the *Historia Brittonum* along with carpenters.[108] One should note equally, however, the monks at St David's in the late eleventh century who did their own building.

The most consistent of suggestions that there was any real specialization of occupations at periods other than the very latest are of two types. Firstly, the consistency of references to herdsmen, and specifically to cow or pig or sheep herdsmen, would suggest that some peasants specialized in such work and were accustomed to spend the greater part of their time in caring for animals. It would be unreasonable to suppose that they did this absolutely exclusively — particularly in winter — but they may well have done so for much of the time. Hence the poets of 'Etmic Dinbych' and *Canu Llywarch Hen* had their cowherds and shepherds; and much more frequently Lives, charters and the *Historia Brittonum* specify both function and occupation of pig-keeping — perhaps for the obvious reason that pigs tend to have been pastured in unenclosed and often uncleared land. Pigs needed a constant watch.[109] The second area of specialization is in the variety of dependants of specialized function resident at and working for lordly centres, both lay and monastic. The *Vitae* often mention the servants of the saints, the peasantry employed by the monasteries to serve, work for and run errands for monks; their duties were doubtless many and varied but they were distinct in their occupations in *being* servants.[110] Some agents of lordly centres had more specialized jobs: the procurators, stewards, *meiri*, agents, who collected renders for their employers and organized their business for them.[111] Some jobs within monasteries (and presumably at kingly lay centres of some pretension) were also more specialized. We often hear of cooks, and occasionally of bakers, butchers and cellarers, people who were specifically concerned with the storing and preparation of food.[112] We sometimes hear of doorkeepers.[113] Again, doubtless these people did not spend their whole time baking or cooking — and they may have been monks — but they may well have spent a good part of it in such activities. Notably, they only appear in association with centres of consumption, that is with centres of wealth.

The Exchange of Goods and Services

In a developed modern industrial economy such as our own in Britain the means of supporting life are many and complex. Few people have direct contact with the land; standard of living is high, which means that the acceptable minimal level of consumption is relatively high and our definition of necessities includes a great range of goods and services; most people, therefore, sustain life by concentrating their skills, labour and resources in one area and exchanging the products of that activity for the range of necessities that they demand. Transactions in which they engage as a consequence are often purely commercial: they buy food; the act of buying it is neither an aspect of some other relationship nor an obligation to continue the relationship. Other and earlier societies often viewed the business of acquiring necessities as part of a wider social relationship, part of the continuing necessary reciprocity without which communities could not hope to survive. The commercial transaction was not the only way of acquiring goods; the idea of sale was not always prominent as a means of acquiring things.

We have seen that in early Wales direct contact with the land and with food production was far more common than in modern industrial societies and far more common than any other activity, and that specialization of occupation was relatively rare until the late eleventh century and almost entirely associated with estate centres before that. Even specialization took place in a predominantly agrarian context, for predominantly agrarian reasons. It would scarcely be controversial to conclude that the range of goods and services available was far smaller than in the modern case; and that basic necessities were fewer. It is quite clear from the range of written material that survives from Wales in this period that the economy was not so simple that there was no exchange of goods between individuals and communities; every group did not entirely provide for its own needs though the circulation and distribution of goods was sometimes effected by means other than commercial exchange. One means was by raiding — cattle raiding in particular is noted in the heroic poetry — though such means are relatively infrequently evidenced.[114] Another was by sale; another by payment for specified services; another by exchanges at an agreed rate. Most notable, however, is exchange accomplished by means of gift. Clearly the ideology of gift conditioned the reporting of many transactions. Men received gifts at feasts; gifts came from God; gifts were given to secure friendships;[115] renders due annually from certain properties were described in terms of gift;[116] a successful attack upon the English was viewed by the attackers as a gift to their enemies.[117] The heroic ethic announced by the poetry depends essentially upon the notion of gift: warriors were attracted to a leader, fought for him, received their gifts of gold, weapons and lands. Generous gift-giving would bring throngs of supporters, therefore, and the distribution of goods depended upon the successful military relationship as much as upon the successful military expedition.[118] The ethic is still evoked in the twelfth-century Life of Illtud, in which the soldier is attracted to Arthur's court and seeks and gets rewards.[119] Gifts from lord to man are another expression of the notion, and Rhun's gifts to Cadog, as supposed by Lifris in the late eleventh century, must imply a similar relationship.[120] The gifts are not merely an expression of thanks for the war well fought; they are equally the symbol of the relationship that will continue between lord and man, which is a relationship of dependence. In one of the charters attached to the *Vita Cadoci*, for example, renders given were described as being in recognition of *societas* (partnership) *and* subjection.[121] The reciprocity of the relationship, however, is underlined by the poetic stress on deserving and meriting the gift: 'he merits no feast-gift who is ignorant of this'; and 'in return for mead in the hall among hosts'. Deserving one's mead is a constant theme.[122] It is extended into the poet's comment on death: the warrior 'got his dues'.[123]

Gift-giving was not restricted to the military context. God sent gifts and clerics gave gifts to each other; David's three gifts of the stag, fish and swarm of bees each had its own symbolic meaning as well; the laity took gifts to the altar, to monks, to hermits from whom they sought advice.[124] Gifts were customarily given at childbirth; and gifts were given normally to monasteries when a child was handed over for monastic upbringing.[125] Occasionally bodies were also given, for burial.[126] Gifts were exchanged in acknowledgment of reconciliation of a dispute.[127] It is presumably in this context that we must also see the donation of lands to monasteries, as is evidenced on a large scale in the South-East from the eighth century especially.[128] Gifts might also be given to other interested parties on the occasion of such donations: to the king that he might ratify them; to others for their good will. Hence, when Gwrgynnyf bought Reathr from King Meurig he gave horses to Cyngen and his son, a sword to Andres, the value of four cows to the king's son, an ox to his foster-father, and a cow to the king's agent.[129] We should perhaps understand the alienation of property, which, unlike wealth, was traditionally an inalienable resource, in the context of the ethic of reciprocity, the acknowledgment of a relationship between God and man.

The fact that the ideology of the gift extends over a range of sources indicates that it was not merely a poetic image. Gift-giving would appear to have been a real aspect of relationships and exchange mechanisms. But gift-giving was not the only means of and attitude to exchange. The perpetual labour of the slave of the Colloquy merited a reward, his wages; the association between labour and payment is explicit.[130] When Llancarfan granted sanctuary to anyone, then a 'payment' of a ewe with a lamb, or 4d., was expected: even this arrangement was reciprocal, as goods were to change hands in recognition of the service performed.[131] The approach, however, is nearer to the modern one, nearer to the commercial transaction which terminates the relationship; the person who sought sanctuary might be an outsider, one with whom there was no previous or current relationship. The pirates who helped in political struggles might receive treasure for their assistance, as did those of 1088 who helped Rhys ap Tewdwr.[132] The man with a torn eye might expect income from displaying it: he could expect a 'reward' from the passers-by with whom he had no relationship.[133]

The ideology of exchange was developing by the tenth and eleventh centuries. The Colloquy's pilgrim journeying in foreign parts entered into negotiations in order to find his means of support: 'Let's do an exchange over food and drink.... give me food... and I'll give you silver, gold, bronze'.[134] The notion of exchange is there; the machinery of payment is there; the notion of payment is not there. A century or more later there were merchants who 'exchanged' wares at the river mouth and merchants from Wales may have been present at the battle of Clontarf in Ireland in 1014, since merchants from 'Britain' are distinguished from Saxons and Franks.[135] Sale and purchase, both notionally and actually, are evidenced infrequently but consistently throughout the whole period. Other machinery did not displace this. Gildas therefore complained of those who would purchase the priestly office; indeed of those who would sell all that they had so that they could make journeys if they could not buy office locally.[136] (Journeys required money or exchangeable goods because of travel outside the known community.) The warriors of *The Gododdin* gave their lives in 'payment' for their feast of mead; though the ideology of gift is so strong in this poem, the ideology of sale is not absent.[137] For the poet of *Canu Llywarch Hen* deceit was viewed as sale; for the drafter of eighth-century charters some exchanges of land were sale; for Lifris, Cadog had to pay the price for land, and Gildas had a bell that he would not sell; a stone was bought so that a memorial might be erected in eleventh-century Glamorgan; the craftsmen of the *Mabinogion* made their goods for sale.[138] It is not merely the idea of sale that is evidenced; some transactions took place that may reasonably be described as 'sale'. Goods were exchanged for a price, with apparently no attendant obligations or relationship. Hence, a Gospel Book was purchased before being handed on to Llandeilo Fawr; freedom was purchased by slaves in the same area in the ninth century; land was bought and sold in the South-East and so was fiscal immunity in the eighth century, and once in the early tenth; a share in fishing rights was purchased some time before the late eleventh century.[139]

In many of these cases the price is stated. The Gospel Book cost a best horse; freedom for four men cost 4lb. 8oz., presumably of silver; fishing rights cost a sword, and a horse plus trappings; the price of land varied; three cows were the price of fiscal immunity. Swords, clothing, horses, dogs, hawks and horns were all used as payment for land, and once, round about 740, a Saxon female slave was included. Clearly no consistent, handy medium of exchange was in use, and this might suggest that the number of such transactions was very limited. Sales cannot have been too rare and unusual an occurrence, however, for sometimes notions of worth were stated. The Llandaff charters include details of sales in which values were expressed both in terms of cattle and in terms of silver. One and a half *unciae* of land at Wonastow, near Monmouth, changed hands for a horse worth 12 cows and another worth 3, a hawk worth 12 and a hunting dog worth 3; another *uncia* changed hands at about the same time for a hawk worth 12 cows, 2 horses worth 6 cows, a *scripulum* (unexplained) worth 12 cows, a horn worth 6oz. of silver, and some unvalued red linen. The very existence of the cattle standard indicates that the communities of the South-East (and all this material comes from the South-East alone) had a notion of value in relation to exchange; price, and therefore sale, was a meaningful concept; and it is notable that the objects of exchange tend to have had a consistent valuation, though those in the Cadog charters have a greater variation. Best horses were worth 12 cows, others worth 3 or 4; swords were worth 12; dogs about 3; and so on. The cattle standard continues in the secular prose tales and *Vitae*: the golden apple worth 100 cows; the *optimas/breyr* worth 450 cows, where the stated value relates to compensation not sale.[140] (The secular tales also go on to give stag values and money values.) The English 'Ordinance of the Dunsaete' cites values in shillings and pence — 30s. for a horse, 30d. for an ox, 12d. for a sheep; these too are compensation not sale values, and their statement in shillings presumably reflects English usage, the language of the record.[141]

The Welsh use of ounces of silver as a guide to some values indicates that they were not unaware of the convenience of precious metals for purposes of exchange. The Life of Samson, already in the seventh century, announced the handing over of silver rods as a gift and there are some indications in the Llandaff material that the use of precious metals increased in the tenth and eleventh centuries. Hence, compensation for damage began to be assessed in terms of silver and gold and references to payment in such metals increased. [142] Samson's silver rods, values expressed in ounces, and compensations expressed in pounds would all suggest that though the use of metal may have increased, it was measured by weight rather than as coin until an extremely late date. References to gold, silver and brass in the *Historia Brittonum* and the Colloquy indicate that some writers were aware — even in north Wales — of coin and its possible varieties, but this is no indication of its use as currency. [143] There is no evidence that any coin was minted in Wales before the Norman Conquest; even the single extant Hywel Dda penny (fig.20) was minted at an English mint at Chester. An imitation

Figure 20. The Hywel Dda penny (photograph by courtesy of the Trustees of the British Museum).

penny of Athelstan was found at Hope in Clwyd but we do not know who was the author of the attempt. [144] There are, however, several coin hoards from Wales in the ninth, tenth and eleventh centuries: 3 coins from Pennard (Glamorgan) deposited c.830, 13 from Bangor c.930, 60 from Laugharne (near Carmarthen) c.975, a hoard of several from Anglesey in the tenth century, more than 20 from Penrice c.1008, 18 from Drwsdangoed (Caernarfon) in the early eleventh century, more than 200 from Llandudno c.1025, several more from Pennarth Fawr (Caernarfon) of the same period. Several of these are quite small, and although some may have to be explained as Viking booty, it is not unreasonable to suppose that they indicate the acquisition of some coin by some Welsh people. [145] The coins are mostly English ones; three more chance finds, of the tenth century, have recently appeared at Caerwent. The implication of their occurrence is that though no coins were being minted in Wales, some people were acquiring those minted elsewhere and using them by weight. It is notable that when the word *nummismatis* ('coins') was glossed in Welsh it was glossed by the word *delu*, 'image'; it is not the aspect of coin as *currency* that impressed the Welsh mind. [146] Both the Annals and the *Brut* record that King Maredudd paid coin for the redemption of captives in the late tenth century. The Annals use the Latin word *nummus*, i.e. 'small coin', and the later *Brut* renders this as *ceiniog*, 'penny'. The reference implies that there was enough coin in Wales to make this exceptional payment — in the exceptional circumstances of Viking attack. [147] It is, indeed, quite exceptional. In the late eleventh century references changed in such a way as to indicate that metal might by then have been used as a standard currency. Cadog offered to fill Gildas's bell with money, or gold; those who took sanctuary at Llancarfan had to pay with a ewe, or 4d.; those who entered David's monastery, wrote Rhigyfarch, could not bring even 1d. with them; several of the renders recorded in Domesday Book for Gwent and mid-Wales included money payments as well as payments in kind. [148]

It would appear, therefore, that though there were recognized standards of value in the eighth century, there was no one medium of exchange at that period; that the use of and reference to payment in precious metals increased notably in the tenth and eleventh centuries, though this largely seems to have been by weight and not as currency, even if coin was used; but that the use of coin as currency was increasing by the late eleventh century. The overall picture would suggest that the amount of exchange conducted by commercial means was very small, unusually so by comparison with the rest of Europe.

If commercial exchange was limited we would hardly expect the importation of many foreign goods, but it is nevertheless quite clear that this did occur and that the category was recognized as special. The notion of 'luxury' is associated with imports from foreign parts. Gildas, writing of the past, referred to the luxuries from overseas that used to be brought by ship along the Thames and Severn and the writer of the *Historia Brittonum* took up this comment, altering it to point out that the ships conveyed riches acquired by commerce. [149] Though the later writer was copying, he had some awareness of the necessary machinery, and when he wrote of Patrick he took the opportunity to point out that his ship was filled with foreign marvels and spiritual treasures; ships were associated with the arrival of foreign goods. [150] The imported pottery of the very early medieval period found at Dinas Powys, Dinas Emrys, Coygan, and Longbury Bank Cave may well have arrived in such a way (see fig.21); as also the fragments of glass for use by the jewel worker at Dinas Powys, or the pin at Castlemartin. [151] Though these are all confined to the earliest centuries, their occurrence is notable and the pottery, though small in amount, remains remarkable in northern Europe. Possibly the silks, wine and gold of the heroic poetry reflect some luxuries which occasionally filtered through to more wealthy patrons. It is tempting to see the copying and glossing of notes of weights and measures — as occurs in the early ninth-century 'Liber Commonei' in the manuscript known as Oxoniensis Prior — as further evidence of preparation for commercial activity, though it appears more likely that this betokens a scholarly and literary rather than practical interest in such matters. [152] However, harbours and ports are noticed, particularly in the later period. The 'chief ports' of the island included Portskewett near Chepstow, and one on Anglesey; the Life of Brynach mentions the port at Milford in Dyfed; that of Illtud notes Illtud's harbour, by his monastery — presumably intended to be somewhere near Llantwit; Cadog sailed from a harbour to Ireland; merchants were accustomed

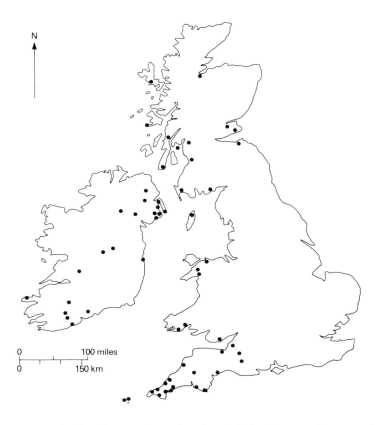

Figure 21. The distribution of British and Irish finds of imported pottery of the fifth to seventh centuries (after C. Thomas, 'Late Roman wares', *Procs. Royal Irish Academy*, LXXVI, 1976, fig.3; *idem, Christianity in Roman Britain to A.D.500*, 1981, 350).

to come to the mouth of the Usk near Newport. Specification of landing rights in Gwent from the ninth century may have a similar import.[153] What we know of the Vikings would encourage us to suppose some considerable sea traffic by the eleventh century, working routes to Chester and Bristol, from Ireland, probably with some associated commercial settlements at places like Swansea and Milford Haven. The presence of recent oriental coins as well as Northumbrian Danish coins in the small hoard of c.930 from Bangor may be associated with such activity, and if so indicates that it had started by a rather early date.[154]

Apart from the luxuries and the sea traffic, further references indicate some transportation of goods — not only by sea — associated with the provision of necessities. Materials from all parts were brought for the building of Gwrtheyrn's citadel; pack horses feature in the triads; travellers came loaded with 'necessities' to St David's, and for that reason the monks laboured to make better roads; Cadog was lucky enough to have horses by which his servants could bring necessities from all parts, quickly.[155] In one scene from the Colloquy the master ordered his servant to stay at home and guard his possessions, for he, the master, had to go off in search of the necessities.[156] Whether or not people came with them or you had to go in search of them yourself, some requirements had to be found from non-local sources, and these appear to have been considered essential.

This evidence points to the existence of some proportion of long-distance trade at all periods, though we cannot even guess at volume; it probably was not great. Awareness of the financial potential of commerce is quite clearly indicated in the eleventh century by the angel's remarks to David: increase your talents by commerce.[157] Whether or not there was any *local* commercial exchange is a more problematic question than that of long-distance trade. There are no references at all to this and one of the charters attached to the *Vita Cadoci* might suggest its absence. Here the tenants were required to carry the due render from their property to the monastic household which owned it, wherever the community might be.[158] They had to carry the render about. Distribution of local produce, therefore, may well have been entirely effected within the estate system, when there were estates; there may have been very little local commercial exchange. There are, indeed, no references at all to markets and only one to merchants and toll, in the very late Life of Gwynllyw. Since the business of local trade is nowadays held largely responsible for the increasing development of markets in western Europe as a whole in the early medieval period, the absence of markets may well be a further indication of the absence of local exchange — except by gift. The deficiency is very marked, particularly by contrast with other areas of Europe.

What then of the towns of early medieval Wales? Again, the pre-Conquest picture is almost entirely negative. As late as the writing down of the secular prose tales, latter eleventh or twelfth centuries, Manawydan and his friends had to go to England to find a town where they could earn a living.[159] Physical evidence of and reference to towns in pre-Conquest Wales is absent. Gildas wrote of the desertion of towns in Britain in the post-Roman period and of their present ruined state in the sixth century.[160] Although we may well suppose some continued occupation of Carmarthen and Caerwent, Caerwent became a monastery and there are indications that Carmarthen was monastic property in the immediate pre-Conquest period.[161] Where Welsh writers noticed towns they tend to be outside Wales: Hereford, York, Tours, Gloucester, Vannes.[162] The pre-Conquest defences of Rhuddlan are almost certainly English, part of the late Saxon *burh*-building programme.[163] The only potential exceptions to this non-urban landscape lie in reference to the Roman fort of Segontium and its continued use (Caernarfon); in the implication that Cadog's *urbs/oppidum* of Llanllywri was some centre of population which needed a church built for its needs, and the attendant implication that his own *oppidani* lived in some such centre; in the possibility of some Viking settlement at Swansea, as indicated by its Scandinavian place-name, or Kenfig, or Milford Haven; in reference to the settlement round the church of Gwynllyw, i.e. at Newport, and the merchants at the mouth of the Usk (it emptied of people when William Rufus came); and in the suggestions of nucleation round about Monmouth from the eighth century.[164] Caernarfon, Llanllywri, ?Llancarfan, Swansea, Milford, Newport and Monmouth are the best candidates, and there is no suggestion that the communities were anything other than exceptionally small by English or European standards nor

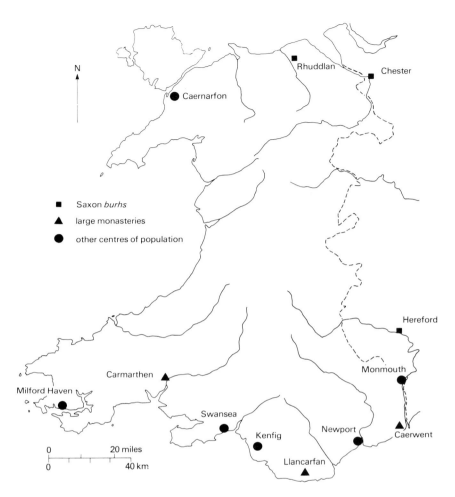

N

■   Saxon *burhs*

▲   large monasteries

●   other centres of population

■ Rhuddlan

■ Chester

● Caernarfon

Hereford

Monmouth

Carmarthen ▲

Milford Haven ●

Swansea

Kenfig

Newport

Caerwent ▲

Llancarfan ▲

0   20 miles

0   40 km

Figure 22. Some possible pre-urban nuclei.

that they necessarily had urban functions (see fig.22). Of course, large monasteries — though ecclesiastical in outward function — may well have performed some proto-urban function, in providing a context for nucleation, larger populations, gathering of movable wealth and greater specialization of function. Cadog's *oppidani* from (?) Llancarfan may fall into this category; so, therefore, would Carmarthen and Caerwent. What of the less well-evidenced monasteries to the north and west? Might we suppose by analogy some comparable function? It is impossible to answer these questions, but on present evidence the picture is not merely one of minimal urbanization but also of minimal trend towards urbanization. This becomes altogether more intelligible when we remember the absence of markets and, apparently, of local trade; it was the latter that provided such a stimulus to urbanization in Europe and England.[165] Without them, Wales could hardly be expected to develop major towns.

3 Social Ties and Social Strata

It is scarcely surprising to find that there were economic distinctions between individuals and between groups. We have already seen widespread evidence of economic dependence in the tenants, the herdsmen and the labourers who worked the lands of both lay and clerical landlords in many areas and at most periods.[1] According to the Lives, even hermits had servants to look after their needs; and the levels of dependence varied from that of the stewards who managed properties and the tenants who farmed for an annual return, to that of the more menial groups whose labour was directed by others. Economic exploitation, which affected people in such varied ways, is itself an aspect of early Welsh society. But social structure is not solely defined by economic inequalities. The bonds between individuals and between groups, and the varieties of association, both voluntary and imposed, form other criteria for distinguishing between the strata of society; they throw a different light on its overall structure and must be considered in their turn.

The Distribution of Wealth

Contemporaries were well aware of a differentiation between rich and poor. It is easy to find evidence of the rich, those with a greater share of available goods. Gildas castigated the 'wicked rich' and Samson's family had 'abundant means'; some were simply called rich; some were distinguished by their possession of rare and precious goods — the rich man who took a bath, the girl with silken clothes; some had the means to give gifts, constantly and bountifully.[2] There *were* differences and men were aware of them, but on the whole they were glad to tolerate them: there had to be people who could give gifts and behave with generosity. Though there is plentiful evidence of the existence of the rich and of the fact of differentiation, there is little evidence of serious poverty until the late eleventh century and later; of course, there were poor people by contrast with the rich, but we hear very little of the destitute. The corpus of poetry, notably, though full of references to the generous, has little to say of the desperate; those who received the goods were already reasonably well-endowed. Only Heledd shivered on her mountain top in a thin cloak and goatskins, leading her single cow after her family had suffered defeat.[3] But even in this poem the point is the contrast between before and after, between the expensive clothes of the days of power and the miserable garments of the days after; and Heledd did have a cow. The poor of the eighth and ninth centuries were poor because they had only a few cattle: the poor householder of the *Historia Brittonum* had only one cow and its calf, a model of poverty which persisted until the late eleventh century — Lifris's hermit Meuthi provided a symbol of ascetic poverty with his 'no worldly goods except one cow'.[4] In the eleventh and twelfth centuries the saintly duty of care for the poor was often reiterated, and although this is partly a reflection of the type of source material — one would expect this preoccupation in hagiographic work — nevertheless there is some reason to suppose that greater degrees of poverty *were* becoming evident, and in any case earlier Lives do not have the same preoccupation. Hence, St David was concerned with his poor peasant neighbour and was distinguished because he gave life to the needy; so, perhaps surprisingly, were those prototypes of knightly valour Cai and Bedwyr; and St Illtud was accustomed to feed the poor in large numbers every day.[5] Not only does concern for the poor become a formal preoccupation, but anecdotes of poverty become commonplace. The master builder Llywri could not find work and was therefore poor; Pwyll went from place to place with an empty bag, which would not fill, dressed in coarse shabby rags and rag boots; a clerk in threadbare clothes received alms; while the annalist of *Brut y Tywysogyon* chose to compliment Llywelyn ap Seisyll by noting that no-one was poor in his time, 1022.[6] All of these may be stock images, but they are images of a different quality from those of earlier years and as such doubtless reflect the changing world.

Both then and earlier the rich were those of predictable political position. Wealth lay with kings, pre-eminently. For Gildas, gold and silver were the chains of *royal* power; Urien was 'gold-king' with wealth all round him; King Maelgwn was distinguished by his golden vestments, and King Paul put on his most expensive clothes to meet St Cadog.[7] Not only kings, however, had the gold and silver and precious clothes. Leaders and successful fighters — the war lords — gave out gold and clothes as well as lands; the same people handed out food and wine and mead.[8] The clergy also shared in this access to consumables and there is widespread evidence of their possession of lands, of renders due to them, and of the amassing of lands by some foundations.[9] Perhaps surprisingly we do not often hear of the stored wealth of the Welsh clergy, beyond the barns of corn stored for the winter or for the short-term benefit. Gildas's strictures against the priests who were greedy for money as well as food and who sold their goods in order to accumulate the means to make journeys are not reflected in the later material.[10] This may be because the clergy were not characterized and categorized as wealthy — they were not associated with gold and purple — but it may also be because they really were less wealthy than the leaders of secular society. Though rich in lands and food, they did not convert their surplus into the precious, lasting symbols of that wealth. If so, this might go some way towards explaining the paucity of ecclesiastical treasure still extant from early medieval Wales: there are very few precious books; there are no costly chalices or reliquaries such as survive from early Christian Ireland; the one surviving gold episcopal ring from Wales is of English origin. Wealth, then, belonged to leaders, both lay and spiritual; it belonged overwhelmingly to those who had military power; it may well have hung less about the clergy than the laity.

Social Stratification

If economic differentiation is clear, distinctions of status or rank are even more so. The law codes are permeated with social stratification and with

Figure 23. A page from Rhigyfarch's Psalter, one of the few surviving early
Welsh manuscripts (photograph by kind permission of the Board of Trinity
College, Dublin).

privilege assessed in accordance with status (*braint*). Indeed, for the lawyers there was more than one kind of *braint:* that of birth, that of land and that of office.[11] Hence, every free man had his proper privilege: the insult done by the perpetration of certain offences against him (*sarhad*) had to be compensated in relation to that privilege; some of his animals and his household furniture were valued in accordance with it; marriage and separation payments were similarly graded; in effect, the higher the status the greater the compensation and value. Hence, this even applies to things owned by a man, for in *Llyfr Blegywryd* we find 'A piped kiln of the king's is six score pence in value. A *breyr's* kiln, three score pence. A kiln of the king's bondman (*aillt*), thirty pence. A kiln of a *breyr's* bondman, twenty four pence' and so on.[12] In the eleventh or twelfth century it was argued that St David had more grace, power and authority than Gildas since God had given him status (*privilegium*, glossed *dignitas*) over the saints of Britain. The clergy of Llandaff, presumably operating on the same principles, attempted to state the extent of their privilege in writing in the so-called 'Braint Teilo', 'privilege of [the church of] Teilo', specifying the privilege enshrined in law.[13] And at least one pre-Conquest account demonstrates the working of this principle in a clear pre-Conquest context, in the South-East: in the case of Bishop Cyfeilliog in the early tenth century, reparation was made to the bishop's household for damage inflicted by King Brochfael 'in accordance with their status and the nobility of their kindred'.[14] Conceptually, therefore, early Welsh society was highly stratified, and that stratification was fundamental to the working of the social system, to the maintenance of balance within communities and to the proper performance of obligations and responsibilities.

We do not lack references to the fact of this stratification in non-legal, pre-Conquest sources: the *Historia Brittonum* records the conversion of all grades (of English, in fact, though the perspective is Welsh); the author of the Colloquy remarked that no-one, of whatever grade, escaped the effects of defeat; Rhigyfarch recorded the meeting of bishops, kings, princes, nobles and all grades of the British people; Ieuan distinguished kings, people (*populi*), clergy and peasants (*coloni*).[15] Much more frequently we find references to persons of higher status, who are more usually distinguished from the mass than is any other group, as in Rhigyfarch's example above. These are the aristocracy, persons variously termed in Latin and the vernacular. It is, of course, difficult to equate the terms of Latin sources with those of the vernacular, and yet more difficult to translate these into sensible modern equivalents. The law codes characteristically use *uchelwr*, literally 'high man', and especially *breyr*, a word derived from **brogo-rix*, 'king of the bro'. Latin sources use *optimates, meliores, nobiles*, literally 'best men', better men', 'nobles', but several others too, and the Latin redactions of the law texts usually render *uchelwr* by *optimas*. There may be no consistency in terminology and approach other than the implication that there were always 'higher, better' people. References to an aristocracy, then, in some way or other, are to be found in virtually every type of material, from the 'noble fostering [of Samson], following the noble custom of noble forefathers' in sixth- or seventh-century Dyfed to the 'inferiors' and 'superiors' of the *Historia Brittonum* in ninth-century Gwynedd, and the action taken by the *optimates* of Ystrad Tywi and Dyfed in 1047.[16]

Was this a nobility of wealth, the top stratum of the economically-differen-
tiated groups, or a nobility whose high status rested on other determinants?
Certainly by the late eleventh and early twelfth centuries the former was
assumed to be so: the noble girl was the one who was dressed in silk, the one
associated with the symbols of wealth; the children of 'gentlefolk' could also
be distinguished by their clothing.[17] It is not so obvious that this was so at
earlier periods, however, for the overt stress of the written source material is
on birth and function rather than wealth itself. It was common to describe
status with reference to birth: Lifris argued that Cadog was more worthy than
David 'by birth'.[18] Noble stocks, noble lineages, noble families are commonly
instanced in the Lives and occasionally in the earlier poetry; Samson's noble
forefathers evidence the same attitude; while the tenth-century 'Ordinance of
the Dunsaete', though written in English from an English viewpoint, nevertheless characterizes the Welsh as 'thegn-born' or 'ceorl-born'.[19] Accordingly,
the marriage of nobles had to be to appropriately noble mates, and conversely
the advance made by a noble to a humble girl was itself ignoble since he was
too high-born for her.[20] Nobles, moreover, did distinctive things: before
Samson, in the sixth century, they did not become clerics; they were warriors
and leaders of hosts, according to the poetry; they were the companions and
associates of kings, and their honoured and honourable servants; they gave
judgments; and by the time of the prose tales they certainly did not do dirty
jobs like shoemaking or cooking.[21] In the South-East, at least from the eighth
century, it was the landowners (classified as 'better men' and 'elders') who
formed the constant element in local meetings, before whom transactions
were performed and disputes presumably settled. Their role in dispute
settlement is certainly clearly evidenced in the Lichfield marginalia, which
concern the area near Llandeilo Fawr.[22]

In the usage of the law tracts, which may be only partly or marginally
relevant to the pre-Conquest period, there are still further types of distinction. The word *uchelwr* seems to refer to the person who had status
because of his maturity: the established head of household rather than the son
who already had *landed* possessions but had not yet succeeded to his father's
household. In fact, Giraldus, reflecting over the past centuries, implied that it
was the *uchelwyr* of the South who had political power, since they were
'difficult to control'.[23] Moreover, the term *bonheddig* (often rendered as
nobilis in Latin texts of the laws and meaning literally 'man of stock') refers
to the man with full rights in the community as opposed to the foreigner
(*alltud*) or the slave (*caeth*) who had less. Here status has a different significance and the notion of nobility has more the meaning of 'freedom' (as also
happens in continental contexts in the early medieval period) and more to do
with free participation — rather like the modern bestowal of the freedom of a
city — than with sheer wealth.[24]

We may say, then, that there is plentiful evidence of social stratification in
early medieval Wales, and of the recognition and classification of some
groups as noble. Though there must have been *some* economic basis to it, it is
notable that 'noble' status seems more often to have been determined by
birth, family and occupation than by wealth alone. One may note again the
persistence of these attitudes into the twelfth century: 'The Welsh value distinguished birth and noble descent more than anything else in the world.

They would rather marry into a noble family than into a rich one', wrote Giraldus.[25] Of course one might expect some regional and chronological variation, and of course in many cases the noble family would have been the wealthiest, but we do not have to suppose that this was necessarily so.

There is little detail of the status and attributes of those groups and persons who were less than noble; for obvious reasons, since the sources are less concerned with them. The *rusticus*, the peasant, passes by from time to time, and in the latest material we hear of cooks, butchers and shoemakers as less than noble. For the most part, however, information is confined to the lowest social group — the slaves. There is absolutely no doubt of the existence of slavery in Wales in the early medieval period and of the capture of some people for slavery by the Vikings in the tenth and eleventh centuries. For much of the time this was no different from the situation elsewhere in Europe — slavery was normal — but there is some reason to think that the rate of manumission, the freeing of slaves, in the ninth and tenth centuries was less than in other parts. By the twelfth century slavery was relatively uncommon in western Europe; incidental references to slavery in Wales, the presence of greater numbers of slaves in the late eleventh century in western parts of England, Cornwall especially, and their persistence in the later medieval law tracts would suggest that this was not so in Wales.[26] Hence, even the late Lives have anecdotes of slaves and slavery which suggest that the notion was not uncommon: there are no introductory words which refer to the practices of former bad times, as might be expected. St Carannog tamed a dreadful serpent, so that it came to him just like a slave does who obeys his master. Rhigyfarch remarked upon the *ancillae*, female slaves, who waited on the wife of the pagan Baia, who met St David, and — as commanded by the wicked wife — took off their clothes and gambolled around in a vain attempt to seduce his monks. Other tales are neither so charming nor so titillating. Lifris seemed to glory in relating that St Cadog's curse ensured that the progeny of Meuthi's servant would be subject to others for ever; and that Cadog ensured that a thief was condemned to perpetual servitude.[27] Though we can mark the existence of and reference to these slaves, we cannot say much about their lives and conditions. The poet of 'Etmic Dinbych' made a political point in preferring the slaves of Dyfed to the dependent peasantry of Deudraeth, and the poet of *Armes Prydein* emphasized the fundamental nature of the social stratification and theoretical lack of mobility by commenting that after the slaughter slaves wore crowns; so great, so terrible was the social upheaval that the slaves came out on top.[28] The tale of the thief in the *Vita Cadoci* indicates that some slaves may have achieved their low status in punishment for crimes committed — penal slavery, as was judged (but not effected) for one case in Gwent in the mid-tenth century, and as is implied by provision for the sale of thieves in the law tracts.[29] The greater proportion of material, however, would suggest that hereditary slavery was more normal. People were born slaves as they were born nobles, and references to the act of enslavement almost invariably mention the progeny as well as the men enslaved. The Llandaff charters record an instance of one rich man giving himself and his offspring, and their lands, into perpetual servitude in recompense for the murder of a boy, so voluntary slavery can also be envisaged. More frequently this charter material records how slaves

Figure 24. A record of manumission in Wales, added to the Lichfield Gospels in the ninth century, Lichfield MS 1, p.218 (photograph Courtauld Institute of Art; reproduced by kind permission of the Dean and Chapter, Lichfield Cathedral).

changed hands: they might form some part of payments, like the Saxon woman handed over round about 740; they might be handed over together with lands granted to the church, like the estate of Llandenni c.760, or two men and their offspring c.885, or the two men and their paternal inheritance given c.980.[30] These were grants made by pious landowners, for the sake of their own or their family's souls; the slaves simply changed owners. It is these latter instances which call to mind the fact that the slave was indeed a chattel; he could be transferred from one owner to another, with apparently no voice in the transaction. This does not necessarily mean that material conditions were bad for him or life unpleasant; it does mean that he lacked the freedom to consider how he would use his labour or body and, though he himself had a worth and was entitled to a small compensation for insult, he had only a very limited privilege recognized by law. The worth of his animals and his household goods therefore finds no place in the graded lists of the law

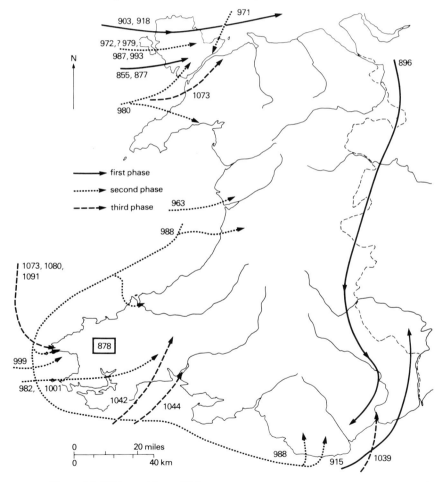

Figure 25. Viking raids on Wales.

tracts: loss of or damage to them was not compensatable in accordance with his status. That material conditions were not necessarily bad is made very plain by the one crucially important record of manumission that survives, a record of the ninth century from Llandeilo Fawr, written into the margins of the Lichfield Gospels (see fig. 24):

> It is necessary to inscribe some letters to the effect that the four
> sons of Bleddri have given freedom to Bleiddud son of Sulien and his
> seed for ever, for a price; and this is the confirmation that he gave
> four pounds and eight ounces [of silver presumably] for his freedom.
> [It was done] in front of suitable witnesses, of the laity Rhiwallon
> [and so on], of the clergy, Nobis bishop of St Teilo's, Sadyrnwydd
> priest of St Teilo's, Dubrin and Cuhelyn the bishop's son... and
> Sulien, the scholar who faithfully wrote this. Whoever shall preserve
> this decree of freedom for Bleiddud and his seed shall be blessed; he
> who does not preserve it shall be cursed by God and by Teilo, in
> whose Gospels it is written.[31]

Manumission clearly *did* occur in Wales, even if we have few records of it, and slaves could purchase their freedom; they must therefore have had the means to save and accumulate precious metals as did their fellows in nearby England. At a roughly comparable period Alfred legislated to allow slaves free days on which they might perform their own transactions.[32]

The attacks of the Vikings introduced a new element into the pattern of slavery in western Britain: the possibility of capture and transportation (see fig. 25). The same had happened in the late Roman period when the Irish had come raiding, carrying off the young Patrick. So, the Colloquy includes *captivi* in its ideal monastic household.[33] In 987, so the Annals record, 2,000 men were captured by the 'Black Gentiles', and 50 or so years later Gruffudd descended upon Gwynllŵg with the Orkney pirates and carried off the people. Transportation was not inevitable, however, for Maredudd is supposed to have ransomed some of the Black Gentiles' captives,[34] but the problem of slavery was clearly intensified by the Vikings' arrival.

Lordship and Dependence

Although we cannot determine the details of the relationships between slaves and their owners, the very phenomenon of slavery reminds us that some individuals were personally dependent upon others. By all modern standards they were not free. Slavery is the most extreme form of dependence but there is good reason to think that it was not the only form of dependence prevalent in early Welsh society. Both the laws and the charters, as well as incidental narrative comment, make it clear that in Wales, as in much of western Europe in the same period, there was a tenant peasantry that was in some sense 'unfree', like the *ministri*, servants, and herdsmen of the saints noted in the eleventh- and twelfth-century *Vitae*.[35] Without being slaves and without being treated as the property of their masters, these tenants were less than free to dispose of their own labour; they were often hereditarily tied to their position as tenants. Hence, they might be born with an obligation to return a certain specified render to the owner of the property that they rented. As far as we know, therefore, they had little choice about the fact of their tenant status, although there is nothing to suggest that they were subject to the excessively burdensome demands that were made on tenant peasants in other parts of Europe and in Wales at a later period. We do not know if they had the power to negotiate upon or change the terms of their tenancies; we do not know if, though born into the position, they had the ability to detach themselves from it. If slaves could purchase freedom, however, it seems unlikely that it was totally impossible for some tenants at some periods to negotiate upon tenancies. There is, after all, quite plentiful charter evidence of transactions in hereditary tenancies, and of the alienation of some of them — in the eighth century particularly — to the church. They do not appear to have been subject to arbitrary payments demanded by their landlords, and there is no pre-Conquest evidence which suggests that they were liable to perform labour service in addition to or as a part of the rent owed for their properties. (The post-Conquest law tracts, however, clearly envisage labour service owed to the king by 'bond tenants'.[36]) The personal status of these tenants, therefore, was almost certainly less restricted than that of some of their contemporaries in England and western Europe and certainly less restricted than that of their equivalents in later centuries. Obedience was, however, expected, as is evident from Lifris's tale of the fate of the servant who would not obey the saint: he was burned to death.[37] Though there is a temptation to suppose that they constituted the non-military section of society, as occurred in most parts of western Europe by the eleventh and twelfth centuries, this was not necessarily so in Wales, and there is a most suggestive fragment in Lifris's Life of Cadog which bemoans the slaughter of a peasant army — 'uiris rusticani agminis trucidatis' — as a result of a dispute between some heirs to property: the implication is that the peasant dependants of the contending heirs were involved in fighting out the dispute.[38] Lifris also has a number of chapters detailing the ways in which persons might become subject to the 'service of Cadog': those strangers setting sail but being driven back to Cadog's harbour of Barry should be allotted to his service; those of certain families committing perjury on the Gildas Gospels or the Gildas bell should be taken half-naked to Llancarfan by the clerics who met them. These obscure references may be to the existence of subject tenants or to slaves.[39]

The tenant peasant was therefore in some sense bound, and it is common to refer to him in modern works as 'bondman', 'bond peasant'. The existence of bonds between men, whether imposed or voluntary, is fundamental to early Welsh society, and at the other end of the social scale, among the 'nobles', there is evidence of a different sort of bond, a free association in which the exchange of goods and services was the symbol of goodwill and of mutual support. This bond is the one represented by the military association, an association crucial to the notion of 'lordship' in the vernacular poetry of early Wales. The rhetoric and the images of the ideal are very familiar, and have already been considered in the context of exchange mechanisms. The 'lord' gathered his warband of warriors around him in his hall; he feasted them and provided for them; in return they fought for him. The most famous expression of the idea is that presented in the poem known as *The Gododdin*, the long set of stanzas on the heroes who did not return from the expedition to 'Catraeth', probably Catterick in Yorkshire. Central to the theme of this poem is not merely the defeat which the poet mourns but the contrast between the feasting before and the corpses after, the dual aspects of the bargain and of the relationship.

> From the retinue of Mynyddog they hastened forth; in a shining array they fed together around the wine-vessel. My heart has become full of grief for the feast of Mynyddog, I have lost too many of my true kinsmen. Out of three hundred wearing gold torques who hastened to Catraeth, alas, none escaped but for one man...
> The exalted men went from us, they were fed on wine and mead. Because of the feast of Mynyddog I have become sorrowful, for the loss of the harsh warrior. Shields resounded like the thunder of heaven before the onslaught of Eithinyn.[40]

The warrior, in the words of the poet, gave 'courage in return for mead':

> He slew a great host to win reputation, the son of Nwython slew a hundred princes wearing gold torques so that he might be celebrated. It was better when he went with a hundred men to Catraeth. He was a man reared and nourished on wine, of generous heart; he was a blessed, active man, he was wearer of a broad mailcoat, he was fierce, he was rash, on the back of his horse. No man put on armour for battle — vigorous were his spear and his shield and his sword and his knife — who would be better than Nai son of Nwython.[41]

When the battle was over, if there were survivors, then the lord still had his companions; the 'beer-drinking host was usually about him'; Cynddylan's retinue sang songs about the fire with their lord.[42]

The images of the relationship are very clear and are consistently sustained through the corpus of poetry of supposed sixth- or seventh-century and of ninth-century origin, though the vernacular terminology of what we describe as 'lordship' is extremely complex and varied and would repay close study. Though the poet of *Canu Aneirin*, in particular, had a predilection for mentioning the faithfulness of the followers, there is nothing in this material which insists on the duty of loyalty to the same extent as in Anglo-Saxon poetry, particularly of the Late Old English period, and there is nothing to suggest that the warrior's service was lifelong, an obligation undertaken in young manhood and sustained until the death of either party. Although there is clear evidence here, therefore, of the literary celebration of a type of relationship common in practice and also celebrated in literature in most of western Europe, there is nothing to suggest that the relationship became institutionalized into a framework of lifelong commitments in the way that it did in England and on the Continent. There, from the seventh and eighth centuries until the late medieval period, comparable associations were transformed from the early warbands similar to those described by the Welsh poets to the developed territorialized apparatus of vassalage, homage and fief, the norms of European feudalism. Indeed, the question must be asked if these relationships existed in 'real life' in Wales or if they were merely a literary notion, produced for the entertainment of aristocratic patrons.

The answer must surely be that they *did* exist, even if we cannot assess what proportion of the nobility was associated or if there were significant changes in obligations and expectations over the long period with which we are concerned: Gildas referred to the military companions of his sixth-century kings, the warbands with which they were familiarly associated; the Llandaff charters give some hints of companions who moved about the South-East with their respective kings, appearing at witnessing ceremonies with them, and of the scurrilous companions of ninth- and tenth-century aristocrats; clerics might see themselves as dependants of God, *homo dei* and *servus dei*, echoing the language of European feudalism; the late Saints' Lives proffer anecdotes which incidentally avert to such relationships. [43] It would appear from Gildas, therefore, that the practice was already familiar in the sixth century, and the anecdotal incidents of the Lives are particularly valuable in indicating a continuing consciousness of it. Illtud was supported in the royal household, serving as a noble soldier till he moved to his own household; Lifris presented most figures of secular authority in the company of their military companions — Maelgwn was *dominus*, 'lord', of his soldiers. [44] The Llandaff charters would also indicate that a very small proportion of the individuals had been endowed by kings; their estates may have been the reward for faithful service. [45] The hints are few, but they are positive.

A very high proportion of the above cases refers to the companions of kings, and the exercise of military lordship may well have been essentially a kingly thing, though the Llandaff material makes it clear that this was not exclusively so. Kings were called lords, whether they were the kings of Dyfed who were served by Samson's parents, the kings — *rhi* — who were the warrior lords of *Canu Taliesin*, or the kings like Gwynllyw who were lords of the late *Vitae*, and this emphasizes the political implications of lordship: the lordly relationship affected military capacity. [46] Occasionally, therefore, the language of lordship was used to express a connection between royal power and power over people: 'son of a rightful king, lord (*udd*) of the men of Gwynedd'. [47] Translation of lordship into a description of the relationship between ruler and subject — common in medieval England — is, however, rare. In these contexts it is more usually reserved for more personal relationships.

The dependant of a military lord, therefore, was not merely a servant, for he also received support. This also applied to other dependants. The peasant had his tenure; and though he might have been tied hereditarily to his tenancy, and have had to produce some annual return, it is more than likely that in a good year he would produce sufficient surplus to support himself and family and more. The warrior clearly also received some economic support in the gifts that came to him. Political support is also implied: the lord was the person with at least the military capacity to provide defence, 'defender of the country', 'bulwark of the people'. [48] Social support, too, is implied for the warrior in the milieu provided by his lord:

> Wine, bragget, and mead, Reward for valour,
> A host of singers, A swarm about spits,
> Their torques round their heads, Their places splendid. [49]

The practice of fosterage — the sending of noble children for training and upbringing to the houses of noble associates, whether equal or unequal we cannot say — gave substance to many of the relationships so established. Ceredig, the fosterling, of *Canu Aneirin*, of 'refined manners', provides evidence of the existence of the practice in the warrior society and it was clearly still prevalent in the twelfth century when it was noted by Giraldus. [50] More of it is implied by the occasional reference to a *nutritor* in the Latin texts, surely 'foster father' rather than 'nurse'. Hence, Gildas mentioned the fosterers of royal children; Samson was not so much nobly 'nursed' in accordance with the custom of his family but 'fostered in a noble household'; and one foster parent received an ox when gifts were distributed in the course of the sale of the Villa Reathr in the South-East. [51] We know from early Irish evidence, which is much more plentiful than the Welsh, that the relation-ships of fosterbrothers and fosterparents could be close and binding, and the practice of fostering therefore played its part in cementing the network of social relationships of aristocratic families.

The Family

The support provided for dependants was not the only source of support in early Welsh society and the associations of the dependance network were not the only type of close relationship, for blood relationships were of conside-rable importance as a social institution:

> It is I who know what's good,
> The bond of blood, noble man

Heledd crooned from her mountain top. [52]

There cannot be any doubt that the strength of the family bond is prominent in early Welsh material, and is much more generally distributed than references to lordship. It is not merely the bond between parents and children, brother and sister, that is noted, but the recognition of the rela-tionship and some association between the members of a wider family group. References to a man's kindred are not uncommon: Bivatigirnus, whose life is commemorated on a sixth-century tombstone from Llantrisant in Anglesey (see fig. 27), had been an 'example to all his fellows (*cives*) and kinsmen (*parentes*), in character, in discipline and in wisdom'; Tudfwlch and his kindred (*cenedl*) played a part together in claiming property in the Llandeilo Fawr area in the eighth century; Cadog asked the giant whom he raised to life in Scotland to identify himself with reference to his *cognatio*, his family, 'set of relations'; Cadog made a pilgrimage in honour of the souls of his kindred; in south-east Wales in the early eleventh century Cadwallon's family (father and cousin) were present to hear his admission of guilt after he had been accused of fighting in the bishop's household, and an unnamed member of the bishop's household had his kin (*parentela*) present when an agreement was reached with Rhiwallon who had wounded him; according to his twelfth-century biographer, the noble Gwynllyw remained a supporter, not a suppressor, of the principle of kinship (*parentelae*), and he accordingly supported his family's rather than his own individual interests. [53] The institution of the kindred, the wider family, is acknowledged in many areas of Wales, at most periods. Furthermore, the question of descent — one of the commonest modes of emphasizing and defining family relationships — is, if anything, even more frequently noticed.

It is one thing to be aware of the wider relationship, however, but another to acknowledge this relationship as a constant influence in daily life. It remains normal in modern Western European societies to be aware of the existence of grandparents, cousins, even great-grandparents, and to associate with them on some occasions; we retain an awareness of the wider family and — albeit inconsistently — we sustain some relationship. It is important, therefore, to consider what role the kindred played in earlier societies before jumping to the conclusion that it was necessarily different from our own. First comes the question of definition: did the term 'kindred' refer to all related persons or to a specific group of them? Most societies which recognize a social function for the kindred are precise in their definition of it: it does not represent all related people but those within limited degrees of relationship, related either through the father or through the mother. The Welsh laws make some clear statements about the structure of the Welsh kindred(*cenedl*): it was patrilineally defined, that is through the male side, though this did not exclude women from participation in, for example, payments for homicide (see fig. 26). For some purposes, such as these homicide payments, the effective kindred extended as widely as to the fifth cousin; for others, such as inheritance, the sharing did not go beyond the second cousin. The four-

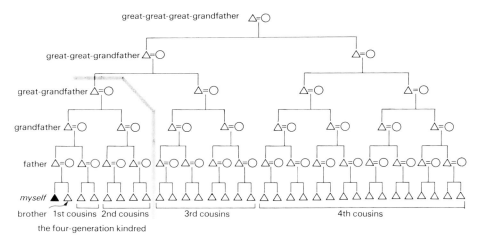

Figure 26. A six-generation patrilineal kindred.

generation group of the latter would therefore include father, grandfather, great-grandfather, brothers, uncles, first and second cousins. There was a head of kin, *pencenedl*, who was responsible for representing the group in some transactions. Women neither joined nor left the kin on marriage, for the mother's kin retained some responsibility for the payment of *sarhad* (compensation for insult) and *galanas* (life price) for homicide committed by a son, and the legal rules on the involvement of maternal kin are complex. A woman's status was, however, affected by marriage: hence, the *sarhad* of a

married woman was assessed in accordance with the *braint* of her husband. [54]
The post-Conquest law tracts, therefore, are clear in identifying kindred,
although it is notable that its composition varied in accordance with its
function and that the position of women is not straightforwardly classifiable.
The details of degrees are not echoed in pre-Conquest material but it is interesting to note that the Colloquy, in instancing its ideal family, confines itself
to the three-generation group (plus children): the pilgrim says 'I was reared in
Ireland/Britannia/Frankia, and I left, deserted, sent away all my substance
and my household and my attendants and all that I had, and father, mother,
grandfather, grandmother, brothers, my wife, my daughter, my sons, my aunt
and all my friends'. [55] Constant reference to the involvement of cousins —
from the political rivalries of cousins chronicled in the eleventh-century *Brut
y Tywysogyon* to the clerical interests of cousins in the seventh-century Life
of Samson — at least supports the notion of a concern that went beyond the
nuclear family group.

Moreover, proper terms do exist in the vernacular for referring to the
different degrees of relationship, and are also used occasionally in Latin texts.
Hence, grandfather, grandmother and aunt of the Colloquy's list are all
glossed in the vernacular; the generically used 'cousin' is sometimes replaced
by the more specific 'first cousin' (*cefnder*, in the *Bruts*), or *fratruelis*,
'father's brother's or brother's descendant', as in Rhigyfarch; *patruelis*,
'father's brother's descendant', is glossed *ceintir*, i.e. *cefnder*; and one early
Christian monument from Glamorgan even uses *pronepos*, 'great-grandson'. [56]

Much more frequent than degrees are indications of an interest in descent,
the defining principle in determining family composition, and hence in determining status. The triads note the 'saintly lineages (*llinys*)'; Illtud's father
Bican came from a distinguished kindred, of noble descent; Cynan was of the
'line of Cadelling'; the men of the North were identified as the men of Coel's
line, the descendants of Coel Hen, and Heledd wept for the loss of her family,
the 'seed of Cynddrwyn'. [57] Seed, stock, race, line, all are words commonly
used in defining and identifying the position of individuals as against each
other, and the very practice of remembering and recording genealogies, long
lines of descent, emphasizes the significance accorded to the fact of descent
itself. Indeed, the writer of the Life of Brynach, when making the conventional introduction on the distinction of the saint's stock, took time to
remark upon the solace offered by relatives. [58]

It cannot be denied that the idea of the kindred, the structured family
group, had some significance in early Welsh society. There is much to
suggest, however, that the smaller group of the nuclear family was the
immediately operative family unit for many Welsh people. The two notions
are not mutually exclusive. Gildas remarked that the British ought to fight for
their wives and children — those nearest and closest — and that the priest
should rule his household like any other paterfamilias, strongly and well.
Cadog's masterbuilder Llywri travelled about with his children, looking for
work; the poor householder of the *Historia Brittonum* lived with his nine
sons. A range of material insists on the closeness between parents and
children. [59] Sons normally inherited their father's property. All of these references stress the significance and tightness of the nuclear unit, even if
occasionally other hints suggest that the residential group could have been

larger than that of the nuclear family, augmented by siblings and/or grand-parents; the listing of the Colloquy cited above might be read to indicate the same.[60] As for family size, there are only a few indications. The poor house-holder was remarkable for his nine sons — and was 'poor' largely because of them; another 'poor' householder of the Llandaff charters was visited with the misfortune of having seven sons because he could not abstain from inter-course with his wife, as St Teilo had recommended.[61] He too was unfortunate in his fertility, and — by implication — unusual. Samson's aunt had three sons already before his own mother conceived, and he himself in the end had five brothers and a sister. The Llancarfan charters refer variously to family interests in property: two brothers and a sister; the three sons of a donor; the two brothers killed by a jealous uncle. The Llandeilo and Llandaff charters have some similar material; the four brothers who sold freedom to Bleiddud; the four brothers who granted land c.708; the three who granted land c.855 and another three who did the same c.864; the two sons who gave their consent to a transaction c.750 and the two who were *hereditarii* c.1030; the two and three slave brothers who were the objects of grants in 885 and 955 respec-tively.[62] The material is fragmentary, but is consistent in suggesting that two, three or four surviving male children was the norm, and consideration of the survival pattern in royal families supports the conclusions — though there is good reason to expect a deviant pattern here, given both the greater access to resources and greater chance of political annihilation.[63]

Perhaps surprisingly, it is also possible to find some evidence of affective relationships within the family, hints of personal affection and emotional responses. Samson's mother looked after the child Samson, even concerning herself with the quality of his play; Hengest proclaimed after the marriage of his daughter to Gwrtheyrn that he would henceforth be as a father and counsellor to him; Heledd wept for her brothers:

> It's not Ffreuer's death grieves me tonight.
> Over brothers' burial
> I wake, I weep, come morning;

Brychan sorrowed at the loss of his daughter; the young Cadog awaited parental consent (not his kindred's) before going to join the hermit Meuthi; as a man he loved his disciple Elli *even more* than a father and mother, but did not fail to rush to attend his father before death.[64] A number of tombstones record the burial together of husband and wife and, once, possibly of mother and daughter (both married). The large sixth-century stone from Llantrisant, Anglesey, is a touching monument not only to a holy woman but to the closeness of husband and wife: 'a most holy woman lies here, who was the very loving wife of Bivatigirnus, servant of God, bishop'[65] (fig. 27). Relation-ships were not always so affectionate, however, and the murder of brothers or cousins is as frequently noted.

If the nuclear family was the unit of everyday association for most people, what was the function of the wider kindred? In the law tracts varying degrees of the kin had responsibility for the debts of its members, for the payment of *sarhad* and *galanas*, for the sharing out of property; and they received compen-sation for ambush and homicide.[66] According to Lifris, when a girl was seized, it was her kin who called the alarm; when an arrest was made, the chief of

Figure 27. The Llantrisant stone (photograph copyright R.B. White).

kindred had to be consulted, and again before a release occurred; when a man was killed, his 'worth' — *galanas* — was paid to his children and land was given to his kin in compensation for the killing; the chief of kindred, in his representative capacity, might receive extra compensation if damage was done to the kin, and he reached his position by the choice of the members. When Tudfwlch 'rose up' to claim disputed lands in the Llandeilo area in the eighth or ninth century, he did so with the support of his kin and committed them to make no future claim. The kin of Cadog, *ex officio*, witnessed the refuge agreement supposedly made with Rhain. The families of Asser and Gulagguin came to an agreement after Asser had killed the latter, round about 940; Rhiwallon concluded an agreement with the bishop and the kin of a member of the bishop's household whom he had wounded, round about 1033; Cadwallon's father and cousin were present to hear his admission of guilt after a fight in the bishop's household, c.1040; Elias received a villa in compensation for the murder of his brother, c.743.[67] The role of the kindred, therefore, in so far as we have any anecdotal evidence, appears to have been principally concerned with property and transactions, and with responsibility at law for offence or injury.

The issue of property is crucial, and problematic, and is the area for which there is the greatest evidence of the operation of the kindred as a significant group. It is perfectly clear that land was heritable: grants and sales were made which conferred perpetual hereditary rights over the properties exchanged — *in ius hereditarium, in propriam hereditatem, hereditario iure* — whether or not this involved total ownership or a right to use some part of the property. The heirs of the donor, or recipient, frequently sustained an interest or obligation.[68] When King Morgan gave Gwengarth a villa in *ius hereditarium* he proclaimed that henceforth no-one but Gwengarth and his heirs should be 'procurator' for that property. If people unjustly took possession of properties to which they were not heir, then disputes, and killings, might arise; inheritance was the usual key to the transmission of property.[69] The law tracts insist that the normal rules for transmission involved the sharing of the paternal inheritance between the sons of the father, with provision being made for daughters' support; and in the event of failure of sons, then the property was to go to first, then second cousins; and in the event of failure of heirs, to daughters.[70] The laws, therefore, while reserving the primacy of the nuclear family, insist on an important rôle for the wider kindred in overseeing and allocating the use of family property rights. The position of the laws is echoed in a number of earlier sources: *Armes Prydein* notes that descent confers the right of possession; family interests in the transmission of property are demonstrated by the involvement of his three sons in a donor's grant recorded in the Llancarfan charters and by the involvement of brothers in donations recorded in the Llandaff charters; very occasionally representatives of a kindred agreed to the alienation of some part of hereditary property in compensation for offences committed in the eleventh century.[71] These interests are also demonstrated by family involvement in the different sort of investment offered by the religious life — Samson's cousin was a deacon in a monastery founded by Samson, and he himself had an uncle also a deacon; Samson's uncle was quickly ordained priest and put in charge of a monastery given to Samson; Illtud's two nephews held office within his monastery and expected to succeed to it; Asser, coming to England from a position of influence at St David's, noted that its archbishop was a relation of his.[72] The only comments upon the division of property are those found in the late Lives: Lifris recorded how Gwynllyw had taken the principal seat of his father's kingdom and the rest of his brothers had divided the remainder between them, in accordance with custom; and the writer of Gwynllyw's own Life also referred to the division. Perhaps surprisingly, one of the Llancarfan charters refers to the shares of two brothers *and* their sister, suggesting the possibility of female inheritance.[73] All of this is entirely consistent with the pattern suggested by the laws, and the succession pattern of the royal families of Wales reinforces it.[74] If we ask how all of this worked on the ground we certainly find problems, but G.R. Jones's suggestion that the pre-Conquest patrimony would have been of *maenol/maenor* size and would not have been subdivided into units smaller than its constituent *trefi* is an attractive solution, though it remains difficult to demonstrate from pre-Conquest evidence (cf. fig. 28).[75] Subdivision was not always welcomed by

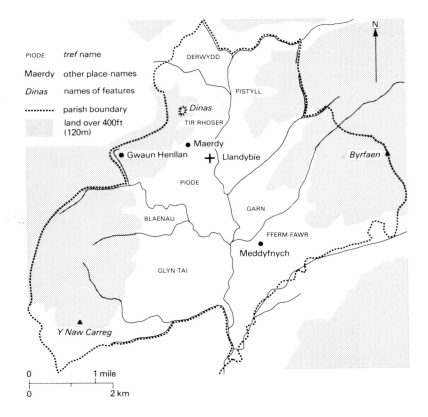

Figure 28. Maenor Meddyfnych and its constituent *trefi* (after G.R. Jones, 'Post-Roman Wales', in *The Agrarian History of England and Wales*, I pt 2, ed. H.P.R. Finberg, 1972, fig.43).

all members of the family, and a corollary of inheritance by brothers was brotherly envy and rivalry, a characteristic of early Welsh relationships emphasized by Giraldus.[76] There are references in the pre-Conquest period to fratricide and to the murder of close relations: Gwyddnerth murdered his brother Meirchion in the South-East in the eighth century and Caradog killed his brother Cynan in the eleventh; King Morgan likewise disposed of his uncle Ffriog; Euan removed his sister's two sons, while the murder of cousins is noted by both the *Historia Brittonum* and Lifris, the latter adding that the deed was done 'for envy'.[77]

If the interest of the family, in the persons of sons or occasionally the wider kindred, in property and its inheritance is easily demonstrable, it is nevertheless clear that automatic inheritance of this type was not the only method of transferring property rights from one individual to another. Lands *were* alienated: they might be the subject of a deathbed grant, alienated by will; they might be given away — almost invariably to the Church, but very occasionally to a secular individual whom the donor wanted to benefit, as King Morgan did when his follower Gwengarth saved his eagle; they might be sold.[78] Though there are certainly cases in which the involvement of the donor's family was noted together with the details of the donation, it cannot be overlooked that in vastly more cases there are no such indications. In the majority of the Llandaff charters alienation of property appears to have been a matter for the donor alone, without a hint of the restraining hand of the kindred. This is not necessarily inconsistent with the prescriptions of the laws: it is possible that, although the interest of the kindred remained residual and was active in the case of failure of near heirs, the kin did not necessarily exert a restraining hand on the attempts of its members to alienate their portions. If so, then the role of the kindred in relation to property was less decisive than in some other early societies, and probably less so than that in contemporary Ireland.

Marriage was a related issue, since it too involved powers over and alienation of some property. Pryderi, therefore, bestowed his mother — and land — in marriage.[79] Family interest in the arrangement of marriages has already been noted: Culhwch's men bargained for Olwen, but her father first had to discuss it with her four great-grandfathers and four great-grandmothers. Cadog bestowed his aunt in marriage; and Samson's parents married each other with the mutual agreement and consent of their respective fathers.[80] Marriage was a matter for negotiation and bargaining, and the bride, as proposed for Rhiannon, could end up marrying someone that she neither chose nor wanted. When Gwrtheyrn demanded Hengest's daughter for himself, he duly promised to give whatever was demanded of him in return.[81] Normally the girl had to be 'suitable'; she should have had no attachments before her marriage; she should certainly be a virgin. If all went well, then at the appointed time the exchange was made: the girl went to her husband, who paid the maiden-fee, *amobr* — payment in recognition of her lord's (usually her father) protection of her maiden status. She herself came with material support from her family (*argyfrau*). Welsh law also adds a further payment, the *cowyll*, from her husband to the girl herself — her morning gift, in recognition of *her* gift of herself.[82] The idea of reciprocity in the arrangement of a marriage was at the forefront. Gildas even referred to a public wedding, though the terms of his reference suggest that this was unusual. [83] Though clerical writers insisted on the 'lawfulness' of marriage contracts, their concern was essentially with marriage within the forbidden degrees, and a petulant irritation at marriage within four or five degrees of kinship was still being expressed by Giraldus in the twelfth century. [84] According to Gildas, Maelgwn's first marriage was unlawful (reason unstated), but as if that were not enough, he had rejected his wife to take on the wife of his brother's son; even this was not enough for him for he soon killed her (and her first husband) in order to take on a third wife, apparently legitimately for she was a widow. King Constantine of Dumnonia, on the other hand, married lawfully but set aside his lawful wife in favour of successive adulteries. [85]

Gildas's complaints against the sixth-century kings of western Britain are a reminder that marriage was considered normal for adults and that separation was possible in this society. Cynddylan died when he was still unmarried, the poet troubled to remark, and Culhwch's father was expected to take another wife when his mother died; childless marriages — at least for royal couples — gave sufficient cause for termination. [86] There is no indication of what happened to the deserted and rejected wives, although presumably their kin took responsibility. The law tracts go into considerable detail on procedure for separation: a woman's *cowyll* remained her own property; if they separated before the end of seven years of marriage she was entitled to her *agweddi* (rather like the English 'dower'); after seven years she had a right to half of the husband's property. [87] Widows are almost invariably presented as highly respectable and respected members of society — the object of sympathy when deserted and widowed by their warrior husbands, the model and symbol of chastity. But if Rhigyfarch thought that St David could have been a support to widows and orphans, he cannot have supposed — or imagined his audience would have supposed — that the kindred structure was necessarily always there to provide the support. [88]

The position of women as such is virtually impossible to assess. By the time that 'Culhwch' and the *Mabinogi* were written down wives were seen as the dispensers of gifts, but this allows the woman a more significant rôle than is usually indicated. Women were not warlike, and were incapable of resisting attack; women were unarmed, though they might carry arms to the combatants in a dispute. Women carried the babies, and saw to the development of the growing child. Good women kept quiet, for modesty's sake. And, like most medieval writers, such was Rhigyfarch's view of the subservient position of women that he substituted a king bee for the queen when he used an analogy of the hive. [89] All of this suggests that, following the biblical model, it was common to regard women as inferior and weak. Though this may well have been a characteristic attitude, we should not forget, as we have seen above, that women *could* have their portions of land; though it is very exceptional to find a woman's name among the hundreds of witnesses present at the conduct of property transactions, it does occasionally happen. It therefore appears that women did not normally play any decisive rôle in the conduct of community affairs — they had no political voice — but that in some circumstances they could do so.

Amongst aristocratic society at least, therefore, kindreds supplied a network of relationships; and marriage might create alliances between those networks. Samson's parents were part of a double intermarriage: two brothers had married two sisters, and the *Historia Brittonum* records not only the continuing interest of father and son-in-law in their girl's new kin, but of the capacity of a girl's father to afford protection to his son-in-law.[90] There remains the problem of the extent of the family's social responsibility. Now, the law tracts suggest that it was the kindred of the killed man who should receive compensation in the case of homicide — father, mother, brothers, sisters, wife, but *not* children; though with a reservation that if the kin failed to exact *galanas* and *sarhad* the king should do so.[91] The pre-Conquest material does not consistently support that position. On the one hand, there is the statement that the worth of the death of one of Cadog's race should be paid to the kin; on the other, the statement that land should be given to the kin of the dead man and his worth to his children; and there are at least two examples of kings demanding the worth, plus compensation, for the killing of their men. The Llandaff material supplies examples of the payment of an estate to a man as the price for the killing of his brother, c.743; and of agreement reached between kindreds as a result of the killing of one member in the mid-tenth century; and of an agreement reached c.1033 between the families of a wounded man and his attacker, even though the wounded man was in fact a member of the episcopal household (which association might have been expected to take precedence over that of the family).[92] These examples suggest that it was common for the kindred of a man to take an interest and be involved in cases of damage; but that the worth was something that went to the nearest relatives, while some further compensation may or may not be paid to the rest of the kindred; and, further, that this was not necessarily the case and that powerful political figures who had a military following were likely to demand the life price of one of their followers, presumably as lord, as against the interests of the man's kin if he had one. It is notable that King Meurig was held responsible in the mid-eleventh century for the assault made by one of his companions, Caradog: this taking on of responsibility for offences committed, the corollary of receiving compensation, would strongly support the possibility, at least in the later part of the period.[93] There is some comparable development at a slightly earlier stage in Anglo-Saxon England: King Alfred's requirement that fighting for a lord would not involve a man in vendetta reflected the changing rôle of the kindred in social functions like the receipt of compensation.[94] Kindred interest may have been the norm in pre-Conquest Wales, but it could be overridden by other interests, and was somewhat loosely and inconsistently defined. Moreover, there are no recorded instances of feud in the pre-Conquest period: the principle of compensation appears to have been accepted rather than that of killing in return. Notably, however, the law tracts prescribe against the taking of vengeance (*dial*) and the root meaning of *galanas* ('enmity', hence 'kindred enmity') must imply some more aggressive practice in the far distant past. The only records of vengeance concern Bleddyn, who would 'do no injury unless injury was done to him', whose blood was avenged by Trahaearn, in the late eleventh century, and Rhodri — who was avenged by God.[95]

The kindred therefore had some rôle in controlling the allocation of property rights and some responsibility for the good behaviour of its members and, together with the lordship structure, provided many of the social functions performed by the modern state; they supplied some machinery of social control and the balance between the interests of different kindred groups was itself some guarantee of social stability. There are also indications that the rôle of the kindred — as in other parts of Europe — was increasing in the tenth and eleventh centuries. The individual's personal security depended on the combination of lordly interest and kindred support rather than upon action taken by the king or state officers. Whether or not the kindred structure reached through all levels of society is impossible to determine, but it is very unlikely to have extended to slaves and foreigners, and rather unlikely to have extended to tied tenants. The personal security of these groups must therefore have been a fragile thing and the pre-Conquest world lacks evidence of any machinery adequate to support them.

Reviewing the status distinctions and the bonds of dependence and lordship, it is tempting to synthesize the results. If the law tract terminology and concepts are applicable even to the last few centuries of the pre-Conquest era, then some correlations suggest themselves. The *bonheddig*, the 'man of stock', translated by *nobilis* in Latin, was presumably the man who had a kindred, as well as the man with full rights of participation in community activities. As such, he was presumably the man who was distinguished from the peasant tenant, for whom neither kindred nor lordship ties provided social support. This leaves very interesting questions which remain unanswered. Were there status distinctions within the 'noble' class? Though the warriors were dependent, they appear to have been men of stock, to have been dependent but free. Were they (and/or their families) an élite within the 'noble', non-tenant strata? Kings occasionally, but only occasionally, appear to have been an instrument of social elevation. Were the companions and warriors of kings, those patronized by kings, an élite? How, if at all, does the notion of a free peasantry accord with this? Maybe, as the 'gentleman' tag of the later medieval period might suggest, the term *bonheddig* covers strata which stretch from untied peasant to warrior hero. These are questions which we cannot yet answer with respect to the pre-Conquest period. It remains extremely important to think about them.

Groups and Associations

The social groupings of which we have the greatest evidence in the pre-Norman period are those supplied by the family, wide and small, and those surrounding the person of a lord, either in the household or as his band of warrior supporters. It is not until the twelfth century that we begin to hear of any urban or work associations — the shoemakers' council and fellow townsmen — but there is a little evidence of associations other than the family and the warband.[96] These are the groupings which might broadly be termed national and local, and which may have some relationship to the developing political structure of Wales. At the widest level there is a clear consciousness of the community of Christians, 'the baptized', to which the early Welsh belonged. They identified themselves in this way, particularly in the face of attack from the pagan English.[97] From the eighth century there is good evidence of their consciousness of themselves as Britons, the original inhabitants of the island of Britain, a consciousness that was repeatedly expressed in the ninth and tenth centuries. Hence, a 'History of the Britons' was written; kings began to call themselves — or be called — kings of the Britons; the notes with the Bamberg cryptogram referred to Merfyn of Gwynedd as 'king of the Britons'; poems like *Armes Prydein* were written in praise of the Britons, with an appeal to all fellow countrymen, *Cymry*, to unite against the English.[98] There was some real feeling of common interest, between the literate and educated groups of Britons at least.

Occasionally descriptive terms were used to express this: we hear of the 'race' of Britons (*gens, natio*), and of other groups like Saxons or Angles.[99] The vernacular term *llwyth*, 'people', is sometimes used, as in the Lichfield Gospel marginalia; though usually assumed to refer to a kin group, it does not mean kin and may imply a wider association. Very occasionally there is mention of *cives*, 'citizens', members of the community; only once does this occur in a context which specifies the size and nature of the community — the 'citizen of Gwynedd' who is recorded on a sixth-century inscribed stone from Penmachno in Gwynedd. Here is a population group larger than the kindred, but smaller than the community of British.[100] Reference to Elmet (Elfed) and *Ordous* on similar stones may possibly have a similar significance.

At other periods, usually much later, there are references to regions within Wales: Argoed, Arwystli, Builth (in the early ninth century), Brycheiniog, Cedweli, Ceredigion, Cynllibiwg, Cynllaith, Dogfeiling, Dyfed, Edeirnion, Ergyng, Glamorgan, Morgannwg, Glywysing, Gower, Gwent and Gwent Is Coed, Gwrtheyrnion, Gwrinydd, Gwynllŵg, Penychen, Rheinwg, Rhos, Rhufoniog, Ystrad Tywi, and so on; the list would be considerably increased by the addition of twelfth-century sources: Elfael, Maelienydd, Tegeingl, and so on (see fig. 29).[101] We have problems if we try to relate these territorial designations to evidence of local group feeling. There is no doubt that these terms were used to refer to specific and recognized areas. In most cases, however, there is no indication of any common feeling or sense of identity of the people who lived within the areas, as happened with the citizen of Gwynedd. But there are comments which indicate the attachment of individuals to their 'country'; he was a 'lover of his country' or 'defender of his country'.[102] We know, therefore, both of the consistent use of territorial names and also that people might feel attached to their own area. We cannot normally, however, make an equation between the regional name and the group feeling. We do not know if the lover of country saw 'country' as meaning Britain or Wales or Gwynedd or Gwynllŵg or some combination; or if and how attitudes changed over time. Certainly, one apparent association, the iron age tribe of Demetae, gave its name to the region of south-west Wales, Dyfed; but, though there are some other possible examples of this, it is an uncommon naming pattern. In Gwent, in the late tenth century, action was taken by the nobles (*uchelwyr*) of Gwent; in the eighth and ninth centuries quasi-judicial action was taken by the *meliores* (established land-owners) of Gwent and Ergyng; in the eleventh century treacherous action was taken by the *uchelwyr* of Ystrad Tywi.[103] In south Wales at least, therefore, there seems to have been some awareness of community of interest among the landowners by the ninth, tenth and eleventh centuries. Is it proper

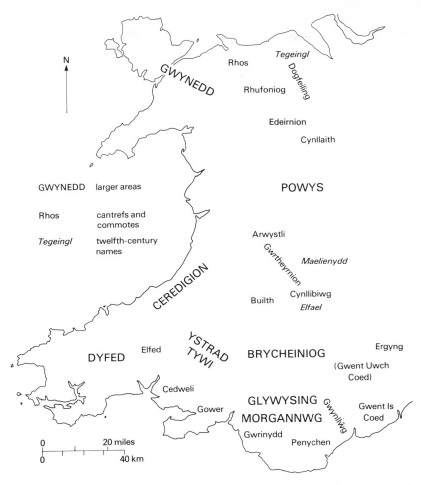

N

GWYNEDD

Rhos

Tegeingl

Dogfeiling

Rhufoniog

Edeirnion

Cynllaith

GWYNEDD   larger areas

Rhos   cantrefs and
            commotes

Tegeingl   twelfth-century
            names

POWYS

Arwystli

Gwrtheyrnion

Maelienydd

Builth

Cynllibiwg

Elfael

CEREDIGION

YSTRAD TYWI

Elfed

DYFED

BRYCHEINIOG

Ergyng

(Gwent Uwch
Coed)

Cedweli

Gower

GLYWYSING

MORGANNWG

Gwynllwg

Gwent Is
Coed

Gwrinydd

Penychen

0   20 miles
0   40 km

Figure 29. Regions named in pre-twelfth-century sources (after M. Richards, *Welsh Administrative and Territorial Units*, 1969).

to assume the pattern to be characteristic of all Wales? Only the highly educated Ieuan, right at the end of the eleventh century, articulated a consciousness of the relationship: he says that he is born 'of the race (*gens*) of Britons' but that Ceredigion is his country (*patria*) and he goes on to define Ceredigion in terms of physical boundaries — the sea, two rivers and mountain block.[104] Here is a piece of territory to which the writer is attached, with which he identifies; it is smaller than the contemporary kingdoms.

The problem is further complicated by political interests: did the kings of the early medieval period exert their authority over already formed communities? Or did they form the communities by the very actions they took in taking control? Indeed, how far was the 'country' loved by the individual the 'country' ruled by the king? Clearly not much in Ieuan's case. Did either, or both, correspond to the classic *gwlad*, 'country', of later historiography?

(In the Juvencus manuscript *gwlad* is used to gloss *regia caeli*, 'royal court of heaven'.)[105] How far were the regional names indicative of administrative units?[106]

Most of these questions cannot be answered at present, but everything would indicate that the answer is not simple, and that there was no necessary coincidence between the self-awareness of a local community, the extent of a king's control and the terms of territorial designation. Boundaries of political units certainly fluctuated. Did the boundaries of local associations fluctuate too? There *was* an awareness of groups and associations outside the family and the warband, apparently a growing awareness; it is attractive to suppose — though unproven — that the growing awareness, rather than contributing to the political development of pre-Norman Wales, created tensions which did not always coincide with kingly ambitions — and which prevented the significant consolidation of any political machine in this period.

4 Secular Politics

Whatever the correlation between kingdom and population group, the attributes of lordship — leadership and dependants — were most commonly associated with kings in the vernacular sources, and the privilege inherent in early Welsh social stratification is most clearly demonstrated by the powers, activities and very existence of kings and their families. Indeed, the Welsh word for king — *brenin* — is etymologically related to *braint*, 'privilege proper to status', and originally seems to have meant 'the privileged one' (and 'freeman' in its legal sense.)[1] Control of dependants gave kings their capacity for political action, a control supported by access to economic resources. Though partly shared with clerics and nobles, it was the kings themselves who dominated political life.

Wales was not a single political unit in the early Middle Ages and the pattern of political development within and between kingdoms — as also between ecclesiastical 'provinces' or spheres — is an extremely complex one. It is difficult to grasp, difficult to unravel, difficult to present. To force the pattern into some coherently-unfolding story is to falsify and mislead, for there was no gradual development towards a consolidated kingdom nor towards increasing governmental and administrative sophistication, as in nearby England. Two things immediately strike the twentieth-century observer, from the distance of 1,000 years and more: firstly, whatever the complexities of their relationship, there were a few continuously prominent kingdoms, the hearts of which lay in the dispersed and more easily exploitable areas of lowland. The Llŷn peninsula and the island of Anglesey in the North-West, the corresponding peninsula of the South-West, and the rich lands of Gwent and the Vale of Glamorgan in the South-East were a constant focus for political activity, while the lowlands of the North-East and middle borderland had a conspicuous rôle in the early period. Secondly, the kingdom of Gwynedd, anchored in the North-West, has a prominence which seems to surpass all others. This is partly because Gwynedd was the last part of Wales to be conquered by the English, and as such was considered the centre of resistance and hence of Welsh political identity. But it is also because the kings of Gwynedd often acted outside their own kingdom and sometimes made claims to some wider hegemony. Though our evidence is fragmentary, both observations offer some clue to understanding the nature and complexities of political activity in early medieval Wales. In the long span of political development, the contrast between the South-East and other parts of Wales was not so stark as it was in some other respects, and it is a contrast which was almost entirely removed by the eleventh century.

The Fifth-Century Hiatus

In the Roman period, Wales had been part of a large Empire whose central government had followed the person of the Emperor whether he was in Rome,

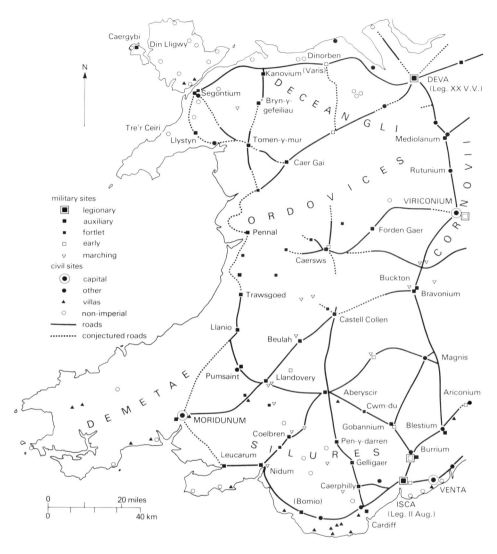

Figure 30. Roman Wales (after D. Moore, *Caerleon Fortress of the Legion*, 1975, fig.5).

Milan, Ravenna or elsewhere. Wales was only a part of one province of Britain, the province known by the fourth century as Britannia Prima, which probably had its provincial capital at Cirencester, with a provincial governor responsible through the tiers of provincial administration to central government, and ultimately to the Emperor, for taxation and judicial business especially.[2] By the late Empire all free members of the provinces had Roman citizenship. We know that the South-East formed the *civitas* of the Silures, the appropriate unit of local government, responsible to the provincial governor for the collection of taxes, with its own *ordo* of a 100 or so local men, sitting in the *civitas* capital at Caerwent (Venta Silurum) and dealing with the registration of transactions and management of public works in the locality.[3] A reasonable case can be made for the existence of a further *civitas* in the South-West, of the Demetae, with its capital at Carmarthen (Moridunum), but there is no good evidence to suggest that the rest of Wales shared the *civitas* structure.[4] The rest may have been divided into *pagi*, rural districts of local government, as the later name Powys — from Latin *pagenses* — might suggest; or it might possibly have been administered as a military zone, from the headquarters of the *dux Britanniarum* at York. In the early centuries of Roman occupation the mountains had been straddled by a network of forts, but since the second century most of these had been abandoned as the sites of permanent military occupation.[5] We may reasonably conclude, therefore, that the inhabitants of mid- and north Wales were no longer hostile to the Roman presence, but there is, of course, very little evidence that Roman habits and institutions were widely adopted in these areas. Some continuing military presence at Caernarfon (Segontium) was necessitated by the requirements of defence, against Irish raiders in particular, and this must have provided some focus of local integration into the Roman system. And Castell Collen, Caersws, Y Gaer (Aberyscir) and Gelligaer may all have been occupied by soldiers in the fourth century. Otherwise, in the late fourth century, Forden Gaer in the midlands was definitely refortified for defensive purposes, as was Cardiff in the South, while a fleet base may have been established at Caergybi, near Holyhead; coins may suggest military occupation at Kanovium.[6] Mineral resources were exploited by central government for some time, the gold mines at Dolau Cothi being worked until the third century, while lead was certainly being taken from Flintshire until the late fourth century.[7]

Roman Wales, therefore, was always a frontier zone. It was a long way from the Mediterranean centre of politics; it was some distance from its own provincial capital. We cannot be sure that the customary Roman machinery of local government was used over the whole of Wales, though we know that it was in some parts. We cannot expect, therefore, that the local aristocracy would have had the political experience common to most parts of the Empire, and we have to admit that for most of the third and fourth centuries — as indeed for the fifth — we have little idea of what was happening.

It is likely that the garrisons of Caernarfon and north Wales were severely depleted when the usurper Magnus Maximus left Britain for the Continent in 388.[8] Contact with central government was terminated in the early fifth century and the effects of this seem to have been very gradual in Britain as a whole; given the third- and fourth-century background, we might expect those effects to have been even more gradual in Wales.[9] There is good evidence, however, of Irish settlement in west Wales, and in the south-western peninsula in particular, although it is impossible to specify numbers and density. The evidence lies in the several notices of raids in the fourth century and possibly later from continental sources, in the fact of the re-fortification and refurbishing of coastal forts like Caernarfon and Cardiff, in the distribution of tombstones inscribed with the distinctive Irish 'ogham' alphabet and of place-names (see for example fig. 31), in the suggestions made by later Irish traditions and by Irish names in some genealogies. At a local level, the metal objects found at Lesser Garth, Radyr, may well be Irish in origin.[10] It is difficult to date the period of settlement, as opposed to raids, although most modern scholars would not dispute a period within the fifth century. The combined implications of Irish and Welsh genealogies would suggest a time shortly after 400 for settlement in the South-West; while the 'ogham' script was used to commemorate the more precisely dated King Gwrthefyr (Vortipor) in the mid-sixth century.[11] The writings of Patrick suggest that the search for slaves encouraged the early raiders, but we cannot rule out the possibility that internal Irish political problems provided the

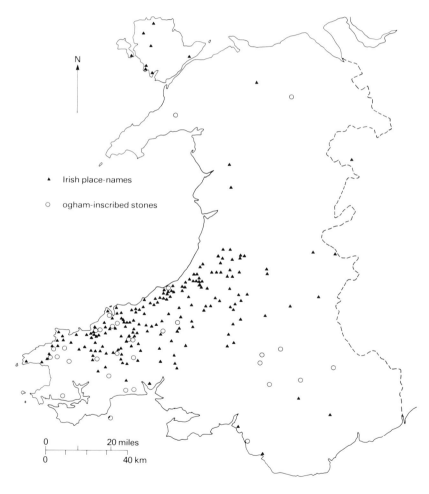

Figure 31. Indications of Irish settlement in Wales (after *ECMW*, fig.2; M. Richards, 'The Irish settlements in south-west Wales: a topographical approach', *J.Royal Soc.Ant. Ireland*, xc, 1960, fig.3).

stimulus for settlement abroad — as the tradition of the expulsion of the group called Déisi, driven from Meath to Leinster, and from Leinster overseas, would have us believe.[12]

Welsh tradition, as recorded in the early ninth century in the *Historia Brittonum*, remembered and honoured other immigrants: the movement of North Britons — from the eastern Lowlands of Scotland — led by Cunedda of the Votadini.

> A great king, Maelgwn, ruled among the Britons, that is in the district of Guenedota, because his great great great grandfather, Cunedag, had come previously from the North with his sons, of whom the number was eight, from the district called Manau Guotodin, one hundred and forty six years before Maelgwn reigned, and expelled the Scots [that is the Irish] with immense slaughter from those districts; and they never returned again to inhabit them.[13]

Contemporary and later historians believed that Cunedda was the ancestor of the principal royal lines of north-west Wales and thereby attributed to him a significant part in the establishment of the post-Roman political framework. The genealogies of Harleian MS 3859 make him, therefore, not merely the great-grandfather (*sic*) of Maelgwn but the father of Dunaut, Meriaun, and Ceretic, the eponymous ancestors of Dunoding, Meirionydd and Ceredigion respectively. Influenced by the historical perspective of the ninth and tenth centuries, modern commentators have sought to give substance to the tradition by supposing some planned movement of the Votadini, at the direction either of the late Roman government or of some successor British government, in order to meet the Irish problem.[14] Irish immigration certainly does not appear to have been as dense in the North-West as it was in the South-West and close contacts between the Britons of north Britain and those of Wales are suggested by the preservation of northern traditions in a Welsh cultural milieu — much of the corpus of Old Welsh poetry mourns or celebrates the lost heroes of the North. The movement, however, entirely lacks contemporary notice and its circumstances are quite beyond reconstruction. It *could* have happened, but we cannot be sure that it did and the nature of the record casts severe doubts on its historicity. A similar model suggested for the South-East in the preface to the Life of Cadog is demonstrably absurd.

The fifth century presents us with an extremely unsatisfactory void. The re-occupation of hill-forts characteristic of this period must have a defensive import: a site like Dinorben near Rhyl can surely only have been inhabited for defensive reasons.[15] Against whom was defence necessary — the Irish, or other raiders, or local enemies? In the case of a fort like Degannwy the enemy must surely have been sea-borne. The fact of Irish settlement is reasonably established, though we can say very little about it. The migration of some of the Votadini is by no means established, and we can say even less about it. It would not be unreasonable to suppose some British immigration into Wales from eastern parts of Britain in the latter part of the century, in response to increasing English settlement there: it is difficult to explain otherwise the influence of spoken Latin, with its vocabulary of Lowland Romanized civilization, on the British language.[16] Others have suggested some Gaulish immigration, on the flimsy evidence of the incidence of Gaulish formulas on inscribed stones; it is not impossible.[17] We may suppose some changes in population, then, and some in density of settlement; but we cannot say much about them. Still less can we comment on leaders and internal politics. No early sources associate either Ambrosius or Gwrtheyrn (Vortigern) with Wales and there is no positive reason to do so. Their localization by later sources may simply arise from the attraction at a late date of the few named persons from the fifth-century hiatus to the remaining British areas. Arthur may well have existed, in the years round about or shortly after 500, but again there is nothing in the early sources which would argue for an association with Wales.

The Emergence of the Kingdoms

After such an unwelcome string of negatives, it is worth pausing to observe that by far the most significant political development of this period must be the fact that kingdoms did emerge. By the early sixth century we know of several in Wales, as also in other parts of Britain and on the Continent; by the early seventh century we know of more. About the middle of the sixth century the cleric Gildas wrote his denunciation of contemporary kings and clerics, of which the following is a small sample:

> Why are *you* senseless and stiff, like a leopard in your behaviour, and spotted with wickedness? Your head is already whitening, as you sit upon a throne that is full of guiles and stained from top to bottom with diverse murders and adulteries, bad son of a good king (like Manasseh son of Hezekiah): Vortipor, tyrant of the Demetae. The end of your life is gradually drawing near; why can you not be satisfied by such violent surges of sin, which you suck down like vintage wine — or rather allow yourself to be engulfed by them? Why, to crown your crimes, do you weigh down your wretched soul with a burden you cannot shrug off, the rape of a shameless daughter after the removal and honourable death of your own wife?[18]

Whether or not one believes the charges and sympathizes with the moral standpoint, the work is clearly of immense importance in identifying particular kings, at least two and possibly three of whom were Welsh. By 540, then, kingdoms had emerged in Britain, and the manner of reference to them suggests that they were no new creation at that date: Gwrthefyr (Vortipor) was already growing old, and was 'bad son of a good king'; Maelgwn had removed the king, his uncle. Gildas wrote, therefore, in at least the second generation of the kingships.

In the early medieval period practice in referring to kingdoms was inconsistent: sometimes a king was named but not his kingdom; sometimes he was called king of a group of people, like Gwrthefyr above; sometimes he was called king *in*, but not necessarily *of*, a named province; the limits of the kingdom did not necessarily coincide with the limits of a region (neither of which are really able to be defined with any precision). The term Gwent, for example, was consistently used for the modern territory of that name (and occasionally more), but only sporadically for a kingdom. All of this makes for complication; hence, in order to make discussion intelligible, I shall use consistent terms, but with the proviso that this does not necessarily reflect the early medieval usage and that territories fluctuated.

Using the clear evidence of Gildas in association with the fragments drawn from other sources, it is possible to identify four Welsh kingdoms of the sixth century; for convenience, these may be termed Gwynedd, Dyfed, Powys and Gwent. Slightly later evidence from the Llandaff charters locates further minor kingdoms in the South-East in the late sixth century and the appearance of a major new dynasty there in the early seventh century. Other fragments indicate the existence of kingdoms in eastern and western mid-Wales in the eighth century, Brycheiniog and Ceredigion respectively. Since

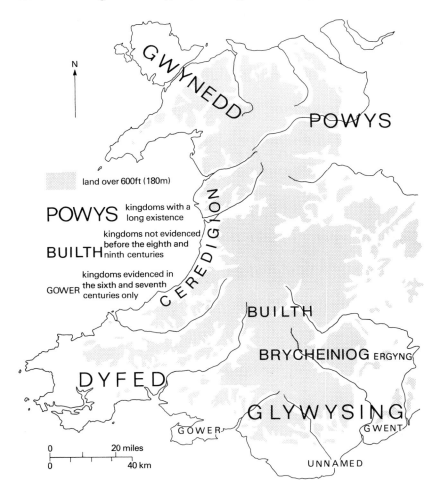

Figure 32. Known kingdoms of early Wales.

information is so scarce, we cannot be sure that this represents the total number of early kingdoms nor that the earliest references reflect their emergence, and the possibility of additional candidates will be considered shortly (see fig. 38).

The kingdom of Gwynedd (Guenedota) in north-east Wales is well-evidenced from an early period: Gildas called its king, Maelgwn (Maglocunus), the 'island dragon... first in evil, mightier than many both in power and malice, more profuse in giving, more extravagant in sin';[19] the Welsh Annals record his death, as *rex Genedotae*, 'king of Gwynedd', round about 547; writing of the next century, Bede recounted the energy and savage tyranny of his later successor Cadwallon, *rex Brettonum*, 'king of the Britons', fighting against the Northumbrian kings.[20] Cadwallon's own father is remembered on his early seventh-century tombstone at Llangadwaladr, in

Figure 33. The Llangadwaladr stone (*ECMW* no.13; reproduced by courtesy of the University of Wales Press).

Anglesey, where he is hailed as 'Catamanus rex sapientisimus opinatisimus omnium regum (Cadfan, the most wise and most renowned of all kings)'[21] (see fig. 33). These names also occur in the Gwynedd genealogy of Harleian MS 3859, as does that of Cadwallon's son Cadwaladr, mentioned in the *Historia Brittonum*.

In the South-West, we have already noted the tyrant of the Demetae, Gwrthefyr, whose memory is also preserved by the stone in the churchyard at

Castelldwyran in Carmarthen, inscribed in Latin and 'ogham',[22] and whose name occurs in the Harley genealogy of Dyfed. The seventh-century Life of Samson, referring to the sixth century, names the province and nobility of Demetae and classifies Samson's paternal ancestors as *ministri terreni regni*, royal servants.[23] The combined sources indicate a kingdom of Dyfed. The Life of Samson also refers to the province of Gwent, to the east of the Demetae, while the Llandaff charters not only name Iddon as king of Gwent in the very late sixth century, but locate his grants and his appearances precisely in northern Gwent, the later Gwent Uwch Coed.[24] Across the river Monnow, still west of the Wye, the same charters reveal the existence of a kingdom of Ergyng (Ercic[g]) for at least two generations in the late sixth century, and further west a minor royal enclave — unnamed — in the region of Cardiff, and another in Gower in the seventh century.[25] Other kings are named but they cannot be precisely located.

In the South-East, in the seventh century, however, there appeared new kings near the mouth of the river Wye, who gradually exerted authority over the minor kingdoms and eventually, acquiring their lands, absorbed them, partly by a policy of marrying into the existing dynasties. The pattern of distribution of grants and witnessing of these kings, Meurig ap Tewdrig and his descendants, as evidenced by the Llandaff charters, allows us to reconstruct their gradually extending influence from coastal regions to the whole of the South-East, until, in the second quarter of the eighth century, we find no further traces of minor kings. This situation remained until the tenth century, when new intruders began to undermine the control of Meurig's dynasty. Until then, the kingdom, whether under the control of a single king

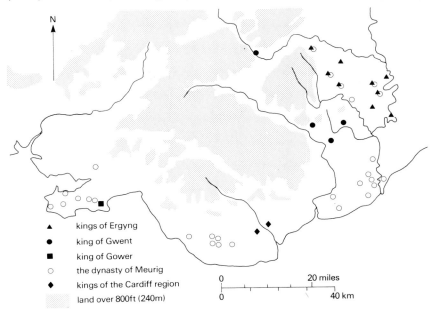

Figure 34. Kings of the South-East in the sixth and seventh centuries (after W. Davies, *An Early Welsh Microcosm*, 1978, maps A-D).

or shared by several members of the family, was known by the new term of 'Glywysing', after Glywys, the supposed ancestor of the dynasty. 'Gwent' remained in use as a regional name but not as a term proper to the kingdom (see fig. 34).

Powys, in the east midlands, is more problematic since the term itself is not used in association with kings or kingdom in sixth-century sources and does not certainly so occur until the ninth century (*AC* 808); the existence of a dynasty in the area is, however, usually accepted. The Annals refer to the death of Selyf (Selim), son of Cynan, at the battle of Chester in about 616, while Bede refers to the participation and subsequent flight of one Brochfael (Brocmail) at the same occasion. [26] All three names also occur in the Harleian collection of genealogies — with Brochfael as Selyf's grandfather — in genealogies which include known later kings of Powys; and Cynan, son of Brochfael, is commemorated as a successful member of that family in the famous early praise poem of *Canu Taliesin*. [27]

> The lineage of Cadelling, immovable in battle...
> The son of Brochfael, boundary-extending, conquest-seeking...
> All around the world under the sun — they are subject to Cynan.

Since his raids reached Anglesey, Dyfed, Gwent and Brecon, he presumably moved out from a base in the North-East. Certainly by the ninth century then — and arguably by the seventh, if we accept the earliest date for *Canu Taliesin* — these leaders were believed to have belonged to the Cadelling, the dynasty which supplied the later kings of Powys. The statement of the same relationships in a number of independent sources would support the possibility that that dynasty was already active in north-east Wales in the late sixth century. But even if they were not related to the main dynasty, the early evidence remains sufficient to indicate the activity of a family of leaders in that area at that date. [28]

The mid-Welsh kingdoms cannot be evidenced before the eighth century, but became clear at that period. The Llandaff charters note several kings of Brycheiniog (*Brecheiniauc*) in the middle of the eighth century, conflicting with each other and making land grants. They are associated with properties on the upper waters of the Usk — near Llan-gors, Llandeilo'r fân and Llanfihangel Cwm Du. [29] Asser also referred to the royal line of Brycheiniog in the later ninth century, in the context of the southern kings' oppression by Gwynedd, while the men of Brycheiniog are noted from time to time by the Annals. [30] The *Historia Brittonum* comments that Ffernfael (? and his father) rule in Gwrtheyrn's original kingdom, in the region of Builth, from which we must presume another early ninth-century kingdom: 'It is Fernmail, son of Teudubir, who rules now in the two regions (*regiones*) *Buelt* and *Guorthigirniaun*. Teudubir is king of the Builth region, son of Pascent'. [31] Whether or not it had any subsequent or earlier history is difficult to say. To the west, the death of the first named king of Ceredigion (*Cereticiaun*) is mentioned by the Annals in 807.

Though we may have some confidence in the *existence* of the above named kingdoms at the times specified, in most cases it is not worth speculating on origins or extents. Though the ninth- and tenth-century genealogical collections often assign a Roman imperial or a Christian ancestry to contemporary royal lines — that of Gwynedd was supposedly descended from Anna, the cousin of the virgin Mary, that of Dyfed from Constantine the Great, that of Powys associated with Magnus Maximus — and though some of those genealogies include Roman names (like Aetern[us] and Patern[us] and Tacit[us], the immediate ancestors of Cunedda), we cannot comment on the relationship between the dynasties which emerged and their Roman or Romanized forefathers.[32] In many cases it is reasonable to assume some connection with Roman Britain. Continuity of nomenclature, for example, is often marked: the kingdom of Dyfed (Demetae) must at some stage have represented the political unit of the iron age and Roman Demetae of south-west Wales. The problem, therefore, is not so much the *fact* of the connection but the nature of it. In England, a good case can be made for the significance of the late Roman city, *civitas* capitals in particular, as the focus of political power for the families which made themselves kings.[33] Gloucester, Cirencester and Bath had three kings associated with them by the late sixth century, even if each one did not constitute a single, separate kingdom.[34] A similar case might well be made for Gwent: it was the *civitas* capital, Venta Silurum, which gave its name to the early kingdom and to the region, although the city no longer appears to have been a significant political focus in the late sixth century. Much, much later, tales surface which tell how King Caradog vacated the city for a site near the coast in order to allow a monastic community possession of and maybe shelter in it.[35] Comparably, it was the town of Ariconium, Weston-under-Penyard on the eastern bank of the Wye, which gave its name to the kingdom and region of Ergyng. On the whole, however, Wales was not a land of Roman cities and it would clearly be unsatisfactory to use the analogy of cities in England as a general aid for understanding its development. Cities were not necessarily useful. The families which elevated themselves and assumed titles of independent authority presumably utilized whatever sources of power and wealth were available. Hence, the movement to hill-forts like Dinas Powys near Cardiff or Dinas Emrys in Snowdon, both occupied in the fifth to seventh centuries, and the re-occupation of abandoned military forts, like that of Y Gaer near Brecon, is almost certainly associated with the political change, whatever the defensive requirement, with the redistribution of power and with the gathering of resources to maintain it. Since, however, we do not know when titles were assumed, we are in no position to assess the relative value of different sources of power.

Changes in population may also have provided a stimulus for the founding of kingdoms, both to defenders against immigrants and to the leaders of movements. The occurrence of Irish names in the Dyfed genealogy, and the circumstance of the preservation of 12 generations of that genealogy in an apparently independent Irish context, must suggest the intrusion of the Irish not merely into the land of Dyfed but also into the political control of it in the fifth century.[36] Gwrthefyr, after all, was commemorated both in Latin and in Irish alphabets. The tradition of Cunedda's settlement in Gwynedd, and the division of political authority between his sons, whether or not it is true in detail, provides a further credible context for the emergence of kings and kingdoms. Yet another context is suggested by the tradition of Gwrtheyrn's association with Gloucester, as reported even less reliably by the *Historia Brittonum*, in implying the displacement of unsuccessful British leaders from

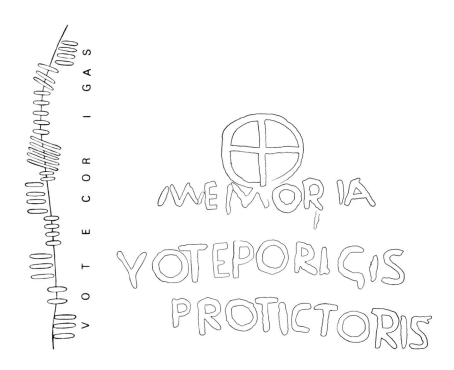

Figure 35. The Castelldwyran stone (*ECMW* no.138; originally published in *Archaeologia Cambrensis* and reproduced by kind permission).

England: not only was Gwrtheyrn's great-grandfather the founder of Gloucester, but his son Pasgen and his descendants had ruled Builth and Gwrtheyrnion from the death of Gwrtheyrn until the present, it reads.[37] There is no need to believe the lurid details of Gwrtheyrn's travels through Wales, nor the more sober ancestry of Ffernfael, the latest of the line, but the suggestion of expulsion from some place such as Gloucester is quite credible, and the tale, moreover, reminds us that several Welsh regional *and* kingdom names are formed from personal names; hence, Gwrtheyrn and Gwrtheyrnion, Brychan and Brycheiniog, and so on. By contrast, the reconstructed narrative of the slow acquisition of property and power by the dynasty of Meurig ap Tewdrig in the South-East is much more mundane, but it provides a useful indication of the ways in which power could have been acquired.

If comments on origins are highly speculative, then even more are those on the extent of the kingdoms. Many centuries pass before we can speak of known, fixed boundaries, though it is clear that by the eleventh century geographical features were utilized; in many cases it is not possible to associate more than a few named places with the kings of the early period. Once again, the unusually detailed local evidence from the South-East permits much greater precision. The minor kings of the sixth century are only to be found in very limited areas, of little more than 15 miles radius; the first appearances of the new dynasty are very coastal, but by the middle of the eighth century Meurig's great-grandson Ithel can be found throughout the extent of modern Gwent, Glamorgan and south-west Hereford.[38] The same material associates kings of Brycheiniog with Llandeilo'r fân, Llanfihangel Cwm Du and Llangors; much later tradition includes Talgarth too.[39] The Llandaff charters also associate the Dyfed kings with lands near Tenby, Penally, Llandeilo Fawr, Llanddowror, Mathri and Cenarth, while Gwrthefyr's stone lies in Castell-

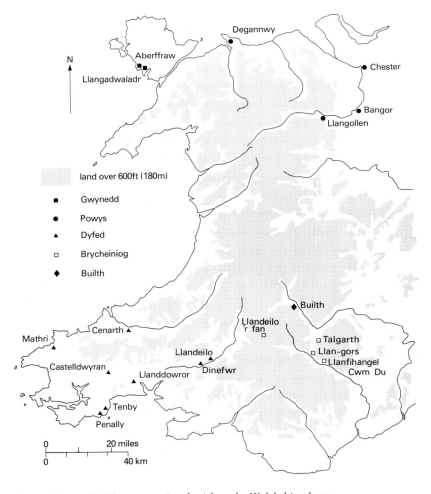

Figure 36. Places associated with early Welsh kingdoms.

dwyran churchyard. By the twelfth century Dinefwr was seen as the traditional 'capital'.[40] In the North, Cadfan's stone is at Llangadwaladr, close by
Aberffraw, associated with the Gwynedd dynasty in the laws and later
tradition, and it is not unreasonable to suppose that the list in the Harleian
collection of genealogies of the sons of Cunedda, eponymous ancestors of
regions of the North-West, represents some view of the extent of Gwynedd in
the mid-tenth century.[41] For Powys, the pillar of Elise (fig. 43) lies near
Llangollen. Early battles were at Chester and Bangor, and the destruction of
Degannwy seems to have led to political disintegration in the early ninth
century.[42] Builth presumably included modern Builth (see fig. 36).[43]
However, there is no need to suppose that all the land of Wales formed part of
some kingdom by 600 or even 700, and there may have been more kingdoms
than those of which we have sure knowledge.

The possibility that there were more kingdoms is a real one, given a
number of additional hints. The annal for 816 of *Brut y Tywysogyon* almost
casually refers to a kingdom of Rhufoniog overrun by the Saxons.[44] This may
be a late amplification of the original annal or it may indeed reflect the
wording of an early contemporary record. The *Vita Cadoci* envisages
kingdoms of Rheinwg and/or *Reinmuc* somewhere outside the South-East.
One early inscribed stone from Llanaber, Ardudwy, commemorates Caelestis
the (?mountain) king (*rigi*).[45] There are no clues to explain this, but it strongly
supports the possibility of the existence of more un-noted kings. The other
additional hints derive from two principal sources: genealogies and poetry.
Even the earliest genealogical collection, Harleian MS 3859, records more
lines than there are known kingdoms. Some of these clearly relate to the
North of Britain and are not relevant for present purposes. Others, however,
are associated with named regions of Wales by later genealogical collections,
and there is no reason to question these associations — particularly since they
occur in the parts of the collection concerned with known Welsh kingdoms. If
the intention of the Harley collector was to record known royal lines then it is
possible that the additional lines represent further independent kingdoms.
This is not necessarily implied, however, for even supposing that the
collector's interest was in royal and not merely aristocratic families, it is
possible that he was recording different branches of the same family with
claims to the known kingships, just as the English collector of genealogies in
BL MS Vespasian B vi recorded the several lines descended from Pybba, father
of Penda, three, six and seven generations before, each of which had supplied
kings of Mercia in the seventh and eighth centuries: Aethelred (674-716) from
Pybba through Penda; Aethelbald (716-57) from Pybba through Eowa; Offa
(757-96) from Pybba through another son of Eowa; Coenwulf (796-821) from
Pybba through Coenwalh.[46] Since we have five lines of the North-West all
supposedly descended from Cunedda, and since one king of the line which
was subsequently associated with Rhos seems to have been king of Gwynedd
in the late eighth century, the possibility is considerable.[47]

The potential additional royal lines are those for Rhos (no.3 in the Harleian
collection), Dunoding (no.17) and Meirionydd (no.18) — all descended from
Cunedda. Of these, two names of the Meirionydd line are usually identified
with the 'Iudris' and 'Brocmail' of the Annals, who died c.632 and 662 respectively. They are not termed kings in the record: it is therefore impossible to

say whether they were kings of Meirionydd or more or less successful con-
tenders for the kingship of Gwynedd — Idris was strangled in the year after the
great Cadwallon's death and Brochfael died some 30 years later, 20 years
before the death of Cadwallon's son Cadwaladr. An interest of Idris and
Brochfael in Gwynedd is therefore quite possible. We can make no comment
on Dunoding but Rhos, as noted above, supplied one Gwynedd king in the
late eighth century and *may* have been ruled by Cynlas in the mid-sixth
century: the Rhos line includes a *Cinglas* three generations after Cunedda and
eight generations before the late eighth century, while a *Cuneglasus* is named
but not located by Gildas.[48]

There are, further, problems of the lifespan of these kingdoms: a case can
clearly be made for the existence of kingdoms of Rhos and Meirionydd in the
sixth and seventh centuries respectively. We know that a kingdom of
Ceredigion was recognized in the ninth century, and the Ceredigion
genealogy similarly traces descent from Cunedda. Even though the number of
generations back to Cunedda is less than those for the lines of Gwynedd,
Rhos, Dunoding and Meirionydd, the implication is that the Ceredigion line
had a pre-ninth-century history, and possibly therefore that so did the
kingdom. If we accept all of these suggestions, Ceredigion may have belonged
with the sixth- and seventh-century kingdoms; if we do not, then it may have
been a development of the central period.

The second problem area lies in the suggestions surrounding the families
dominant in Powys in the seventh century. There is a relatively large corpus
of poetry of the ninth century which mourns the death of Cynddylan and
family, once dominant in Shropshire, that known as 'Canu Heledd', part of
the larger corpus known as *Canu Llywarch Hen*. According to the poems,
Pengwern is in ruins, the well-known lands by the Tren (i.e. Tern) are empty,
all Powys grieves since the defeat of Cynddylan and his brothers, and Heledd
his sister keens alone from her mountain top.[49]

> My brothers were slain at one stroke,
> Cynan, Cynddylan, Cynwraith,
> Defending Tren, ravaged town....
> White town between Tren and Trafal,
> More common was blood on the field's face
> Than ploughing of fallow....
> The hall of Cynddylan, dark is the roof,
> Since the Saxon cut down
> Powys's Cynddylan and Elfan....
> It's not Ffreuer's death I mourn for tonight
> But myself, sick and feeble,
> My brothers and my land I lament....
> Heledd the hawk I am called.
> O God! to whom are given
> My brothers' steeds and their lands?[50]

The message is powerful; it bewails the end of a local ruler; it locates the river
Tern in Shropshire, and names further places in the neighbourhood — the
river Severn, the Wrekin (Dinlle Ureconn), Ergal (cf. High and Child's Ercall),
Baschurch, Meheli (Eli, near Newtown), and two Rhiw rivers probably near

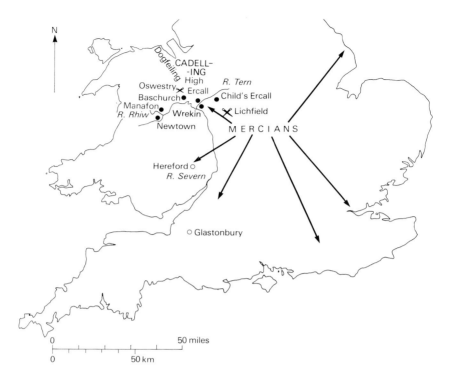

Figure 37. Places associated with the family of Cynddylan.

Manafon (Dwyryw) (see fig. 37);[51] it associates the family with the fortunes of Powys. (Pengwern is often identified with Shrewsbury, on the authority of Giraldus, but there is no early support for this.[52]) From the perspective of the poet, Powys was clearly associated with Shropshire and the lands over the modern border, a perspective reiterated by Giraldus in the twelfth century. No appropriate genealogy occurs in the Harley collection, but there is another, probably earlier poem, 'Marwnad Cynddylan', which relates how Cynddylan, ruler of Dogfeiling, and his brother Morfael fought at Lichfield from beyond the Tern, apparently against the Christian British population.[53] One line of *Canu Llywarch Hen* associates Cynddylan with the cause of Penda of Mercia at the battle of Maserfelth (near Oswestry); Penda's descendants are known to have been in control of the Wrekin area by the late seventh century, while the Harley genealogy for *Glastening* comments that Glast, the eponymous ancestor of Glastonbury, came through Lichfield, and was father of Morfael.[54] This is a difficult area, for the material is late and sometimes garbled, but certainly ninth-century tradition seems to have seen this family as active in the west Midlands — initially in association with Penda of Mercia — and then ousted. Given the control of this area by Mercia by the late seventh century, this is quite credible; and it is not impossible that some survivors went south, to the Glastonbury region. The material, therefore, would suggest a lost dynasty of the west Midlands, central marches and east Wales, thriving in the early seventh century but soon displaced.

This has some significance for Powys. The Cynddylan family was associated with Powys in ninth-century tradition — we cannot be certain of anything earlier — while the line of Cadell was identified with the Powys kingship by the ninth century; and the line of Cadell already seems to have been politically active by the early seventh century. If the Cynddylan traditions contain even a speck of truth, then there must have been *two* Powys lines in the early seventh century or *two* branches of the Cadelling, one in the far North-East, and one in the east midlands and marches. [55] The removal of Cynddylan and his family and the establishment of the English in Shropshire and Herefordshire would then have allowed the Cadelling to intrude their

Figure 38. The known kingdoms of early Wales, with some possible additions.

influence south into the middle borderland of Wales, the western extremity of Cynddylan's area.

We can summarize the situation in the early period as follows: after the hiatus of the fifth century, we know of major kingdoms in north-west and south-west Wales in the early sixth century, Gwynedd and Dyfed respectively; of several minor kingdoms in south-east Wales and the Cadelling dynasty in the North-East in the late sixth century; of the establishment and expansion of a major dynasty in the South-East in the seventh century; of Brycheiniog in the eighth century; of Builth and Ceredigion in the very early ninth century. There may, in addition, have been kingdoms of Rhos, Meirionydd and Dunoding in the sixth century and later, and of Powys in the midlands for a short period in the seventh century, while Ceredigion may have had a pre-ninth-century history (see fig. 38). It is extremely important that we are aware of these possibilities, but equally that we are aware they may do no more than reflect the historical perspective of the ninth century. With so many uncertainties, no overall trend is perceivable; in the South-East the trend was for smaller kingdoms to be replaced by larger, and for the dynasty to strengthen its own position. Elsewhere, the implication of the certain evidence is that new kingdoms were emerging in the eighth century, but this may be an impression misleadingly conveyed by very uneven material. In the present state of research, however, I should prefer to take the implications of the certain evidence — a complex pattern of dynastic strengthening in some areas but emergence of new kingdoms in others.

The Expansion of the Kingdoms

The pattern of development in the ninth, tenth and eleventh centuries is much clearer, and is dominated by the expansion of Gwynedd. For most of the period, however, the South-East stands apart and it is only in the eleventh century that it was seriously drawn into the politics of the rest of Wales. The dynasty of Meurig ap Tewdrig continued to rule Glywysing, though the later ninth century saw two branches of the dynasty sharing royal functions there and the loss to the English of political control in Ergyng. The movement towards consolidation — of kingship and of territory — that had characterized the first century of activity, had already reached its peak under Ithel, who was sole king from c.715-45. From then, the kingship was shared by brothers and sometimes by cousins until the middle of the tenth century when Morgan ab Owain, known as Morgan Hen or Morgan the Old, became dominant. Monarchy, therefore, was not a norm and we should think of there being several kings within the kingdom at any one time. Asser, when writing of the Welsh kings' relationship with King Alfred of Wessex, distinguished between kings of Gwent — the brothers Brochfael and Ffernfael — and the king of Glywysing — Hywel ap Rhys — but it is clear from the charter evidence both that there was no consistent territorial division of the area and also that Hywel was active as king *throughout* the South-East. Brochfael, Ffernfael and Hywel did not control territories which slotted together like a jigsaw puzzle, and in the early tenth century, therefore, the contemporary kings Gruffudd, Cadwgan and Cadell — all descendants of Hywel — did not succeed to pre-

defined pieces of the jigsaw. They moved, as kings, within the whole
available area. There is much to suggest, however, that the one who was
called king of Glywysing was in some sense pre-eminent.[56] Until the eleventh
century the term Glywysing was used of the whole, while Gwent was used of
the eastern part of that whole.

Under Morgan, c.930-74, there were changes; for, like Ithel 200 and more
years before, he did not share his kingship with other members of the family
after the early years. Some considerable impression was made, for the South-
East was henceforth known as Morgannwg and/or Gwlad Morgan, that is,
Morgan's land. But at the very time that dynastic complications seemed to be
easing, control of Gower was lost and the pattern of kingship in the South-
East was further complicated by the intrusion of new families. Round about
950 one Nowy ap Gwriad, of unknown origin, appeared in Gwent calling
himself king, and he was followed in kingship by his son Arthfael and
grandsons Rhodri and Gruffudd ab Elisedd. A little later another stranger is
found as king in and of Gwent, Edwin, c.1015, and about the same time one
Rhydderch ab Iestyn settled there. He too was followed in kingship by his son
Gruffudd — also king of Dyfed — and his grandson Caradog. The last of the intruders was the immensely energetic Gruffudd ap Llywelyn, a Gwynedd king,
who campaigned in the South-East in mid-century and effectively ruled all
Wales from 1055 to 1063. The intrusions invoked political chaos for most of
the eleventh century. Morgan's descendants, the old dynasty of Meurig ap
Tewdrig, still remained kings, retained properties throughout the area, and
sometimes called themselves kings of Morgannwg. More usually, however,
the title was appropriated by Rhydderch and his line, acting from their

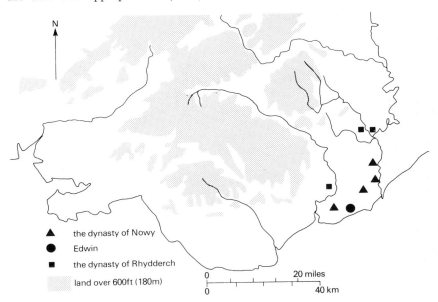

Figure 39. Intrusive dynasties in the South-East in the tenth and eleventh
centuries (after W. Davies, *An Early Welsh Microcosm,* 1978, maps I-J).

property base in Gwent and certainly claiming some general hegemony over the whole of the South-East, and according to the *Liber Landavensis* occasionally over all Wales (see fig. 39). By the 1070s and the arrival of the Normans the effects of such contradictory tendencies — and of Gruffudd's success — was to undermine the notion and practice of any general hegemony of the South-East, and to confine both the old dynasty and the term Morgannwg to the area subsequently and still known as Glamorgan. The long-term trend, therefore, was for the establishment and early consolidation of a single political unit in and of the South-East, called Glywysing and later Morgannwg; for kingship characteristically to be shared and/or multiple within that single unit; and for its ultimate, and partly consequential, fragmentation on the eve of the Norman Conquest. It is scarcely surprising that the Conquest of the South-East took so short a time. For most of the period, horizons were extremely close: we do not hear of expeditions to other parts of Wales, or contacts with other Welsh kings until those kings started to intrude in the 1020s. In the late ninth and tenth centuries, some contact was sustained with England, and for a period kings of Glywysing attended the English court. [57]

In the opposite corner of the land lay the kernel of the most dominant, most long lasting of the early kingdoms of Wales: Môn — Anglesey — the island stronghold of Gwynedd. The kings of Gwynedd frequently crossed their borders and looked outwards — at first to a wider Britain, and then throughout Wales. There is much to support the notion that the Gwynedd kings claimed some superiority amongst British kings, a superiority that was not institutionalized but might well have been widely recognized. Gildas called Maelgwn 'first in stature and also power'. [58] The early material within the *Historia Brittonum* emphasizes the special position of Gwynedd: Maelgwn was *magnus rex*, 'the great king'; [59] the inscription of Cadfan's memorial stone makes him the best of all kings; [60] Bede referred to Cadwallon as king of the Britons and presents him as the focus of resistance to the English; [61] the Annals repeat the reference in 754, calling Rhodri *rex Brittonum*, 'king of the Britons', as do the *Annals of Ulster* of his son Cynan, s.a. 815 (= 816); [62] so does the message accompanying the early ninth-century Bamberg cryptogram: 'Merfyn, glorious king of the Britons'; [63] the eleventh- and twelfth-century Saints' Lives of the South-East use the same terms, and frequently make the raid of a Gwynedd king the occasion for miraculous intervention by the saint. [64] In the latter part of the ninth century the kings of Gwynedd attempted to realize these claims by raiding and harrying outside Gwynedd. For this reason, the kings of the South-East, of Brycheiniog and of Dyfed went to Alfred for protection, a pattern which was sometimes repeated in the next 200 years. Expansion is the outstanding characteristic of Gwynedd's pre-Conquest political history, and is well documented from the change of dynasty that took place in the early ninth century. So strong was the legend of Cunedda that the kings of Gwynedd continued to trace their descent from him even after changes in the male line: Merfyn, the 'glorious king' of the Bamberg cryptogram, who died in 844, owed his membership of the family to his mother Esyllt, the daughter of Cynan ap Rhodri. [65] According to the later genealogists of Jesus College MS 20, his father was Gwriad, descendant of the legendary Llywarch Hen, of Powys association and ultimately of northern origin.[66] Whether or not he came from Powys, he may well have profited from the instability in the succession to the Gwynedd kingship which marked the late eighth and early ninth centuries. Caradog of Rhos, a branch of the family that was not associated with Anglesey — the line of Maelgwn and Cadwallon — had been strangled as king of Gwynedd in 798, and his death was followed by some years of conflict between Hywel and Cynan, the sons of Rhodri, of the Anglesey branch. The laconic entries of the Annals dwell a little on the years 813, 814 and 816: 'War between Hywel and Cynan, and Hywel was the victor'; 'Hywel from the island of Môn triumphed, and Cynan expelled him from there with great contrition of his army'; 'Hywel was again expelled from Môn. King Cynan died'. Hywel died in 825, and the next we hear is the death of Merfyn, his brother's daughter's son. The change of line accompanied, if not occasioned, new vigour in the Gwynedd kingship. Merfyn's son Rhodri was the issue of his marriage with Nest of Powys, which

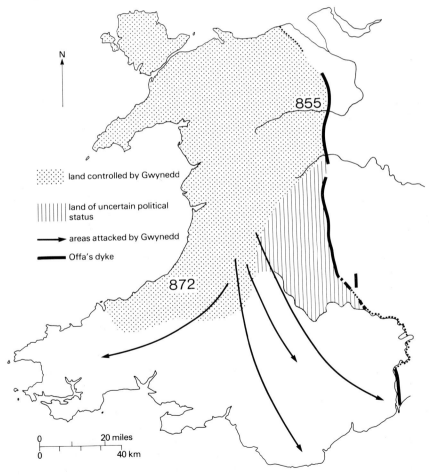

N

...... land controlled by Gwynedd

||||| land of uncertain political status

——▶ areas attacked by Gwynedd

━━ Offa's dyke

855

872

0   20 miles
0   40 km

Figure 40. The expansion of Gwynedd in the late ninth century.

kingdom he acquired at the death of Cyngen in 855; and Ceredigion was absorbed in 872 (see fig. 40). Rhodri was now master of the whole of north Wales, with a geographical range unequalled since that of the Gwynedd kings of the seventh century, and his success in absorbing Powys and Ceredigion suggests considerable military and political capacity. His ability is also indicated by his victory over the Danish leader Gorm in 856, one of the few Welsh kings to be so credited and the only one to earn the epithet 'Mawr', the Great. Though he was eventually forced into exile in Ireland by the Vikings (in 877) and was killed by the English a year after that, his fame outlived his own generation and by the twelfth century he was regarded as having ruled all Wales; it is from him that many of the tenth- and eleventh-century kings of Gwynedd and of Dyfed traced their descent.[67] After Rhodri's death his son Anarawd with his five brothers harried southern and midland Wales.[68] It was in response to this that the kings of Dyfed, Brycheiniog and the South-East sought protection of Alfred of Wessex. How effective such protection can have been is doubtful, for Anarawd not only made alliances with the Danes, but — after defeating the English in 881, in revenge for Rhodri's death at their hands — he visited Alfred himself and acquired soldiers for use in his own aggressive campaigns.[69]

If the ninth century was the period *par excellence* of Gwynedd's expansion, then the tenth represented the fruits of that policy in the establishment of a close relationship with Dyfed. Rhodri's grandson, Hywel ap Cadell, known as Hywel Dda (Hywel the Good), had married Elen, daughter of Llywarch of Dyfed (who died in 904), and by this action seems to have acquired the kingship of Dyfed.[70] Though both kingships remained separate, both were now in the hands of the Gwynedd family, and remained so for much of the tenth and eleventh centuries. Indeed, for a period after the death of Idwal, son of Anarawd, in 942, Hywel held both kingships, thus effectively ruling more than half of Wales. His signature always took precedence on English charters over those of the remaining Welsh kings. At his death in 949 or 950, however, the Gwynedd kingship returned — by battle — to the descendants of Anarawd (Iago and Idwal ab Idwal) and essentially remained in their hands — still often with several kings in association — until 1039 (see fig. 47). For one brief period, in the meantime, the Dyfed branch of the Gwynedd line returned to Gwynedd, in the person of Maredudd ab Owain, Hywel's grandson, from 986 to 999: 'Maredut son of Owin killed Catwalaun son of Idwal and possessed his kingdom, i.e. Wenedocia'.[71] Moreover, a generation later, in 1039, Iago ab Idwal, king of Gwynedd, descendant of Rhodri and Anarawd, was killed by Gruffudd ap Llywelyn, who appeared from Dyfed, and whose father had married into the Dyfed line.[72] Gruffudd exercised the kingship of Gwynedd for the next 25 years, during which time he contended with the kings of the South; at the death of Gruffudd ap Rhydderch, which he brought about in 1055, having already the defeat of the other kings of the South-East in hand, he became in some sense ruler of all Wales, 'most noble king of the Britons', as the Annals call him, until his own death in 1063 at the hands of the English, after effecting considerable devastation on the borders.[73] Only in 'some' sense was he ruler, however, for Gruffudd spent most of his reign campaigning to establish and maintain his own position: he had little time for 'rule' in any real sense of the word. After his death, moreover, the old pattern

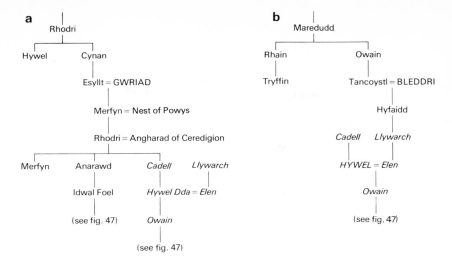

Figure 41. The royal dynasties of *a* Gwynedd and *b* Dyfed. The names common to both dynasties are shown in italics.

returned: after two half-brothers of Gruffudd received Gwynedd and Powys from Harold of England, the Gwynedd line eventually reappeared in the person of Gruffudd ap Cynan, arriving from Dublin in 1075 and surviving until 1137 to fight a long, hard and eventually successful battle against the encroaching Normans.[74] Unlike the South-East, Gwynedd's horizons were always distant.

The development of the South-West is obviously closely associated with the North-West in the tenth and eleventh centuries, but not nearly so much beforehand. As in Gwynedd there were changes in the dynasty in the ninth century: the old line, the line of Aergol and Gwrthefyr, survived through male descent until the death of Tryffin in 814 (see fig. 41b).[75] Marriage into that line, from unknown origins, produced kings in the ninth century, and marriage again by Hywel Dda of Gwynedd to Elen effected yet another change of blood. While lacking the claims to overall superiority sustained by Gwynedd, Dyfed too had expansionist tendencies and raids on the western borders of Glywysing were common in the tenth century.[76] After Hywel, the kingship was most frequently in the hands of his descendants, ultimately, that is, the descendants of Rhodri Mawr of Gwynedd. For much of the eleventh century, however, intruders prevailed. After Maredudd's own successful intrusion into Gwynedd in 986, the power of the main dynasty slackened, and there followed a series of four kings of Dyfed who did not belong to it: Aeddan, Llywelyn, Rhain and Rhydderch ab Iestyn. Llywelyn at least associated himself with customary sources of power by marrying Angharad, Maredudd's daughter; as far as we know, the others did not adopt such devices.[77] Rhydderch, as we have seen above, had already established himself in Gwent, calling himself king and claiming some general hegemony over the South-East. In moving to Dyfed, he brought the political ambitions and horizons of the South-East into line with those of the rest of Wales and in so doing undoubtedly contributed to the growing political chaos of the South.

His efforts were not immediately sustained, for on his death in 1033 the old line returned to the kingship, in descent from Maredudd's brother Einion, in the persons of Hywel and Maredudd ab Edwin.[78] Eleven years later, the intrusion from the South-East repeated itself as Rhydderch's son Gruffudd, already king in Gwent, returned to take the kingship and contend with the other Gruffudd, Gruffudd ap Llywelyn, already king in Gwynedd and son of the earlier Dyfed intruder.[79] And this eleventh-century trend of combining political interests in South-West *and* South-East is reflected in the use of a new term, *dextralis Britanniae* and Deheubarth, for the whole of south Wales.[80] Eventually, in 1055, Gruffudd ap Rhydderch was killed by his enemy, and Gruffudd ap Llywelyn took Dyfed as he had taken the rest of Wales.[81] At Gruffudd's death, the old line of Dyfed returned yet again with a second Maredudd ab Owain, Hywel's nephew, whose successors contended with and ultimately largely succumbed to the Norman encroachment. But the battle was longer and harder than that for the South-East: until the death of Rhys ap Tewdwr in 1093 — hailed by *Brut y Tywysogyon* as the final overthrow of the kingdom of the Britons — progress was slow, and it took much of the next two generations to colonize and appropriate. At the death of Henry I in 1135 much of the South-West was in Anglo-Norman hands, but still not solidly enough to prevent the Welsh revolts of the reign of Stephen. The successors of Rhys continued to have vigour enough for opposition.[82]

The complicated and interwoven pattern of dynastic history characteristic of Gwynedd and Dyfed does not dominate the development of the remaining kingdoms of early Wales, the 'unsuccessful' kingdoms of Builth, Brycheiniog and Powys. It is difficult to say anything about Builth: only one ruler is known, the Ffernfael of c.800 already mentioned above. By the late eleventh century it must have been, if loosely, assimilated into the kingdom of Gwynedd, but unlike Gwynedd proper appears to have been conquered quickly, by Philip de Briouze, lord of Radnor, certainly by 1100 and probably by 1096.[83] The fate of Brycheiniog is comparably difficult to detect. The sharing of names for three generations with the Dyfed genealogy might suggest some association in the eighth century — but this is unproven and unprovable. Like the other kings of the South, King Elise of Brycheiniog suffered from the raids of Gwynedd in the ninth century and sought the protection of Alfred. The English connection was sustained into the tenth century, for Brecon kings were still attending the English court in 934, although in 916 Aethelflaed had invaded from Mercia and captured the queen.[84] We last hear of grants made by a king of Brycheiniog round about 925, when King Tewdwr, son of Elise, stole the bishop's foodrent and eventually agreed to a judgment at Llan-gors and to the compensation assessed, although it was subsequently commuted to a land grant.[85] Whether or not the kingdom was absorbed by Gwynedd or by the South-East after this, or if the line continued independent, we do not know. The genealogies of Jesus College MS 20 go no further than Elise's grandson.[86] The Norman Conquest was again quick, and Bernard of Neufmarché had a foothold by 1088, and was established by 1093.[87]

What happened to Powys is clearer. From the seventh century the kingdom had been subject to attack from the English, and particularly from the midland kingdom of Mercia as its kings rose to pre-eminence. In the eighth century, Offa had raided several times, presumably before the construction of

Figure 42. Offa's Dyke on Spring Hill, Clun Forest (photograph Ernie Kay, Offa's Dyke Association).

the dyke which bears his name (fig. 42).[88] A century later Asser believed it to have been built at his direction, and there is no good reason to question the attribution.[89] (*Brut y Tywysogyon* follows him and assigns the erroneous date of 798 to the construction.) Whatever the precise intention of this imposing work, it must have had the effect of limiting movement through the marches; it created a border.[90] The dyke did not stop the English penetration of Wales, however, even if it stopped Welsh penetration into England, for the land was overrun by the English in 822, the citadel at Degannwy destroyed, and according to the Annals Powys was conveyed into the power of the English. In the middle of the ninth century Cyngen of Powys could still remember that his great-grandfather Elise had annexed land for Powys away from the power of the English, and he had erected a 12ft pillar, now near Llangollen, in Elise's honour (fig. 43).[91] Cyngen survived the English onslaught, but not that of Gwynedd. Merfyn married Cadell's daughter — Cyngen's sister — Nest; their child Rhodri took Powys in the year of Cyngen's death, 855; thenceforth it was ruled as part of Gwynedd and had no history as a separate kingdom until the later eleventh century.[92] Ceredigion met a similar fate, Rhodri marrying the sister of Gwgon, the last known king of the area. Its pre-ninth-century history is obscure: later tradition suggests that Arthgen's father Seisyll added Ystrad Tywi to make Seisyllwg — but there is no early evidence of this and it is notable that ninth-century annals refer to the unit as Ceredigion, not Seisyllwg.

Relationships within and between the early kingdoms of Wales form an exceptionally complex pattern for a relatively small area with a relatively small population, but some trends are clear. The most obvious of the developments is that kingdoms did emerge in the vacuum created by the disappearance of the Roman Empire in the West. We might try and object that the small size and unsophisticated administration of these petty states scarcely qualifies them to be kingdoms, but however small and primitive in organization these might appear beside later medieval and modern kingdoms, they are quite justifiably regarded as such: Latin sources use *rex* (king) and *regnum* (kingdom) when describing them, and no other terms of political authority, just as the same sources sometimes use *rex* to refer to a Roman emperor; descriptions of behaviour, which are admittedly few, imply that rule and authority were transmitted dynastically; those which survived were regarded as kingdoms by external observers. Moreover, the phenomenon is not confined to Wales: new kingdoms emerged all over the former Empire, from that of Syagrius in northern Gaul, to that of Odoacer in Italy, to that of Ceredig in Strathclyde. In Wales, there were undoubtedly several by the mid-sixth century. The second obvious characteristic is the constancy of dynastic continuity (or, the predominance of the idea of dynastic constancy); until very late in the period, most changes in the kingships took place because of marriage into the controlling dynasties. Once established, moreover, the units tended to retain their recognizable identity; kingdoms might be conquered or absorbed, but new units did not emerge. Thus, Gwynedd, Dyfed and Glywysing/Morgannwg had some sort of continuous history from their early emergence in the sixth and seventh centuries until the eleventh century. The ninth century was a period of change and new directions: dynastic change in Dyfed and Gwynedd preceded expansion; Powys and Cere-

Figure 43. The pillar of Elise (*ECMW*, pl.xxxvi; reproduced by kind permission of the Honourable Society of Cymmrodorion).

digion were absorbed. Expansion stopped at the distinction between Dyfed and Gwynedd; although, from the early tenth century, the descendants of Rhodri Mawr ruled both, the kingdoms remained separate, even when both were in the hands of the same man. Interaction between them was, however, constant and is one of the characteristics of the political history of the tenth and eleventh centuries. The last century of full independence was marked above all by dynastic instability, and by some fluctuation in the stability of the units. This latter is most marked in the South-East, where charter evidence allows us to see the carving out of new kingdoms; if we had such detailed evidence for other areas, especially the South-West, we might well be able to fill in a comparable pattern. Unknowns thrust themselves into the old-established kingships, and into new kingships too; tradition no longer seemed sufficient to sustain royal families or kingdoms. In the South-East, the property base of the old dynasty of Meurig ap Tewdrig was clearly inadequate to sustain the family and withstand challenges; there are doubtless further explanations to be sought — in the nature of warfare, the loyalty of retainers, increased mobility of persons and property, and decreased respect for the power of local social institutions. [93] In the eleventh century too south-east Wales, which had remained very separate and had a different background, became drawn into the politics of the rest of Wales: its kings sought to expand; its resources became the goal of northern and western leaders. Of these, Gruffudd ap Llywelyn stands out as the most dramatically successful: ruler of all Wales, his eight-year elevation lends a spurious air of unification. The impression is misleading: ideas may have been grander, but institutions were not, and at his death the chaos of contention within and between Gwynedd, Dyfed and Morgannwg, old dynasties and new intruders, returned once more. The extending grandeur of ideas is nicely demonstrated by the titles which the annalist of the Bruts conferred upon the prominent kings of the tenth and eleventh centuries, expanding those of the contemporary annals: 'head and glory of all the Britons', of Hywel Dda, 'foremost and most praiseworthy king of all the Britons', of Llywelyn ap Seisyll, 'head and shield and defender of the Britons', of Gruffudd ap Llywelyn. [94] By contrast some aspects of the complex of regional identities had clarified by the ninth century; with Morgannwg fully drawn towards the North and West, and away from England, these identities had a political reality which had more strength than the idea of unification. And once clarified, they persisted long after the Norman Conquest: Giraldus still remembered the centre of Powys in the twelfth century.

Wales and England

Two factors significant in the political development of early Wales have received only brief mention: the influence of England and the influence of the Vikings. We do not have to subscribe to the old cliché that the battles of Dyrham and Chester, c.577 and 616 respectively, cut off the British of the South from those of Wales and from those of the North to recognize that the English settlement over much of south-eastern Britain had a politically and culturally confining effect. There is nothing to suggest that the creation of some wider kingdom or empire of the Britons was thwarted by those battles. The British were politically fragmented, even if the kings of Gwynedd hoped for some presiding superiority. But the very fact of English settlement in the midlands can hardly be ignored. After some very early indications of Saxon penetration in south-east Wales in the late sixth century it is quite clear that initially relations between the English and the British of Wales were not entirely hostile. [95] We have seen that Cynddylan and his brother(s) may well have been fighting with the Mercian Penda before their fortunes changed and they lost power in the west Midlands and east Wales. The Gwynedd kings are much more certainly associated with Penda. Bede railed at length on the wickedness of Cadwallon for consorting with the pagan: 'Cadwalla, although a Christian by name and profession, was nevertheless a barbarian in heart and disposition. . . . Nor did he pay any respect to the Christian religion which had sprung up amongst them. Indeed to this very day it is the habit of the Britons to despise the faith and religion of the English and not to co-operate with them in anything any more than with the heathen'. [96] Together they were responsible for the death of Edwin, who, later tradition maintains, had been fostered by Cadwallon's father Cadfan. [97] With Mercia established in the mid-seventh century, and Cadwallon dead, co-operation seems to have ended, Cynddylan's family was ousted, and the Gwynedd kings withdrew from English politics. The kings of Mercia continued to be an irritation for the next 200 years and the ealdormen and earls of Mercia after them; raids were sporadic but constant even after the building of Offa's dyke in the late eighth century. Powys was not the only kingdom to suffer: the battle at Hereford in 760 would have been the business of the king of Glywysing, as was the death of Meurig in 849 and ravaging by the ealdorman in the reign of Alfred; Offa ranged over the south Welsh in 777, and Coenwulf over Dyfed in 818; it was the Saxons who strangled Caradog of Gwynedd in 798, ravaged in Snowdon and Rhufoniog in 816, killed Rhodri Mawr and his son in 878. [98] The very brief terms of reference to these raids in the Annals suggest that their object was as much political as acquisitive: it is the *vastatio*, 'devastation', that is recorded, not merely the raid or expedition. The intention appears to have been to cause damage as well as take booty. The characterization of Saxon victory in 818 and 822 as taking parts of Wales 'into their power' (*yn eu medyant, in sua potestate*) makes the same political point, an attitude also reflected on Cyngen's pillar. [99] Just what practical force English domination had is difficult to say, but it was apparently viewed as a real threat for some years in the early ninth century. Ithel of Glywysing, however, seems to have reached agreement with Aethelbald of Mercia in the mid-eighth century, after ravaging west of Hereford, but notice of such meetings is rare. [100] English influence does leave its mark in place-names west of Offa's dyke in the middle of the marches and the failure of Powys to re-establish an independent political identity in the tenth and earlier eleventh centuries emphasizes not merely the power of Gwynedd but that of England too. It seems highly likely that north-east Wales, and certainly Clwyd, was politically dominated by English kings for much of the later period. Indeed, though English aggression may not have been continuous the problem certainly persisted long after the clarification of a frontier, and the 'Ordinance of the Dunsaete' took care to insist that no-one crossed the frontier between English and Welsh without a guide. [101]

The changing political structure of England itself, with the rise of Wessex and the establishment of an English monarchy, meant changes in the relationship. The southern Welsh kings took the initiative of going to Alfred to seek protection from Gwynedd, and Asser commented that they accepted

Alfred's lordship — political superiority — in so doing.[102] Soon the very object of their fears, Anarawd, was making his own alliance with Alfred and making his own promise of subjection, if Asser's word is to be trusted.[103] Accordingly, the Welsh seem to have assisted Alfred at Buttington in 893.[104] The English desire for domination was pursued through the tenth century, extending the attempts of Egbert of Wessex in 830 and Burhred of Mercia in 853, whose subjection of 'the Welsh' is laconically recorded by the *Anglo-Saxon Chronicle*, and whose request for Alfred's assistance against the 'midland Britons' was noted by Asser.[105] Alfred's daughter Aethelflaed, the 'lady of the Mercians', moved against Brycheiniog in 916; further 'submissions' are recorded, of the brothers Hywel and Clydog of Dyfed and Idwal of Gwynedd to Edward in 918, and of Hywel again and Owain of Gwent to Athelstan in 927, the former reference implying a previous submission to Aethelflaed.[106] Much later, William of Malmesbury recorded that agreement had been reached between Athelstan and the Welsh kings, fixing the Wye as boundary and establishing an annual tribute payable to the English monarch of hounds, hawks, 20lb of gold, 300lb of silver and 25,000 oxen.[107] The record is a late one, early twelfth century, and there is no evidence that this tribute was paid, but it is not unthinkable that such a meeting took place. The south Welsh poem *Armes Prydein* — probably of early tenth-century date — appropriately looks forward to the day when, the English ejected from the land, the taxes will not be paid:

> The stewards of Caer Geri will lament bitterly,
> in valley and on hill, some do not deny it —
> not fortunately did they come to Aber Peryddon,
> afflictions are the taxes they will collect.[108]

Later in the century, King Edgar accepted the submission of six kings of Britain at Chester; Florence of Worcester, writing in the late eleventh century, named Iago and Hywel (of Gwynedd, uncle and nephew) among others from Scotland and the Isles.[109] It is as difficult to specify what such claims of submission by tenth-century English writers meant as it is to understand what ninth-century Welsh writers implied by English political domination in the North and Midlands but there is very good evidence of the appearance of Welsh kings at the English court in the period between 928 and 956. Hywel of Dyfed, Idwal and Iago of Gwynedd, Tewdwr of Brycheiniog, and Morgan, Owain and Cadwgan of Gwent/Glywysing all witnessed English charters, where they are described as *subreguli*, 'sub-kings': the implication is one of dependence.[110] It is quite possible, therefore, that tribute was paid for some years. Appearances *are* limited, however, to these years and the claims of submission do not continue into the eleventh century. The attitude of Edward the Confessor, on the other hand, has much to suggest that he considered the whole of Wales already subject, and in 1056 he forced Gruffudd to swear loyalty to him.[111]

Conflict between English and Welsh continued during this tenth-century period and beyond, despite the friendly relations implied by appearances at court. The ravagings went on, 942 Gwynedd, 949 the South East, 967 and 978 Gwynedd, 983 and 1012 Dyfed, ravagings which were often carried out by the earls of Mercia, political successors of the Mercian kings.[112] The last century before the Norman arrival saw a further development as Welsh kings used

English leaders for their own political purposes, an extension of the policy of Anarawd, and a practice complemented by the use of Vikings. In 983 Hywel ab Ieuaf of Gwynedd campaigned with earl Aelfhere against Einion of Dyfed; in the 990s Edwin, Einion's son, used English forces to ravage his uncle's, Maredudd's, lands in Dyfed; in 1046 Gruffudd ap Llywelyn co-operated with earl Sweyn of Hereford, and nine years later with Aelfgar, the would-be earl of Mercia and his Hiberno-Danish supporters.[113] Conversely, part of Ealdred bishop of Worcester's levy in 1049 was Welsh.[114] In the last resort, the English became a source of fighting bodies and military competence. This must betoken the end of the hard lines of cultural separation — the English were no longer the massed enemies of the mass of Welsh. Some Welsh, at least, could see them as allies, a comment both on the changing policy and capacities of the English government and on the Welsh consciousness of political identity.

The presence of the English was therefore one determinant of political relationships and political activity throughout the period. Initially and latterly a potential source of support in the political programmes of the Welsh kings, they were more consistently an irritant — especially to the eastern and midland kingdoms — by raiding and ravaging, and Powys may for long periods have been controlled by the English. In the tenth century, the submission

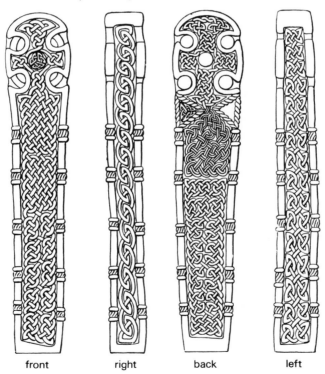

front   right   back   left

Figure 44. The Llanynys Cross (*ECMW* no.65; originally published in *Archaeologia Cambrensis* and reproduced by kind permission).

first articulated by Alfred's court circle seems sometimes and in some ways to have been admitted in other areas too; some tribute must have been paid, if we are to believe the cries of *Armes Prydein*. Contacts must certainly have been close in mid-century and English influence is apparent not only in the framing and terminology of Welsh laws, but in the use of English names, and presence of English people in the South-East and middle marches.[115] It is nicely demonstrated by two surviving monuments from Llanrhaeadr-ym-Mochnant in the North-East: a ninth-century cylindrical cross shaft is decorated in Mercian style, while an eleventh-century grave slab bears the hybrid Anglo-Welsh name Gwgan mab Elstan. And there are other English (and Scandinavian) style crosses in the borderlands at Llanynys (Brecon) (fig. 44) and Whitford (Clwyd), the style of which in their turn influenced the design of crosses further west.[116] That influence was not one-sided, of course, and it is indicated at least by the flow of books and intellectual attitudes from Wales — as from Brittany — throughout the tenth century.[117]

Wales and the Vikings

From the middle of the ninth century Wales, like England, was subject to attacks from the Vikings. These came from a number of different directions and affected Wales in different ways. Between 852 and 877 there were attacks by Vikings described as Gentiles or Black Gentiles, the latter from Dublin, on Anglesey and the North, on Gwynedd essentially; despite his earlier success against them Rhodri of Gwynedd was forced to flee to Ireland.[118] In 878 Asser records that a Viking force wintered, probably for the first time, in Dyfed and for the next few decades parts of Wales suffered a backlash from attacks that were directed elsewhere: Brycheiniog and Gwent in 896 took the brunt of Haesten's army of pirates and Danes which had ravaged England for the past 14 years; in 914 a force came up the Severn, harried the Welsh coast and captured Cyfeilliog, bishop in Ergyng; in 903 and 918 Dublin Gentiles came to Anglesey again, Ingimund having been expelled in the first case.[119] After a lull, the second half of the tenth century saw constant attacks upon Anglesey and the monasteries of the North and upon Dyfed; and as the century turned Bishop Morgenau of St David's was killed by them: 'Because I ate flesh I am become flesh', he revealed in a vision to an Irish bishop, as Giraldus rather gleefully relates.[120] In 989, the year after a heavy attack right round the coast of Wales, Maredudd of Dyfed (and Gwynedd) paid tribute in an attempt to keep them away.[121] This was not the end of the problem. The Gentiles of Dublin and elsewhere were still attacking the north-west and south-west peninsulas in the 1040s and were only deflected by alliances made by Gruffudd ap Rhydderch, which sent them to south-east Wales and Gloucestershire, to 'do evil' up the river Usk, and confound the dynasty of Meurig ap Tewdrig, his rival in Morgannwg; Meurig ap Hywel had actually been captured by them in 1039.[122] Finally, a spate of attacks on St David's in the 1070s and 1080s rounded off the pattern, as Gruffudd ap Cynan came in from the Danish community of Dublin to re-establish the old line of Rhodri in Gwynedd (see fig. 25).[123]

It is clear from the above summary that St David's and Anglesey were constantly the object of attack, and that the mid-ninth and second half of the tenth centuries were the worst periods. As far as the sources specify, the Viking enemy normally came by way of Ireland and their attacks on Wales were presumably related to the activities of the fleets travelling and working the Irish sea. Only occasionally did the English Vikings impinge on Wales, and that was more usually in the South-East. Whatever we think about the numbers of Vikings involved, they clearly caused disturbance and upset. The Annals comment that in 1049 the whole of southern Wales was deserted 'for fear of the Gentiles'. The coin hoard evidence, though slight, would support the notion that there was some dislocation. Coin use in Wales seems to have been too little, however, for this to supply any useful index of density or frequency and in several cases the hoards clearly point to commercial activity *by* the Vikings rather than a Welsh fear *of* them. [124] It has been suggested, not unreasonably, that the problem of Viking attack was much worse in the late tenth and eleventh centuries because of the beneficial effects of co-operation with the English in the earlier period. [125] Bishop Cyfeilliog, after all, was ransomed from the Vikings by an English king.

At least some of the Welsh, however, saw the Scandinavians as more natural allies than the English:

> and there will be reconciliation between the Cymry and the men of Dublin, the Irish of Ireland and Anglesey and Scotland, the men of Cornwall and of Strathclyde will be made welcome among us

so the poet of *Armes Prydein* remarked in the early tenth century. [126] And in some senses coastal Wales, at least, must have formed part of a Hiberno-Norse world which stretched from Limerick and Dublin to Chester and York. Some Vikings were utilized by Welsh kings: as early as the time of Anarawd, alliances were made with York, while in the late tenth century Maredudd hired Gentiles to ravage Glamorgan; and both Gruffudd ap Rhydderch and Gruffudd ap Llywelyn had similar policies. The former used Vikings in south-east Wales and against Gloucestershire; the latter used the Hiberno-Danes of Aelfgar in 1055 and acted with Magnus from Limerick, in 1058. [127]

Some Vikings, moreover, must have settled in Wales, even if the numbers were few and the sites largely coastal. There is some Norse tradition of settlement in the country, reflected in later saga, and the prevalence of Scandinavian names for islands and coastal features — particularly in north-west Wales, Flint and Pembroke — suggests it too (see fig. 45). [128] The large hoard from Llandudno looks like Viking booty rather than local savings while the isolated finds on northern and southern coasts look like the effects of commercial activity. Indeed, the coastal features may well have been navigation points for the Vikings working the main routes along the north and south coasts, into Chester and Bristol, and a plausible case has been made for the establishment of supportive commercial colonies at Milford Haven and Swansea, with perhaps some inland settlement in Pembroke. [129] It may even be a Viking ship, 70ft long, that was discovered in Newport in the last century. Even so, evidence of settlement is extremely slight and seems to have had little effect on Welsh life, language and institutions. Indeed, perhaps the most notable of effects are those upon the style of decoration used on the

Figure 45. Scandinavian place-names in Wales
(after H.R. Loyn, *The Vikings in Wales*, 1976, map 2).

great crosses of the tenth and eleventh centuries, like those at Penmon
(Anglesey) (fig. 46), Whitford (Clwyd), Nevern (see fig.51) and Carew
(Pembroke). These and other fragments, particularly located in north-eastern,
north-western and south-western extremities, share decorative elements with
other monuments from the Hiberno-Norse world, including Scandinavian

right back left

Figure 46. Part of a free-standing pillar cross from Penmon (*ECMW* no.38; originally published in *Archaeologia Cambrensis* and reproduced by kind permission).

Northumbria.[130] The Scandinavian culture area was wide but the precise nature of the culture and the means of its propagation still elude us.

Anglesey is especially problematic. Though it had come to be known as Anglesey, 'Ongul's Isle', by the late eleventh century, rather than by its Welsh name, Môn, it was after all the traditional seat of the kings of Gwynedd and time and time again the heart of Welsh resistance. Anglesey, moreover, was the focal point in the battles which determined the Norman withdrawal from the North in 1098. The only thing that makes sense of the place-name is to suppose either that the repeated attacks upon Anglesey did result in some limited period of Viking domination and/or that the sustained contacts of Gruffudd ap Cynan with his Dublin Hiberno-Norse background somehow influenced the island's description by outsiders. Neither point is really satisfactory. There can be no doubt, however, of the political and cultural associations of Gruffudd; and it was the appearance of a Norwegian fleet off Anglesey which seems to have decided the issue for the Normans in 1098.

The attacks which the Vikings made on Wales were presumably for booty — both movable goods and persons — for use by the trading fleets; where attacks were constant, then it suggests that supplies were constant.

St David's, attacked at least seven times, and Anglesey even more, must have had considerable powers of recovery, and therefore considerable resources on which to draw. The drain which this constituted may have been partly responsible for the lessening powers of the later leaders of Wales, but one cannot establish a direct relationship. Like the English, the Vikings had become a source of fighting men for the Welsh kings in the eleventh century. As such, they tended to intensify the fragmentation; they certainly did not provoke unification, as happened in England, and do not appear to have attempted or wanted the establishment of political units of their own. There is no Welsh kingdom of Dublin. The Vikings kept passing by; they came, they plundered, they were utilized as allies; they left their art-styles; but they left little trace of their presence and little suggestion that they were a significant determinant of political relationships and developments.

5   Kings, Law and Order

If kings and kingdoms were the characteristic manifestation of power in early Welsh society, then we must ask what sort of states the kingdoms were, what sort of relationship existed between king and subjects. Any notion of democratic rights and of citizen participation in the disposition and exercise of power within the community would, of course, be highly anachronistic. Perhaps surprisingly, public expectations of kings — in so far as this can be assessed from the doubtless partial comments of contemporary writers — were of beneficence; the institution was useful. Rhodri and Hywel, after all, earned the epithets 'Great' and 'Good' respectively. The annalist of *Brut y Tywysogyon* commended Bleddyn for his gentleness and his defence of the weak as well as for the terror he inspired in war.[1] As early as the sixth century, Gildas had clearly expected that kings should not only honour clerics and Christian principles but that they should provide defence and protection, chase after thieves, make judgments, imprison offenders and persecute evildoers.[2] Poets and other writers, however, most consistently stressed the military capacities of kings: the ruler was a true ruler (*rector*, *rwyfadur*, 'governor', 'steersman') by virtue of his deeds and his forcefulness;[3] the *boldest* king (*teyrn*) was the one most honoured;[4] he should be a good horseman and a skilful leader;[5] he should extend boundaries, seek conquest;[6] his magnificence resided in his soldier-like qualities.[7] Kings should correspondingly, like all leaders, have wealth: generosity may have been seen as the proper use of royal and other wealth but Gildas had already characterized gold and silver as the 'chains' of royal power.[8] The image of the wealthy king persisted until much later;[9] but, by the eleventh century, the image of the king as plunderer was also common: the Saints' Lives voiced the viewpoint of the local population who had to suffer the king on expedition as opposed to that of the poet who told tales of such expeditions for the benefit of the companions in the king's hall. Kings Maelgwn, Rhun, Rhain, Caradog, Edgar arrived in person, or sent their agents, to plunder, lay waste and cause havoc amongst an otherwise peaceful rural population.[10]

The consistent requirement, then, was that the king be powerful, and effective; the consistent view was that he should be wealthy, whether for the benefit of himself or others. Both early and late there were also expressed the hopes that a king might be more: Gildas hoped for public service as well as protection, and commented that rule purely by force was a bad thing;[11] *Canu Taliesin* asks for wisdom and honour — 'a falsehood is not good concerning a king';[12] the *Brut* praises Bleddyn for his mildness and mercy; the Life of Gwynllyw maintains that it is the king's role to keep the peace.[13] At times some notion of social and public responsibility accompanied the role. It is a key problem, then, to discover how often and how far this was recognized and influential; and how much the preservation of order was the domain of kings.

Selection and Elevation

How was a king made? Gildas complained that cruel kings had been chosen in the years before the Saxon revolt, chosen for their cruelty to replace the less cruel, chosen by those who anointed them.[14] In this suggestion of clerical king-making lies one of the few indications of any procedure of elevation other than the recognition or exercise of superior force. It is not impossible that in the years shortly after central Roman government had lost contact with Britain, kings had sometimes been chosen, but it is well to remember that Gildas wrote of a period of which he had very little knowledge himself. This cannot be good evidence for the greater part of early medieval Wales, and indeed, when writing of his own times, Gildas made other procedures explicit.

Of elevation rituals there is little indication. Apart from Gildas's anointing, the tale of 'Branwen' refers to royal investiture, albeit in Ireland, but we do not know what was involved or indeed if the reference is more than a borrowing from some literary model. It is seriously to be wondered if there were rituals (though there were clearly symbols of royal power).[15] If not, their absence is curious.

Secondly, the idea of legitimacy — rather than selection — always seems to have been significant. It is quite clear from an early date that many believed that some people had a right to be kings and some did not: usurpation was possible but scarcely desirable. Gildas dwelt upon the moral requirements of kingship, and moaned that the unjust king was a tyrant, whose tyranny disqualified him from kingship. Legitimacy, for him, lay in the proper exercise of kingship. Although reference continued to be made to the fact of legitimacy — the poet Aneirin sang of the son of a 'rightful' king (*mab brenhin teithiauc*)[16] — the association of a strong moral requirement disappeared and the only indications we are given of what constituted legitimacy are those which emphasize birth, and native blood.

All available contemporary evidence indicates that kingship was a family affair, that it passed from one member of a royal family to another. Gildas complained of his own times that Maelgwn of Gwynedd had removed the king, his uncle, in order to make himself king.[17] The early fragments in the *Historia Brittonum* noted that Maelgwn reigned because his great-great-great-grandfather had arrived in the area 146 years before; and the later, elaborate tale of the destruction of Benlli was quoted in order to explain the origin of the kings of Powys: the poor but hospitable man, Cadell, was blessed with the prophecy that in future kings would come from his seed. The compiler noted triumphantly that all his sons had indeed been kings and that the whole of Powys had been governed from their offspring.[18] The truth of the tale is immaterial: the perspective of the early ninth century envisaged that kings should be descended from kings. The observation may appear trite to us with our knowledge of the way hereditary kingship dominated and conditioned much of the political history of medieval and early modern Europe. But this did not have to happen; what is interesting is that it did happen, and did so in the very early medieval period. A little later than the compiling of the *Historia Brittonum*, Cyngen of Powys erected his pillar, inscribing for all to see, preserving in the most durable material available, the message of his own descent, and referring to the kingdom of Powys as an inheritance, *hereditas.*[19] The message, of course, is precisely the same as that conveyed by the recording of genealogies: dynastic dominance and dynastic continuity. The extant genealogical collections are witness to the expectation of family interest in the kingships from at least the ninth century, and a case can be made for an earlier date: it is difficult to explain the collection and preservation of the long genealogies which terminate at dates before the ninth century — like no.4 of the Harleian collection, for the Isle of Man — without supposing some pre-ninth-century practice of genealogical recording. More than this, the practice — and the expectation — very often seems to have been for sons to succeed fathers. Magnus Maximus was thought to have associated his son Victor with him in government;[20] the poet of *Canu Taliesin* vowed that he would stay loyal to the sons of the king (*teyrn*).[21] Even at the period of greatest political dislocation and of most intrusions, in the early eleventh century, the notion continued: the annalist of *Brut y Tywysogyon* expanded the usually terse entry to comment that an Irishman, Rhain, pretended that he was the son of Maredudd because he wanted to be king; hagiographic writers adorned their saints with supposedly royal fathers, and characteristically presented them spurning the earthly kingdom that was rightly their inheritance.[22] Further, though there are many instances of contention in the later period, there are also many occasions on which sons *did* succeed fathers: it was a common occurrence. In Gwynedd, for example, there is good evidence that Rhodri Mawr was succeeded by his son Anarawd, who was succeeded by his son Idwal, who was succeeded by his sons Iago and Idwal, in the ninth and tenth centuries (assuming that notice of their actions, rule, deaths and so on by the Annals implies kingship); in Dyfed, Hywel Dda was succeeded by his son Owain, who was succeeded by his son Maredudd (his brother Einion dying before his father), in the tenth century; in Glywysing father-to-son succession ran through four generations from Morgan to Athrwys in the seventh and eighth centuries.[23] The examples could be multiplied. Occasionally there is clear expression of the notion that the kingdom should be shared between the sons of the departing king, as would be the appropriate succession practice for property in accordance with the principles of Welsh Law. Late in the eleventh century, Lifris explained in the Preface to his Life of Cadog that, long before, the sons of Glywys had shared their father's kingdom, their respective portions being signalled by the names of the regions within that kingdom: just as the whole was known as Glywysing, after the father, Gwynllŵg took its name from his eldest son Gwynllyw, Edeligion from Edelig, and so on.[24] Notably, at a later date, the Life of Gwynllyw emends the same story by adding the comment that the eldest could have taken the whole but did not.[25] Precisely the same attitude as that of Lifris is evidenced by the disposition of genealogies and their relationship to the sons of Cunedda — Meirion ap Cunedda and Meirionydd, Ceredig ap Cunedda and Ceredigion, and so on.[26] Indeed, the number of occasions on which sons jointly followed their fathers or contended with those who did are such as to suggest that this attitude was current; action by the 'sons of N' is the frequent designation in annals of the tenth and eleventh centuries.

If the expectation was that sons should succeed fathers, and the practice was that this was often so, nevertheless the long-term consequences of allowing the succession of more than one son took effect from time to time, and especially from the tenth century. Several sons succeeded and then son's sons succeeded; kingship might then be shared or disputed between cousins; it was logically impossible to permit both the sharing by brothers *and* successions by *all* sons without division of the units or strife between the candidates. Hence, already in the sixth century, Maelgwn removed his uncle — his father's brother — in order to take the kingship himself; in Glywysing two descendants of Rhys ab Ithel, of uncertain relationship but clearly not brothers, were kings in the ninth century, while the brothers Morgan and Cadwgan ab Owain and their first cousin Cadell ab Arthfael were all kings in the period c.930-42;[27] the Annals record the succession to Gwynedd in 1073 of Trahaearn the *cousin* of Bleddyn. In effect segmentation, that is alternation between different branches of the same family, became characteristic. In

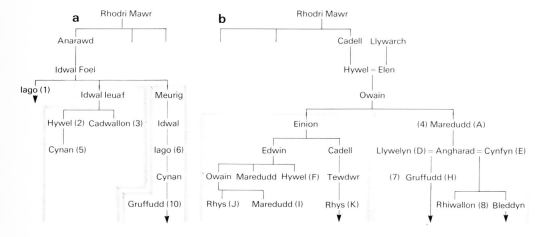

Figure 47. Segmentation in *a* Gwynedd (numerical order indicates kingship; no.9 belongs to a distant branch) and *b* Dyfed (alphabetical order indicates kingship; B, C and G are intruders).

Gwynedd, Hywel followed his uncle, Iago, in 979, and was followed by his own brother; after the intrusion of Maredudd (his third cousin) came Hywel's son, and then Hywel's son's second cousin, Iago. In Dyfed, Maredudd was succeeded in 999 by two intruders, and then by his own son-in-in-law, who was succeeded by another intruder; and then his nephew's son Hywel, followed by his son-in-law's son, Gruffudd. Though the kingship was retained within the five-generation group in the case of Gwynedd — from Idwal Foel — and four-generation group in the case of Dyfed — from Owain — (apart from the complication of intruders) each kingship became a matter for contention. In Gwynedd it was between the descendants of Meurig and of Idwal Ieuaf ab Idwal, two 'segments' of the family; and in Dyfed between the descendants of Maredudd and of Einion ab Owain (see fig.47).[28] In fact, all were descendants of Rhodri Mawr, and the intruders in Gwynedd were Dyfed kings — four generations from Rhodri in Maredudd's case, six in Gruffudd's. If anything — though there were more intrusions in Dyfed — this made Dyfed 'superior' to Gwynedd in the eleventh century, in that the Dyfed branch of the family could exert family control over the two units: Dyfed took over Gwynedd's superiority. This never happened with the Gwynedd branch until the time of Gruffudd ap Cynan, after the Norman Conquest had begun. Father-to-son(s) succession therefore appears to have been common, both in practice and in theory, but on occasion kingship was shared or passed over more than one degree of kinship, and by the twelfth century the consequences of this practice had in effect replaced father/son succession by segmentation.

By the time the laws were recorded some conceptual sophistication is evident. These recognize the existence of an heir to the throne, the man expected, the one next in line, as the vernacular terms *gwrthrych* and *gwrthrychiad* literally indicate. The tracts also use another term for 'heir to the throne', *edling*, a borrowing from the Anglo-Saxon 'aetheling', a word originally meaning 'noble' and later 'second to the king', (and hence potentially heir to the throne).[29] The existence of the terms in Welsh and their use in legal tracts means that at least by the twelfth century and probably earlier there existed a notion that there should be a single heir and that he should be recognized before the death or departure of the outgoing king. The comments of hagiographic writers in the late eleventh and twelfth centuries about the position of the eldest son would support the currency of such notions at that time,[30] and the tale of 'Culhwch ac Olwen' also refers explicitly to the privilege of the aetheling.[31] A case can be made — from the existence of the term *gwrthrychiad* and the comparable term and institution of *tánaise ríg* in Ireland — that such notions were present at much earlier periods and inherent in Welsh kingship. This is not impossible, and some instances of father to son succession might support it, but it remains notable that the institution as such is not mentioned in any early source, and that behaviour argues against any general acceptance of the notion; the adoption of the English term (which itself carries no implication of a *single* heir in the Saxon period) in preference to the Welsh suggests that the institution at least went through some changes in Wales. We have to conclude on the basis of present evidence, therefore, that designation of a single heir to the kingdom was not a common practice for much of the period.

The Powers of Kings

The deepest impression conveyed by our inadequate source material is of the virtually unrestrained power of kings to move about the land plundering and causing havoc, in a fury of wilful exploitation. Indeed, one is tempted to wonder whether kings had any rôle beyond purely selfish aggrandisement. Institutionalized limitations seem to have been few, but there must have been a real practical limitation afforded by the availability of resources and the ambitions of the royal kin. As long as kingdoms remained small, there can never have been so large a surplus as to sustain unlimited exploitation: too little can have been produced to allow for any very great build-up of power. And as long as kingship was a family matter, the ambition of cousins or brothers — or sometimes the common interest of the group — must often have prevented unrestrained action. There are occasional hints of other sources of restraint. These are essentially two: the corporate will of a king's people, his subjects, and the practical and psychological powers of clerics. In the tale of 'Branwen' Matholwch's (Irish) 'people' objected to two persons that he was maintaining, and protested that he must give up either the two offending satellites or his kingdom; in his dispute with Ligessog, according to the Life of Cadog, Arthur was forced to submit to the judgment of the assembled clerics and elders; while passages of the *Historia Brittonum* refer to consultation with elders at crucial stages of the Hengest/Gwrtheyrn story.[32] The information is slight, but clearly a number of different writers envisaged the possibility that representatives of the community might attempt, sometimes even successfully, to have a restraining effect upon the actions of kings. That they could envisage the possibility suggests that this may have happened sometimes, and the occasional references by the Annals to action taken by the 'men of Brycheiniog' or the 'nobles of Gwent', who respectively killed King Ithel in 848 and Einion ab Owain in 984, suggests further that sections of the community had the political capacity not merely to comment but to act.[33] There are also a number of suggestions of the significant consultative role of groups of 'elders'.[34] It is, moreover, quite clear that clerics, like the prophets of the Old Testament or like the contentiously outspoken Columbanus in sixth-century Frankia, thought that they had a right to pronounce and to expect that their pronouncements would be heeded. There is little indication, however, as there is from Ireland, that they might have taken up arms in order to enforce their especial viewpoint. Gildas's long tract is a first-hand demonstration of the lengths to which an outraged cleric might go in denouncing his contemporaries, though it contains no evidence that the wicked necessarily listened or changed their ways. The early penitentials explicitly prohibited bad kings from ritual prayer offerings,[35] and much later it was claimed that David had been the corrector and instructor of kings, and intercessor for them.[36] The Llandaff charters are full of claims that kings were not only made to do penance and pay compensation for their offences but that they were forced into penitential exile for perjury and murder. While the claims for the early period are extreme and largely incredible, there is no good reason to question those for the tenth and eleventh centuries, and it would seem that bishops were able to succeed in their demands for heavy compensation for offences committed against them at that time — often assessed in synod. After his appropriation of food from Bishop Libiau in the early tenth century, for example, King Tewdwr of Brycheiniog was forced to agree to a huge compensation payment; it was — interestingly — only after the intercession of the bishop of St David's that the payment of much gold was commuted to a land grant.[37] In the South-East, at least, it appears that though kings certainly had the nerve to attack and plunder churches and clerics, they nevertheless were sometimes prepared to admit fault. Slight though it is, this does at least constitute some restraint.

The existence of limitations must tacitly admit the possession of some powers, and there are some indications of specific powers that were exercised and acknowledged. If kings would sometimes listen to clerics, they also had some control over clerical office itself. In the sixth century, control was such that kings were able to put up the posts for sale: the greedy clerics who grabbed 'the name of priest but not the priestly way of life' bought their tainted priesthoods 'from the tyrants and their father the devil'.[38] Such abuses may not have continued, but the Llandaff charters contain a number of examples of royal appointment of clerics and we still find it assumed at the end of the period that Maelgwn must have installed Kentigern as bishop at Llanelwy and that Meirchion — through his steward — had control over prelates.[39]

From the sixth to the eleventh centuries, kings moved about with soldiers (*milites*): we might term this a warband, a military retinue, a band of thugs, a bodyguard, depending upon our own perspective or that of the recording source, but the armed (mounted) band, the group with easy recourse to violence, were the king's companions throughout and there seems to have been little change over the centuries.[40] The Life of Cadog even supposed that King Paul went to visit St Cadog in all humility, along with a retinue of 12 picked soldiers. Hence we find comments like the following:

> Each went on campaign, Eager in combat,
> His steed beneath him, Set to raid Manaw
> For the sake of wealth, Profit in plenty,
> Eight herds alike of calves and cattle.[41]

Here the context is glorious, the raid deemed honourable, the leader (the poet's patron Urien) a hero, his loss a tragedy. Is this really any different from the expedition of Rhun ap Maelgwn who came 'from the North with a numerous company of the nation of Gwynedd on an expedition, that he might rob the possessions and treasures of the southern Britons and utterly lay waste the land'? 'When they had come to the borders of Gwrinydd, they formed a camp in Cair Trigguid. And when the men of Gwrinydd had seen them, they fled from them frightened, hiding themselves in woods and thickets and holes and caves of the earth.'[42] The poem celebrates royal behaviour in at least the ninth (and possibly the early seventh) century; the other, from a hagiographic work of the very late eleventh century, condemns it. Kings had force, and used it.

Perhaps surprisingly, the *Historia Brittonum* associated King Benlli with some rule-making power: he decreed that everyone should be at work by sunrise, on pain of death.[43] This is surprising since it is customary to suppose that Welsh law — like Irish law — was lawyer's law, the distillation of centuries of practice, preserved by professionals with immense care.

> The laws of the Welsh were not the creation of any legislator, owing their origin to the royal fiat and capable of being altered by the same authority. They were the ancient customs of the race, handed on in each tribe as a precious heirloom from generation to generation, preserved by the tradition of the elders, and having the sanction of immemorial antiquity. In order to annul or modify them, nothing short of the assent of a national conclave was sufficient;

so run the comments of the most distinguished historian of medieval Wales.[44] Lawyer's law there may have been, but even Irish law allowed for kings to make ordinances in particular circumstances and there is nothing inconsistent in supposing some royal law-making function alongside the preservation and application of traditional law. In the Welsh case, the very fact that some parts of the extant legal collections are strongly influenced by English practice indicates that changes took place, and the best explanation for these particular changes remains the influence of the kings who spent time at English courts in the mid-tenth century. [45] The extant texts are, after all, associated with the name of King Hywel, though later kings, such as Bleddyn, are associated with enactments. Accordingly, the hagiographic writers endowed kings, not lawyers as might be expected, with the power of determining privilege: it was Arthur who prolonged the period of *nawdd*, protection, which the monastery of Llancarfan could bestow; it was Maelgwn, Rhun and others who confirmed the distinctive attributes of that protection; it was Gwynllyw and his successors who gave permission for trading to take place and tolls to be collected. [46] It would be foolish, therefore, to suppose kings were necessarily disassociated from the law-making process; it is clear that kings made decisions and highly likely that by the tenth and eleventh centuries they influenced traditional law, made comments which they expected to be obeyed and played some part in regulating relationships in the community. It is equally clear, however, that they were not the sole source of law for centuries after the Norman Conquest.

The rôle of the king as a source of privilege is also demonstrated by the relatively large amount of material that deals with the powers of the king in relation to land. Kings were donors, of lands, churches, 'cities' and of immunities; a royal grant might comprise not merely land but exemption from any fiscal or other obligations that owners or residents might normally be expected to meet. [47] Kings might also confirm the donations of other donors: donors: hence, Gwengarth — having been given a villa by King Morgan — gave an annual render of beer, bread, flesh and honey to Llancarfan and also a valuable sword to one of its clerics; the cleric then gave the sword to Morgan so that he should confirm the donation, as he subsequently did. [48] Some few of the Llandaff charters include royal consent and/or guarantee phrases which appear to be genuine. However, this did not always happen, so there is no suggestion that royal confirmation was essential or that the king necessarily had an interest in all private property; it suggests rather that the involvement of the king gave some guarantee that he and his descendants would not renew their interest in their own alienated property and gave an extra binding force to the grant — an extension of the privilege kings might bestow. It is again notable that most of the Llandaff consent phrases reflect the desire of the recorder of a transaction to have royal acquiescence rather than any institutionalized royal power to convey it. [49] At a very late date comments were made which suggest that kings controlled the use of all land, in confirmation of the view of the law tracts that 'the earth is the king's' and that service of some kind was due from all land. [50] Hence, occupation of waste land was only possible by permission of the king, a permission that was not easily given and might be withdrawn. [51] Something of the same is suggested much earlier by the *Historia Brittonum* where the settlement of foreigners is at the disposal of the king and huge tracts were made over to the newcomers. [52] In this case it is not merely the allocation of rights in land which was in the king's gift but full political control of it, and the circumstances were the exceptional ones of the English settlement. The case, therefore, though apparently relevant, is not really comparable, and it remains difficult to find early evidence of the powers of kings over all land in their kingdoms.

Kings acted as judges and made and gave judgments, in person or by proxy. Although he specified the existence of professional judges, Gildas complained of the bad judgments made by his tyrannical kings: 'they take their seats as judges but rarely seek out the rules of right judgment'. *Canu Taliesin* celebrates Gwallog not merely as hero but as judge too; Lifris referred to the past judgments of the agents of kings and their significance in establishing precedent; conflicting traditions were noted and debated in the case of Arthur and Ligessog; Meirchion's agent made accusations in the king's name and took property on the basis of having made the accusations — plaintiff and judge all at once; judgment supposedly took place in the court of King Caradog. [53]

The most striking power available to kings was their capacity to demand some income, as of right, from their subject population. It is often difficult to distinguish between the demand for tribute made by kings upon subject kingdoms — the perks of overkingship and political domination — and the demand for taxes made from subjects. Indeed, it is to be wondered if contemporaries recognized a distinction between them, since the same terms were used to refer to both. However they viewed them, the existence of both forms of income is very clear by the tenth and eleventh centuries, and of the former at earlier dates. Early ninth- and tenth-century reflections on past developments assume that the corollary of political conquest was the taking of tribute: the British owed *census* to Rome; when subject, the Picts owed *vectigal* to the Saxons; the Irish made a food payment (*bwyttal*) to Arthur, in recognition of his political superiority. [54] The attitude continued into the eleventh century with the tales that the Gwynedd kings came again and again to the South-East to collect tribute (*census, tributum*), by force, with soldiers, thus unjustly occasioning much panic and despair. [55] The expectation, clearly, was that political conquest involved payments from conquered to conqueror. On a number of occasions in this period there is evidence that this *did* happen: some payments (*tretheu*) seem to have been made to the English king Athelstan; hostages as well as tribute were sent by the Dunsaete to the West Saxons; Rhys ap Tewdwr paid a huge *census* to the Irish Gentiles in 1087 (the latter to stave off attack, but by its very payment an acknowledgment of potential conquest). [56] It is reasonable to suppose, therefore, that political conquest could involve the payment of tribute to the conqueror for as long as he seemed to have the capacity to reinforce his demands; it would be unreasonable to suppose that this was institutionalized or that there was much machinery to effect it, in view of the changing nature of political relationships; the taking of tribute must in most respects have been indistinguishable from the plundering raid.

Taxation within the kingdom is a much more difficult problem. It is a commonplace to suppose, on the basis of the evidence of the (very late) law tracts, that the payment of render (*gwestfa*) once a year to the king from the free kindreds was a norm, and that direct payment (*dawnbwyd*) was made twice a year by servile or 'bond' peasants, and that this was territorially organized. [57] The law tracts specify in detail the constituents of this render and present an elaborate administrative structure in which the essential unit of royal organization was the commote (a notional 50 *trefi*). Although there is no reason to question that this fiscal structure was common by the twelfth century and later, it is not easy to find evidence that it was in operation throughout the early medieval period. Indeed, unless we are to believe that kings always existed or that they simply utilized some pre-existing structure of payments made to landlords, it is difficult to see how such an apparatus could have been there from the beginning, given the political fluctuation of the early period. Even if we allow the utilization of some pre-existing structure, we must envisage the development of machinery which distinguished between the landlord's and the king's portion — since it is clear that the king did not in any sense 'own' all land; and even this cannot account for everything, unless we suppose that all land had been tenanted. It is extremely unlikely that there was no development at all. Such evidence as we have suggests that by the eleventh century kings might expect to take exactions from their own subjects, exactions that were certainly assessed by territory rather than by head. The Lives accordingly nod favourably at grants of land that were free from royal exactions (*exactio, census, tributum*) that had been made to monasteries, and make much of the 'unjust' attempts of royal agents to extort payments for their masters.[58] For the South-East, information is more detailed, given the corpus of charters, and a number of those from Llancarfan specify freedom from royal exaction (*seruitium, exactio, census*) in similar but more precise contexts. Sometimes this freedom followed the involvement of kings in a third party's transaction, as in the example cited above, and sometimes it followed a royal grant. It is normally associated with the direct participation of the king in the transaction in some way.[59] The Gwengarth charter recorded after the Life of Cadog goes on to specify that henceforth no 'procurator' will trouble the territory, except for Gwengarth who now owns the land. If the dates that I have suggested for these charters are reasonable, then there is no doubt that they provide unusually early evidence of fiscal obligations to kings in the South-East, evidence appropriate to the very late seventh and eighth centuries. In the case of the material collected at nearby Llandaff, there are some comparable indications. Here it would suggest that some machinery of taxation had developed by the eighth century, in Glywysing, partly as a consequence of the consolidation of the kingdom.[60]

Further references clarify the ways in which such taxes were paid. Most would have been paid in kind rather than coin — despite *Brut's* notification that Maredudd levied a tax of a penny a head in 989, an unwarranted elaboration of the Annals' original entry (though payments *to* the Gentiles are most likely to have been paid in metal, and this at least opens the possibility that some collection of metal was made in order to raise the payment).[61] While Meirchion's steward came round collecting and sent the returns to the royal fortress, and Maelgwn expected 100 cattle and calves to be sent every year from each rural district, Math and Gilfaethwy went on circuit themselves, and when travelling Maelgwn dropped in to demand supper at any likely community — not merely 'bond'.[62] Hospitality, and the billeting of royal officers and animals, must have been as common a form of render as the collection and presentation of foodstuffs at some royal centre.

Royal powers, therefore, certainly extended to taxation in the later period and seem to have done so in Glywysing from the eighth century. There is no reason why this should have been peculiar to Glywysing unless it be argued that machinery would develop more quickly, given the denser agricultural exploitation. Other demands are not specified, though the references to royal exactions *and* service in charters and Saints' Lives might suggest that they could amount to more than render. Three very late references would suggest that the obligation to serve in the king's host — to go on expedition for a period — was common by the late eleventh century: Cadog's inheritance was exempt from all royal exactions except for the obligation to send men (number unspecified) to serve for three days and three nights in the royal host, taking their food with them; the men of Ergyng sent representatives to lead the king's army when it was called out against an enemy; and exemption from military service is also specified in Llandaff's demands from the king of Morgannwg expressed in the earlier portion of 'Braint Teilo'.[63]

Administration

Successful demands for taxation and military service presuppose some sort of administrative machine, unless the kingdom was small enough and the resources were scarce enough for the entire operation to be carried out by the king himself, by visitation and personal contact. Some element of this may well have persisted into the conquest period, for the late hagiographic writers still refer to yearly royal circuits as well as to the hospitality obligation. It is likely, however, that some machinery of collection had already evolved by that time — even without the elaborated structure of the laws, since there are a large number of references to royal officers, occasionally with specific reference to tax collection (the 'procurators' of the Llancarfan charters). From the kings' *ministri* of seventh-century Dyfed, to Benlli's *praefectus* in Powys, to the *praepositi* of people and of king in the Colloquy and in eleventh-century Glamorgan, to the *cynweissyat* of the Triads, officers (*swydawc, swydwyr*) of the tales, and the *meiri* of much of the poetry, we do not lack references from most periods and most areas to the agents of kings — though it is notable that the highly detailed evidence of *Liber Landavensis* has none.[64] One tale, 'Branwen', even goes so far as to detail arrangements that were made when the ruler went on a journey overseas: seven 'stewards' (*kynueissat*) were left to take charge of the island, with one named as chief. The same tale also details the constitution of the levy, drawn from 154 districts (literally 'countries').[65] References to officers are extremely unspecific and suggest that — unlike the detail elaborated by the laws — there was little or no differentiation of function: officers were to execute the king's business, whatever it might be, supervising his own estates or collecting render from those of others. Further, though references are relatively plentiful, they do not in themselves suggest that there were large numbers of such agents.

Correspondingly, the late hints that we have of territorial divisions — whatever the explanation for their origin — may well have been used for administrative and/or fiscal purposes. Already in the tenth century the Colloquy indicates some awareness of administrative subdivisions in its garbled references to the tribune who was chief of two villas, the *commes* (*sic*) in charge of the *civitas*, and the *dux* in charge of 12 *civitates*. The terms and units probably derive from literary models, but they point to the writer's recognition of the value and/or fact of administrative subdivision. [66] By the twelfth century the commote was already the fundamental unit of admin- istration with its proper court and the fiscal substructure detailed above. In the previous century references to distinctively Welsh units begin: the seven *pagi* (districts) of Glamorgan, the 154 districts (*gwledydd*) of 'Branwen', the fiscal *pagi* supposedly exploited by Maelgwn. [67] At the same time, occasional references to regions which are classified as cantrefs and commotes in subsequent centuries indicate that the regional substructure was already forming: Gwent Is Coed, Ystrad Tywi, Cedweli, and so on. There can be no doubt that the administrative framework of Wales was taking shape before the Norman Conquest; but there is little to suggest that it had a long history — as an administrative device — before then. [68] Development is implied, then, in the 100 or so pre-Conquest years.

The existence of administrative devices other than those designed to implement the royal will appears to have been almost entirely limited to the deliberations of notables, and how far these had an administrative rather than a consultative function is arguable. They require mention, however, in the total administrative scheme. Apart from the deliberations of notables, we must not forget the so-called 'magistrate' from Gwynedd and the *publici*, public persons as opposed to private, mentioned by Gildas in the sixth century. [69] This pair of words conjures up an impression of officials with public responsibility and a sense of public duty, people who were not devoted to the furtherance of their own or some exploiter's interests, and it is customary to suppose them the dying remnants of late Roman administration. They may have been descendants of the membership of local *ordines* or even of some layer of the provincial administration; they may have been performing some task of public organization which had its origins in earlier requirements. It is highly unlikely, however, that at that period, four or five generations after the end of contact with central government, such persons were continuing to perform late Roman administrative duties in a late Roman way.

The notables are more serious. Elders, counsellors, 'good men' (*gwyr da*) are noted as often as royal officers and sometimes appear as an alternative authority, sometimes as the natural advisors of kings. The Llandaff material contains very explicit evidence of the meetings of such groups of elders (*meliores, seniores*), particularly in the seventh and eighth centuries, often without a king, for the purpose of regulating transactions; membership was drawn from narrow areas, from the prominent local landowners who did not owe their position to the king. A similar function is implied by at least one of the Llancarfan charters, where King Meurig confirmed a grant in the presence of his *seniores*. And six or seven of the *meliores* of Ergyng were obliged to accompany the English sheriff to the shire court in the mid-eleventh century, presumably an English harnessing of an older Welsh machinery. [70] The Lichfield marginalia include the very explicit narrative of the process of settlement of a dispute, in which the *degion*, 'good men, worthies' — again without royal interference — insisted that agreement be made between Tudfwlch and Elcu over a land claim long contested (see fig.48). [71] Records from other areas which are, of course, different in type, often present the

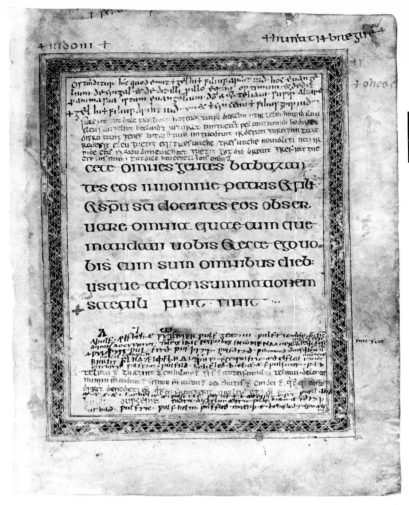

Figure 48. A Welsh record of dispute settlement from the Lichfield Gospels, Lichfield MS 1, p.141 (photograph Courtauld Institute of Art, reproduced by kind permission of the Dean and Chapter, Lichfield Cathedral).

elders in association with the king; they are his natural companions, natural advisors. Gwrtheyrn supposedly deliberated with his elders (*maiores natu*) when wondering what to do about the Saxons in Britain, while the scribe of the fabulous section of the Colloquy glosses the 'patrician who sits beside the king' with *hinham*, 'elder'.[72] It would be interesting to know if there was indeed some regional difference; if the elders of the South had a tendency to meet alone and conduct business apart from the king, while the elders of the North and West worked with him. In both cases, there is some sense of the unsophisticated but functional assembly, the meeting of notables, the occasion on which major decisions affecting the whole people were taken.

The restraining effects of such groups upon kings has already been noted. And certainly the preface to the Dunsaete Ordinance in the tenth century refers to the agreement made by the councillors of the Welsh with the English witan. An advisory and negotiating function is here quite clear. Kings, therefore, do not appear to have been the sole makers of policy and decisions.

The administrative machinery of early medieval Wales was extremely rudimentary. The kings did not consolidate or institutionalize political power; they had no need, therefore, of any more sophisticated administrative machine.

Law and Order

With only a minimal administrative machine, and a propensity to plunder, it is scarcely to be expected that kings would have been in the forefront of law enforcement. Indeed, the first question to be asked is to what extent kings and their officers felt any responsibility for 'order', for keeping the peace, for preventing damage to person and property. The assumptions of the modern tag 'law and order' invoke the weight of the state (and hence the king) behind peace-keeping; but, of course, this was not so in many early medieval societies. Damage was prevented by recognition of the benefits of acceptance and mutual support within the community and not by deterrent regulations or officers handing out penalties. Peace was maintained, damage was made good and disputes were settled with reference to customary rules and procedures, often administered by local worthies like the elders discussed above. Only gradually did kings assume responsibility.

In one sense, the central rôle of the king was to provide protection against damage caused by persons outside the community — other kings and their followers; and to ensure compensation to the community by the distribution of booty acquired by reprisal. As long as kingdoms were small this was a real possibility. But kingdoms grew and political relationships changed. In a society in which ravaging and raiding were a norm — both for plunder and for political devastation — there cannot have been much law and order by the standards at least expected in modern societies. It is easy to overstress this: life, for the most part, went on; people recovered, rebuilt their houses, sowed a new crop; with less to lose, it was easier to start again, and the tales of the local population taking to the woods and caves at the news of the raiders' approach probably convey a valuable insight into the way ordinary people managed. However, already in the sixth century Gildas painted a gloomy picture of civil dislocation; although external wars had stopped, civil wars had not; kings were given to plundering and terrorizing; individuals engaged in the unrestrained murder of their enemies.[73] This was but the beginning. Damage caused by raiding came on at least three levels: the local plunderer, the foreign king, and pirates — especially Vikings. In the South-East, Llywarch seized Eicolf and all his goods and animals round about 940; in c.1025 Rhiwallon attacked the church at St Maughan's and attempted to make off with booty; 20 years later Caradog carried off Seisyll's wife; these are but a few instances.[74] It is quite clear from the terms of reference that seizing food and cattle was not the only object of such activities, for both devastation and the capture of persons are specified, and, in Viking raids, churches were burned. 'The second Unrestrained Ravaging [occurred] when Arthur came to Medrawd's court. He left neither food nor drink in the court...'; King Edgar ravaged churches and settlements in Glamoragn; armed pirates landed with Gruffudd in the estuary of the Usk and went away with precious goods and people: 'The iniquitous pirates, seeing that the church of Saint Gwynllyw was barred, reckoning that precious articles were inside for safety and protection, broke the bar and after breaking entered as violators. Whatever precious and useful thing was found, they took...'. Indeed, Giraldus selected this propensity to live by plunder, theft and robbery from both foreigners and neighbours as one of the outstanding Welsh characteristics in the twelfth century. [75]

Thieving, presumably plunder by locals, plunder without a political aim, plunder not necessarily supported by military force, was a common complaint; [76] so much so that it was occasion for comment when cattle fed freely in the fields, without watchers and without protection. [77] The most frequently-cited objects of theft are animals: pigs, sheep, cattle, the easily movable sources of wealth and of support. Rules for following the track of stolen cattle are the preoccupation of the Dunsaete Ordinance: 'If anyone follow the track of stolen cattle from one river bank to the other, he must hand over the tracking to the men of that land' and so on. [78] The Life of Illtud relates how two thieves came from Brycheiniog to Glamorgan, stole a herd of pigs from their sty, drove them through the woods at night, but lost their way and ended up where they had started. [79] This late, but very detailed, tale conveys a nice impression of the way theft was carried out, just as the educational narrative of the Colloquy dramatized a different aspect:

> 'Brother, if you are experienced, show us the way we must go.'...
> And the one who knew said 'Go this way and go off to the right or
> left; it won't fail you, but will lead you to the city in peace '. 'Have
> you heard if there are bad men and robbers on the road we must
> take?' And he said 'There are not' and they arrived at the monastery
> in peace. [80]

Travel was dangerous, and there is much to suggest that often one could neither venture out nor stay at home without fear of harm to body or property. Heavy penances for theft — at least a year, and two years or exile for a second offence — indicate the concern with which it was viewed. [81]

Community action against such dangers was clearly expected, and independent individual action condoned in the case of the thief caught red-handed. The swineherd who came upon the holy Cadog and, thinking he disturbed a thief, rushed at him with his spear, was berated for his lack of perception rather than for his action; the people of Gwynllŵg refrained from killing the plunderers who tormented them — as they would normally have done — because they were the men of Cadog's uncle. [82] Death sentences for theft are noted by both the *Historia Brittonum* and the story of 'Manawydan'; and penal slavery by the Life of Cadog. [83] The Dunsaete Ordinance, although primarily concerned with English/Welsh relations, spells out the steps of community action against theft: the man who owns the land must take up the search, and compensate or put down a pledge within nine days if unsuccessful; six men of good repute must swear good intention if anyone be challenged for pursuing the track; right must be done within nine days, and so on.[84] When a girl was seized, her kindred mounted horses and blew horns, and the arms-bearing men of the community turned out to pursue her capturers; at an earlier date, the 'Stanzas of the Graves' refer to the cry *not* raised against thieves.[85] Only Gildas mentioned a royal responsibility for the pursuit of criminals, and he did this in a context of their failure to do so. After the sixth century, it seems to have been viewed as a community rather than a royal responsibility to deal with disturbance, prevent a recurrence and acquire compensation, unless the king's share of the plunder legitimately taken in cases of homicide in eleventh-century Ergyng be viewed as a Welsh rather than English institution.[86]

Theft is by far the most frequently cited offence against individual, family or group. Others such as abduction, bloodshed, assault, arson and trespass do occur.[87] Killing, however, and the penalties for it, were understandably the greatest concern. The planned poisoning, the blow from thieves, the workmen who joined together to kill the master builder, are all duly condemned.[88] Procedures for dealing with killing are only lightly sketched, however; redress was certainly expected — by the dead man's family or lord — but we have little detail of the manner of achieving it.[89] The implication of the story of Arthur and Ligessog, who had killed three of Arthur's men, is that the murderer was only safe from Arthur if he could gain protection (*nawdd*) from some greater power; eventually resolution and redress was achieved through the meeting and judgment of notables, lay and clerical. Procedure in this case involved pursuit by the injured party and ultimately compensation to him after a judgment in accordance with established rules. The killing was treated as a dispute between bodies.

If information on the procedure for dealing with killing is only lightly sketched, the principle fundamental to the resolution of the dispute thereby initiated, and to the resolution of all offence and damage, is clear — that of compensation for the injury done as opposed to that of the fine paid to the state. In the early tenth century King Tewdwr of Brycheiniog stole Bishop Libiau's foodrent, and it was eventually agreed that, as compensation, the king should make reparation by handing over five times the worth of the bishop's household and seven times the worth of the bishop himself, an amount that was assessed at 700 mancuses of gold; a little earlier King Brochfael had come into conflict with Bishop Cyfeilliog, and a similar assessment had been made. The poet of *Armes Prydein*, at a similar period, asked that the invading Saxons should be asked to compensate for the damage they had done before they were allowed to leave the land of Britain:

> When they come face to face with each other, the Cymry will take care
> that the foreigners shall not go from the place where they stand
> until they repay sevenfold the value of what they have done,
> with certain death in return for their wrong.[90]

The principle is therefore clear, and it is notable that the compensation that was paid was not merely the equivalent of the property stolen but a greater amount, and, moreover, an amount calculated in accordance with the status of the damaged party. Every man correspondingly had his 'life price', his worth if killed, again in accordance with status. The 'Ordinance of the Dunsaete' pronounced a modification for cases of inter-racial killing: if a Welshman killed an English man or *vice-versa*, only half of the *wergild* (the appropriate English term) should be paid, whatever the status. In the tale of Arthur and Ligessog, Lifris recounted the dispute among the judges of the South-East when they tried to assess the worth of Arthur's men — 3 cows each or 100; later King Maelgwn came to demand the worth of his killed men and it was argued that 450 cows was the worth of every *optimas*, 'noble', of Cadog's progeny.[91] In the South-East, the Llandaff charters sometimes specify the compensation due for killing or procedure after it; Elias received an estate of about 500 acres in compensation for the murder of his brother, in the mid-eighth century; Asser and his father came to agreement following the murder of Gulagguin in the mid-tenth century.[92] Moreover, compensation was due not merely for physical damage done but for the insult afforded by certain offences. Insult, therefore, could be as great a damage as theft of property or attack on person, and had to be comparably treated. This is the notion expressed in the laws as *sarhad* (or very occasionally *wynebwerth*, 'worth of face') and is fundamental to the conceptual structure that informs the laws.[93] The honour of a man — or of a group — was therefore as precious a thing as his body and property, and damage to it was equally compensatable: dishonour was done to Pwyll to the 'value of 100 stags'.[94] A further aspect of offence that required compensation, an aspect largely unfamiliar to modern criminal procedures, is that of the offence caused by the infringement of a person's or institution's powers of protection (*nawdd*). Damage done to an individual who was protected by a third party might oblige the offender to compensate the third party as well as the person injured. Hence, in Lifris's tale about Arthur and Ligessog, no-one except St Cadog would give Ligessog protection for fear of Arthur, and the point of the story is to stress the dire consequences of the insult done to the saint by Arthur's pursuit of Ligessog rather than those of Ligessog's original murder; Cadog's powers of protection were extended by Arthur and confirmed by other kings. In a different context, his protection was specified as lasting seven years, seven months and seven days and a night's lodging throughout the district.[95] A comparable though more generalized claim was made for St David, who, by the agreement of the bishops, was to have superior powers of protection wherever a homicide or offender sought the shelter of land consecrated to David.[96] In this reference the temporal interpretation of the institution — protection for a prescribed period — very familiar in (though not exclusive to) early Irish contexts, has been transformed into a territorial one: David gives protection over areas of land. And it is this aspect which survives to be noted by Giraldus and others in the twelfth century and to be preserved and elaborated in the law tracts:

> Around (the churches) the cattle graze so peacefully, not only in the churchyards, but outside, too, within fences and ditches marked out and set by bishops to fix the sanctuary limits. The more important churches, hallowed by their greater antiquity, offer sanctuary as far as the cattle go to feed in the morning and can return at evening. If a man has incurred the hatred of his prince and is in danger of death, he may apply to the church for sanctuary and it will be freely granted to him and his family. Many people abuse this immunity.[97]

The compensation in these cases seems to have been assessed by notables, presumably the worthies who met to discuss matters of importance, witness transactions, resolve other civil disputes.[98] All the material suggests that clerics took part in such meetings, and it is evident that the church was more or less concerned with problems of order, even when they did not directly affect church interests. Penance for murder was again high: 3 to 13 years, according to the status of the murderer; when Euan killed his sister's sons, he was cursed by Cadog until he came to confess and redeem himself; the numbers of south-eastern aristocrats who came to synods in the tenth and eleventh centuries to make grants in penance for offences — from abduction and rape to theft and murder — is evidence of the same concerns.[99] Perjury was regarded as especially serious and might condemn the offender to perpetual servitude.[100] Clerics were interested enough to be involved — obviously, for they stood to gain from penitential action — but, perhaps surprisingly, they seem to have had some effect, for their interference was not merely in cases of damage to themselves. The law tracts would make every landowner a judge in the South, perhaps a reference to the continuation of these meetings of notables, and also indicate the presence of professional judges in the North; and there are some few references in the pre-Conquest material to judges who may have been comparable professionals. Interestingly, these are all in southern contexts. Llancarfan's concern with immunity from the judgment of kings, bishops and nobles is presumably a negative aspect of the same differentiation: Llancarfan will have its own judges, its own judgment place and its own book of procedure. Presumably, therefore, it is outside the normal processes of dispute settlement, and presumably the same applies to (or was claimed by) Llandaff as the church of Teilo in the late tenth century or early eleventh century when it produced a privilege (the so-called 'Braint Teilo') exempting the community from judgment by the king of Morgannwg and mentioning *sarhad* in particular.[101] The judges consulted in the Ligessog case were specifically distinguished from the nobles, clerics and elders assembled by Cadog, and the context of their involvement in this case would suggest that the judges were distinct from the others in the corporate process of finding a resolution because they knew — or had much greater knowledge of — the law: hence, some judges assessed the worth of the dead men at 100 cows each but the 'most *skilled*' assessed it at three.[102] Similarly, in the famous case of 955 recorded in the Llandaff charters, the violation of the sanctuary of St Arvans by six of King Nowy's household in pursuit of a homicidal deacon was held to be Nowy's responsibility by the very famous man Blegywryd, and compensation had duly to be paid to the bishop.[103] The implication of the record is that the judgment turned upon the knowledge of Blegywryd. The 'professional' judges were the lawyers, performing a role similar to that of the judge in a modern English criminal court.

There is virtually no useful detail of procedure: Llancarfan had its own procedure for finding judgments and there were set days for pleading in Gwynllŵg.[104] Witnesses might be noted; accusations could be met by denial, but they might require the oaths of many men: that of 60 men was required for the denial of slaying someone in the protected area (refuge) of Gwynllŵg; or accusations might be denied by the defendant by oath taken on a holy relic

— like that of the thief who foolishly attempted to proclaim his innocence on the Gildas Gospels.[105] These are but hints but they emphasize both the procedural significance of oath-helping and the power and interest of clerics in the process; in the end, however, as with the compensation material, their greatest significance is to emphasize that there were standard procedures.

The machinery for dealing with disturbance, therefore, included the community pursuit of thieves, and private pursuit of murderers, encouraged by the denunciations of clerics. There is no suggestion of royal involvement in the catching of offenders. Once caught, the offender was expected to make compensatory payment, in accordance with the judgment of notables — perhaps with the advice of a professional judge, a 'lawyer' — and often to do penance in addition to compensation. In the latest period, imprisonment and corporal punishment of various sorts emerged. In the South-East bishops imprisoned offenders while waiting for settlement, clearly a way of enforcing settlement without fighting; while kings threatened blinding, mutilation and beating for offenders.[106] These are new trends, heralding new procedures and new principles.

Private security, therefore, was limited, as was royal responsibility for it, and though there are indications of a growing royal involvement by the late eleventh century, it would appear that kings had little to do with maintaining the peace, taking action on disturbance and administering law before that time. They were, after all, some of the major perpetrators of disturbance, especially when they ceased to be effective protectors against the intrusion of foreign kings. Law there was in plenty, but not necessarily royal law.[107] There were customary procedures. There was a clear notion of law, of lawful behaviour, of persons outside the law — outlaws.[108] There were persons skilled in the law and respected for such. There is a huge corpus of distinctively Welsh law from the twelfth century and later and, whether or not we believe the association made by post-Conquest jurists between King Hywel and its collection, it is perfectly clear that much of this corpus has a pre-Conquest origin and pre-Conquest relevance. The pre-Conquest context is made perfectly clear by the fragments of Welsh law in Ergyng which are preserved in the Herefordshire Domesday.[109] Law was associated in the literate mind with peace: Gildas thought that the Romans had brought law and peace; Lifris thought that plunder was contrary to law and right; the author of the Life of Gwynllyw thought that laws were increasing in his own time and the citizens law-abiding.[110] Law was also, and maybe more strongly, associated with the preservation of privilege, that is with the preservation of order in a different sense: maintaining the right balance, enshrining the proper disposition of things and seeing that everyone got his due. By the eleventh century churches, in particular, were attempting to specify this privilege, as guaranteed by law, in writing. 'Braint Teilo', therefore, associates the two ideas: 'Here is the law and privilege of the church...'; the writer of the Life of Padarn notes the *lex*, law, due to all churches.[111] To see this society as 'lawless' is therefore unthinkable: law was plentiful, but its relationship to the state and the king, its principles and its functioning, were different from those we expect in a modern society.

So, for much of the early medieval period, kings had few functions beyond the military, though there are hints that the notion of some greater responsibility was developing by the later eleventh century, possibly under the influence of wider contacts. Kings made war and made judgments, as did any notable; they did not govern in any of the usual senses of the word; they were exploiters, whose greatest success lay in fostering some development of the machinery of exploitation.

6 The Church – Institutions and Authority

Surprisingly little is known about the pre-Conquest Welsh church, considering how much has been written about it; and it is quite impossible to consider or compare it with the Irish church in any real sense, as is the common temptation. Romantic views of a Celtic church, spanning Celtic areas, with its own institutional structure and special brand of spirituality, have often been expressed, but have little to support them, especially with reference to Wales.[1] We are extraordinarily ignorant, beyond our knowledge of the existence of clerics and their capacity to influence kings and others. Some fundamental questions about ecclesiastical institutions are raised by the very assumptions that are common: in what senses was the church in Wales a monastic church? Were there monks and monasteries? Were there *many* monks and monasteries? Were they so dominant as to determine the character of the church? Were they so dominant as to control all ecclesiastical institutions and personnel? Should we, in fact, consider abbots rather than bishops the controlling members, invested with the greatest fiscal and jurisdictional powers? Were there federations of monasteries displacing, in effect, the customary European prominence of the territorial bishopric? The popular view of the Celtic church assigns a power to monastic institutions which is difficult to support in Wales, though the questions need to be asked; it also assigns a special sanctity, a habit of selfless denial and self-willed endurance, to its members. The 'Age of Saints' figures prominently in most surveys both of Welsh history and of medieval ecclesiastical history, and the image of sixth-century Wales as a source of missions and the hope of a new asceticism has had a powerful influence. The picture presented by the Lives of Saints produced in Brittany and in Ireland, as well as in Wales, in the central Middle Ages is of dozens of ascetics wandering through the western world, making new foundations as they travelled. Whether or not the historical perspective of these Lives — which has much to do with a developing cult of saints — has any relevance to the events of 500 years earlier remains problematic. It is useful, therefore, to attempt some definition of the evidence of contemporary material rather than accept unquestioningly the interpretation of later hagiographers.

Foundations

Though the elaborations of later tradition and inferences made from the distribution of dedications would suggest many more, we have early notice of some 35 religious foundations in Wales before or at the Conquest, outside the evidence supplied by charters (see fig.49).[2] To these we might reasonably add the church of Presteign, which stands on pre-Norman foundations.[3] The

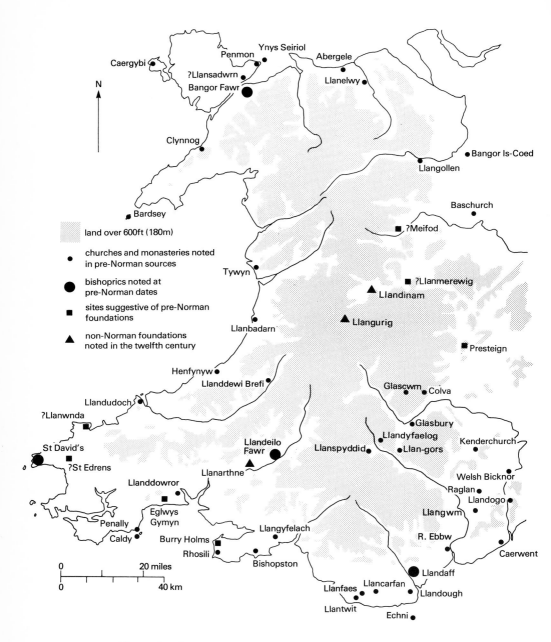

Figure 49. The well-evidenced religious foundations of early Wales (see fig.50 for further detail of the South-East).

number would certainly be increased if we had more early documentation, and possibilities are suggested by different types of evidence: houses at St Ishmaels, Rhoscrowdder, Llandeulyddog, Llandeilo Llwydarth,? St Issells near Tenby and ? Llangenau in the parish of Clydai are named in a portion of the law tracts which must have some pre-Conquest origin; places like Llandinam, Llangurig and Llanarthne were twelfth-century churches which were not Norman foundations; early churches may be indicated at places like Llansadwrn in Anglesey by the presence of a tombstone commemorating Sadyrnin, as Sir John Lloyd suggested; concentrations of early Christian inscribed stones at sites like Llanwnda and St Edrens *could* have a pre-Conquest import, though they may have been brought together after the Conquest; the evidence of structures beneath medieval churches at Burry Holms, St Patrick's Chapel, St Justinian's Chapel, suggests earlier churches; the late tenth- or eleventh-century cross at Nevern almost certainly points to the existence of a major pre-Conquest church within two or three miles of the present structure (see fig.51); the undated physical evidence of settlement on islands like Gateholm, Grassholm and Priestholm (Ynys Seiriol) could have an eremitic significance; and the equally undated enclosures which surround modern churches like Eglwys Gymyn, Llanmerewig and Meifod could represent early cemetery boundaries in the first two cases and the boundary *vallum* surrounding a monastery in the latter.[4] The distribution of the known sites is quite strikingly coastal, hugging the lowland, occupying the good lands, within easy reach of the main lines of communication.[5] Four have associated bishops — Bangor, St David's, Llandeilo Fawr, Llandaff — but we have very little information about the rest; Bardsey and Bangor on Dee certainly had monks; there was a monastic community on Caldy island and Llantwit was a 'great monastery'. Notice of burning and plundering indicates that they *were* permanent religious settlements, but tells us no more that. The evidence that we have suggests that these foundations were settlements rather than isolated churches, though the settlement might itself have been isolated, and hence that churches were attached to religious communities rather than lay villages.

Even allowing that the population was minimal, the number of named sites is very small, much smaller than casual references to churches and monasteries would suggest. An early narrative source like the Life of Samson refers to un-named foundations made by Samson's pious relatives so often that it suggests that there were many that have left no mark. In this context the evidence supplied by the charters of the South-East is of paramount importance, for it fills in the framework supplied by other sources. The Llandaff charters refer to 36 monasteries in the South-East, and a further 38 *ecclesiae*; this latter term, literally meaning 'church', is very commonly used to refer to monasteries, though not always so in eleventh-century records.[6] There appear to have been over 50 monasteries, therefore, in the South-East, mostly small ones with limited resources but well positioned on the good lands (see fig.50). It is very difficult to know whether the analogy of the South-East is applicable to other areas of Wales and whether records of the transfer of property elsewhere would reveal a similar phenomenon had they survived. Any comment on this is necessarily very speculative, but a few observations may be made. Firstly, although the virtual absence of charters from areas outside the South-East is merely a negative point and cannot conclusively demonstrate anything, on balance present evidence would suggest that the deficiency is in itself significant and that there are scarcely any charters because there were fewer transfers of property, and fewer houses to record them. This is understandable, given the different Roman background of the South-East, a possibly different tenurial structure, and almost certainly higher population and more easily exploitable resources; all such considerations would make for greater mobility in the 'land market', and mean that alienation of property to the Church was easier. Secondly, the

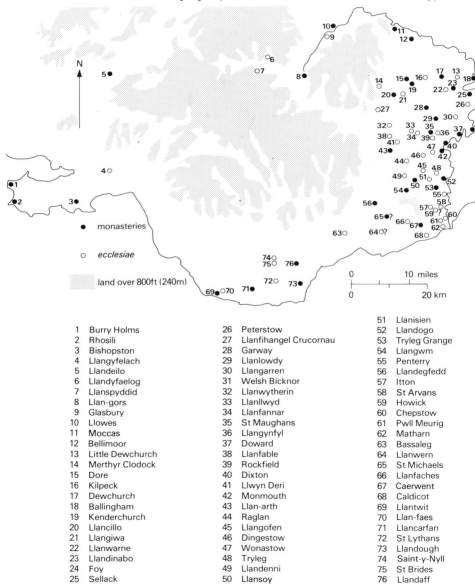

N

● monasteries

○ *ecclesiae*

land over 800ft (240m)

0   10 miles

0   20 km

1 Burry Holms	26 Peterstow	51 Llanisien
2 Rhosili	27 Llanfihangel Crucornau	52 Llandogo
3 Bishopston	28 Garway	53 Tryleg Grange
4 Llangyfelach	29 Llanlowdy	54 Llangwm
5 Llandeilo	30 Llangarren	55 Penterry
6 Llandyfaelog	31 Welsh Bicknor	56 Llandegfedd
7 Llanspyddid	32 Llanwytherin	57 Itton
8 Llan-gors	33 Llanllwyd	58 St Arvans
9 Glasbury	34 Llanfannar	59 Howick
10 Llowes	35 St Maughans	60 Chepstow
11 Moccas	36 Llangynfyl	61 Pwll Meurig
12 Bellimoor	37 Doward	62 Matharn
13 Little Dewchurch	38 Llanfable	63 Bassaleg
14 Merthyr Clodock	39 Rockfield	64 Llanwern
15 Dore	40 Dixton	65 St Michaels
16 Kilpeck	41 Llwyn Deri	66 Llanfaches
17 Dewchurch	42 Monmouth	67 Caerwent
18 Ballingham	43 Llan-arth	68 Caldicot
19 Kenderchurch	44 Raglan	69 Llantwit
20 Llancillo	45 Llangofen	70 Llan-faes
21 Llangiwa	46 Dingestow	71 Llancarfan
22 Llanwarne	47 Wonastow	72 St Lythans
23 Llandinabo	48 Tryleg	73 Llandough
24 Foy	49 Llandenni	74 Saint-y-Nyll
25 Sellack	50 Llansoy	75 St Brides
		76 Llandaff

Figure 50. Religious foundations in the South-East.

Communities

What, then, can be said of these communities? Firstly, although the recognition of monasticism as a distinct vocation is clear from an early date, we should not expect communities like the rigidly ordered and standardized Benedictine houses of Europe in the central medieval period. There may have been some such communities, with a clearly regulated and moderated day, and a controlled balance between manual labour, prayer and worship, but variety was almost certainly as characteristic. Community life seems to have been the norm throughout the period, whether or not the community was composed of professed monks, for we hear nothing of the isolated cleric. (Though if recent suggestions that some early churches developed in association with long cist cemeteries, in accordance with C. Thomas's models of ecclesiastical topographical development, are correct, this may indicate a different type of religious complex.[20]) Bishops had their households too. Indeed, Asser referred to St David's as the home of a bishop but also as *monasterium*; the same is implied for Llandeilo by the witnesses to the Lichfield charters; Llandaff was certainly a *monasterium* before it became the seat of a bishopric.[21] There was, then, no incongruity in placing the seat of a bishopric in a monastery; no distinction of type was seen between the two communities; and there may have been no actual distinction of type between the two, particularly by the ninth and tenth centuries. Indeed, it is highly likely that the distinction between those members of a religious community with monastic vow and those without became less and less clear as time went on. After the middle of the tenth century abbots stop being mentioned in the South-East and the representatives of communities are merely called priests or *sacerdotes*. This, together with increasing references to priests, suggests a change from houses of professed monks with monastic and non-monastic clergy to houses in the later period essentially composed of secular clergy.[22] Moreover, observers of the twelfth century complained to the *claswyr* in Wales, members of religious communities whose property rights were hereditarily transmitted, since they seemed so unlike the reformed houses of the rest of western Europe.[23] Rhigyfarch, like Asser, still viewed the episcopal community at St David's as monastic — *monastica classis* — though it is perfectly clear that bishops married and produced children, as was also the case at Llandaff at the same period, and (for monastic officers) at the closely related houses of Llanbadarn and Llancarfan.[24] They may all have considered themselves monks, but if so their vocation did not require celibacy, and their way of life must have had little in common with the popular image of the cloistered monk either now or then in contemporary continental Europe. Although there are references, therefore, to monks and monasteries at all periods, and though community life seems to have been the normal expression of religious vocation (until quite late in the eleventh century when the beginnings of some sort of diocesan organization began to develop in the South-East[25]), by the late eleventh and twelfth centuries communities which were considered monastic had practices which were not very 'monastic' in the usually accepted sense. Some continuation of the earlier distinction between members who were professed monks and those who were not may possibly have been sustained, however, for the law tracts distinguish between the 'monk' or canon who was a member of a hereditary corporation and the *diofredawc* (popularly *meudwy*), the celibate.[26] Whether or not the celibate pursued his more rigorous practice alone, within established institutions, or with a few fellows in a more strict community is not at all clear.

We can make no useful observations about the size of communities. Bede referred to the hundreds at Bangor on Dee in the early seventh century and the triads specify 2,400 there.[27] Neither figure is very credible. The only other indications are those of the late Saints' Lives, where numbers are invariably very small — 7, 11, 12.[28] The charters also imply small communities and small numbers for the greater proportion of cases, though the presence of lectors at some probably indicates larger establishments.[29] Presumably powerful foundations like Llancarfan, Llantwit, Llanbadarn, Mathri, Tywyn and Clynnog were larger, but we have no idea by how much. The only excavated possible religious sites are those at Ynys Seiriol, Gaerwen, Arfryn (Bodedern, Anglesey), Llandegái (near Bangor) (see fig.65), St Patrick's and St Justinian's Chapels (St David's), and Burry Holms (Gower) (see fig.52). Only Ynys Seiriol supplies reasonable evidence of possible living quarters, and these are very limited in size. Some of the hut groups at nearby Penmon may have been associated with the monastery there but it is difficult to specify date and precise relationship. We can therefore get little indication from physical remains except to note the contrast between the large enclosure round Meifod and the huge size of the Norman church at Tywyn on the one hand and the smaller enclosures at Eglwys Gymyn (see fig.11) and Llanmerewig on the other.

Figure 52. The religious site at Burry Holms (photograph Terrence James; copyright reserved).

Evidence about practice is similarly incomplete, but there are some indications of it at the beginning and end of the period. Gildas, as ever, is useful, despite his verbosity and apparent inconsequentiality, particularly in this case because he presents two alternative and opposed modes of behaviour. There were monastic rules and monastic vows, clothing proper to abbots, a code of behaviour proper to chaste widows; the machinery of ascetic devotion was known and established. On the other hand, the clergy made long journeys in pompous style with elaborate retinues, manoeuvred for the purchase of clerical office, failed to help the poor and teach the people, and lay about in drunken stupor. [30] Though ideals were in the air, normal practice was scarcely attuned to them. At about the same time, the preface on penance which is attributed to Gildas — there is no need to suppose it is his own work — insisted on obedience to the abbot, presumed that manual labour was usual in monastic communities and made some detailed provisions about penitential diet; the monastic priest or deacon guilty of a sexual offence should do no penance for three years;

> he shall have bread without limitation and a titbit fattened slightly with butter on Sunday; on the other days a ration of dry bread and a dish enriched with a little fat, garden vegetables, a few eggs, a British cheese, a Roman half-pint of milk in consideration of the weakness of the body in this age, also a Roman pint of whey or buttermilk for his thirst, and some water if he is a worker. He shall have his bed meagrely supplied with hay... [31]

Here is a strict limitation, decreasing the bread ration in accordance with the high status of the offender (monks without orders received more bread when doing penance for the same offence) but it is not unduly hard; and if eggs, cheese, fat and vegetables formed the stuff of penitential diet the normal diet for professed monks must have been palatable and quite substantial.

The Life of Samson supplies the greatest detail about both practice and ideals, though it must represent a Breton rather than a Welsh statement of the latter; insofar as it provides evidence of contact between Wales and Brittany then those ideals must be at least relevant to the Welsh perspective. The acceptance of the notion of a rule is again explicit: living the monastic life means living in accordance with a rule. [32] One incident gives some indication, perhaps a surprising one, of the contents of that rule, for in introducing the tale of the attempted poisoning of the youthful holy Samson the writer mentioned that the constitutions of the monastery included the prescription that herbs should be gathered and prepared 'for the health of the monks'. [33] Concern for the potential of widows echoes that of Gildas for we hear again of an order of widowhood. [34] Details of the practice expected included the shaving of heads and the obligation of manual labour: even the abbot Piro 'worked with his hands all day' on Caldy. [35] Three monasteries in Wales provide an anecdotal context for the young Samson's ascetic development, and in so doing supply some details of variant practice. Large numbers, eating and drinking, communal life, attention to administration and conversation were the norm at Illtud's Llantwit: the monks were in the middle of life and affairs. [36] Caldy was more isolated. Situated on an island, its physical setting proclaimed withdrawal and we are told that Bishop Dyfrig was himself accustomed to withdraw there for his Lenten retreat. Indeed, this was the community to which Samson was drawn when he left Llantwit in search of greater poverty and greater abstinence, and the writer of the Life clearly used it as a model of more ascetic, cenobitic life, whether or not it actually was such. Nevertheless, the plentiful feasts, the abbot's intoxication and Samson's eventual introduction of a 'proper rule' would suggest that though the community was a withdrawn one and though hereditary interest was not the chief mechanism for the disposition of its property — the brothers in council chose a new abbot together — it enjoyed a far from uncomfortable life-style and was scarcely the model of a rigorous asceticism.[37] Of the third we are given much less detail, for this was the 'fort' and cave to which Samson retreated with his three companions when he left Caldy, dissatisfied with the quality of the life it offered.[38] The writer's message is clear: though there was variety of practice among the monasteries of the south-east of Wales, no established community offered a rigorously ascetic experience. Indeed, Samson's new community is neither described nor presented as a 'monastery', although it had a water supply and living quarters were constructed in the fort and an oratory in the cave. The implication is that the community was too small, too unstructured and too simple to deserve the term and is presumably what the writer had in mind by calling Samson 'hermit' not monk. The implication is also, of course, that a few such isolated communities did emerge in the context of the ascetic movement of the mid-sixth century, the ideal of which this Life does much to publicize. Practice at such communities is only lightly sketched. The relationship of cave and fort seems crucial: the small but supportive community resident in the fort, the cave the opportunity for personal withdrawal and retreat. Samson would withdraw to the cave for a seven-day fast, fed only lightly and occasionally by the brothers from the fort. One might imagine this sort of eremitical occupation in the caves with known artifacts of the early medieval period, like Radyr near Cardiff and possibly Bacon Hole in Gower. The practice, of course, is not confined to this Life or to Wales and Brittany, and is known elsewhere in the early medieval period: Bede wrote of Cuthbert's retreat on Farne which remained important even after he became bishop of Lindisfarne; Adomnán of Columba's personal writing hut, within the monastery of Iona.[39] For the others life presumably consisted of gathering the means of support and sustaining life; the community which was too small to specialize functions and to benefit from intensively labouring at busy times can have had little time for activities other than those of self-support.

More specifically, the practice demanded of and occasionally sustained by the real ascetic is described with reference to Samson's personal habits throughout his life rather than with reference to his cave near the Severn. As we might expect, poverty, the renouncing of property, the restraint of bodily appetite, were all demanded. Samson encouraged his true followers to give up all their goods to the poor; while he himself was distinguished by refraining from either heterosexual or homosexual expression and even had doubts about visiting his sick father because of the necessity of re-entering the home in which he had been 'carnally born'; he himself neither ate flesh nor allowed himself to become intoxicated.[40] Long vigils were a feature from an early age, in the pursuit of the conscious wakefulness that might produce the semiconscious trance of communion with God. Samson therefore worked with his hands or prayed all day, while working all night on the mysteries of Holy Scripture. He did not sleep in a bed, but reclined against a wall so that, achieving a state of spiritual ecstasy, he prepared his mind for the visions that would direct him further.

> On a certain night when he was preparing to sing the Paschal Mass and, following a custom of his, after partaking of the blessed bread, had determined to stand wakeful till dawn at the altar by himself alone, nay, rather, with God also with him, as he was praying on that very spot in ecstasy, he lost consciousness altogether, and as he stood there, he saw a mighty man shining with great splendour come and stand by him, and at first, as I have heard he afterwards related to his father, he himself was terrified by the immensity of this apparition; and he heard a word of comfort for him not to fear and which said to him 'Be of good cheer, saint of God, and play the man, for God holds thee dear and true; now therefore listen without fear to my words. For indeed I have been sent to thee by my Lord; of a truth thou oughtest to tarry no longer in this country, for thou art ordained to be a pilgrim, and beyond the sea thou wilt be very great in the Church'. [41]

At the other end of the period, and from a different perspective, Giraldus dwelled upon the physical context and the meaning of this type of eremitical life when he discussed the settlement at Llanthony which had preceded the foundation of Augustinian canons there in the twelfth century:

> In the deep vale of Ewias, which is shut in on all sides by a circle of lofty mountains and which is no more than three arrow-shots in width, there stands the abbey church of Saint John the Baptist.... It is a site most suited to the practice of religion and better chosen for canonical discipline than that of any of the other monasteries in the whole Island of Britain. It was originally founded by two hermits, in honour of the eremitical way of life, in solitude and far removed from the bustle of everyday existence. ... It rains a lot there because of the mountains, the winds blow strong, and in winter it is always capped with clouds. The climate is temperate and healthy, the air soothing and clement, if somewhat heavy, and illness is rare... the monks gaze up at the distant prospects which rise above their own lofty roof-tops, and there they see, as far as any eye can reach, mountain peaks which rise to meet the sky and often enough herds of wild deer which are grazing on their summits. Even on a clear day, the sun's round ball is not visible above these lofty mountain tops until the hour of prime, or maybe just before. This was formerly a happy, a delightful spot, most suited to the life of contemplation, a place from its first founding fruitful and to itself sufficient. [42]

After the time of Samson we have little indication of practice — beyond the 'continuous prayer' demanded by the triads of the three perpetual harmonies — until the prescriptions of the Saints' Lives. [43] The early twelfth-century

Lives nod dutifully towards the by then expected reformed monastic practice: labour, prayer, obedience, fasting, chastity, adherence to a rule; and occasionally specify the greater demands of the ascetic — washing in cold water, sleeping on a mat, dressing in skins and goatshair.[44] They say little, however, of requirements for entry beyond vague generalizations about the conversion of rich men and handing over of oblate children. The rather earlier Life of Cadog has some similar anecdotes, making comparable points — a life for the tonsured monk of singing, reading and praying, and of manual labour — though it must be noted that the proportion of this long Life which demonstrates any such concern is extremely small.[45] All of this, in any case, is extremely unspecific and probably reflects general attitudes of the late eleventh century and later. The most detailed comment comes from the late eleventh-century Life of David by Rhigyfarch, who was particularly explicit on the rules associated with St David himself. Monks were confined within the cloister and isolated from the world, living a life in common, subject to a rule and promising obedience to the abbot, whose permission was required for all things.[46] The would-be entrant was to undergo the trial of waiting at the door of the monastery for ten days, to demonstrate his intensity of purpose, and then be admitted to work hard at the entrance before he was finally allowed full admission to the community; no fees were to be taken from him — a useful hint that this was the usual practice.[47] Once a member of the community, life was rigorous and idleness not tolerated in case it encouraged lust; daily labour, therefore, bearing yokes on their own shoulders, was to be the norm — 'each his own ox' — and after work in the fields, reading, writing or praying. In the evening, the bell would ring for worship and prayer in church, where the monks would stay till nightfall, chanting psalms and then praying for three hours, and there was prayer again at dawn; a regular weekly vigil happened on the eve of the sabbath till after dawn in the first hour of the Lord's Day. Poverty was essential; private possessions were not tolerated and attracted heavy penances, for all essential property was to be held in common. Material comfort was to be limited: clothing was to be cheap, and skins much utilized; diet was limited to bread, vegetables, salt and 'temperate' drink (David was traditionally *aquaticus*, 'water-man'), though the old and the sick and travellers were allowed more; conversation was to be restricted to matters of essential communication.[48] Chastity, modesty, patience, humility, compassion and charity were all encouraged.[49] The model accords well with the ideals of moderately ascetic cenobitic practice expounded in Mediterranean areas in the late and post-Roman periods, ideals which were to become so prominent in Western Europe in the central middle ages: restraint, awareness, a measure of solitude guaranteed by the support and the overseeing of fellows, and underwritten by obedience to the master and to the rule, designed for those normal men who could not hope to emulate the extremes of self-denial achieved by the true ascetic but who might hope to achieve some genuine contemplation — the translation of Samson's message into practical terms.

This is, of course, a statement of ideals. As such it is an extremely valuable comment on the way some clerics in west Wales were thinking in the late eleventh century. It could even contain rules formulated by David and his contemporaries and handed down to future generations. Certainly some of the prescriptions — especially those concerned to guarantee proper behaviour in church — are close to those of the early penitential material discussed above. However, how far this applies outside the obvious cases and how far the ideals represent any sort of *practice* current in the late eleventh century is lost to our inspection.

The formal statements of rules are few. Physical descriptions are hard to find and as yet archaeology does not suggest much to augment the picture, though the cells which underlie medieval structures on Priestholm (Ynys Seiriol) may well have a monastic significance of this period. A church, 5ft square, lay beneath the twelfth-century church, and three or four rectangular 'cells', 12ft wide and of varying lengths, were enclosed by a dry-stone boundary wall. On the southern coast, at Burry Holms in Gower, a wooden church lay beneath that of the twelfth century (see fig.52); associated structures were not sufficiently defined, but a turf wall, with palisade added later, surrounded the complex. (It is also possible that the large settlement on Gateholm was monastic, although the absence of religious objects and of any structure which looks like a church must make this unlikely (see fig.13).)[50] The written evidence contains a few hints: apart from the occasional indication that the monastery was a separated place, marked off from the world by well-defined bounds, the late Lives suggest that a church and/or oratory, together with distinctive eating and sleeping quarters and a house for guests, formed the consistent constituent components of the complex.[51] There is little hint of private individual cells, but there must have been additional buildings for reading and writing, especially for the work of designated scribes. A number of Lives go out of their way to specify that the work of construction was performed by the monks themselves, often after the theoretical establishment of the community: David's monastery was built in Rosina Vallis after he had gathered together his band of followers; Brynach's companions took their tools to cut down the trees and prepare to build; Beuno constructed his hut in a deep valley; though most of Cadog's monks were engaged in building, two were given special permission to remain behind and read.[52] This may be the wishful implementation of the ideal of manual labour, for the Life of Cadog equally presents Cadog sending off his workmen to construct a new community near Neath; and traditions of foundation are sometimes transformed in later material into records of building (establishment becomes construction, becomes building).[53] But new communities, supported by their own labour, must have done some proportion of their own construction work.

The range of officers mentioned gives some hint of the nature and potential complexity of communities. As might be expected, the earliest material — though it might well include several monastic priests as members — does not specify many different functionaries beyond the abbot. The Life of Samson mentions only the cellarer, the monk in charge of the storeroom; the charters of the Lichfield Gospels mention the *scholasticus* who had written the record; the charters appended to the Life of Cadog refer to procurators, priors and *praepositi*, men responsible for managing income and for acting as deputies for the abbot.[54] The Llandaff material adds merely a smith and the occasional steward in the early period, but in the tenth century begins to specify scribes, stewards (*equonimi*), teachers (*doctores*), not to mention one cook and a medical doctor.[55] In one splendid scene the Colloquy specifies the full composition of its idealized community: seniors, *sacerdotes*, presbyters, boys and dependants, who included a cook, a baker, a doorkeeper and herdsmen.[56] The eleventh-century Lives are fuller: the Life of Cadog with steward, cook, sexton, doctor, messengers to look after relics, grave-diggers, *praepositi*, officers with special responsibility for kitchen, consulate and bakery; the Life of David with scribe, doorkeeper (who was a senior), cook, steward and *praepositus*.[57] In most of these contexts it is clear that *praepositus* and prior both refer to deputies of the abbot, either the monk who acts for him when he goes away or the monk who acts as head of some dependent community. We may say, therefore, that the monk with responsibility for overseeing food supply and the scribe were consistent elements at most periods. For the rest, the overall impression is one of increasing specialization in which the business and property of the monastery became sufficiently complex to require the professional attention of one of its members; this in its turn suggests some general growth. The Colloquy and the Lives differ by alternatively classifying cook, baker and so on as dependants and as full members of the community. There is no reason why there should not have been distinctions between those places which separated intellectual and necessary service functions and those which did not, especially given the variant attitudes to the requirement of manual labour for monks. Indeed, the Life of Cadog numbers soldiers and workmen among the members of Cadog's household, in addition to the officers specified.[58] It also includes children, and the number of sources which include boys as members of monastic households — whether incidentally, receiving training and scaring off the birds, or descriptively, as in the case of the Colloquy above[59] — would suggest that here too was a constant element; as constant as the priests who became increasingly prominent, in the South-East at least, and probably in general.[60] The presence of boys also serves to explain the meaning of the designation 'seniors'. There may be here, therefore, another of the structural differences between that type of religious life which was usually called monastic and that called eremitical: the hermit had companions but the structure of his community was less complex, the functions less (or not) specialized, the very young not present.[61] And the distinction may also correspond to the distinction between monks noted in the later law tracts — the canon of a corporation as opposed to the *meudwy* — as cited above.

One final aspect deserves discussion: that of heredity and its significance in the monastic and clerical structure. From the start, the existence of a married clergy is demonstrated by the comments of Gildas and an inscription on a tombstone from Llantrisant on Anglesey, erected to the memory of the loving wife of the *sacerdos* (priest or bishop) Bivatigirnus, herself described as a 'most holy woman'.[62] The practice was still current in the episcopal community of Llandeilo Fawr in the ninth century, where Cuhelin, son of the bishop, was among the clerical witnesses of the purchase of manumission by Bleiddud.[63] Clerical celibacy was not expected, and at St David's later in the ninth century the archbishop — whether or not he was himself married — allowed members of his family into the community, for Asser averts to his own relationship with him.[64] Expression of family interest was also sustained in non-episcopal monastic communities. Such was the fear of Illtud's nephews, members of the Llantwit community who expected to succeed their uncle as abbot, that they mixed poison with Samson's herb tea in the hope of despatching the threat that he might displace them. Needless to say, Samson suspected the treachery, tried out the potion on the cat, and observing its immediate effect declined to drink it and exposed the plot. The holy man's objection can scarcely have been to the hereditary interest, however, for later he himself placed his uncle in charge of one of his own dependent monasteries; while the connections of his family within the monastic life appear to have been sustained for at least two generations.[65] One of the Llancarfan charters cites the fact that abbot Paul numbered his own brother among his monastic household.[66] The same pattern is not so clearly reflected in the late Saints' Lives (possibly already reflecting the reforming interest of Western Europe), yet we know of at least two major families — that of Llancarfan and that of Llanbadarn — with sustained and strong hereditary interests not only in the offices and properties of the monasteries but also in the bishoprics of Llandaff and St David's, both of whose late eleventh-century bishops (Herewald and Sulien) were married.[67] Moreover, it was the burden of twelfth-century reformers' complaints, Giraldus among them, about Welsh monastic life that sons succeeded to benefices by hereditary right rather than election.[68] The Llandaff material, besides specifying the relationships of Bishop Herewald and his family, is more detailed on other communities of the South-East. Already in the seventh century there was evidence in Ergyng of the succession to office by sons, and in the ninth, tenth and eleventh centuries some clerical families who were members of communities can be traced over several generations: Bleinwydd, his son Cadien, Cadien's three sons and his grandson all appear in clerical witness lists in Gwent; while the steward Bledgur was succeeded by his steward son Cyfeilliog.[69] Marriage of the clergy therefore appears to have been common from the outset, accompanied sometimes by the hereditary transmission of office within monasteries and without; with the blurring of the distinction between monastic and non-monastic houses (and the dominance of community life), the hereditary transmission of office (and hence of control over community property) appears to have become characteristic.

Relationships between Clerics and Monks

Monks in orders, monks not in orders, non-monastic clergy are all evidenced in different contexts at different periods. This poses the problem of the relationship between monks and clergy and between monastic and non-monastic clergy, as also of the relationship between the different grades of clergy. Did some groups or individuals have powers of direction over others? Were there connections and associations between them? Who were the superiors, if any? The three major orders of clergy — bishops, priests and deacons — are easy to find and some of the minor orders too. Hence, we have reference to bishops (*episcopi*) and priests (*presbiteri*) from all periods and in all areas except the North-East (from which there is very little material anyway, so the deficiency cannot be counted significant). Deacons are specified both in the early penitential material, the Life of Samson, one

Llandaff charter (no.218) and the late Lives; lectors in the penitential material, the charters attached to the Life of Cadog and those of the Llandaff collection; and other or 'minor' orders in the penitentials, the *Historia Brittonum* and some of the late Lives. The institutions of the church were therefore supplied with such grades of clergy as might be found anywhere in Western Europe, though there is no information on function sufficient to detect any difference between Wales and the Continent. Complications are presented by the use of the term *sacerdos* in some sources, referring to the priestly office and hence any cleric who dispensed the sacraments, for this word might legitimately have been used of either priest or bishop in the early medieval period. Gildas, therefore, wrote of the 'sacerdotal seat of the episcopate and priesthood' (*sacerdotalem episcopatus vel presbyterii sedem*), betraying his consciousness of the alternative usages.[70] In early Wales the term occurs in inscriptions, as well as in the writings of Gildas, the Lichfield and Llandaff charters, the Colloquy and Rhigyfarch's Life of David.[71] It is to be found, therefore, all over Wales and in both early and later periods, though there is some tendency for the early usage to be northern and the later to be southern. It would be convenient to suppose that some sources used *sacerdos* in preference to *episcopus* and others used it in preference to *presbiter*; there is some reason to see this in the inscriptions of the North-West, which do not use *episcopus* at all and do use *sacerdos* and *presbiter*, while the Lichfield Gospel charters, on the other hand, have *episcopus and sacerdos* but not *presbiter*. *Sacerdos* may have signified 'bishop' in the North-West, therefore; and it may have signified 'priest' in Llandeilo further south. Such an explanation is unfortunately too simple, for other sources (Gildas, Llandaff charters, the Colloquy, Rhigyfarch) use all three terms, while two of those (the Llandaff charters and thè Colloquy) use them in ways which suggest that they had alternative meanings. Each clearly states that both priests and *sacerdotes* were members of monastic communities, and distinct from the *episcopus* who visited and inspected from time to time. Each implies that the status of the *sacerdos* was higher than that of the presbyter. It is possible, therefore, that in the South this term was used in the tenth and eleventh centuries to refer to consecrated bishops with no administrative responsibility.[72]

The problem of ecclesiastical authority is complex, and has several aspects. We know that some foundations were called bishoprics; we know that bishops are not infrequently mentioned; we have evidence of the administrative and jurisdictional responsibility of some particular bishops. There is every reason to suppose that the precursor of the community of St David's was the seat of a bishopric, known as Mynyw, from at least the eighth century, since the Annals provide an almost unbroken sequence of episcopal obits. Indeed, Giraldus supplied a list of 44 pre-Conquest bishops and arch-bishops of St David's.[73] The relationship between the supposed site of David's original foundation at Rosina Vallis and the sites of old Mynyw and modern St David's is obscure but some continuity of community is reasonable even if sites changed. There is very good reason to suppose that there was a bishopric located somewhere in the eastern part of the South-East from the late sixth to the early tenth century, possibly located at Welsh Bicknor or somewhere near Kenderchurch (Llangynidr) in Ergyng or

Glasbury;[74] and another at Llandeilo Fawr on the western edge of the South-
East in the eighth and ninth centuries. The episcopal associations of both of
these places had petered out by the tenth century but their archives and
traditions — and possibly communities — were transferred ultimately to
Llandaff, certainly by the early eleventh century when it had acquired
episcopal status itself. There would appear to have been at least one bishop
operating in the South-East from the sixth to the twelfth century.[75] Beyond
this, we know of a bishop of Bangor round about 800 and in the tenth century,
and it is widely assumed that Elfoddw, 'archbishop of Gwynedd', who died in
809, worked from Bangor, though this is not stated in any early source; the
bishopric is well evidenced from the period of initial Norman contact.[76]
There are no pre-Conquest references to any bishopric at Llanelwy in the
North-East, and the see of St Asaph was not founded there until 1143; it is not

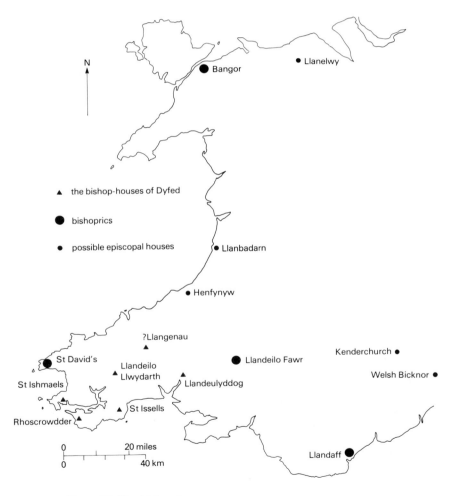

Figure 53. The bishoprics.

impossible, however, that the house of Llanelwy had some pre-Conquest episcopal tradition.[77] Twelfth-century Llanbadarn also claimed episcopal associations, associations which were admitted in some of the material from St David's, and it is again by no means impossible that this powerful house on the west coast — a long and difficult journey from both St David's and Bangor — also had a pre-Conquest episcopal tradition.[78]

The number of bishoprics is therefore few, even allowing the maximum possibilities, and they are well scattered. Given the geographical relationship of the 'sees' and the consistent stress of the sources on episcopal authority, there is every reason to suppose that the bishops of those houses exercised some sort of territorial responsibility for the areas adjacent, without supposing that those areas were formalized into a full diocesan structure.[79] This does not preclude the possibility of the presence of consecrated bishops, without administrative responsibility, in some communities, as may be indicated by the presence of *sacerdotes* in the later period. The precise relationship between the six so-called 'bishop houses' of the law tracts, which had abbots, some in orders and some not, and St David's, is not clear, though the implication must be that they were closely associated with St David's rather than independent bishoprics.[80] In the South-East, which is so much better evidenced, there were clearly some changes. We know nothing of the origins of these bishoprics or of their relationship to the late Roman ecclesiastical administration of Britain. As might be expected, however, the sees are planted in the best-resourced areas, not far from major royal centres.

What of the relation of these bishops with each other? Many sources have a preoccupation with authority and pre-eminence. Only two pre-eleventh-century sources use any term of authority superior to that of bishop: the Annals refer to Elfoddw as 'archbishop of Gwynedd' in 809 and Asser, later in the ninth century, used the same term of Nobis of St David's.[81] Later, Rhigyfarch repeated the claim for St David's, as does a very late triad, and the law tract on the seven bishop houses of Dyfed maintained that St David's was the principal see in Wales; the twelfth-century interpolations of the Book of Llandaff make both Dyfrig and Teilo archbishops; another triad invokes the 'chief bishop' of the three regions.[82]

Indeed Rhigyfarch and his successors were well-nigh obsessed with the theme of the status of St David's: Gildas had acknowledged David's primacy; a third or a quarter of Ireland 'served' David; David was consecrated to the archiepiscopate by the patriarch of Jerusalem, thereby elevating him above Teilo and Padarn; a synod of all the bishops of Britannia consented to David becoming metropolitan archbishop of them all; David's *civitas* (monastery) was made the metropolis of the whole country; David was chief overseer and chief protector; all bishops surrendered monarchy and primacy and submitted to his protection; the hearth kindled at Rosina Vallis sent smoke rising upwards to fill the whole island and Ireland too, symbolizing David's pre-eminence in a manner immediately recognizable to all who saw it:

> near the spot there was a certain chieftain and magician, called Baia, an Irishman, who sitting within the ramparts of his citadel, whilst the beams of the sun were scattered over the world, felt faint at the sight of such a portent and trembled... [His wife asked what was

wrong.] To this he replied, 'I grieve to have seen the smoke rising out of Rosina Vallis... for I regard it as certain that the kindler of that fire shall excel all in power and renown in every part that the smoke... has covered'. [83]

It is perfectly clear that St David's made serious claims for metropolitan status in the twelfth century and reasonable to suppose that Llandaff opposed these by claiming that it had had its own archbishops in the past. [84] The late references have to do, then, with the situation of the early Norman period and have no necessary bearing on the previous state of affairs, although it is fair to point out that the St David's claim argued for a continuing and ancient metropolitan status. The only serious suggestions of archiepiscopal authority come, therefore, from the Annals and Asser. Does the term 'archbishop' in those sources imply metropolitan status comparable to that of the archbishops of Canterbury or York, with some practical powers of interference in the elevation of new bishops and powers of calling synods, at the least? Elfoddw was certainly held responsible for the synod which changed the Easter cycles in Wales; but this is an isolated instance of such activity. For the most part, what is notable is the lack of any such initiative. Moreover, if Asser's description of his relative is striking, even more striking is the absence of the term in the large number of references to bishops of Mynyw (St David's). Its isolation suggests that there was no institutionalized archbishopric, and therefore that the term was purely honorific. It may in fact have reflected the pre-eminence which the bishops of the 'sees' had in relation to any consecrated bishops without administrative responsibility who resided in their own or other communities, although it could also indicate some desire for metropolitan powers in the ninth century, comparable to those expressed by Armagh in the preceding century. The form of the Annals, kept at St David's from the late eighth century, suggests contact with Armagh and opportunities thereby for influence. [85]

The late Saints' Lives are explicit on the subject of episcopal powers: episcopal permission was necessary before Gwynllyw could become a hermit, before a church could be founded, before Illtud could establish his cemetery; [86] Bishop Padarn made appointments and Bishop Dyfrig granted Illtud 'magistral responsibility'; [87] bishops were to consecrate churches, confirm baptism, impose ecclesiastical degrees, and to make visits of inspection to monasteries. [88] All of this material is consistent on the controlling, legitimizing hand of the bishop and on his powers of inspection and confirmation. The Life of Padarn even implies that a bishop had a right to demand payments from the churches of his territory, when it presents Samson travelling the *parrochiae* of Brittany to collect his tribute and Padarn 'controlling' all the churches of Vannes, except one. [89] Although it is consistent, it nevertheless remains the perspective of a late period. Apart from noticing the presence of bishops and the implication of superior status at earlier periods, it is difficult to find material which explicitly details their powers and behaviour. Indeed, the most usable detail is that contained in the Life of Samson; consecrations and ordinations, appointing a cellarer to Caldy, convening the council which was to choose an abbot. [90] The visitation of monasteries and convening of synods occurs elsewhere, and in the South-East in the ninth, tenth and eleventh centuries (and quite possibly before), bishops certainly had a major rôle in this. [91] We may suppose, then, that bishops had a clear administrative function and a controlling interest in the religious life of Wales, but we cannot say much about the nature of that control.

Bishops were not the only religious with powers of control. Already at an early date the discretion of an abbot over his community was emphasized, [92] and it would be unreasonable to suppose that the powers of an abbot over his immediate personnel were not respected at all periods; there is always an emphasis on obedience. Some abbots appear to have had greater influence, however, for they had powers over dependent communities in addition to their powers over the personnel near at hand. It is perfectly clear that some monasteries were more prominent than others — Illtud's monastery 'will be first among those of the district', so he is promised [93] — and clear that their prominence did not merely consist in greater size or fame or influence but in the powers of control they exerted over lesser monasteries and the number of such communities that were so dependent. Already in the seventh century, therefore, Samson not only founded communities, but was 'given' some that already existed; in so far as the Life details the effect of such gifts, then it tells us that Samson retained powers of appointment within the dependencies. [94] We have to turn to the Life of Cadog and to the charters attached to this Life for more detail; though this work is late it clearly in these respects presents material and attitudes that are pre-Norman and is therefore of crucial importance in any attempt to understand the (non-unitary) structure of the early Welsh Church. There is no need to believe every detail, but the principles are important. Llancarfan was, therefore, Cadog's 'principal monastery', as Lismor was a principal *civitas* of Ireland; the abbot had monasteries in Scotland and in the surrounding areas of Wales; the abbot had rights of appointment of his successor and of *praepositi* and *principes*; Cadog, indeed, was so powerful that only he should have had the authority to call synods: David was roundly snubbed when Cadog returned to find that the latter had done so in his own absence. [95]

The charters expand on the implications of such dependencies: when Cadog built a church he installed the prior-*cum*-procurator so that he could expect hospitality on his travels; when Elli built a church and monastery and proclaimed them 'subject' to Cadog he assigned provisions for three nights in summer and three in winter to Cadog and arranged that the abbot of Llancarfan would preside in any change of administration. [96] There was, then, a financial benefit from dependencies as well as an interest in appointments. Both the presentation of the two saints of Cedweli who 'submitted' to David, and the one church of Vannes which was *not* subject to Padarn, seem to be indications of a comparable relationship. [97] The Llandaff material is explicit on the lands, churches and communities dependent on the house of Teilo (originally Llandeilo, but claimed by Llandaff in the twelfth century); here all are presented as property, as if that was the only interest. [98] It is reasonable to suppose, therefore, that there existed some types of monastic federation in Wales, as there were in contemporary Ireland.

Some idea of the spheres of influence of the prominent houses may be gained from the distribution of dedications to their principal saints (see fig.54). In the case of Cadog and Teilo there is good evidence that a large proportion of dedications represents churches which were dependent upon the main houses of Cadog and Teilo (i.e. Llancarfan and Llandeilo Fawr) in the pre-Conquest period, and regarded as properties of those houses.[99] The dedication pattern does not exclusively represent properties, however, for — as is well known — some dedications arose for reasons other than those of relationship with the main house; incidental connections, late medieval cult,

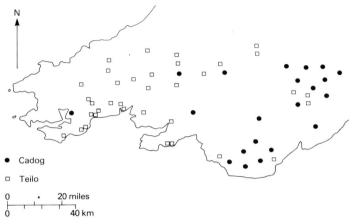

Figure 54. Dedications to Teilo and Cadog in south Wales (after E.G. Bowen, *The Settlements of the Celtic Saints in Wales*, 2nd edn 1956, figs.9a and 15).

friendly associations, might all account for them. Churches represented by very scattered dedications, in particular, and those at some considerable distance from the main house, do not seem ·to have had the same institutionalized dependent relationship.[100] Hence, federated communities appear to have been regionally confined to areas within easy reach — not more than a few days' journey or 50-60 miles' radius — of the main house, and they are unlike the great scattered federations which we assume, probably wrongly, to be typical of Ireland. If the analogy of Teilo and Cadog dedications be applicable, then this would suggest comparable federations in other areas of Wales: that of Illtud, basically in Glamorgan, dependent upon Llantwit; that of David over much of the South, dependent upon St David's and its predecessor; that of Padarn in the midlands, dependent upon Llanbadarn; that of Tysilio in the east midlands, dependent upon Meifod; that of Beuno, in the North-West, dependent upon Clynnog.[101] The number is not large; the distribution is not exceptionally wide; the widest distributions are those of David and Beuno.

Some abbots, therefore, had powers of direction and control over lesser religious institutions which were associated with them. We cannot comment upon the circumstances in which such relationships were established except to note the occasions of voluntary 'submission' cited above; where there is evidence, it appears to have been gift — by the founder or incumbent, or by the owner of the land — which established it. The relationship between these greater abbots and the bishops is therefore of considerable interest: were they, too, subject to episcopal control? No comment at all can be made upon most areas of Wales, except to note the prominence of the bishop of St David's in all sources, a prominence which suggests powers of interference in all ecclesiastical matters in the South-West. In the South-East, though there are many difficulties of interpretation of the evidence, bishops seem to have had the power to command the attendance of major abbots and many clerics at their meetings, for witnesses to the business transacted there tend to be drawn from a very wide area; the bishop moved in the company of the great abbots. [102] Whatever the abbots' powers in relation to their own federations, therefore, they seem ultimately to have been subject to the direction of the bishops of the South-East. As far as we can assess it, it seems to have been an episcopally dominated church, though a church largely consisting of monasteries.

Ecclesiastical Income

As might be expected, all available source material suggests that landed property formed the basis of support and of income for clerics and religious communities of all types, even those described as hermits, and there are relatively many references to grants of property to particular individuals and to communities. Of these, the corpus of charters is the most explicitly relevant, but the Saints' Lives are dotted with references to grants made by kings and pious converts, while we are fortunate in possessing a few inscriptions which record such grants from areas outside the South-East (in which part the corpus of charters is concentrated), like the early stones from Llanddewibrefi and Llanllŷr, in Ceredigion (see fig.55). [103] In several cases it is clear that churches and their accompanying dwelling houses were surrounded by the land which provided support for the community: 'the church of Kilpeck with its estate around it' in a charter of c.850; 'the monastery (*podum*) of St Buddwalan with two and a half *unciae* of land surrounding the monastery', in a charter of c.620; the monastery of the old Roman city of Caerwent supported from the fields outside the city, the *ager suburbanus*, literally 'suburban estate'; the church and accompanying territory for those serving the church supposedly founded by King Edgar in honour of Illtud. [104] The church and community was notionally the centre of a unit of production — and probably sometimes physically so too: in a number of cases from the Llandaff charters the focal position of the church and settlement within estates whose bounds can be traced is notable. [105]

The landed basis of support is, of course, entirely what one would expect of this area in this period. The question of the utilization and exploitation of that support is more difficult. Monasteries had herds: Llancarfan's sheep on the island of Echni (Flatholm); Llantwit's pigs that a thief attempted to appropriate; the herds of sheep and goats of the idealized community of the Colloquy. [106] They also had barns, crops that had to be protected from the birds, and threshing floors. [107] The care of animals and the cultivation of land required labour. Since manual labour was required of some communities, necessary labour was sometimes supplied by the religious members of the community, creating an almost entirely self-supporting religious unit. But some communities did not demand manual labour of their members, and in

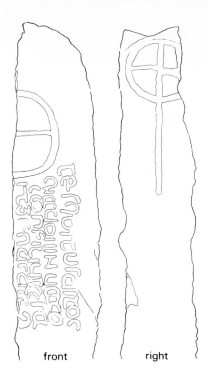

front right

Figure 55. The Llanllŷr stone: 'The small waste plot of Ditoc. Occon, son of Asaitgen, gave to Madomnuac' (*ECMW* no.124; reproduced by courtesy of the University of Wales Press).

this case labour must have been supplied by others — dependants resident in the community but vocationally distinct, or dependants resident nearby, working the fields, taking something for their own support but labouring essentially for the upkeep of the monastery. We hear, therefore, not just of dependants but also of stewards whose business it was to supervise labour and its product. [108] Here, the income for the community came as directly from the properties owned as in the former case, though the means of realizing that income — the hands that gathered it — were different. Some communities were involved in yet more sophisticated enterprise: renders were received from scattered properties and/or churches with their surrounding lands. Here the surplus product was channelled into the stores of some prominent institution, and monks and clergy lived off the labour of a distant and disassociated population. They made a business, in effect, of landlordship. Such renders might be returned as hospitality obligations: the abbot of Llancarfan established a community in Gwent so that he might have somewhere to be entertained when travelling in that area; the feast demanded by and provided for the Bishop of Llandaff in the early eleventh century was collected at St Maughan's but consumed by the greedy Rhiwallon who got there first; the abbot of the Colloquy took his whole household to the house of a neighbour to consume the meal prepared for them. [109] Alternatively, regular payment might be made of bread, flesh, oxen, sheep, beer and/or honey, that is of food ready to consume; [110] and officers with a responsibility for the collection and management of it appear from time to time.[111] Very occasionally, both hospitality and render occurred together.[112]

We should expect, therefore, considerable variation both in the relative amount of income received by communities and in the methods used to realize that income. Some houses were exceptionally wealthy — the seats of bishops and the heads of widespread federations with their network of dependencies. By the late eleventh century in the South-East there are already hints of complexity and sophistication in the administration and allocation of resources; certain portions of the income were regularly set aside for certain purposes: grave-diggers got their food and income from sanctuary — and relic-keepers 4d. or a ewe and lamb — but not a portion of land reserved to their own use.[113] A monastery like Llancarfan must have been an exceptionally complex institution by the time of the Conquest. There are also occasional references to fish and fishing rights, indicating the utilization of water potential as well as land. Stretches of the Usk, Dore, Wye, Dee, Clwyd and upper Severn were developed as fisheries by the eleventh century, as we have seen — a sophisticated exploitation; the monasteries of Llancarfan and Llan-faes secured a fish supply from the rivers Usk and Neath, and fishing rights changed hands in the neighbourhood of Llandeilo Fawr and Cardiff.[114] Land was not, therefore, the only source of income.

There are finally some rare references to harbours: Cadog's harbour and Illtud's harbour, and the landing rights specified on the Severn at Caldicot, Pwllmeurig and Matharn from the late ninth century may have a commercial significance; if so, the gathering of toll on goods passing through those harbours would have supplied further income.[115] There is not enough material to suggest that this was substantial.

Figure 56. Gateholm Island in the middle distance with Skomer Island on the horizon, from Marloes Beach (photograph Terrence James; copyright reserved).

The Powers and Immunities of Clerics

A corollary of the power to collect renders from their own scattered properties was the privilege of exemption from the capacity of others to tax their lands, and claims of exemption from the fiscal demands of kings and secular lords are commonplace in the Lives and in the corpus of charters. It was clearly considered that ecclesiastical lands ought to be immune from such payments to secular authorities, whether or not this was so in practice. In some Llandaff charters there is every reason to believe that such exemptions were admitted, especially in the eighth and ninth centuries, while the charters appended to the Life of Cadog sometimes record that payments were made in order to secure exemption;[116] hence the latter establishes that such exemptions cannot necessarily have been admitted as a matter of course but that they could and did happen.

There was a further aspect of immunity: the range of privileges and benefits associated with the legal notion of *nawdd*, 'protection', a power possessed in a large measure by clerics, whose status was high.[117] Like the property rights that were recorded and publicized by the Lives, so too was this right of sheltering offenders and the accused from pursuit and from legal process. In practice it meant more than the familiar right of sanctuary since a large territory (*nodua*, '*nawdd* place') might afford protection and since the period of legally recognized protection would vary with status. The Life of Cadog emphasizes the point in its several examples, the most extreme being the case of Ligessog, who fled to the protection of Llancarfan from the wrath of Arthur, after he had killed three of Arthur's men. So insistent was the narrator on the power of Llancarfan's protection that he records that the compensation fairly assessed as due to Arthur turned to nothing when paid by Ligessog: the cattle turned to ferns. His point was that Llancarfan's powers of protection were so great that they should even override the justly made settlement in a justly prosecuted grievance.[118] The Life of David was more explicit, arguing that all the bishops of the British agreed that David's protection:

> should apply to every ravisher and homicide and sinner, and to every evil person flying from place to place...in every kingdom and each region where there may be land consecrated to holy David. And let no kings or elders or governors, or even bishops, abbots and saints dare to grant protection in priority to holy David. In truth, he provides protection before every person and there is none prior to him, because he is head and leader and primate over all the Britons.[119]

Communities would seem, therefore, to have hotly contended for superior powers of protection, in themselves both an acknowledgment of status and a source of greater influence, since they conferred both the power to thwart the action of others, and the power to demand payment or favours from the one protected. Such extreme claims as those of St David's can hardly have been generally admitted or murderers would have roamed unharmed from one David property to another, but the principle of protection exercisable by communities is emphasized in the law tracts and the Llandaff material suggests that at least in the tenth and eleventh centuries major clerics were powerful enough to demand and receive compensation for the violation of their protections. Assault, abduction, rape and murder were all perpetrated by kings and nobles within ecclesiastical protected areas, in Gower, Gwent and Glywysing, and all were atoned for.[120]

The power, moral and spiritual, to enforce recognition of status and to demand compensation for the infringement both of the privilege attached to status and of protection appears to have been the greatest weapon that clerics had in their dealings with kings and with the laity, for we do not hear of clerics taking up arms to defend their rights and properties. Cadog, so Lifris claimed, negotiated with kings; bishops occasionally acted as intercessors for kings — like Lunberth of St David's for King Tewdwr of Brycheiniog in the tenth century[121] — and the judgment of clerics was sometimes utilized in secular cases. References to this begin already with Gildas, are implicit in much of the later Llandaff material, and are sometimes explicit in the Lives.[122] We might suppose that the dread power of Cadog's curse was one of the weapons invoked by the clergy of Llancarfan to establish a negotiating position and in the Life Lifris did much to emphasize and publicize tales of the horrors which befell those who offended the saint: the peasant who refused to give him some live coals was burned to death and his threshing floor cursed for ever; the robbers who tried to make away with the monastery's stores were swallowed up by the earth; wolves that attacked his sheep were turned to stone; King Rhun and his men were blinded when they attacked Cadog's barn.[123] Fasting also seems to have been used by clerics in order to gain power and win points, in order to better their rivals. Hence, Cybi fasted in his dispute with Cruibthir, in order to get God on his side; Cadog's monks fasted for three days to get God to restore the broken bridge; Cadog *and* the local community fasted before their meeting with the angry King Maelgwn; Germanus and the British clergy fasted and prayed for three days and nights, in their battle with Gwrtheyrn and the Saxon enemy; Patrick fasted for 40 days and nights on the summit of mount Eli.[124] Clerics, then, might well demand to be the correctors of kings and to be able to compel kings to obey them, but they could do little to meet the application of sheer force.[125] They remained subject to the plundering raids of kings and aristocrats, and even St David's could not avoid the ravages of King Hyfaidd.[126] Though wealthy, their power remained essentially spiritual and moral; this could be very great, but it was necessarily a fluctuating thing, and monks and clergy could not therefore guarantee their position against a particularly aggressive secular power.

7 Christianity and Spirituality

Belief

The religious culture of early medieval Wales is overwhelmingly Christian, and even if it be objected that material is short, nevertheless the import of the material that we have is remarkably consistent. Early in the sixth century Gildas was already referring to pre-Christian times and practices as to the distant past: 'I shall not enumerate the devilish monstrosities of my land...some of which we can see today, stark as ever, inside or outside deserted city walls: outlines still ugly, faces still grim. I shall not name the mountains and hills and rivers, once so pernicious, now useful for human needs, on which, in those days, a blind people heaped divine honours.'[1] Two to three hundred years later the *Historia Brittonum* averted to paganism as the peculiar practices of foreign people; Geata, the compiler commented when writing of the Saxon invaders, was the son of a god, but this was not God Almighty but the offspring of an idol which they worshipped in their blinded way, as heathens do.[2] There is a minimal tradition of conversion, also preserved in the *Historia Brittonum*: Patrick preached for some time in Britain before baptizing and preaching in Ireland; Bishop Germanus came to Britain to preach, with the result that many were saved but many also remained unconverted.[3] This suggests that from the perspective of the ninth century it appeared that there were still unconverted Britons in the fifth century, but this is all. There is no other hint of memories of conversion, unlike the situation in early Ireland where conversion tales figure prominently from the early medieval period. The only other references to paganism occur in the late Lives, where the comments refer to non-British areas — Cadog preaching and converting in Scotland, Carannog living amongst unbelievers in Ireland[4] — or in material with strong Irish connections: Rhigyfarch wrote of the Irish *magus* Baia and his wife who came into conflict with David, fearing lest the saint's spiritual power be more effective than their own.[5] Even reference to Ronnwen, the pagan woman of the triads, has a foreign context for she was the Saxon Hengest's daughter, the one so desired by Gwrtheyrn.[6] In the face of a total absence of references to the British who were not Christian and the absence of any tradition of conversion or of pagan practice and practitioners, we must conclude that Wales was an essentially Christian country in the early medieval period. The contrast with material from and bearing upon Ireland is particularly notable.

If early medieval Wales was Christian, then we cannot avoid the problem of the date of conversion and the question of whether or not Welsh Christianity arose directly from the Christianity of Roman Britain. It is clear that Christianity — if not universally accepted — was well established in Roman Britain by the late fourth century. Written references to British bishops and priests, to structures for Christian use, and pavements and objects with Christian symbols on them, to Christian burial practice within Roman cemeteries like Poundbury, and at temple and villa sites, have all been collected and amply discussed in the last generation. We know that a clerical hierarchy was established, which suggests that the Christian community existed in some numbers: there would scarcely have been need of pastors without a flock; we know that Christianity could be socially and politically advantageous, or at least not disadvantageous, for in the early fifth century the Caesar Constans was a monk and Patrick's father was a decurion; we know that the faith was vigorous enough to produce both adherence to a major heresy — Pelagianism — and some missionary activity outside the Roman provinces.[7] All of this testifies to the strength of the religion in late Roman Britain, though it would be unbalanced to forget to note that some pagan temples of the late fourth century — places like Lydney and Maiden Castle — were also well patronized. There is also difficult but cumulatively convincing evidence of British Christianity surviving in the post-Roman period: this consists not merely in the references to certain named British Christians, but in circumstances such as the surviving Christian community at Wall/Lichfield; the oriented cemeteries, without grave goods, on new sites (cf. Cannington, fig. 57); the presence of British Christian communities

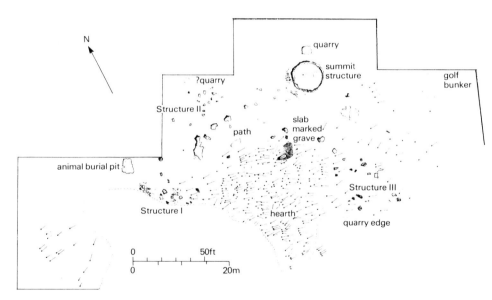

Figure 57. The cemetery at Cannington (reproduced from P. Rahtz, 'Late Roman cemeteries', in *Burial in the Roman World,* ed. R. Reece, CBA Res.Rep.22, by kind permission).

indicated by 'Eccles' place-names; the corpus of ecclesiastical terminology borrowed into Irish from British Latin; and possibly the imported wares bearing Christian symbols to be found in western Britain.[8] Welsh Christianity of the early sixth century was structurally entirely consistent with that of Roman Britain, with its clerical hierarchy and minor monastic element; and Gildas wrote of an obviously long-established church — one which was wealthy and corrupt. Hence, given all of the above considerations, given the absence of pagan and conversion traditions in early medieval Welsh material, and given the circumstance of some westward migration of British population in the immediate post-Roman period, it is highly likely that the early Christianity of Wales had some continuous relationship with that of Roman Britain. Conversion of the 'Welsh', therefore, had taken place before the medieval period began. This is not to say that there were no changes, for it is notable that the distribution of early inscribed stones — which bear inscriptions and have letter forms which have Christian African and Gaulish parallels — is concentrated in west Wales, and notably sparse in the South-East.[9] Fifth- and early sixth-century stones in Gwynedd, in particular, could indicate Gaulish and African/Spanish contacts.[10] This strongly suggests new Christian influences. Other changes are obvious: the urban basis of Romano-British Christianity clearly disappeared, as did the rôle of metropolitans; changes in burial practices involved not only the adoption of new sites, but a different relationship with the settlement pattern and some tendency to focus on the 'holy place'.[11]

What did Christianity mean for these people of Wales in the early middle ages? The most frequently cited implication of belief was the promise of an afterlife. The warriors who did not run away but stayed to fight to death would see the 'joyful land' of Heaven, where they would make a perfect union with the Trinity, and the believer would surmount the trials and punishments of life — even beheading — by being escorted to heaven by the angels hovering above.[12] By the eleventh and twelfth centuries a set-piece on the transitory nature of earthly life, the hollow treasure of the earthly kingdom, the momentary allurements of the world, was an almost invariable introduction to the saintly biography.[13] The afterlife was not only a goal and a reward; in the intervening centuries it had become the only real value; life was as nothing. Hence, Lifris more than once introduced the image of life as a prison: if the giant, Caw, were to heed Cadog's teaching, then his soul would eventually leave the prison of the body for eternal glory; while Cadog himself effected many miracles after he had left 'the prison-house of this false world'.[14] The joy and the immediate reward of belief is communicated much more successfully than this, however, by the ninth- or tenth-century *englynion* of praise written into the Juvencus manuscript:

> The world cannot express in song bright and melodious, even though the grass and trees should sing, all thy glories, O true Lord.
> The Father has wrought such a multitude of wonders in this world that it is difficult to find an equal number. Letters cannot contain it, letters cannot express it. . . .
> He who made the wonder of the world, will save us, has saved us. It is not too great toil to praise the Trinity. . . .
> Purely, humbly, in skilful verse, I should love to give praise to the Trinity, according to the greatness of his power.[15]

Besides the benefits of Christian belief there were also the obligations, and the other constantly noted aspect of what Christianity meant for the ordinary man was the moral requirement. Sin brought judgment and trials, and these would begin already in this world:

>And it was not only this vice that flourished, but all those that generally befall human nature — and especially the one that is the downfall of every good condition nowadays too, the hatred of truth and its champions and the love of falsehood and its contrivers: the taking up of evil instead of good, the adoration of wickedness instead of kindness, the desire for darkness instead of sun, the welcoming of Satan as an angel of light. ... A deadly plague swooped brutally on the stupid people, and in a short period laid low so many people, with no sword, that the living could not bury all the dead. But not even this taught them their lesson. ...In just punishment for the crimes that had gone before, a fire heaped up and nurtured by the hand of the impious easterners spread from sea to sea. It devastated town and country round about, and, once it was alight, it did not die down until it had burned almost the whole surface of the island and was licking the western ocean with its fierce red tongue.[16]

Thus Gildas, with Old Testament vehemence, and Old Testament analogies, described the fortunes of the provinces of Roman Britain in the series of fifth-century onslaughts upon them. The theme was to be echoed in the following centuries: the compiler of the *Historia Brittonum* took care to point out that the Saxons ruled Britain not because of their superior prowess but because of the sins of the Britons; likewise the author of the Colloquy, pursuing a somewhat contrary view of past events but a similar moral standpoint, insisted that God had given victory to the Britons because they were meek and poor, and because they had trusted in God and had accepted the body of Christ before battle, whereas the Saxons were proud and because of their pride God humiliated them.[17] Fighting the heathen was expected of the believers, the baptized.[18]

Gildas was the most specific on the moral qualities expected of the Christian: whoring, adultery, lust, pride, greed, office-seeking (ambition), the pursuit of wealth, lying, sport, entertainment, indulgence in leisure were all abhorred. The priests of his acquaintance were denounced, therefore, because they grabbed at all they wanted, encouraged strange women to intimacy, were fat, held their heads high, all the while yawning at the precepts of the holy men.[19] The requirement of modesty and humility, the attack against pride, is one that was often repeated, although the Colloquy's answer to the question 'How do you live well?' is a simple one: 'pray without intermission, don't indulge in too much talking, and give alms'; in other words, it asks for commitment, restraint, charity.[20] By the time the Lives were written down the requirements had become conventional: chastity was regularly advocated, innocence admired, purity associated with virginity; Rhigyfarch asked for patient long-suffering, charity and compassion as well, although he left room for vengeance and the power of the curse, the preoccupations of Lifris.[21] Indeed, Cadog is remarkable far more for his powers of destruction than for anything that smacks of humility; he is the type of pride.[22] In the Lives, then, we have gone full circle, celebrating the qualities that Gildas denounced while advocating others for the layman; there is an ambiguity of attitude in some of this material (the earliest examples of the latest phase) which does not slot easily into either conventional moral requirements or the earlier tradition. The interests of the abbot of Llancarfan outweigh the didactic impulses, but if monks and clerics failed to keep the precepts, nevertheless they remained the model for the ordinary man.

The Cult of Saints

A characteristic concomitant of Christianity in the medieval period was the elevation of selected human beings as intermediaries between God and men, with some increasing tendency towards the veneration of these individuals on account of the potentially beneficent effects of their influence. The saint was, or had been, human, but his special qualities gave him access to the deity in a manner denied to ordinary man so that he might tap the power which was at the source of all things, both life and fortune; grants were made, hymns were sung, festivals were held in his honour so that he might use his influence to secure good fortune for the world. Communities would adopt their own special protectors, and would invest particular saints with particular care and responsibility for particular areas. Cult, relics, saints and miracles are an expression both of the way man feels about the supernatural and a practical means of coping with it. Wales was no different from the rest of Christian Europe in adopting this device of mediation between the human and the supernatural, and in its recognition and celebration of the spiritual potential of some individual men and women. There are plenty of references to saints, in particular and in general, to the fact of sanctity, and to the significant role of the saint in the formal and informal organization of the religion. Indeed, although it is rare that the rôle of the saint as mediator is explicitly noted in early Welsh material, the poet of *Armes Prydein* is very clear about it:

> Through the intercession of Dewi and the saints of Britain
> the (foreigners) will be put to flight as far as the river Ailego.[23]

The saint, *sanctus*, was already making his appearance in the sixth century as the ancient authority for certain penances, and as the venerated holy man of Llansadwrn — *beatus Saturninus* — buried with his holy wife; he appeared as the patron of Llandeilo in the eighth and ninth centuries; as the protector of the Welsh against the Saxons in the tenth century; and, of course, as protector, benefactor, corrector throughout the corpus of eleventh- and twelfth-century Saints' Lives.[24] The saint, so reads the *Historia Brittonum*, achieves everlasting life along with the elect of God; while it was considered that David's monastic community was itself a community of saints, holy men set apart from the rest of the world.[25] (*Sanctus* — or *sant* in the vernacular — is the Latin term usually employed for these men, but *beatus* occurs too with no implication of lesser status; the Greek-derived *agius* was also used of David, while we occasionally hear of confessors and of martyrs, influenced presumably by the European hagiographic tradition.[26])

Who were these saints? Far and away the most frequently mentioned of the saints is David — Dewi; his prominence is not confined to south-western sources and he was invoked in the South-East as early as the seventh and eighth centuries.[27] Pre-eleventh-century references to other local or British saints of any note are limited to Teilo and Gildas, both in the ninth century, although the Breton Lives name Illtud, Samson and Pyro already in the seventh century and Paul in the ninth, and Irish sources mention Beuno and Deiniol by 800;[28] the Llandaff material, however, is particularly valuable in preserving the names of some saints venerated in highly localized contexts: Buddwalan, Cingualan, Cynfwr and Cynfarch in the seventh century; Cadog, Illtud and Docgwin from the seventh to the eleventh centuries; Titiuc in the eighth and ninth centuries; Dingad in the ninth; Iarmen and Febric in the tenth; Clydog, Tatheus, Mirgint, Cinficc, Huui and Eruen in the eleventh century.[29] The corpus of late Lives widens the range of references to the sanctity of Teilo, Cadog, Illtud and Gildas, but also adds some more — Padarn (who also occurs in the late eleventh-century *Martyrology of Ricemarch*), Gwynllyw, Nonnita, Boducat and Martrun, Aeddan, Modomnoc, Cybi — while an inscribed stone from Merthyr Mawr adds Glywys, the St Asaph material Gwrwst, Terillus and Deiniol, and the tract on the so-called children of Brychan, 'De Situ Brecheniauc', at least Cynog, Dedyu, Cynon and Cynidr to the number.[30]

Two observations may immediately be made. Firstly, there is a clear tendency for the veneration of local men, some so localized that nothing at all can be said of them, and the more detailed the evidence the greater the tendency; this process was already happening by the seventh century. Secondly, some local saints gained a following outside their own immediate locality — and even outside Britain — David, Teilo, Cadog and Gildas being the most notable. Gildas was already being cited in Ireland at the end of the sixth century; together with David his festival was noted in the martyrologies of Tallaght and of Oengus (29 January, 1 March) of c.800, the former of which also notes those of Beuno of Clynnog and Deiniol of Bangor (21 April, 11 September); Cadog and/or Docgwin (Doco) was noted at least by the tenth century.[31] Veneration was not confined to local saints: Michael was already occurring in the eighth century; Oswald, Cuthbert, Brigit, Columba, Patrick, Germanus (later confused with Garmon), Faustus and Martin from the ninth; Mary and Peter from the tenth; Brendan, Maedhog, Mochutu and Andrew in the eleventh.[32] Invocation of the Holy Trinity was, if anything, the commonest of all — as indeed were dedications to the Holy Trinity — occurring from the seventh century; and its selection as the distinguishing concept of Christianity was emphasized by the compiler ·of the *Historia Brittonum*, who not only made Patrick set captives free in the name of the Trinity but convert others to the *faith* of the Holy Trinity.[33] The calendar in BL MS Cotton Vespasian A xiv (fig.58), which might be expected to provide evidence of festivals celebrated in east Wales at the time of the Conquest, really adds nothing beyond the saints already named in the Vespasian collection of Lives and a few local saints from the area of St David's. All are of no certainly earlier origin than the twelfth century.[34] It is perfectly clear, then, that the notion of sainthood was accepted in Wales, and that a large number and wide range of saints were acknowledged, from the apostles and a few of the Irish saints to very obscure local men.

By the tenth and eleventh centuries, saints could have territory, privileges, powers of protection.[35] The house at Llandeilo was dedicated to Teilo, its community was the community of Teilo, its lands the lands of Teilo. Grants

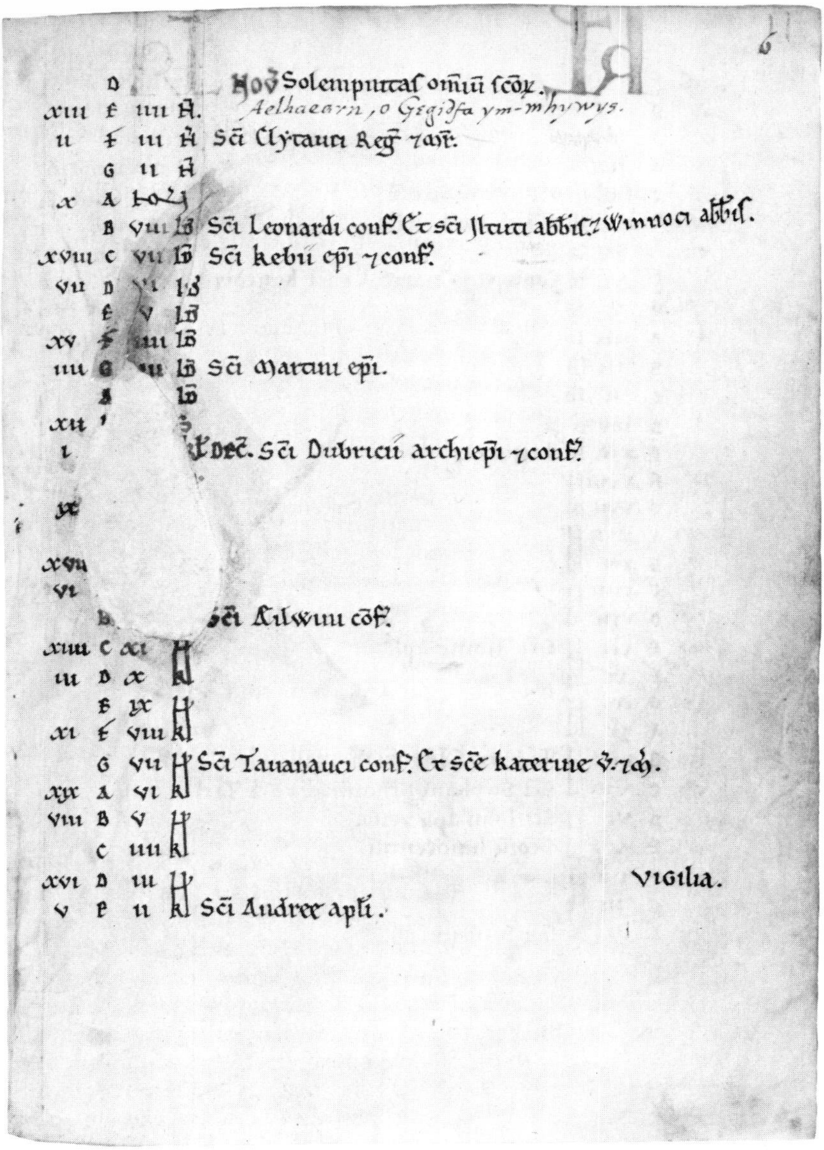

Hoc Solempnitas omiu scox.
Aelhaearn, o Gigidfa ym-mhrvwys.

xiii f iiii A.
ii f iii A Sci Clytauci Reg 7 ası̃t.
    G ii A
x   A ʎoʎ
    B vii Iɜ Sci Leonardi conf. Et sci Itura abbiꝰ Winnoci abbis.
xviii c vii Iɜ Sci kebii epi 7 conf.
vii D vi Iɜ
    f v Iɜ
xv f iiii Iɜ
iiii G iii Iɜ Sci Martini epi.
    ɜ Iɜ
xii i ɜ
i   ʎ Dec. Sci Dubricii archiepi 7 conf.

ix

xvii
vi
    b.   sci Kilwini cõf.
xiiii c xii
iii D x A
    E ix A
xi f viii A
    G vii A Sci Tauanauci conf. Et sce katerine ɜ. 7ch).
xix a vi A
vii B v A
    c iiii A
xvi D iii A   vigilia.
v   f ii A Sci Andree apli.

Figure 58. A calendar from ?Monmouth, BL MS Vespasian A xiv, f.6A (copyright The British Library).

of property were made to God, of course, but they were also made to the saint of the house which received them — *deo et sancto N et in manu abbatis*, as the charters often read, '[given] to God and St N into the hands of the abbot'. The saint's territory was therefore the territory of the community of the church which owned the saint as its protector; the privilege of the saint was the privilege possessed by that community in accordance with the status assigned to it in Welsh law; the protection of the saint was the legal quality of protection that the community could offer, and not merely the supernatural protection that the saint could give.[36] Communities had these powers and privileges of right, but chose to identify themselves with reference to different saints; in sinking their identities in those of their guardian saints — like many others in Western Europe — they could not fail to emphasize their all-seeing presence and thus power. Hence, the sixth-century Teilo was cited as witness to the ninth-century transactions recorded in the Lichfield Gospels; like God he is witness in heaven.[37]

How, then, were saints made? The recognition and veneration of non-Welsh saints is part of a general European phenomenon. Once Christianity was accepted and the idea of sainthood itself was adopted, then knowledge of the cult of European saints was transmitted; they came as part of the package of Christianity. But a very high proportion of the saints named above are of purely local significance, and it is clear that the habit of creating, recognizing and venerating local saints had developed at a very early stage — by the seventh century. How were local saints made? This is an exceptionally difficult question, but at least two, related, processes are indicated. Firstly, the only early clues are those contained in the Life of Samson: exceptional purity and moral stature, together with ascetic practice, made Samson something of a local wonder wherever he went; he earned, by popular acclaim, the designation *sanctus*. Secondly, in other cases it appears that the founder or establisher or supposed founder of a church or community earned it by the act of foundation alone. Where we find the church or community of St N, at a very early date, with no evidence of the recognition of that saint at any other place or in any other context, then the implication is that St N was the founder: hence St Buddwalan at Ballingham c.620, St Cynwal at Rhosili c.650, St Cyngwr(?) at Bishopston c.650, St Tisoi at Llansoy c.725.[38] Whether or not our inference that they were the founders is correct, it was certainly the inference made by the local population, and it is perfectly clear that saints could be mistakenly created because of misunderstandings of this type. Dinebo was supposed to have been the saint who founded Llandinabo, by a simple argument from the place name: Llandinabo must have been St Dinebo's *llan* (church). We know, however, from early forms of the place-name — *Lanniunabui* — that the only personal name contained here is Inabwy, while we know further from charter evidence that this man was a priest of early association with the church, and later a bishop.[39] In some cases such inferences of foundation might be reasonable: the inscription mentioning the blessed Saturninus (Sadyrnin) is to be found at Llansadwrn, Sadwrn's *llan*, which is dedicated to Sadwrn; there is a good chance that this saint *was* associated with the place. Founders, then, were made into saints and supposed founders too. In other cases, early associates, or donors, or first incumbents might be remembered in the place-name and in the dedication; and these too could achieve 'sanctity'. Hence, the church at Garway in Ergyng, the early form of which name is *Lann Guorboe*, Guorboe's *llan*, was first served by the priest Gwrfwy, *Guorboe*.[40]

We have no means, of course, of assessing the historicity of most of these 'founding' saints, given the absence of early material: we do not know if Cadog or Buddwalan or Cynwal existed, although we can say that they were certainly thought to have existed in the seventh century. Some may well have been founders, or first incumbents, or donors; some were clearly not. Evidence of the veneration of a saint, therefore, is irrelevant to the issue of the historicity of that saint; it is no comment at all on his acceptability outside the locality of which he was selected; it *is* a valuable comment on the local acknowledgment of sanctity and its continuing local force. For the essential characteristic of this material and this evidence is that sanctity is locally conferred. Hence, Lifris commented that the people went to venerate Michael of St Michael's mount in Cornwall; Rhigyfarch that Dewi was the term used by the 'common people' for David; the writer of the Life of Gwynllyw that verses on Gwynllyw were composed in the vernacular by a professional versifier. [41] Sanctity in this area and at this period had nothing to do with canonization, with reviews of life and works by venerable committees of powerful clerics, with submissions and reports. It was, instead, to do with conscious or unconscious selection by a local community, either recognizing some especial quality, or willing that there had been that quality.

What then constituted sanctity, what was the special quality, what was necessary for the recognition of sainthood? The simplest answer to this problem is that, as far as the evidence we have will suggest anything, some combination of good works and outstanding moral qualities together with the power to work miracles — the product of the access to the deity achieved by self-denial and contemplation — was the essential requirement. The proportions vary with time. The contrast between the model saint portrayed by the early Life of Samson and the models of the late Lives is therefore very striking. In Samson's case the stress is upon the ascetic, upon rigorous self-denial and personal struggle; [42] the discussion of his moral qualities is detailed, explicit and often repeated; consideration of miracles is slight and occasional, and the miracles performed tend to be about confrontation with and overcoming evil — dragons, serpents, a witch — and are not of the more extreme kind. The late Lives certainly have conventional passages which dwell upon ideal qualities, but these tend to be concentrated in pious introductions and to be detached from and unrelated to the real narrative content of the works (and therefore to such parts of the content as might have had a pre-twelfth-century origin). The emphasis on miracles, on the other hand, of many and various types, is notable, while the most striking quality of their saints is not compassion or humility but power, a quality also noticed by Giraldus, who commented that Welsh and Irish saints seemed more vindictive than others. [43] David cursed the bees that followed Modomnoc so that they never again flourished in his settlement, and he withered the hand of the man about to strike the saint. [44] Cadog caused the barn and its attendant servant to be consumed by fire, for insubordination; he occasioned the death of two disciples of his when they carelessly left his book behind on Flatholm; he killed his steward for dereliction of duty and deficiency in looking after the resources of the community. [45] Cadog, especially, is the saint of the curse, whose power over the elements and over life and the natural world is manifest as much through his capacity to cause damage as it is to bring relief. The same ideal qualities, in a much less concentrated form, were invoked earlier by the writer of the *Historia Brittonum*: by the agency of St Germanus the wicked tyrant Benlli was consumed by fire which fell from heaven, as was Gwrtheyrn together with his wives and citadel (just to be sure, the compiler went on to give an alternative fate for Gwrtheyrn of being swallowed up by the earth); by the same agency, materials for building Gwrtheyrn's citadel had already disappeared once. The ruler who refused to believe in Illtud's body and altar lost his life.[46] The saint, then, is the man who had access to supernatural powers and could call upon them for the purpose of controlling both man and the natural world around him. His access might also be demonstrated by his power to bring about more beneficial developments, rather more in accord with the European miracle-working tradition.

In this context, therefore, we find what amount to catalogues of miracles performed through the agency of the saint. Theoretically it was not the saint who worked the miracle but God, through his saint. He had *virtutes* — powers of access to God — the common and technical early medieval term used in association with miracle-working; it is twice used in the *Historia Brittonum*, of Martin and also Germanus.[47] Once, indeed, in the Life of Cadog, the admission is made that miracles are worked by the power of God, working through Cadog,[48] but much more commonly the presentation of miracles in these Lives ignores the source and excessively elevates the agent, to the extent that the agent appears to be the source. The range of miracles is great.[49] A few healing miracles, usually very unspecific, are included: David cured a blind monk, restored sight, brought the dead to life; Cadog caused a barren woman to conceive, 'cured the sick', resurrected Llywri, headless but carrying his head; the *Historia Brittonum*, in a flush of enthusiasm for Patrick, records that he 'gave sight to the blind, cleansed lepers, brought hearing to the deaf, cast out devils, raised nine men from the dead' in a list that entirely lacks detail of names and places.[50] But, unlike much of continental European hagiographic material, the saint as healer is not a dominant image. The emphasis, rather, where it is not on the saint as curser, is on control of the elements and of matter. Cadog could carry burning coals, David could bring warmth to the bubbling waters at Bath; both caused springs to emerge from dry land, could divert rain from falling where it might cause harm, as on books; and the river Taff narrowed for Cadog to pass.[51] Both saints emerge as a source of plenty and fertility: David turned water into wine and Cadog water into mead; fish crowded to the end of the line when Cadog arrived to be entertained; a mouse brought him grains of corn when he spent time in a famine-struck area near Brecon.[52] More modestly, but with an eye to the same principles, the cow killed by the hospitable peasant for Germanus and eaten, recovered next day.[53] The mouse was not the only animal harnessed to the will and benefit of the saint. Stags were yoked, salmon caught missing books, wild boars tamely pointed out good building sites.[54]

This access to power is the chief demonstration of sanctity by the eleventh century, the evidence of the man's ability to pass into the world of the spirit. Correspondingly, the deity gives signs of his favour: lights shine and birds sing in celebration of the arrival of the chosen ones.[55] Angels are sent with messages directly from heaven and the special quality of the saint is revealed by his capacity to perceive them, by his openness to such messages. There is a contact between the saint and heaven already while he is still in life. Such are the qualifications for sanctity and for continuing reverence.

Relics

By the latest periods the saint in person was not the only miracle worker. Objects, and even places, that had been associated with him were seen to confer relief from suffering, for miracles from this agent are almost entirely of a healing nature. Hence, those people who went to venerate Michael at St Michael's Mount often had recourse to the healing well nearby. The local patronage of such wells, each under the care of its peculiar saintly patron, is something that continued till very recent times in Wales — at places like St Seiriol's well at Penmon; Holywell (Flint), where a large medieval structure still advertises its powers; and the well at Llangybi (Caernarfon), where one can still see the steps by which the sick entered the water — although in most cases we have no evidence that this was continuous from the early medieval period. Five wells in Glamorgan are still associated with St Cadog, for example, including one noted in the early sixteenth century near Aberkenfig and one in the early nineteenth century near Gelligaer.[56] Other features could be selected: the stone which had weighed down the body of Cadog's murdered builder Llywri remained to mark his grave and to heal many diseases, especially urinary ailments; Gildas's bell raised two people from the dead; the Patriarch of Jerusalem's gifts to David, of altar, staff and bell, survived to work miracles after his death, 'numberless', but unspecified (see, for example, fig. 59).[57] The most attractive of all of these was the staff of Padarn, called Cyrwen, which had the virtue of bringing peace: those in dispute who swore upon it would find a resolution for their problems. Rhigyfarch's

Figure 59. The Llangwnnadl bell (by permission of the National Museum of Wales).

brother, Ieuan, the scribe of Corpus Christi College Cambridge MS 199, decorated his work with a poem in honour of this staff, clearly one of the major relics of the house of Llanbadarn, the family house of Ieuan's family:

> Much accomplishing, much loved, it gives protection,
> Its holy power reaching the limits of three continents.
> No other relic can be compared with Cyrwen —
> A wonderful gift — Padarn's staff. [58]

Of a comparable sanctity were the books into which records were written of grants made — the Llancarfan charters in the Book of Cadog, the Llandaff charters in the Chirograph of Teilo — and oaths might be sworn on such holy books. Records were sometimes written into the margins of Gospel Books themselves, as were the Llandeilo charters in the Lichfield Gospels, preservation in that context conferring an added sanctity and underwriting the curses that would be fulfilled should the properties recorded be violated or appropriated. [59] And, just as associated objects might have acquired the saint's miracle-working powers, so associated or supposedly associated places acquired an aura of holiness and a miraculous potential. Tatheus, so it was thought, built a church on the spot where the girl, Machuta, was murdered by sheep thieves (though he transported her body to Caerwent); and a church was built over the stone where Nonnita was supposed to have given birth to David. [60]

It was bones, however, that had or were seen to have had the greatest powers. The *Passio* of Cadog's Life announces quite explicitly that those who possessed some of the bones of Cadog — or of his disciples — would be able to perform miracles, drive off demons, and ensure abundance and fertility. [61] By this time, the cult of relics was well established in Wales, both in the original sense of the relic of the saint's own person — his bones — as well as in the secondary and subsidiary sense of the relic of his belongings discussed above. Cadog's own relics were guarded in his tomb in Italy, lest any Briton steal them and their miracle-working properties be lost, while at home in Wales others contended that their shrine held his relics and they sometimes moved it about to avoid the possibility of theft. [62] These relics were taken in procession, carried to meet invaders of the land, carried by appropriate messengers to those who sought the protection of the saint, for which payment was duly received. [63]

The deposit of the true relic, the bones of the saint, created the holiest places; and by the eleventh century shrines, portable or otherwise, containing the relics, already tended to be housed in churches. Cadog's shrine, with a gilded wing, rested in his church at Llancarfan, and there was a basilica over his tomb in Italy; in 1089 the shrine of David was stolen from his church. This was not always so. According to his Life, Illtud, upon receiving the miraculous gift of a holy body and an altar, which arrived from over the sea in a boat, buried the body in a cave — *lingarthica spelunca* — and placed the altar over it; henceforth, miracles were performed at the site. [64] Here, in one anecdote, we find spelled out the association of the holy burial with the sacred place and the consequent performance of miracles there. These statements are late (though the essence of the tale occurs in the ninth-century *Historia Brittonum*), but the attitudes they reveal are comparable to those to the martyr's burials of the Continent in the very early medieval period, where the deposit of bones created the *martirium*, which might become a focus for local devotion and/or other burials. Gildas shows that veneration of the martyr's tomb was already happening in Britain in the sixth century, and the Welsh word *merthyr*, used in place-names signifying church or cemetery, is a direct borrowing from Latin *martirium*. Though it is clear that the burial places of some of the major saints was not known by the twelfth century,[65] indicating that commemoration was not consistent, Wales nevertheless seems in general to have shared the European experience and approach. Rhigyfarch and Lifris, indeed, were aware of the rationale behind the borrowed word and noted the association between the merthyrs of Wales and the burial places of martyrs. Though early references are few, therefore, it is reasonable to suppose that Welsh attitudes developed like those in mainland Europe: an early respect for the burial places of martyrs became a respect for the burial places of holy men, 'saints', and an expectation that miracles might be performed there. They might be ordinary extended burials or non-extended deposits of bones in a shrine that was accessible to the population. The burial places (sometimes in cemeteries, sometimes not) were marked simply at first, but surrounding walls and eventually churches might be built to house them, particularly in the latter case. The special grave, therefore, sometimes preceded the construction of special churches (cf. fig.60).[66]

In some cases archaeological evidence both suggests the location of some very early shrines and confirms that the marking of special graves happened in Wales, as elsewhere. At Arfryn, Bodedern, on Anglesey, excavation of an early cemetery revealed more than 90 north-south and east-west aligned

Figure 60. Some special graves at Cae Capel Eithin, Gaerwen. Phase 3: a clay floor sealing two central graves, with a new grave inserted in the doorway (photograph R.B. White; by permission of the Gwynedd Archaeological Trust, Crown copyright reserved).

graves around a central focus: a ring of posts surrounded a pebble floor which lay over another grave. An early tombstone with the simple inscription 'Ercagni' (i.e. [grave] of Ercagnos) was found elsewhere on the cemetery site and it is possible that it stood upright at the foot of this grave. Another marked grave was found at Llandegái in Gwynedd, with a rectangular slot, 12ft by 14ft, to the south of rows of inhumations, and yet more at Cae Capel Eithin, Gaerwen, on Anglesey (figs.65,60).[67] Specially marked graves like this recall the better-known example of the young girl's grave in the huge cemetery at Cannington, Somerset, which formed one nucleus of a large fourth- to seventh-century cemetery and appeared to have a worn pathway to the mound which covered it (fig.57).[68] We cannot, of course, comment on why these were specially marked graves. The discovery of burials beneath some churches may possibly point to a similar beginning, and point to a process in which the special grave, or the shrine, ultimately became the focal point for the building of a church. At Pennant Melangell, near Llangynog, there is a cist grave within the apse of the church and a shrine, possibly of the twelfth-century. Under the walls of St Justinian's Chapel (near St David's) — itself the latest of a complex series of buildings — was another long cist and a small stone structure covered with white quartz pebbles and containing a few bones, possibly indicating just such an early shrine and just such a sequence of development as in the classic continental models.[69] Outside the church-yard at Parc-y-cerrig Sanctaidd (Llansadyrnin), stands a structure, 1ft 8ins x 2ft, which may be interpreted as a *leacht*, the altar-like feature found commonly on open sites in early Ireland. This one has stone foundations and was associated with water-worn pebbles; nearby stands a cross-inscribed tombstone of seventh- to ninth-century date, quite possibly *in situ*. The discovery of several sub-church burials — like the long cists at St Patrick's Chapel — may on the other hand point to circumstances in which early, undeveloped cemetery sites developed to include churches.[70]

Bones, objects and places were an attraction, for specific thaumaturgic reasons and for sheer curiosity. The saints themselves made visits to the relics of the apostles, and others made trips to the bones of a saint's disciples.[71] Evidence of pilgrimage as such is of two types: the planned journey to the holy place, and pilgrimage, *peregrinatio*, in the other sense, the journey without a particular end except to detach the traveller from the familiar and supporting social context and to free him to fight the spiritual battle against self. This latter occurs in the early penitential material of the sixth century and in the tales of saintly travels; both exile (presumably temporary) and perpetual pilgrimage are prescribed as penances for the monk repeatedly guilty of theft and for the man who defiled his mother.[72] The notion is periodically recalled after that. Evidence of pilgrimage in the usual sense is largely confined to the eleventh century, except with respect to Rome, though Wales was on the route for Irish pilgrims travelling to the Continent. We know of those who passed through the monastery of Caldy Island and through Merfyn's court in Gwynedd in addition to the contacts implied by Irish material at St David's and Llanbadarn, by the influence of Irish decorative styles in the eighth and ninth centuries on the crosses of west Wales, and by the spread of some Irish cults (see fig. 61).[73] Journeys to Rome are evidenced from the seventh century, when the Irish who had been visiting

Figure 61. Fragment of a sculptured cross slab from St David's (*ECMW* no.377; originally published in *Archaeologia Cambrensis* and reproduced by kind permission).

Rome called at Caldy and met Samson on their return journey, and the Annals record a succession of kings who went there in the ninth and tenth centuries.[74] The Colloquy makes Rome the goal of its ideal pilgrimage and the late Lives have this as a commonplace: Cadog, for example, went seven times to Rome, so Lifris maintained, travelling through the holy places of Gaul and Italy on his way.[75] At this late period, Jerusalem was almost as popular a place of pilgrimage as Rome itself, while Cadog even reached the river Jordan.[76] In all of these examples the pilgrim is himself a noted saint (or a king); these are not the journeys of the ordinary believer. At the very end of our period, however, hints are given of pilgrimages undertaken by other people, and pilgrimages to more local centres. Hence it was the 'people' who were drawn to St Michael's Mount in honour of Michael, and who came to Llancarfan on the day of Cadog's festival to hear mass 'as usual'; William the Conqueror might have been king, but it was to St David's that he went in 1081, not Rome — for prayer, as the Annals described it, for pilgrimage as did the *Brut.*[77]

Much the same pattern is true of festivals as such. Until the eleventh century we only hear in Wales of the great festivals of the Christian church, Easter and Whitsun.[78] At that time the celebration of local festivals, like that of Cadog at the house of Cadog, or of Pedrog, Tatheus, Patrick, begin to be evidenced.[79] The surviving Welsh calendars hint at the celebration of more, certainly in the eleventh century and possibly at earlier dates.[80]

Lay Participation

Popular involvement in pilgrimage and festivals marks one stage in the increasing lay participation in religious ceremony, and by the late eleventh century popular practice was often absorbed in the formal ritual presided over by clerics. Hagiographers of the eleventh and twelfth centuries were fond of instancing lay participation in religious experience: there are the locals who gave praise in finding a bridge restored through the prayers of Cadog, the people who waited for the word of David at the synod of Brefi, the sick rich man who gave up his goods and prayed for three days for relief at the church of the martyr, the peasant who asked David to intervene in his favour against a prolonged drought.[81] These are, however, very partial witnesses. Other types of evidence, from earlier periods, though less colourful, probably give a better insight into the manner (though not, of course, the amount) of popular involvement in the practice of Christianity. In his account of the fortunes of post-Roman Britain, Gildas remarked that some of those who fled from the Saxons did so singing psalms.[82] One ninth-century inscribed stone from Caldy invites all those who walk past it to pray for the soul of Cadwgan, though this is on a monastic site, while invocations to God to protect and guide the souls of the departed are not infrequent in the early poetry.[83] The intercession of David would lead the Welsh and their allies to victory over the invading Saxon; that of Padarn might lead people to heaven.[84]

Where any statement is made, then the spiritual health and welfare of the ordinary person would certainly seem to have been in the hands of the Christian God or his agents. The occasions on which the laity came into contact with the professional Christian — monk or non-monastic cleric — seem to have been relatively limited. Only in the eleventh century do we hear of preaching to the people: Rhigyfarch claimed that David had preached to the multitude on Sundays and that some of the laity, at least, had entered churches in order to hear the preaching of the Gospel; Lifris claimed that Cadog had preached to the masses after the Palm Sunday procession.[85] Services only appear in monastic contexts. If 'going to church' was a customary part of weekly or monthly life, then it goes quite unnoticed by the sources that we have. Presumably, in any case, there were few churches outside monastic contexts before the mid-eleventh century. Samson's parents, indeed, were accustomed to go to church at festivals; churches otherwise seem to have been utilized by the local population as places for storing their valuables: the pirates who came to Gwent assumed that goods would be stored in the churches, and we know that people were accustomed to take even clothes and food there. The church was a place for very special occasions, and also a convenient local lock-up. The Colloquy, interestingly, despite its variety of scenes from religious life, has no scene of the people in church; we hear virtually nothing of any provision for regular ministry to the people, and nothing of parishes and parochial organization until the twelfth century.[86] Mass was a special case. The oft-noted line from *Canu Aneirin* seems to suggest that at least by the ninth century fighting men went to church to take communion before battle: 'Cibno does not tell, after the uproar of battle, that he got his dues though he took communion'.[87] This does not, of course, imply that the taking of communion was a regular event, and is presumably comparable to the communion taken at the deathbed; it was administered to Samson's father as he lay dying, though he subsequently recovered.[88] Otherwise, the singing of mass and taking of communion was reserved for the saints themselves, or their monastic followers. Samson himself went to his own oratory to sing mass every Sunday; David took the Body and Blood after preaching to the masses on Sundays.[89] We do not — as we might expect — hear of the taking of communion regularly by the laity.

For most of the population the occasions of greatest involvement with the institutionalized rituals of the Christian Church were the occasions of birth and death, and the appropriate ceremonies of baptism and burial. As far as we can see, the *rites de passage* accompanying birth and death were entirely monopolized by the Christian clergy, and just as there are no hints that the population was other than Christian so — perhaps surprisingly — there are no hints of alternative practices. Some of the earlier material makes the connection between baptism and conversion, as was, of course, its prime significance in a partly pagan world, and accordingly the poems of *Canu Taliesin* characterize the Christian British community — as against the pagan Saxons — as 'the baptized'. Baptism, often mass baptism, of the Irish and English was therefore the symbol of their acceptance of the new faith.[90] Despite the adoption of infant baptism, the rite continued to be seen as a sign of spiritual regeneration: even if he was but recently born, man was born again into his new spiritual potential.[91] As for the practices themselves, we have no clue other than the fact that according to the *Mabinogi* the practice of earlier centuries was considered to be in some way different from that of contemporaries.[92]

Burial is widely attested and there are no hints of other methods of disposal of the dead; inhumation seems to be generally implied — by the coffins, the planks, the biers, the oak which are constantly invoked as a symbol of the loss of dear or respected ones — but the deposit of ashes is not in itself impossible.[93] Certainly excavation and chance finds provide overwhelming evidence of inhumation.[94] The grave itself is a constant concern of much early Welsh poetry, a thing at once of celebration and of grief. The early lament, 'Marwnad Cynddylan', ends each stanza with a reference to the grave where the poet will lie; it is both the inevitable outcome and the recurrent device that gives shape and meaning to the poem:

> ...I shall mourn till I enter my oaken grave
> Cynddylan slain at his power's height.
> ...I shall mourn till I enter my quiet oak
> Cynddylan slain, loss that pierces deep.
> ...I shall mourn till I enter the steadfast earth
> Cynddylan slain, famed as Caradawg.
> ...I shall mourn till I enter circling staves
> Cynddylan slain, famed for majesty.
> ...I shall mourn till I enter the field's surface
> Cynddylan slain, each border's renown.
> ...I shall mourn till I enter travail's acre.
> Cynddylan slain, praised by all patrons.[95]

For the writer of *Historia Brittonum* burial places might be the focus of wondrous tales and the poems known as 'Englynion y Beddau', 'Stanzas of the Graves', were written to celebrate the burial places of the heroes of the past, an attitude which has something in common with the attitude to the burial of holy persons:

> The graves which the rain wets, —
> men who had not been used to being provoked:
> Cerwyd and Cywryd and Caw.
>
> The grave of Rhun son of Pyd is in the rippling of a river
> in the cold in the earth;
> the grave of Cynon is at Rheon ford.
>
> Whose is the grave on the mountain,
> he who had led hosts?
> The grave of Ffyrnfael the Generous, son of Hywlydd.
>
> The grave of Siawn the proud is on Hirerw mountain
> between the earth and his oaken coffin,
> smiling, treacherous, of bitter disposition. [96]

The detail is always of the body laid in the earth — 'he laid his head in the earth' — sometimes within a coffin, sometimes not; sometimes with a stone marker, sometimes under a pile of stones, sometimes under a heap of earth, sometimes with no mark, once with a briar. [97] There are, of course, plenty of surviving tombstones in the form of inscribed stones scattered over Wales,

Figure 62. The 'judgment day' stone from Llanlleonfel (*ECMW* no.62; reproduced by courtesy of the University of Wales Press).

bearing sometimes only the name of the dead — in Latin and/or ogham script — sometimes the words 'here lies', sometimes a longer message: 'silent in the shroud Iorwerth and Ruallaun [lie] in the tomb, silent they await the coming of the judgment', from Llanlleonfel, Brecon (fig. 62); 'Carausius lies in this heap of stones', from Penmachno, Caernarfon; 'the body of Cyngen lies beneath [this stone]', from Meirionydd; and so on.[98] The implication of most of the stanzas is of burial in isolated places — on the hillside, by the stream, in the valley, once in the homestead (*tref*) — and a few incidental references would support this practice. Gildas refers to the burial of the British in the ruins of their houses, which cannot but remind us of the burials in the ruins of the Llantwit Major villa; the *Historia Brittonum* records Gwrthefyr's request for burial by the rock where the Saxons first landed; Cadog buried Llywri near the place where he was killed, with a stone to mark the spot.[99] With the exception of the burial of a murdered girl — itself classified as martyrdom — burial within churches seems to have been restricted to the saints themselves; it was reserved for the most holy and their immediate followers.[100] Clearly by the eleventh century burial rights had developed and were viewed as some sort of perk for the community which owned them. Lifris records that Gwynllyw's deathbed grant to Cadog was that kings, leaders and nobles of his land (Gwynllŵg) were to be buried in Cadog's cemetery at Llancarfan, while exiles and women dying in childbirth were to be buried at his own.[101] This is clearly related as if to indicate some sort of privilege; and we must assume that it brought some financial benefit. The evidence of a few direct gifts of bodies for burial, together with a land grant, would support the notion: Cynfelyn gave land and his body to Llancarfan; Awst and his sons gave Llan-gors and their bodies for burial; Bledrys gave Cairnonui for his own burial.[102] Other evidence from Llancarfan suggests that goods willed to the community by the sick should be allocated for wake offices (for them).[103] All of these considerations suggest that by the late eleventh century burial, within the cemetery of some community, was normal at least for the aristocracy on payment of due fees to the community. By then cemetery burial is much more frequently evidenced, and the Lives are full of references to it.

An early (maybe sixth century) inscribed stone from Aberdaron at the west of the Llŷn peninsula, which records the burial of a priest together with a multitude of the brethren, would suggest the existence of cemeteries at a much earlier date.[104] It is, of course, reasonable to suppose the existence of cemeteries attached to religious communities virtually from the time of their foundation. It is, therefore, worth considering the possibility that, while cemetery burial was usual for members of religious settlements, it was not necessarily so for the lay community until the eleventh century (if so, one must wonder what rituals accompanied these lay burials). The presence of female and child skeletons, as at Llandough, is not decisive proof of lay use, and as yet the archaeological evidence of burial, which is relatively plentiful, is not specific enough in date to resolve the problem.

Surviving physical evidence of burial practice really has two aspects: the location and distribution of inscribed tombstones and crosses, the 'early Christian monuments' of Wales, and the discovery of early cemeteries. In many cases we have no reason to suppose that the stones now mark the place of burial, for many have been moved to more recent churches and cemeteries, but it is notable that stones of Nash-Williams's Group I, of the fifth to seventh centuries, still tend to be scattered in distribution and located in isolated places. Their positioning supports the implications of the written comment. (Long cist burials are occasionally in isolated positions too.) Moreover, there is reason to think that one or two are still in their original positions: that mentioned above at Llansadyrnin stands outside the modern churchyard, near the supposed *leacht*; [105] 'Maen Madog', at Ystradfellte in Brecon, more than 12ft high, of fifth- to sixth-century date, stands at the side of the road, exposed high on the mountain, commemorating Dervacus son of Justus; there may have been a burial in the hole beneath the platform above which it now stands; at Llanddetty, on Ystrad mountain, stood another; and the famous pillar of Elise, near Llangollen, set up by Cyngen to commemorate his grandfather, stands on a barrow, like the cross at Llanfynydd (Carmarthen) which once stood on a small cairn. [106]

The cemetery evidence consists largely of 'long cist' burials (inhumations in stone-lined graves), though occasionally we find simple dug graves. Many, though not all, long cist burials — which are particularly characteristic of the British lowlands of Scotland, Wales and the West Country — are assumed to belong to the few centuries after the Roman period. This is because their lack of grave goods (and the frequent west-east orientation of bodies) would imply a Christian rather than pagan burial practice; because they are characteristic of British rather than English parts of Britain; and because their frequent discovery away from modern cemeteries suggests a practice current before it became common for churches to be attached to cemeteries, as happened increasingly in the early medieval period. (In the Roman period burial had been away from residential centres. Only gradually were cemeteries associated with churches and only gradually, if at all, did churches become focal to rural settlements. [107]) Clearly the answer is not quite so simple, since we do frequently find long cist cemeteries in association with Christian sites — implying continuity of practice and therefore not necessarily an exclusively early date; since the nucleation of settlement round churches is not characteristic of Wales anyway; and since the absence of associated finds makes it difficult to say anything conclusive about them. However, some long cist cemeteries in Wales may reasonably be associated with Christian practice: that at Arfryn, cited above, because of its orientation and focal grave, and notably because of its association with a very early inscribed stone; that at Caldy, on a long-established monastic island, oriented, near the church, with an inscribed stone nearby; that at Llanwnda (Pembroke), with at least 14 oriented burials, a seventh- to ninth-century tombstone in the farmyard, and eight more in the church a couple of miles away. [108] At St Elvis (Pembroke) and Llanllwni (Carmarthen), at Pennant Melangell, at St Patrick's and St Justinian's Chapels, at Burry Holms, there are more, either under the present churches or on church sites. [109] Other, sometimes large, burial sites — Llanfeithin near Llancarfan, St Ishmaels, Llandegái, Cae Capel Eithin (Gaerwen) on Anglesey, Ramsey Island off the coast near St David's (which recently produced an inscription in Anglo-Saxon script, of eighth- or ninth-century date (see fig.63), or Pentrefoelas (Denbigh), where about 40 graves were found in the early nineteenth century, and an inscribed stone and

Figure 63. The Ramsey Island inscription (by permission of the National Museum of Wales).

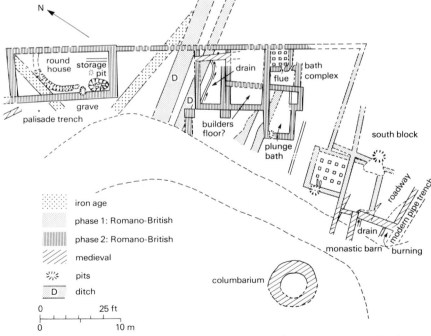

Figure 64. The site at Llandough: interim plan (after Henry Owen John, by permission of the Glamorgan-Gwent Archaeological Trust).

possibly a chapel were associated — may also be of this period.[110] Only at three sites, Caerwent where graves were dug in the ditch of the Roman town, Bayvil where graves were dug into an iron age bank (see fig. 66) and Llandough (fig. 64), where burials were found very near the Roman villa *and* the medieval church, do we have any good evidence of dating: radio-carbon analysis indicates dates for burials centring on the fifth, sixth, eighth, ninth and tenth centuries at Caerwent, on the seventh century at Bayvil and on the eighth century at Llandough.[111] In the other cases, though the attribution to the early medieval period as a whole is not unreasonable, the conventional limitation of them to the fifth, sixth and seventh centuries may well be misleading.

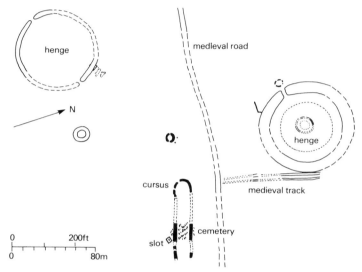

Figure 65. The site at Llandegái (after C. Houlder, 'Llandegái', *Antiquity*, XLII, 1968, fig.1).

The practice of placing inscribed tombstones on barrows has already been noted, and there are also some long cist burials placed in barrows in Dyfed and Anglesey. At Treiorwerth, three long cists with no grave goods and 'fairly strict' east-west orientation are inserted in top of a bronze age barrow, and the excavator noted two other instances of this, and two inhumations without cists, on Anglesey. At Rhoscrowdder (Pembroke) a single long cist was placed in the top of the barrow; at Brownslade a large number of burials — dug graves, long cists, oriented and non-oriented — were inserted.[112] Clearly in some cases Christians used older, pagan burial sites, although it would be false to suppose necessarily continuous use. The cemetery at Cae Capel Eithin, Gaerwen, is associated with a bronze age burial site, and that at Llandegái (fig. 65) lies across the (?bronze age) cursus, close to two bronze age henge monuments in a site of exceptional complexity and long use.[113] Interestingly the church at Meidrim is inside a promontory fort and that at Eglwys Gymyn inside an earlier earthwork.

The clear re-use of pre-Christian and prehistoric sites for Christian purposes in these latter cases means, unfortunately, that we cannot assume that all long cist burials on sites of undisputed later Christian use were in fact Christian: we may simply be uncovering evidence of sites of long-standing ritual use, pagan and Christian. Until more modern investigation of these sites has been undertaken, therefore, the questions will remain. For the moment there is evidence both of isolated and of cemetery burial, with an implication in the written evidence that cemetery burial for the laity became more common as time passed; there is evidence that some burial sites attracted later churches and some were a sort of holy focus, pagan and/or Christian; there is implied, in the relatively large number of burial sites discovered, especially in the South-West, which do not occupy the sites of modern cemeteries and modern settlements, either a considerable shift in cemetery siting or the collapse of associated settlements. We cannot, at present, go further.

If the entry to and exit from life were the most significant occasions of recourse to the church for ordinary people, two other areas constituted the greatest demands which the clergy might make upon the Christian communities in their care: the giving of alms and the doing of penance. As cited above, the Colloquy's advice to those who wished to live well and be good Christians was to pray, keep quiet and give alms; the giving of alms was one of the constantly proclaimed obligations of Christian life. A chief complaint of Gildas against the clergy themselves was that they failed to give alms, though he does note that offerings were commonly made to churches by

Figure 66. Cist grave cut through defensive bank at Y Gaer, Bayvil, containing bone dated ad 665 ± 60 (photograph Heather James, copyright the Dyfed Archaeological Trust).

the people, and then plundered by the priests.[114] The warriors of *Canu Aneirin* were accustomed to present gold and gifts to the altar, as did — much later — the army noted by the Life of Gwynllyw; gifts were 'customarily' made at childbirth, according to Rhigyfarch, a preliminary to the blessing of the newborn.[115] Apart from such special occasion gifts, we know of land grants, often made specifically for the soul of a named person; some of the records from both the Llancarfan and Llandaff collections specify that such grants were made in alms, and it is easy to understand how, in a society with no monetary economy, the giving of land became an acceptable, possibly normal, means of meeting the almsgiving obligation.[116] Another charter, from Llandeilo, records the gift of a Gospel Book; other forms of grant were obviously possible.[117] Some people, at least, took the obligation seriously.

Just as some charters specify almsgiving as the main reason for donation, others indicate penance, and this appears to represent some change from the practices advocated in the early church. The penitential material of the sixth century is very explicit about the performance of penance, which was to apply to the laity as much as to those who had taken monastic vows. Penances were prescribed, therefore, for theft, manslaughter, adultery, political treachery (giving directions to the 'barbarians'), perjury and sexual offences.[118] The nature of the penance to be done is described in terms of years or days, and the implications are that for the periods described diet and material comfort was to be restricted, sometimes severely; for very serious offences, penitential exile might be recommended. In the case of monastic penance the restriction might vary from missing one meal to omitting flesh and alcohol and most fats for several years; for the laity there is no direct specification, but presumably something comparable was envisaged, on a lesser scale. Incidental comments suggest that something of this survived till the end of our period: Gwynllyw and his wife wore hair clothing, ate barley bread with ashes, water, cresses and herbs, washed in cold water only; Rhiannon sat by the gate in poor clothes, like a servant girl; one man was bound up in rusty iron bands.[119] The penitential grant, however, is much more precisely and much more commonly evidenced than these extremes during the period. The Llancarfan charters record grants made in penance for fratricide and for murder in addition to 14 years of penance. The Llandaff charters record penitential donations for murder, perjury, abduction, assault, bloodshed and theft, from the seventh century onwards, and also include one interesting claim of penitential exile to Brittany enforced in the early eighth century on Gwydd-nerth for the murder of his brother. So, for example, Gwrgan was supposed to have made a penitential grant of an estate of six *modii* after he had taken his stepmother as wife in the early eighth century; King Arthfael gave land at Llanmelin in the late tenth century to Bishop Gwgon as penance for the murder of his brother; and King Cadwgan gave land near Llandaff c.1070 in penance for his attack on Bishop Herewald's nephew, and so on.[120] Even Lifris argued that Cadog's parents fulfilled the penances imposed upon them by founding churches and granting them with their territories to Llancarfan as dependencies.[121] The suggestion, therefore, is that in practice the require-ment of personal hardship and restraint implicit in the notion of penance was commuted to a requirement to make donations; grants were made in lieu. This must represent some considerable deviation from the original moral and spiritual purpose. It seems very likely, therefore, that almsgiving and penitential donation were between them responsible for much of the donation to the church that took place in Wales in the early medieval period, and are fundamental to understanding the alienation of property. They also indicate some considerable participation by the aristocratic laity in the business of the Christian religion and some considerable acceptance of and adherence to its precepts, in a manner which contrasts notably with their absence from regular ritual. Participation may well have meant something to the early Christian Welshman rather different from the experience of the believer of the central and later Middle Ages.

Epilogue

Even if it is impossible to write a satisfactory history of early medieval Wales, the questions that have to be asked and the problems which a modern survey discloses indicate that the undertaking is not without its value. Wales should take its place in the pattern of Europe's development and, despite the problems of source material, Wales has its own intrinsic interest. Its area may have been relatively small and its economy relatively poor, but it was not isolated in the early Middle Ages and it also shared characteristics with many other parts of contemporary Europe. It was Christian, and newly Christian, like much of Western Europe; life was supported and wealth was accumulated on the basis of an essentially non-monetary economy; security for the individual was provided by a delicate balance of kindred and lordship structures, structures which also provided the machinery of control over persons; and kingship emerged and was sustained as the most typical institutionalization of political superiority.

Reflecting upon Welsh development between the fifth and the eleventh centuries, the reader will notice some distinctive characteristics and also many problems. Of the former, the influence of geographical determinants is especially marked, for again and again the mountain served to isolate the low-land foci of ecclesiastical and political power, distributed almost centripetally in the four corners of the country. Likewise, settlement was markedly coastal, and churches, villages and ultimately towns were strung around the rim of the landmass. Though this country was relatively poor, it is notable that we hear very little of personal poverty; but by contrast, whatever the relative economic status of the majority of the population, their relative social status was depressed: the sources continued to emphasize the importance of slavery at a time when manumission was becoming increasingly common in Europe as a whole.

Such contrasts serve to identify some of the problems and others are all too evident. Given the number of monasteries and their survival into the twelfth century, why does so little pre-Conquest Welsh material remain? Why was the continuity of the early Welsh archive tradition broken? Why was Welsh development so unlike that of Ireland? Wales lacked ecclesiastical treasure on the Irish scale; it lacked religious institutions of an Irish type, though there were many churches and monasteries; it lacks evidence of proliferating over-kingships. One reason for the difference probably lies in the direct and indirect influence of the Roman past on the political institutions of early medieval Wales. But even here there are problems: a new type of kingship emerged, but what was the relationship of this with the regional groups whose self-awareness became evident by the tenth and eleventh centuries; and what part did the notables, who might often have a restraining effect upon the king, play in the inter-relationship between the two? Some of the evidence might suggest that — rather than acting *for* the group — a king might act for self and dynasty, regardless of group interest, so that there was no necessary coincidence of powerholders with interest groups. The tensions so created may go some way to explaining why, if Wales shared many characteristics with early medieval Europe, it did not develop along parallel lines. By the eleventh century there was no noticeable trend towards urbanization, towards feudalization, towards the consolidation of monarchy nor the sophistication of administration. Such omissions are very curious and the lack of an adequately exploitable surplus, together with particular political factors like the consistent thrusts of English aggression, may have to be drawn into an explanation.

Though there are problems, some of the material suggests lines of development and is particularly suggestive of long-term political trends. In some senses it was the Roman period which gave political shape to Wales for it was in the first and second centuries A.D. that the marches became a military frontier area and acquired their border character. Thus was Wales isolated from south-eastern Britain, and English settlement in the fifth, sixth and seventh centuries merely intensified a process which had already begun. It took time, however, for a distinctively Welsh cultural identity to form, largely because the area never achieved a single political identity. For much of the early middle ages Wales was essentially a land of four kingdoms, each with its lowland focus in one of the four corners of the country. For many centuries the south-eastern kingdom, Glywysing, initially distinguished by its much more intensively Romanized past, had a distinctive and separate history and few contacts with the rest of Wales. By the eleventh century, however, not only was it sharing the political and social trends of the other kingdoms, but its political fortune was closely linked with that of the South-West and occasionally with the North. The eventual integration of the South-East into a network of distinctively Welsh cultural associations and social institutions points the contrast between the development of this area and that of the North-East. Though it had belonged to the 'lowland zone' in Roman times while the North-East belonged to that of the highland, by the eleventh century much of this northern quarter had been conquered by and integrated into the kingdom of England. The contrast is nicely demonstrated by the line of Offa's Dyke (see above, fig.42). The Dyke effectively bisects the Marches: its northern course runs along the edge of the Welsh mountain mass, separating the north-eastern lowlands from the north-eastern highland and placing those lowlands very firmly in the kingdom of England; in the midlands, however, the Dyke turns sharply east, and eventually turns again to follow the river Wye flowing south to the coast; this southern line of the boundary keeps the south-eastern lowlands in Wales. When the line was drawn — presumably in the late eighth century — the lowland base of the north-eastern kingdom was thereby detached and Powys was confined to the uplands, while the lowlands of Glywysing in the South were left untouched. It is therefore easy to see why Gwynedd could absorb Powys half a century later and why the latter kingdom did not regain its independent status for more than 200 years. Indeed, much of the North-East must have been effectively English — or rather Mercian — during the eighth century; correspondingly, the exclusion of the South-East from English control is presumably to be explained in terms of the politics of the eighth century.

There were, of course, some friendly contacts between English and Welsh and influence travelled in both directions; Asser, after all, went from St David's to King Alfred's court in the late ninth century and English kings continued to call on the Welsh tradition of learning in the tenth. Despite this, it is clear that the Welsh suffered from English raids intermittently but constantly during the eighth, ninth, tenth and eleventh centuries; and evidence of long-ranging English raids is much more impressive than that of Welsh raids on England, which tend to be confined to the borders.

The nature of contacts with the people to the west is much more elusive, particularly in the later centuries. Cultural contacts with the Hiberno-Scandinavian world are closely demonstrated by the art styles of inscribed stones and great crosses, but their political and social context is at present unclear. By the eleventh century north Wales was undoubtedly in touch with Scandinavian Dublin, as the careers of Cynan and his son Gruffudd amply demonstrate. Concentrations of Scandinavian place-names and of Hiberno-Norse styles of decoration along the north coast, together with the recently discovered (?) Viking hoard near Llandudno, argue for some Scandinavian settlement and also for the possibility of periods of Scandinavian political control. It is exceptionally interesting to note in this context that the Irish overking who took control of Dublin in the mid-eleventh century — Diarmait mac Mael na mBo — claimed to be king of the British (i.e. Welsh) as well as the Irish and Scandinavians. It is possible that when he took Dublin he also took over a sphere of political influence which included North Wales. These are mere hints of such a possibility, but they are extremely suggestive hints.

Despite the acute political problems of the immediate pre-Conquest era, it is in that period that a distinctive Welsh cultural identity clarified and consciousness of that identity began to be expressed. Already in the ninth century a 'History of the Britons' had been compiled: in the tenth, the poet of *Armes Prydein* exhorted the British to unite together and, with their allies, expel the English from the island of Britain; and the more powerful kings of the tenth and eleventh centuries sought titles which might express the range of their new ambition of ruling all the Britons. So strongly did this develop that, in spite of the Anglo-Norman Conquest, the Welsh bequeathed a legacy of distinctively Welsh language and literature and law to the later middle ages and the modern world. The South, and the ecclesiastical centre of St David's and its patron saint in particular, became the focus of Welsh feeling in the late eleventh century; and if there were Vikings in Anglesey and English in the hinterland of Chester, this is scarcely surprising. St David's was already famous in the ninth century and its saint had a widespread cult even before that date; the trends of the tenth century were such as to emphasize the significance of Dyfed, particularly under kings like Hywel Dda and Maredudd. It was St David's, therefore, that struggled to become the seat of an archbishopric for Wales in the twelfth century; it was to St David's that William the Conqueror travelled, for pilgrimage and prayer in 1081; and it was a member of the episcopal family of St David's who voiced the national lament at the coming of the Normans: 'Our limbs are cut off, we are lacerated, our necks condemned to death, and chains are put on our arms... liberty and self-will perish'.

Though the poet rightly perceived that the political consequences of the

Norman coming were disastrous for Welsh rulers, their conquest did not destroy the fact that a distinctive character had been determined for Wales; in its formation, the experience of the early Middle Ages had been crucial.

Appendix: The Source Material

The sources for the history of early medieval Wales are few, fragmentary and difficult to use. For this reason they are also difficult to classify, and do not fall neatly into the categories of source material available for later, better-evidenced periods. They are often incidental and uneven in their coverage, producing patterns and emphases that must mislead the modern researcher, professional and amateur alike. Since the written sources frequently only survive in manuscripts written centuries after their composition, to the problem of scarcity is added the problem of corruption: mistakes and omissions were made in copying; additional material was added; content was sometimes changed. Such changes have occasionally been detected by the modern scholar, but much fundamental source study remains to be done. It will be some time before the potential of the meagre amount of material available can be realized. Till then, we cannot even know the date of composition of much of it: where precise indication is lacking, as it so often is, then deductions have to be made from the type of script or type of spelling or type of language in which the piece is written or from internal references and allusions.

The earliest written documents that survive from Wales are of no earlier than ninth-century date. These include the first of the charters written into the margins of the Lichfield Gospels,[1] the fragments of scholarly notes collected in the 'Liber Commonei', which is part of the manuscript known as Oxoniensis Prior,[2] a copy of the long poem by the fourth-century Juvencus on the story of the Gospels, with accompanying Welsh glosses and poems,[3] a copy of the fifth-century educational work by Martianus Capella called *De Nuptiis Philologiae et Mercurii*, with more glosses, a copy of Ovid's *Ars Amatoria*, and a copy of the *De Consolatione Philosophiae* of Boethius.[4] This undoubtedly curious miscellany of largely scholarly works therefore supplies the earliest contemporary written material, although since both the Juvencus, Martianus Capella, Ovid and Boethius manuscripts are themselves copies of earlier works they supply only minimal contemporary comment. An earlier script and an earlier witness to contemporary development is provided by the corpus of inscribed stones, which begins already in the fifth century and is particularly rich for the fifth- to seventh-century period.[5] The inscriptions are clearly of paramount importance in any consideration of post-Roman Wales and their significance — as also that of the marginalia in the Lichfield Gospels — cannot be over-emphasized. We should not forget, however, that early contemporary notice of Wales is sometimes to be found in the works of writers outside the area. The comments of the monk of Jarrow, Bede, from the early eighth century, of the *Anglo-Saxon Chronicle* from the ninth century at the latest, of ninth-century Anglo-Latin vocabularies from Canterbury, are therefore of especial value although they are few in number.

The Welsh corpus of sources also forces us to confront the especial difficulty of the relationship between oral and written material. Some proportion of the written material clearly had an oral origin: one cannot imagine devices like the triads (see p.212) having other than ultimately oral ancestry, whatever the strength of written culture at the time of their recording; one cannot imagine some of the tales in the Saints' Lives having anything other than a popular oral currency. It is possible that some of the genealogical material was memorized over several generations before being committed to writing; it is more than possible that some of the tales which come together in the mid-medieval stories had an earlier oral circulation; it is highly likely that memory of the deeds celebrated by the earlier poems was transmitted orally before being fashioned into the carefully-crafted written works, and indeed that some element of that crafting was an oral rather than a written process. In all of these cases, therefore, though the form in which it is presented may be late, aspects of the content may have been articulated several centuries earlier. This makes the intellectual problems of analysis exceptionally complex and the dangers of drawing conclusions which only pertain to one period immense. We cannot, at present, determine with any precision which aspects or what proportion of aspects are earlier or later; however early a work was created, therefore, its earliness is useless for historical purposes. The poem *The Gododdin* may possibly have first taken shape round about 600 in the days after a battle at Catraeth; the forms in which it survives, however, cannot be earlier than the ninth century; the seventh-century element is not (or not yet) definable; its seventh-century aspect is therefore of no practical use to the historian.

Finally, it is worth observing that a very high proportion of the material that survives from the pre-Conquest period is written in the Latin rather than the vernacular language. Despite the very large corpus of late medieval law texts in Welsh, some of the earliest texts are in Latin. This suggests that, until Welsh literary culture received a boost in the central middle ages, the normal practice was to write in Latin, presumably influenced in part by a prominent clerical culture. It remains possible, however, that the greater survival of Latin texts was determined by the propensity of copyists outside Wales to copy Latin rather than Welsh texts. Nearly every pre-Conquest Welsh book that survives was taken out of Wales at an early date, a circumstance which emphasizes the dis-continuity of archive.

The issues which are raised above cannot be discussed in detail for this is not the place for a full critical discussion. I have tried to indicate here the nature of the sources I have used and the range of critical problems that surround them. Full references to modern critical discussion will be found in the *Bibliography of the History of Wales* published by the Board of Celtic Studies, and its regular supplements. Work in progress can be followed in the volumes of the *Bulletin of the Board of Celtic Studies, Studia Celtica, Welsh History Review*, as they appear. The issues are important, and have a significant bearing on the nature of pre- and post-Conquest Welsh culture and on attitudes to record-keeping. Such questions, in their turn, bear upon the problem of the proper use of evidence and they should always be kept in mind. It may well be that only a small proportion of the material that does survive should properly be used in writing a history.

1   Records

There are no 'official' government or institution-sponsored records of the type that form the stuff of history writing of most parts of Western Europe from the twelfth century onwards. There are no censuses, no tax returns, no records of regular court proceedings, no estate surveys, no accounts; there are no registers of births and deaths, of properties, of transactions; there is no written constitution, no statute book that records legislation, no statement of bye-laws, no regulations from guilds or other corporations. There is therefore scarcely any standardized procedure for written record-keeping, and no implication that the act of making the record in some sense guaranteed its veracity. There are, however, three types of document that must in some sense have been considered records, though the rationale for the making and keeping of such records has to be guessed rather than established, in the absence of more familiar institutional requirements.

The first type of source that may legitimately be viewed in this way are sets of annals, year-by-year surveys of past events. Whether or not the selection of events was biased or ill-informed, whether or not the annalist was accurate, they represent some attempt to capture the past. We possess one principal set of annals for early Wales, known as *Annales Cambriae*, whose entries (in Latin) run from the fifth to the thirteenth century, starting from a notional year 1 in the mid-fifth century, at A.D.445. These are extremely terse in character until very late in the eleventh century, and the following, for the years 798 to 810, is a typical sample (the year numbers, which are usually not given in the text, are those of the notional sequence):

Year [354]   Caradog king of Gwynedd was strangled by the Saxons.

Year [363]   Arthgen king of Ceredigion died.

Year [364]   Rhain king of Demetae and Cadell of Powys died.

Year [365]   Elfoddw archbishop of the Gwynedd region migrated to the Lord.

Year [366]   the burning of St David's.

The Annals survive in four different manuscripts. The earliest is BL Harleian MS 3859, copied round about 1100; the others belong to the thirteenth century. Since the entries in the Harleian manuscript stop at the year 954, it is presumed that this manuscript is a copy of a mid-tenth century compilation; the scribe clearly did not understand the material that he was copying. Material for the last century or so of the pre-Conquest era has to be supplied from the later texts, and that in the Public Record Office abbreviated Domesday sometimes gives better readings even for the fifth to tenth centuries. Whatever the age of the manuscripts, K. Hughes has demonstrated that the creation of the annals was in the first instance the action of the episcopal community at St David's, and it appears that contemporary records were made there from the late eighth until the early thirteenth century; contemporary records were made at other centres, like Strata Florida and Neath, in the twelfth and thirteenth centuries, but these are outside the interest of this book.[6] When the St David's annalist began to keep a regular record in the late eighth century he had to use extant material from other sources to fill in the years between the fifth and the eighth centuries. It seems that for the fifth and sixth centuries to 613 he used material closely related to that in the early Irish annals, possibly acquired form a north British source, and for the seventh and eighth centuries miscellaneous historical notes compiled in the same or another northern British centre, some of which possibly derive from contemporary records.[7] A.D. dates were not assigned to this material until sometime after the tenth (and probably after the eleventh) century, and the sequences of years often suffer confusing dislocations: the entry which corresponds to the year 797 A.D., for example, really applies to the year 796, though that which corresponds to 757 applies to 757. There is no easy guide to this and we await a modern edition to solve the problem. We have, then, in the Annals, brief contemporary records made at St David's from the late eighth century onwards and an adaptation by St David's of material compiled in a northern centre in the seventh and eighth centuries, mostly relating to north Britain and Ireland.[8] The fifth- and sixth-century entries are of virtually no use at all for Welsh history; the seventh- and earlier eighth-century entries, whether made by contemporaries in the North or retrospectively, contain only a little material that relates to Wales.

Related to the Annals are the late medieval collections known as *Brut y Tywysogyon*. These survive in a number of texts, written at different centres, and they constitute vernacular versions of a Latin text which had been based on the Annals, with additional material, compiled in the late thirteenth century. Their significance for the pre-Conquest period lies in the fact that they occasionally have entries which are not to be found in any of the surviving texts of *Annales Cambriae*, but which appear to have been derived from pre-Conquest annalistic material, presumably from earlier texts of the Annals which have not survived. These relate almost entirely to the tenth and eleventh centuries.

The second type of source which has some claim to be regarded as a record is the corpus of charters recording the transfer of rights in property from one person (or several) to another. These are the only documents which are written in accordance with a standardized procedure, a procedure which appears to derive from registration practices current in the late Roman Empire.[9] They tend, therefore, to have a standard form and to use standard Latin formulas; essentially they describe the transaction, naming the persons and properties involved, they list the witnesses present on the occasion, and they add a religious sanction invoking the wrath of God upon anyone who should fail to keep the terms agreed; sometimes they add a description of the bounds of the property and narrative detail about the circumstances which led to the transaction. The latter is particularly true of charters of the tenth and eleventh centuries, and in this respect they go outside the limitations of the standardized procedure. Since they survive in entirely clerical contexts they tend to record grants rather than other types of transaction. The charters are of exceptional importance in that they provide highly detailed, localizable evidence and it is unfortunate that almost the entire corpus comes from the South-East. We have, then, 149 charters contained in the twelfth-century Book of Llandaff or *Liber Landavensis*, which relate to the South, and to the area of the twelfth-century and later diocese of Llandaff in particular, a very high proportion referring to Gwent and Ergyng; they run from the very late sixth to the late eleventh century, although nearly 40 per cent of these belong to the eighth century and another 20 per cent to the second half of the ninth century. They are both corrupt and undated in the form in which they are preserved in the manuscript but it is possible, by analysis of the witness lists and of the formulas, to deduce approximate dates for most of them, to pare away the later accretions, and hence to reconstruct the original texts. Though brief, these still contain much useful detail.[10]

A further 14 charters from the South-East are appended to the Life of Cadog (*Vita Cadoci*) in a manuscript of c.1200, and they relate to the interests of the monastery of Llancarfan. It is impossible to date these precisely, though they are likely to belong to the seventh and eighth centuries.[11] Five more charters, and some fragments, of which three are in mixed Latin and Old Welsh, were written into the margins of the Lichfield Gospels (or Book of Chad) when that book was at Llandeilo Fawr; they relate to the latter area. Numbers 1, 3, 4 and 5 are at least of ninth-century date, since the hands in which they are written may be so dated; it is unlikely that the texts are much earlier. No.2 may be a copy of an eighth-century text, but its hand is difficult to date (though not later than the late tenth century, by which time the Gospels had been moved to Lichfield).[12] As noted above, these texts are of exceptional importance since they represent some of the earliest surviving writing from Wales and are therefore extremely valuable as contemporary witness.

There are in addition a few fragments of charters from other places. These are, principally, an unknown number from St David's, of which only a few odd names survive;[13] a witness list from St David's, or somewhere in its vicinity, which probably belongs to the eleventh century;[14] part of an undatable charter for Clynnog preserved in the fourteenth-century 'Record of Caernarvon';[15] a couple of charters for Llanelwy, probably of immediate pre-Conquest date, recorded in the (lost) thirteenth- or fourteenth-century Red Book of St Asaph.[16]

The remaining type of source which may be viewed as an intentionally compiled record is the corpus of early genealogical material. A genealogy is a pedigree of descent (or supposed descent), which in Wales runs from the most to the least recent member. Hence, 'Owain son of Hywel son of Cadell son of Rhodri', and so on through many generations. The earliest Welsh collection (Harleian Genealogy) is that contained in the same British Library manuscript as the earliest Annals, Harleian 3859.[17] Though the copy is later, the actual collection appears to have been made in the middle of the tenth century, since it begins with the pedigrees of Owain, who died in 954, through his mother and his father, and since Owain is the latest person to be mentioned.[18] This same circumstance suggests at least an element of the 'official' about the collection since it seems to have been compiled for royal purposes and royal propaganda, or at least under royal patronage.[19] It contains 30 genealogies, some of which are extremely short and of obscure provenance, others of which span nearly 40 generations and relate directly to the ancestry of the royal families of tenth-century Wales. The collection is exceptionally important as providing evidence of the approach to royal ancestry in the tenth century, although it does not follow that the ancestry claimed has necessarily anything to do with the actual relationships of those families. M. Miller has demonstrated, for example, how the historical horizon reaches back to the mid-sixth century, sometimes credibly, but not before.[20] It is also clear that some of the short genealogies, which terminate with historically attested persons who died before the tenth century, must derive from written or oral material of earlier dates. They remain impossible to use as evidence for periods previous to the tenth century, however, in the absence of corroborative material.

Though the Harleian collection is the earliest collection of genealogical material, there are more genealogies in other types of source, often embedded within a narrative structure. The *Vita Cadoci* and the *Historia Brittonum*, for example, include material of this type and the latter therefore provides clear enough evidence of the practice of writing down genealogies at least as early as the early ninth century. Evidence of a different sort also comes from an inscribed stone: the so-called 'Pillar of Elise' was erected by Cyngen of Powys (who died in 855) in memory of his greatgrandfather.[21] The long inscription on this large monument includes a statement of five generations of Cyngen's own pedigree, and three generations of an earlier pedigree. Clearly this also supplies undisputed ninth-century evidence of the significance of royal patronage and royal interest in their preservation.

2 Laws

There is an extremely large corpus of distinctively Welsh legal material produced in the late medieval period, in a large number of manuscripts. This falls, very broadly, into three classes of manuscript now known (after Aneurin Owen's classification as Venedotian, Gwentian and Dimetian Codes) as *Llyfr Iorwerth*, *Llyfr Cyfnerth* and *Llyfr Blegywryd*, after — in the two latter cases — jurists named in the prologues, and — in the first — the thirteenth-century lawyer probably responsible for part of the compilation; there is, nevertheless, considerable overlap in the content of these and some overlap in form, and the groups are clearly not entirely independent, especially with respect to the law of land and women.[22] There are about 40 medieval Welsh texts of the laws and a further five medieval Latin texts. Until recently it was believed that the earliest manuscript was in fact a Latin one, that known as Redaction A, from NLW Peniarth MS 28. Since Mr Huws has now demonstrated that this belongs to the thirteenth century, it is clear that it is not even the earliest of the Latin texts, none of which are definitely earlier than the earliest Welsh texts (such as BL MS Cotton Caligula A iii).[23] The process of compilation of law tracts was traditionally attributed to Hywel Dda in the mid-tenth century, and most of the texts carry a prologue pointing out his responsibility, some elaborating the circumstances of his initiative and the instructions that he gave to his most skilled lawyers and clergy. This is not to imply that it was regarded as legislation in the modern sense: Hywel's rôle was to stimulate the collection and rationalization of existing customary practice; and occasionally to prune and improve.

It is perfectly clear that Welsh law had a practical relevance in the late medieval period and that a high proportion of law texts were copied in order to assist lawyers in carrying out their business. The extant corpus does not survive, therefore, merely because of antiquarian interest in an archaic system. It is also clear that the total range of this material, with all its variations, cannot be attributable to the initiative of Hywel, quite apart from the absence of reference to it before the twelfth century. We are therefore confronted with the problem of the existence of a late medieval corpus of law, whose origins were supposed to lie in the distant past, and with the problem of the relationship of this corpus to a real or supposed body of law current in the pre-Conquest period.

It would be ridiculous to suppose that there was no sort of pre-Conquest origin for Welsh law. The existence of thirteenth-century texts, dependent upon earlier exemplars, bears witness to the currency of established and complex legal relationships and concepts in the twelfth century; incidental references to distinctive procedures, such as those found in *Liber Landavensis*, in 'Braint Teilo', and in the Hereford section of *Domesday Book*, indicate that they were current by the eleventh century and sometimes earlier;[24] and those parts of the texts which appear archaic in twelfth-century and later contexts, such as the passage on the seven bishop-houses of Dyfed, are very difficult to explain in anything other than a pre-twelfth-century context.[25] Some part of the practices recorded in the extant texts must have had an earlier relevance and application. The problem lies in establishing what part. At present there is no easily available method of disentangling the later from the earlier and this means that the law texts as such are not useful as evidence for the pre-Conquest period.

It might be expected that even if we have no secular legislation some ecclesiastical legislation might survive since, in ecclesiastical matters, Wales belonged to a wider European association. Canons from church councils survive from many parts of early medieval Europe and it is notable that Ireland produces a particularly rich collection in the eighth-century 'Collectio Canonum Hibernensis'.[26] Unfortunately no Welsh canons survive (the so-called 'Canones Wallici' are of Breton origin) but there is some ecclesiastical material which belongs in an associated category. This is the group of four short Latin penitentials which prescribe penances for sins committed: the 'Preface on Penance' attributed to Gildas, the 'Book of David', and the decrees from the 'Synod of North Britain' and the 'Synod of the Grove of Victory'. In fact neither date nor provenance can be ascertained with precision; the texts occur in two continental compilations of (largely Irish) penitential material of the ninth and tenth centuries respectively, Cambrai MS 625 and Paris, Bibl.Nat.Lat.3182, the latter of Breton origin.[27] The suggestion that these are sixth-century texts is entirely reasonable since they lack many of the characteristics and the severity of the more developed Irish penitentials of the late sixth and seventh centuries.[28] The suggestion that they are Welsh rests essentially on their association with saints Gildas and David and with synods celebrated in the St David's tradition; it is also a reasonable suggestion, but remains quite unproven.

One remaining piece of legal material comes from an English source, the early twelfth-century collection of Anglo-Saxon laws in Corpus Christi College Cambridge MS 383. This is a short Anglo-Saxon tract, of nine clauses, which details an agreement made between the Welsh and the people called

Dunsaete and is hence known as the 'Ordinance of the Dunsaete'. It is concerned almost entirely with arrangements for the pursuit of stolen cattle across the lands of one or the other group, and therefore has something of the character of a border treaty; it also, however, provides arrangements for an Englishman travelling on the Welsh side, and *vice-versa*, and modifies the penalties for killing. Since it refers both to the 'Wentsaete' (i.e. the inhabitants of Gwent) and to the West Saxons it is reasonable to suppose that it relates to arrangements made for the south-eastern borderlands; it was dated by Liebermann to the tenth century, on grounds of content and likely historical context. It is quite possible that it emerged as a consequence of King Athelstan's agreement with the Welsh on the river Wye in 927 but there is no conclusive evidence of this.[29]

3 Narrative Sources

There are a number of narrative sources which in some sense provide surveys of the past in early Wales. The only history is the history of the Britons (*Historia Brittonum*) attributed to one Nennius in a prologue attached to the text in some of the later manuscripts of this work; the attribution has no authority earlier than the mid-eleventh century, as David Dumville has demonstrated.[30] The original work was put together in 829 and survives in about 40 manuscripts, including BL Harleian MS 3859, along with *Annales Cambriae* and the genealogies;[31] none of the manuscripts is earlier than the eleventh century.[32] Though it is clearly intended to provide a survey of the past history of the British it is an ill-synthesized and ill-digested work; the compiler gathered together and transcribed more or less relevant documents of very different types. Its contents, therefore, are very varied, and may be briefly indicated as follows: cc.1-6, computistical work on the six ages of the world; cc.7-30, survey of the geography of Britain, origins and ancient history of the British, with recurrent interest in chronological computation (ch.16 especially), and some in European and biblical genealogy (cc.17, 18), concentrating on the Roman period from ch.19; cc.31-50, the arrival of the English and the inter-relationships of Hengest, Gwrtheyrn and St Germanus; cc.51-5, St Patrick in Ireland; ch.56, Arthur's battles; cc.57-61, genealogies of the early English kings, interspersed with some historical notes of their deeds in northern Britain; cc.62-5, regnal list of late sixth- and seventh-century English kings, together with notes of events in north Britain; ch.66, computations and list of cities of Britain; cc.67-76, the wonders of Britain and Ireland. The varied nature of this work is obvious even from a brief description of contents, though it would be reasonable to point out some consistent interest both in the recording of genealogical material, English, Welsh, biblical and other, and also in chronology (of which genealogy is presumably an aspect);[33] hence, the whole work is marked by computations which attempt to state the passage of time between events: 'From the birth of Christ until the coming of Patrick to the Irish there are 405 years. From the death of Patrick to the death of St Brigit, 60 years. From the birth of Columba to the death of Brigit there are four years', and so on. These are very occasionally related to a fixed point such as the birth of Christ, but more usually they are not; in many cases, the computation can now be demonstrated to be inaccurate.[34] Two other aspects of the compilation require comment: the chapters dealing with St Germanus (and to a lesser extent St Patrick) are distinguished by their exceptionally fabulous nature and involve much telling of wondrous tales; the chapters dealing with the English in north Britain are, by contrast, extremely terse both in their sentence structure and in their content. It is this latter material which has a close relationship with the seventh- and eighth-century section of *Annales Cambriae*, the material acquired by St David's from some north British source, and it is to be presumed that the compiler of the *Historia Brittonum* acquired his material for these chapters from the same or a nearby place. Like the Annals, it appears to derive from northern records of the seventh or eighth century.[35] It is impossible, therefore, to generalize about the value of the *Historia Brittonum.* On the one hand it provides first-hand evidence of the attitude to history writing of a Welshman of the early ninth century. On the other it presents us with edited documents of varying dates and provenances whose origins are not yet sufficiently understood; at the least, however, the latter indicates some of the materials that were available to the historian in the early ninth century.

A different type of narrative source, which nevertheless contains some survey of past history, is the work usually known as 'The Ruin and Conquest of Britain', by Gildas (*De Excidio Britanniae*). Though the work only survives in a tenth-century Canterbury manuscript (BL MS Cotton Vitellius A vi) and in two later manuscripts, it is quite clear from other evidence that Gildas was a cleric who lived in the sixth century; moreover, style and name-forms in the work would indicate a sixth-century date; it was being quoted already in the early eighth century, and substantial extracts are quoted in a ninth-century Breton manuscript.[36] There is therefore every reason to suppose this a sixth-century work, and arguments based upon internal evidence — essentially references to the contemporaneity of named individuals — would suggest a date of composition between 534 and 549, i.e. round about 540;[37] there is no real reason to question the attribution to Gildas. This work is not designed to be a history. It is, rather, a long moral tract, whose purpose is to warn the British contemporaries of the writer that they were doomed to destruction if they did not mend their ways. It is full of biblical quotations; it is written in the language of outrage.[38] Though the concern of the writer was the present and the future, he prefaced his main argument with an account of Britain, of the Roman past and of the coming of the Saxons, by way of explanation of contemporary political relationships (cc.1-26), and this therefore provides some evidence of early sixth-century historical perspective in Britain. We do not, however, know where the work was written. In later tradition Gildas was associated with north Britain and it is not impossible that the work comes from those parts. If so, it is perfectly clear that the writer was well-acquainted with Wales for most of his named contemporaries who can be identified were Welsh. Where this was written is irrelevant to our purposes, therefore, for the writer clearly had access to Welsh information. Moreover, its greatest value to us lies precisely in the comments that Gildas had to make upon his contemporaries; but the historical survey supplies a curious, and occasionally amusing, insight into sixth-century attitudes to the past. The view of the present may be biased and extreme, but it is only rarely that we have anything so personal from early medieval Wales and it is therefore of considerable value.

A third type of narrative source is the corpus of Lives of Welsh Saints. These have a pseudo-biographical form and purport to record the life, deeds and death of the saints who are their subjects, and the miracles that were performed by the saints in life and in death. Though the form is biographical, they include very little straightforward detail on the lives of their subjects and are largely composed of wondrous tales, most of which appear incredible to the modern reader and some of which appear distasteful. They belong to a genre of writing which was extremely common in Christian Europe and share the characteristics of that genre, although the types of miracle performed and the characters of the saints have their own distinctive qualities.[39] The Welsh corpus is very late in date and no Welsh Lives survive from periods before the eleventh century; much of the material in the *Historia Brittonum*, however, has a hagiographical character and may have been derived from an early Life of St Germanus.[40] Though the texts were written down in the eleventh and twelfth centuries they purport, in the main, to deal with very much earlier periods; this distant past is not usually precisely dated, but it is clear that the sixth and seventh centuries are intended because of the introduction of sixth-century characters such as Maelgwn of Gwynedd. Occasionally they refer to later chronological contexts by instancing miracles performed at the tombs of the saints in the lifetime of other known and dated persons. Now, in most cases we do not even have corroborative evidence of the existence of these saints and it is perfectly clear that the Lives do not supply us with any factual record of sixth- and seventh-century events; there are far too many chronological and logical inconsistencies for credibility. In some cases it is not impossible that some aspect of the material written down in the eleventh and twelfth centuries had an earlier origin; a tale may have been repeated over several generations before being recorded; an event may have taken place, may have been remembered, may have become the subject of an elaborated story. If so, in most cases such aspects are not definable and the principal relevance of this corpus of material is therefore for the periods in which it was written down and not for the periods to which it purports to relate. It tells us much about attitudes and something about incidentals in the eleventh and twelfth centuries: since so much of it is anecdotal, we can acquire detail about agrarian practice, or court procedure, or royal officers, quite apart from its more obvious value as evidence for moral attitudes and belief systems.

The main early collection of Welsh Saints' Lives, for there are many versions and variations produced in late medieval and modern periods,[41] is that contained in BL MS Cotton Vespasian A xiv, copied round about 1200, quite probably at Gloucester but drawing upon a Monmouth collection.[42] This includes copies of a number of Lives, as well as an ecclesiastical calendar, a Cornish glossary and the text 'De Situ Brecheniauc'. There are also three Lives (of Teilo, Dyfrig and Euddogwy) in the Book of Llandaff, written in a hand of the 1120s or 1130s. Whether or not they contain any earlier material and whatever the date of the surviving manuscripts, it is perfectly clear that most of these Lives were compiled in the twelfth century at a time when the Welsh church was coming under new influences. They are not strictly relevant, therefore, to the subject matter of this book. Two, however, belong to the late eleventh century, from a time just before and just when south Wales was receiving the Norman impact. They are therefore of exceptional importance for the very latest pre-Conquest period. These are the Lives of Cadog (*Vita Cadoci*) and of David or Dewi (*Vita S.Dauid*).

The Life of Cadog was written by Lifris, son of Bishop Herewald of Llandaff and archdeacon of Glamorgan, at some date between 1061 and 1104 and probably in the 1070s or 1080s rather than later. Lifris was also master (*magister*) of Llancarfan, the principal house of St Cadog.[43] Lifris's work is represented by cc.1, 4, 6-17, 19, 21-31, 33-39, 44[2] of the printed text of the *Vita Cadoci*, many of the rest being interpolations made in the Vespasian manuscript from a later Life of Cadog by Caradog. There are strong arguments for cc.40-44[1], 53-4, 69-70 of the printed text being of eleventh-century origin also; and cc. 55-68 are charters.[44] The Life of David was written by Rhigyfarch of Llanbadarn Fawr round about 1095. His father had been bishop of St David's twice, and it is clear that the family had sustained hereditary interests in both houses.[45]

I have sometimes cited the later Lives for their twelfth-century perspective on the past. Most of them cannot be precisely dated or provenanced, but the following suggestions were made by Wade-Evans: the Life of Brynach (*Vita Bernacii*), late twelfth century, from Nevern or a close associate; the Lives of Carannog (*Vitae Carantoci* I, II), early twelfth century, from Llangrannog or a close associate; the Lives of Cybi (*Vitae Kebii* I, II), before the late twelfth century, possibly from Llangybi in Gwent; the Life of Gwynllyw (*Vita Gundleii*), round about 1130, from Newport; the Life of Illtud (*Vita Iltuti*), round about 1140 or later, possibly from Llantwit Major; the Life of Padarn (*Vita Paterni*), about 1120, from Llanbadarn Fawr; the Life of Tatheus (*Vita Tathei*), after 1130, from Caerwent; the Life of Winifred (*Vita Wenefrede*), from the thirteenth-century manuscript BL Cotton Claudius A v, 1135-8, from Tegeingl.[46]

There are some Breton Lives of an earlier date which relate to Wales and these are considered under the section dealing with non-Welsh sources.

A final narrative source, of yet another type, is supplied by two of the works of Giraldus Cambrensis. In 1188 Giraldus travelled round the perimeter of Wales with Archbishop Baldwin on a preaching tour. He wrote an account of their journey, which includes much topographical description and many anecdotes both of the adventures they had and of stories about Wales that they heard as they went on their journey. This was published in three versions, of which the first is supposed to have been ready in 1191 (*Journey through Wales*, 63-209). He also wrote a 'Description of Wales', an early ethnographic work which attempts to describe the good and bad characteristics of the Welsh, their habits and lifestyle. The first version of this appears to have been prepared in 1193 or 1194 (*Journey through Wales*, 211-74). These are quite obviously works of the late twelfth century, pertinent to that century. They are, however, the closest we can get to a description of the land and people of Wales in the early medieval period and are therefore worthy of some attention. They are, in any case, full of detail and written with great liveliness and vigour.

4 Poems and Stories

The notes in the northern section of the *Historia Brittonum* include references to the poets who flourished in the late sixth century and it is their names that have been attached to late medieval collections of poems of varying dates, Aneirin and Taliesin especially. Most of the poetry attributed to Taliesin, therefore, has nothing to do with the sixth-century poet Taliesin. This particular case highlights the general problem for a historian who wishes to take note of the poetry. It would be simpler to treat them as a strict scholar of literature might do, that is as texts without chronological context, works of art that stand alone — outside context — as works of art. In some real sense they are timeless: many can still communicate to twentieth-century man; and many are the product of repetition over several generations, being slightly re-fashioned with each repetition, and so belong to no one period. If they are in any sense the product of the early medieval period, however, the historian cannot afford to ignore them; they say something about attitudes and values, something about mental culture; they may occasionally note events, procedures, institutions, behaviour. The problems of dating are intensified, the above problems apart, for they survive in manuscripts of the thirteenth century and later; and being almost entirely in the vernacular, their assessment also depends on consideration of the problems of linguistic change.

There can be no doubt of the early date of the two Welsh poems in the Juvencus manuscript, Cambridge University Library Ff.4.42. They are inserted into a ninth-century Welsh manuscript in a hand which is no later than the tenth century; the three stanzas of the first are clearly of ninth-century date, and the nine of the second slightly later.[47] There is also no doubt of the (later) date of the Latin poems written by Rhigyfarch, author of the Life of David, and of those written by his brother Ieuan, between 1085 and 1091, including one in Welsh, into the Corpus Christi College Cambridge manuscript of Augustine's *De Trinitate* (MS 199). Rhigyfarch wrote three poems, a short one on the Psalter, c.1079, in Trinity College Dublin MS 50; the well-known lament on the coming of the Normans, c.1094/5; and a humorous verse on a harvest eaten by mice; both of the latter are in BL MS Cotton Faustina C i. Ieuan wrote a number of two-line verses, an introductory invocation and a long poem about the life and family of his father, all in Corpus Christi College Cambridge MS 199.[48]

The rest is more complex. The corpus of vernacular poetry includes three main groups that were identified by Sir Ifor Williams as being of ultimately early origin, the songs of Aneirin, Taliesin and Llywarch the Old respectively (*Canu Aneirin, Canu Taliesin, Canu Llywarch Hen*). From the mass of later attributions, he identified in the so-called 'four ancient books of Wales', the Book of Taliesin, the Book of Aneirin, the Red Book of Hergest, and the Black Book of Carmarthen, a relatively small corpus of late sixth-/seventh-century date in the first two cases and ninth-century date in the third.[49] The subject matter of the first, a series of elegiac rhyming stanzas, more than 1,000 lines long, concerns the disastrous expedition to Catraeth (probably Catterick) of the late sixth century and forms the long poem known as *The Gododdin*.[50] (There are some interpolated stanzas which do not form a part of this poem.) It occurs in the Book of Aneirin, Cardiff MS 1, of the mid-thirteenth century, in two versions: A has thirteenth-century orthographic characteristics, while B, which is shorter, has Old Welsh orthographic features (i.e. of the ninth, tenth or eleventh century). The subject of the second collection, which consists of 12 short separate poems, concerns a number of late sixth-century heroes of north Britain and their battles, and one — Cynan — of Wales. They occur in the Book of Taliesin, NLW Peniarth MS 2, of the later thirteenth century. The subject matter of the third mostly concerns the misfortunes of another family of northern origin, Llywarch and his sons, localized in mid-Wales, though some stanzas deal with the northern hero Urien. With it are associated the stanzas known as 'Canu Heledd', which treat of another ousted family, localized in Shropshire and east Wales. These are poems of a different type, mostly three-line *englynion*, sometimes described as saga poetry, on account of the suggestion that they constituted the dialogue element in an unwritten prose narrative, thus dramatizing it. These occur in the Black Book of Carmarthen, NLW Peniarth MS 1, of c.1200, the earliest of the medieval collections, and in the Red Book of Hergest, Jesus College Welsh MS cxi, of the late fourteenth century. Much of this material, therefore, though written in Welsh, has subject matter which centres on north Britain, like the Cunedda tradition of the *Historia Brittonum*, and some of the genealogies.

The problems are these: the grounds for ascribing a sixth-/seventh-century date to *Canu Taliesin* and *Canu Aneirin* rest upon their historical and geographical consistency; upon the fact that their language was clearly archaic in the thirteenth century, and that some of their orthographic characteristics were Old Welsh; upon their unusual and complex metres.[51] The grounds for attributing *Canu Llywarch Hen* to the ninth century depend on form and content rather than language and orthography.[52] The orthodox view is that the earlier poems were orally transmitted for at least two centuries, then written down and copied; the present texts therefore contain both oral and scribal corruptions, and *some* interpolations are obvious. It is proposed, then, that they are at the least an amalgam of sixth- to ninth-century material, and possibly sixth- to eleventh-century. No-one, therefore, really suggests that they were unchanged since the late sixth century, although it is customary to refer to them as late sixth-/seventh-century poems; (hence, K.H. Jackson can comment that though he makes no claim that 'the Book of Aneirin is the *ipsissima verba* of Aneirin as they stand' it is 'a modernised and corrupted version of them which nevertheless preserves the essential character and contents, and *broadly speaking* [my italics] the wording, of his work', and T.M. Charles-Edwards writes that 'the historical arguments suggest that the poem is the authentic work of Aneirin... but that we cannot... establish the wording of the original').[53] Whatever the date of origin of these poems, therefore, they cannot possibly be used as evidence of anything earlier than the ninth century; there remains, in any case, considerable chronological insecurity. The original date of these and *Canu Llywarch Hen*, and the circumstances of their transmission, are in any case disputed: some modern scholars have recently pointed out that there is no linguistic argument against a ninth- or tenth-century date and no palaeographic argument against a ninth-, tenth- or eleventh-century date.[54] The matter remains exceptionally uncertain in many respects.

There are other poems which are also generally agreed to be of pre-

Conquest date, though occurring in later manuscripts. These include the lament for Cynddylan, assigned a date in the early seventh century on linguistic and orthographic grounds ('Marwnad Cynddylan'), [55] and nearly 100 *englynion* (mostly three-line stanzas) on the graves of the noble warriors of the past, dated by their latest commentator to the ninth or tenth centuries, on grounds of their language and metrical patterns ('Stanzas of the Graves'). The largest group (73) is to be found in the thirteenth-century Black Book of Carmarthen, though there are others in the Red Book of Hergest and NLW Peniarth MS 98B, a copy of a sixteenth-century manuscript. There is also an interesting poem in the Book of Taliesin which Sir Ifor Williams has ascribed to the ninth or tenth century on grounds of its language; it is called 'Etmic Dinbych', The Praise of Tenby, and is a poem of some 67 lines in praise of the fort at Tenby and its lord. [56] Another interesting poem from the same collection belongs to the same period, and probably more precisely to the years round about 930 when the English Athelstan was establishing himself in Cornwall, reaching agreement with the Welsh kings on the river Wye and probably making demands for tribute. [57] This is the poem called *Armes Prydein*. It is a longer work of nearly 200 lines which not merely calls upon the Welsh and their allies to unite against the English but prophesies that the day will come when the English will be expelled from the land of Britain for ever. Other prophetic poems ascribed to the poet Myrddin could be of comparable date. [58] *Armes Prydein* is dated not only on linguistic grounds, but on grounds of content, context and orthography, and its commentators produce one of the more convincing range of suggestions in the great range of chronological insecurities that surround early Welsh poetry. [59]

The vernacular literary tradition of medieval Wales includes not merely poems but prose works. Though the earliest of these contain references to archaic institutions and are almost certainly the product of some oral story-telling tradition, they equally certainly belong in the form in which they are written down to the century of Norman contact. They are therefore, strictly speaking, outside the period of interest of this book. I have occasionally, however, averted to their contents and it would be foolish to ignore their existence.

The earliest of the prose tales appear to be those known as the 'Four Branches of the Mabinogi', popularly *The Mabinogion*, and the separate tale of 'Culhwch and Olwen'. In fact, the date of their composition is much disputed between c.1060, Sir Ifor Williams's preferred suggestion, and the date of the manuscripts into which they are copied. T.M. Charles-Edwards, for example, has recently argued for a date between 1050 and 1120, though E.P. Hamp has even more recently pointed out that arguments based on linguistic and phonological archaisms are irrelevant for dating purposes. [60] The Four Branches occur complete in the White Book of Rhydderch (early fourteenth-century) and the Red Book of Hergest, and include the separate tales of 'Pwyll', 'Branwen', 'Manawydan' and 'Math'. 'Culhwch ac Olwen' occurs in the same manuscripts and is generally agreed to be the earliest of all the tales. These are stories of magic and of wonders, of giants and the other world. In 'Culhwch', Culhwch has to complete tasks before marrying Olwen, the giant's daughter; in performing them he has a great variety of adventures. In the *Mabinogi*, 'tales of youth', though the hero Pryderi appears in all four of the *Mabinogi* tales, giving some semblance of unity, they are really an amalgam of different themes, elements and stories. Pwyll goes to the Other world; Branwen goes to Ireland; Manawydan goes to England; places in Gwynedd, Dyfed and Gwent are mentioned. (The best way to appreciate their varied character is, of course, to read them.) Such is the variety that there is no agreement among scholars as to their origin and their authorship. Some consider, therefore, that they represent a fusion of different elements of different provenance, a sort of synthesis of ancient story-telling traditions; others consider that they were conscious literary creations; some see an organic unity to the Four Branches while others tend to stress the disparate nature of their elements. Date and provenance, therefore, remain undetermined and pose extremely complex problems.[61]

There is one final class of material which requires consideration in the context of story material — the triads. These are classifications of people, animals and events which occur in threes. Hence, 'Three Pillars of Battle of the Island of Britain: Dunawd son of Pabo Pillar of Britain, and Gwallawg son of Lleenawg, and Cynfelyn the Leprous' (no.5); 'Arthur's Three Principal Courts: Caerleon-on-Usk in Wales, and Celliwig in Cornwall, and Penrhyn Rhionydd in the North' (no.85).[62] The triads are clearly neither poems nor stories in themselves, although sometimes explanatory narrative material is attached to them. They relate, however, to the corpus of story material since they refer frequently to characters in the tales and they therefore have something of the nature of a mnemonic device, or index to the stories, whose principal relevance lay in an oral story-telling context. (Triads also occur in some of the law texts, where it may be considered that they also had a mnemonic significance but one relevant to the learned profession of lawyers and to the oral practice of the law.) The earliest collection of triads is copied into the thirteenth-century NLW Peniarth MS 16, although allusions of triadic type are to be found in some of the earliest Welsh poetry. R. Bromwich has demonstrated — on grounds of content — that the manuscript transmission of the triads must go back to the early twelfth century, and that it is likely that somewhere in south Wales was the place of redaction of the 'Early Version'; she has also produced a strong argument for the existence of some of the triads in oral form as early as the ninth or tenth century, based essentially on the fact that some early twelfth-century characters and elements were substituted for those of the native tradition. Although, therefore, the collections of triads in their present form belong to a period outside the interest of this book, it is not impossible that some of their elements were in oral circulation during the tenth and eleventh centuries. They could not, of course, be taken as they stand as tenth- or eleventh-century evidence.

5 Scholarly and Liturgical Writings

There remain some written materials produced in Wales, or by Welshmen, in the pre-Conquest period, mostly in the vernacular, which may most conveniently be classified as scholarly writings. These are bits and pieces which provide good evidence of the intellectual interests of some Welshmen at this time, interests which are often notably different from those which surface in the post-Conquest vernacular collections discussed above. These fragments are also often exceptionally important for the study of the Welsh language. Apart, however, from the insight that they afford into the intellectual pre-occupations of learned men, they supply relatively little information about events, persons or institutions.

There is, firstly, an extremely curious Latin text, glossed in Welsh, called by its editor 'De Raris Fabulis' (Colloquy). This takes the form of a colloquy, a schoolroom exercise in dialogue form, whose purpose was to provide practice in the exercise of the Latin language and in vocabulary. It therefore commonly provides alternatives for the words it uses and this makes it read very oddly if treated as a straightforward piece of dialogue. Hence, for example, it runs 'Go to the river, or to the spring, or to the well, and bring the clear water... I was reared, or brought up, in Ireland, or Britain, or Frankia'. It is also heavily glossed with Welsh equivalents, particularly for nouns. The content of the dialogue takes the form of scenes from daily life — getting up in the morning, going on a journey, visiting neighbours, and so on. This work occurs in the manuscript known as Oxoniensis Posterior, Bodleian MS 572, and is written in a hand of the tenth century. It is likely that it was written by a Cornishman, but since there are Welsh words both within the text and as glosses it would appear to be Welsh in origin.[63]

The Welsh glosses of the Colloquy provide ample evidence of the linguistic interests of Brittonic scholars in the tenth century. We possess other manuscripts which are similarly glossed.[64] The Cambridge Juvencus, Cambridge University Library Ff.4.42, which contains the earliest copy of poems in the vernacular, is also glossed in Welsh (and Irish and Latin) in a number of hands of the ninth and first half of the tenth centuries.[65] The Cambridge Martianus Capella, Corpus Christi College MS 153, has Welsh glosses assigned to the ninth century.[66] Part of Oxoniensis Prior, Bodleian MS Auct.F.4.32, also known as 'St Dunstan's Classbook', is a manuscript of the *Ars Amatoria* of Ovid and has ninth- to tenth-century glosses.[67] A ninth-century manuscript from the Vatican of Boethius's *De Consolatione Philosophiae*, Vat. Lat.3363, copied at Fleury, has glosses in a Welsh hand of the second half of the ninth century.[68] The great value of this material, apart from its obvious significance for the study of the language, lies in the insight it provides into the Welsh understanding of the meaning of Latin and in the range of vernacular terms that it suggests as equivalents. Its potential has yet to be fully realized.

Presumably from the same school of interests come a few short pieces of miscellaneous content. One part of Oxoniensis Prior, Bodleian MS Auct.F.4.32, is the so-called 'Liber Commonei'. This appears to have been put together at about 820 and contains the 'Alphabet of Nemnivus' (a Latin text with Welsh names for the letters of the alphabet), a Latin 19-year cycle with some calculations on the phases of the moon, and some Latin notes on weights and measures, glossed in Welsh in a ninth-century hand.[69] There is more work on the calendar, this time in Welsh, in a fragment known as the Computus fragment, in Cambridge University Library MS Add.4543. It has been assigned to the early tenth century.[70] These pieces supply further evidence of the interest in computation and chronology which is so clear in the *Historia Brittonum*.

The surviving liturgical works do not really fall into the same category, although they give some indication of a different sort of learned interest. There are two from Wales, and both belong to the very end of the period here considered. The collection of Welsh Saints' Lives possibly made at Gloucester and copied c.1200 into BL MS Vespasian A xiv, also includes a calendar of saints of the type commonly produced as an index of festivals to be celebrated in church services.[71] This was compiled at sometime after 1080, apparently in Monmouth priory, before being copied at Gloucester. Its latest item cannot have been added until 1175 and it includes a Welsh saint who died in 1124 (Caradog). It also had additions made contemporary with the manuscript. It is very brief: it has 84 commemorations, 30 of these relating to the festivals of Welsh or Irish saints. All of those who are not represented in the Lives, except ?Gwynnog (in the forms Winnocus *and* Tauanaucus) and Caradog appear to have been borrowed from a St David's calendar and are local to south-west Wales. It cannot have been produced for strictly liturgical purposes since it omits mention of a number of feasts that must have been celebrated in a priory of that type in the twelfth century. It was presumably compiled for what K. Hughes called 'pseudo-historical purposes', that is, it represents some aspect of research into Welsh saints, almost certainly of twelfth-century origin.[72] If it is any reflection of cult, therefore, it can only represent local cult round Monmouth, c.1200, and local cult near St David's between 1080 and 1200. Its value for our purposes is therefore very limited.

The other is the Martyrology of Rhigyfarch (or Ricemarch), the author of the Life of David, Trinity College Dublin MS 50 (A.4.20). This was written for Rhigyfarch by Ithael, and illustrated by his brother Ieuan (Iohannes), between 1064 and 1082, probably c.1079.[73] It is an abbreviated recension of the Hieronymian Martyrology, and shows virtually no Welsh influence — apart from the inclusion of saints Padarn and Samson, which may equally be explained by Breton influence. It does not include the feast of David. The same manuscript contains a psalter.

6   Non-Welsh Sources

Notice of events, developments and persons in early medieval Wales is not confined to Welsh sources, and though such notice is usually brief and incidental it is sometimes of great importance in signalling items of which we have no other indication. These sources are fully discussed in their own proper contexts and most need only a brief mention here. English sources include the detailed narrative history of the English conversion by Bede, completed in 731 (*Historia Ecclesiastica*); the annals of the *Anglo-Saxon Chronicle*, compiled in the late ninth century at or near the court of the West Saxon kings, from material at least as old as the eighth century (*ASC*); the biography of King Alfred written by Asser in the late ninth century (*Life of King Alfred*); and the survey of fiefs and fiscal obligations undertaken by the English in 1086 for the kingdom of England (*Domesday Book*). The Life is in some sense Welsh for Asser was a Welsh cleric from St David's attracted to King Alfred's court because of the quality of his scholarship. Though the work is largely about English matters, and draws in part upon English annals, it has a little information about Wales and is in any case witness to the cultural sophistication of the St David's school. The text of Asser's work is known only from an early modern copy; arguments against its authenticity were amply considered and countered by W.H. Stevenson in his edition of the work but have been more recently and even more forcibly rejected by D. Whitelock. *Domesday Book* contains valuable information on the borders and eastern parts of Wales, because of early Norman penetration there.[74]

Notable among Irish sources are the Irish annals, preserved in late medieval and modern manuscripts in a range of different versions, of which the most valuable collection for us is the set which goes under the title of *Annals of Ulster*. It is likely that Irish annal-keeping began with an Iona chronicle in the seventh century which was transferred to the mainland in the mid-eighth century and thereafter variously augmented and elaborated.[75] Also useful for early Welsh religious history is the early eighth-century collection of canonical material known as 'Collectio Canonum Hibernensis'; and the martyrologies of the late eighth to ninth century.[76]

There is a corpus of Breton Saints' Lives, material of the same general type as the Welsh Lives but with a stronger biographical and often less miraculous slant.[77] They are also of earlier date. Their significance for this work is that many of the saints they celebrate were supposed to have had a Welsh origin. It is clear that there were contacts between Brittany and Wales in the early medieval period — as demonstrated by the sharing of cult and transmission of manuscripts — and it is therefore nor unreasonable to suppose that Breton authors had information about Wales, whatever the historicity of their hagiographical subjects. In fact, in most cases the amount of reference to Wales is slight and its nature is generalized but a large part of the earliest Life, the first Life of Samson, is about Wales (*Vita Samsonis*). This exists in an early eleventh-century manuscript, Metz Bib.mun.195, and its date has been the subject of considerable controversy. The prologue announces that it was written on the basis of information supplied to the writer in Brittany by a very old man who had been approximately contemporary with Samson, supplemented with information from the saint's mother transmitted through his uncle. This implies an early seventh-century date, since Samson is known to have been alive in Brittany in the mid-sixth century. The seventh-century date was questioned by the Life's editor, Fawtier, who argued for the ninth century, and supplementary arguments have recently been brought forward by J-C. Poulin.[78] Fawtier's case was powerfully attacked by Duine shortly after publication, in favour of the seventh century, and in the light of early name forms and the strong contrast between this work and the known corpus of ninth-century Lives, I am still persuaded by the argument for the seventh century.[79]

The remaining Lives cited in this book are those of Paul, Guénolé, Machutes and Gildas. The Life of Paul was written by Wrmonoc at Landévennec in west Brittany in 884, and survives in manuscripts of the tenth and late eleventh to twelfth centuries (*Vita Pauli*). The Life of Guénolé also comes from Landévennec, was written c.880 by the abbot Wrdisten, and survives in manuscripts of the tenth and later centuries (*Vita Winwaloei*). The first Life of Machutes (Malo) dates from the ninth century and is presumably of east Breton origin, from S. Malo or its neighbourhood; its manuscripts are of the twelfth and fifteenth centuries (*Vita Machutis*). The first Life of Gildas was written in the eleventh century by a monk of Rhuys, on the southern coast of Brittany; the manuscript does not survive, but was described in the early seventeenth century as 'very old' (*Vita Gildae*).

7 Place-Names and Language

Considerable insight into the past can be provided by a study of the names of places; the meaning of a settlement name may indicate something about its foundation or something about the character of an earlier landscape; knowledge of fashions in naming may indicate a chronology of development; appreciation of the language of a name may indicate foreign influences. The Scandinavian names of the islands of Gateholm and Grassholm and Ramsey, of the town of Swansea (probably meaning 'Sweyn's island'), point to Viking influence in Wales, even if it is not yet fully understood; the element *llan* frequently points to the presence of a church, or of an ecclesiastical influence. Knowledge of the modern name of a place is not sufficient, however, and it is important to collect and analyse all early forms of a name before proceeding to make historical deductions based upon them. Unfortunately, the place-names of Wales have not yet received the systematic treatment accorded by the English Place-Name Society to the place-names of England and it is therefore only rarely possible to use place-name evidence in a book such as this. There are a few useful recent studies of small areas; and some older, general surveys, of limited value.[80] However, immense work of collection and analysis was begun by the late M. Richards and some of the results of his labour are available in a miscellany of articles on different elements, in his comments on the names of towns and cities, and in the invaluable *Welsh Administrative and Territorial Units*.[81] We must hope that more of his work will soon reach publication.

Just as a study of the elements of names and their combination can have a historical significance, so does the development of language itself. Words have more than one meaning, and more meaning than their lexical import at any one time. Changes in syntax, vocabulary and pronunciation may indicate something of foreign influences, of the isolation of some groups in a wider community, of the emergence of new institutions and their development. Hence the separation of Brittonic into the separate languages of Breton, Cornish, Welsh and Cumbric says something about the relationships between the peoples of western Britain and Brittany; the borrowing of Latin words into Brittonic can indicate the reception of new ideas, techniques, institutions; the emergence of a new Welsh word for king, *brenin*, in the early medieval period, points to changes in the institution of kingship. The indispensable guide to this technical and difficult but extremely important subject is K.H. Jackson's *Language and History in Early Britain*, which deals not only with language change itself but with some of the historical implications of the changes.[82]

8 Physical Evidence

The evidence of surviving monuments from the early medieval period and that provided by archaeological excavation is often of exceptional importance. The largest corpus of surviving monuments are the so-called 'early Christian monuments', stone tombstones and crosses, sometimes inscribed with a cross, sometimes inscribed with a message, sometimes decorated with ornamental carving. Although some refinements in date and classification may be suggested, another indispensable guide was provided by V.E. Nash-Williams when he published his detailed descriptive list of those known to him in the late 1940s. [83] Subsequent discoveries, of which there are a few, have been published in volumes of *Archaeologia Cambrensis*. [84] There are over 400 of these stones, broadly classified as follows: Group I, simple inscribed stones of the fifth to seventh century, of which there is a large concentration in the north-western and south-western peninsulas; Group II, cross-decorated stones of the seventh to ninth century, usually without words, particularly concentrated in the South-West; Group III, sculptured crosses and cross-slabs of the ninth to eleventh century, of which there is a greater concentration in the South-East than elsewhere; Group IV, transitional Romanesque monuments of the eleventh to thirteenth century, of which there are only 26 examples. The dating of the monuments of Group II is more open to question than that of the other groups because of the relative simplicity and paucity of identifying characteristics of the crosses inscribed upon them. (There are very few of any group in the North-East.) The language of the inscriptions is nearly always Latin, though the famous Group II stone from Tywyn (no.287) is inscribed in Welsh. [85] Though the actual language is commonly Latin, an Irish script, known as 'ogham', is sometimes used on stones of Group I. The messages vary from a simple name in the genitive, implying '[This is the stone] of N' to the exceptionally long passage on the pillar of Elise, which includes narrative and genealogy besides its commemorative message (no.182), to the record of a transaction inscribed on a stone from Merthyr Mawr (no.240). The range of information that may be gleaned from them is therefore much greater than might be expected from a simple collection of tombstones. Moreover, the decorated sculptures reveal a range of artistic influences — Scandinavian and English in particular — which bears witness to cultural contacts in the later centuries, while aspects like the form of script and type of commemorative formula — Gaulish and African/Spanish in particular — perform a similar function for the earlier centuries. The significance of these monuments cannot be over-emphasized.

Other standing monuments which belong to this period are hard to find. The greatest single item is the earthwork known as Offa's Dyke, which runs virtually along the entire border of Wales and is still impressive in its height in most of its stretches. The construction of the work was already being attributed to the eighth-century English king Offa in the late ninth century, and in the absence of any other suggestion there is no good reason to question it. The Dyke has formed the subject of an important monograph by Sir Cyril Fox, but work at present being undertaken by a new generation of archaeologists may well refine old ideas and will certainly add to our understanding of it. [86]

Apart from Offa's Dyke, there are earthworks and hut groups, many of which may belong to the early medieval period — or have been occupied then — but which cannot be associated with any precise period of construction or occupation, either because they have not been investigated or because investigation has produced insufficient evidence of date. I have noted above, where relevant, those which may be assigned to early medieval contexts.[87] The volumes produced by the Royal Commission on Ancient and Historical Monuments, Wales and Monmouthshire, published with reference to pre-1974 counties, attempt to note and describe all existing monuments, of all periods, with dating where known, and they therefore provide some guide to the possibilities. There is no published survey of the known early medieval monuments.

Understanding of these has often been considerably extended by excavation and there can be no doubt that the work of archaeologists, both now and in the past generation, does more to increase the corpus of available early medieval material than that of any other branch of scholarship. Recent sophistication of techniques, like the use of radio-carbon dating, has a particular significance for the early medievalist since it can refine and define chronological contexts in the absence of artifacts. Developments in techniques of soil and mollusc analysis offer the possibility of totally new insights into the changing landscape and economy, in addition to the familiar areas of the development of settlement, burial and religious sites. There is no general guide to the archaeology of early medieval Wales and no comprehensive guide to the archaeology of all periods, although guides to the modern administrative counties are planned. Annual reports, though brief, are, however, produced both in the periodical *Medieval Archaeology* and in the Report of the Council for British Archaeology (CBA) Group 2, entitled *Archaeology in Wales*; fuller accounts can be found in *Archaeologia Cambrensis* and the archaeology section of the *Bulletin of the Board of Celtic Studies*, in addition to those in the several local periodicals. Regular scanning of these reports at least permits acquaintance with new material and developments and is the best method of acquiring such knowledge at present.

Abbreviations

Note Places of publication are given only for works published outside the United Kingdom. In abbreviating less frequently cited periodicals the commonly accepted usage of *Soc.* for *Society*, *J.* for *Journal*, *Trans.* for *Transactions* etc. has been followed. Other abbreviations are listed below.

AC	*Annales Cambriae.* Text to 954 in E. Phillimore, 'The *Annales Cambriae* and Old Welsh genealogies', *Y Cymmrodor*, IX (1888), 152-69; thereafter in *Annales Cambriae*, ed. J. Williams ab Ithel (Rolls Series, 1860). Translated by A.W. Wade-Evans, *Nennius's 'History of the Britons'* (1938), 84-101. References here are by year of entry: i.e. *AC* 869 means *AC sub anno* 869.
AgHR	*Agricultural History Review*
Arch. Camb.	*Archaeologia Cambrensis*
Armes Prydein	*Armes Prydein*, ed. I. Williams, trans. R. Bromwich (Dublin, 1972)
ASC	*The Anglo-Saxon Chronicle*, trans. and ed. D. Whitelock with D.C. Douglas and S.I. Tucker (1961). References are by year of entry in this edition.
BAR	British Archaeological Reports, British Series
BBCS	*Bulletin of the Board of Celtic Studies*
BL	British Library
'Book of David'	'Excerpta Quedam de Libro Dauidis', in *The Irish Penitentials*, ed. L. Bieler (Dublin, 1963), 70-3. References are to clauses of the work.
'Branwen'	*Mabinogion*, 25-40, and *Branwen Uerch Lyr*, ed. D.S. Thomson (Dublin, 1961)
Bromwich, *TYP*	R. Bromwich, *Trioedd Ynys Prydein* (1961). References are by triad numbers.
BT	*Brut y Tywysogyon, Red Book of Hergest Version*, ed. and trans. T. Jones (1955); *Brut y Tywysogyon, Peniarth MS 20*, ed. T. Jones (1941); *Brut y Tywysogyon, Peniarth MS 20 Version*, trans. T. Jones (1952). References are to years A.D.
CBA Res. Rep.	Council for British Archaeology Research Report
Canu Aneirin	*Canu Aneirin*, ed. I. Williams (1938); trans. K. Jackson, *The Gododdin* (1969). References are to the stanzas of the translation.
'Canu Heledd'	*Canu Llywarch Hen*, 33-48; trans. J. Clancy, *The Earliest Welsh Poetry* (1970), 79-86. References are to page numbers of the translation.
Canu Llywarch Hen	*Canu Llywarch Hen*, ed. I. Williams (1935); trans. J. Clancy, *The Earliest Welsh Poetry* (1970), 65-78, 92-7, and also P.K. Ford, *The Poetry of Llywarch Hen* (Berkeley, Cal., 1974). References are to page numbers of Clancy's translation.
Canu Taliesin	*Canu Taliesin*, ed. I. Williams (1960); edition (but not poems) translated by J. Caerwyn Williams (Dublin, 1968); poems partly translated by J. Clancy, *The Earliest Welsh Poetry* (1970), 23-32,

and no.I by I.Ll. Foster in *Prehistoric and Early Wales*, ed. I.Ll. Foster and G. Daniel (1965), 229-30. References are to numbers of the poems in Williams's edition.

Colloquy — 'De Raris Fabulis', Oxford, Bodleian MS 572, in *Early Scholastic Colloquies*, ed. W. Stevenson (1929), 1-11.

'Culhwch' — *Mabinogion*, 95-136; and J.G. Evans (ed.), *The White Book Mabinogion* (1907), 226-54.

Davies, *Early Welsh Microcosm* — W. Davies, *An Early Welsh Microcosm* (1978).

De Excidio Britanniae — Gildas, *The Ruin of Britain*, ed. and trans. M. Winterbottom (1978); and in *Chronica Minora Saec. IV. V. VI.VII*, III, ed. T. Mommsen (MGH AA xiii, Berlin, 1898), 1-110.

ECMW — V.E. Nash-Williams, *The Early Christian Monuments of Wales* (1950).

HG — Harleian Genealogy

Hist. Brittonum — *Historia Brittonum* in *Chronica Minora Saec. IV. V. VI. VII*, III, ed. T. Mommsen (MGH AA xiii, Berlin, 1898), 111-222; trans. A.W. Wade-Evans, *Nennius's 'History of the Britons'* (1938), 35-84, 114-21.

Hist. Ecclesiastica — Bede, *Historia Ecclesiastica Gentis Anglorum*, ed. C.Plummer (1896); *Bede's Ecclesiastical History of the English People*, ed. and trans. B. Colgrave and R.A.B. Mynors (1969).

Journey through Wales — Gerald of Wales, *The Journey through Wales, The Description of Wales*, trans. L. Thorpe (1978); and *Giraldi Cambrensis Opera*, VI, ed. J.F. Dimock (Rolls Series, 1868).

Lib. Land. — *The Text of the Book of Llan Dâv*, ed. J.G. Evans with J. Rhys (1893). References are by charter number, which are also the page numbers of this edition.

Life of King Alfred — *Asser's Life of King Alfred*, ed. W.H. Stevenson (1904)

Llyfr Blegywryd — *Cyfreithiau Hywel Dda yn ôl Llyfr Blegywryd*, ed. S.J. Williams and J.E. Powell (1942); *The Laws of Hywel Dda (The Book of Blegywryd)*, trans. M. Richards (1954). References are to the page numbers of the translation.

Mabinogion — *The Mabinogion*, trans. G. and T. Jones (1949); and *Pedeir Keinc y Mabinogi*, ed. I. Williams (1951). References are to page numbers of the translation.

'Manawydan' — *Mabinogion*, 41-54.

'Math' — *Mabinogion*, 55-75.

'Marwnad Cynddylan' — *Canu Llywarch Hen*, 50-2; trans. J. Clancy, *The Earliest Welsh Poetry* (1970), 87-9. References are to the translation.

Med. Arch. — *Medieval Archaeology*

'Ordinance of the Dunsaete' — *Die Gesetze der Angelsachsen*, ed. F. Liebermann (3 vols., Halle, 1903-16), I, 374-9;trans. in B. Thorpe, *Ancient Laws and Institutes of England*, I (1840), 353-7. References are to clauses of the tract.

NLW — National Library of Wales

'Preface on Penance' — 'Praefatio Gildae de Poenitentia', in L. Bieler, *The Irish Penitentials* (Dublin, 1963), 60-5. References are to clauses of the work.

PPS — *Proceedings of the Prehistoric Society*

'Pwyll' — *Mabinogion*, 3-24.

RCAHMW	Royal Commission on Ancient and Historical Monuments in Wales
RCAHMW *Anglesey*	RCAHMW, *Inventory of Ancient Monuments in Wales and Monmouthshire, Anglesey* (1937)
RCAHMW *Caernarvon*	RCAHMW, *Inventory of Ancient Monuments in Wales and Monmouthshire, Caernarvonshire* (3 vols., 1956-64).
RCAHMW *Glamorgan*	RCAHMW, *Inventory of Ancient Monuments in Wales and Monmouthshire, Glamorgan*, I pts 1 and 3 (1976).
RCAHMW *Radnor*	RCAHMW, *Inventory of Ancient Monuments in Wales and Monmouthshire, Radnor* (1913)
VCH *Hereford*	*Victoria History of the County of Hereford*, I, ed. W. Page (1908).
V. Bernacii	*Vitae Sanctorum Britanniae*, 2-14.
V. Cadoci	*Vitae Sanctorum Britanniae*, 24-140.
V. Carantoci	*Vitae Sanctorum Britanniae*, 142-8.
V. Gundleii	*Vitae Sanctorum Britanniae*, 172-92.
V. Iltuti	*Vitae Sanctorum Britanniae*, 194-232.
V. Kebii	*Vitae Sanctorum Britanniae*, 234-50.
V. Machutis	'La plus ancienne vie de S. Malo', in F. Lot, *Mélanges d'histoire Bretonne* (Paris, 1907), 294-329.
V. Paterni	*Vitae Sanctorum Britanniae*, 252-68.
V. Pauli	'Vie de S. Paul de Lèon en Bretagne', ed. C. Cuissard, *Revue Celtique*, v (1881-3), 413-60.
V. Samsonis	*La Vie de S. Samson*, ed. R. Fawtier (Paris, 1912); trans. T. Taylor (1925).
Vitae Sanctorum Britanniae	*Vitae Sanctorum Britanniae et Genealogiae*, ed. A.W. Wade-Evans (1944).
V.S. Dauid	*Rhigyfarch's Life of St David*, ed. J.W. James (1967); trans. A.W. Wade-Evans, *Y Cymmrodor*, xxiv (1913), 1-73.
V. Tathei	*Vitae Sanctorum Britanniae*, 270-86.
V. Wenefrede	*Vitae Sanctorum Britanniae*, 288-308.

Notes

1 Land, Landscape and Environment

1. E.G. Bowen (ed.), *Wales, a Physical, Historical and Regional Geography* (1957), 267-9.
2. *Ibid.*, 19-28.
3. *Journey through Wales*, 182.
4. *Ibid.*, 96f.
5. D.Thomas (ed.), *Wales, a New Study* (1977), 36-59. The point was emphasized by J.A.Taylor in his survey of the evolution of the physical environment of Wales at a conference on the making of the Welsh landscape held in Cardiff in March 1980.
6. E.Le Roy Ladurie, *Times of Feast, Times of Famine: A History of Climate since the Year 1000* (1972), 290f.
7. Cf. P.J.Ucko, R.Tringham and G.W.Dimbleby (eds.), *Man, Settlement and Urbanism* (1972), 239.
8. Thomas, *op. cit.*, 57f.
9. J.Taylor, 'The role of climatic factors in environmental and cultural changes in prehistoric times', in *The Effect of Man on the Landscape: The Highland Zone*, ed. J.G.Evans, S.Limbrey and H.Cleere (CBA Res.Rep.11, 1975); H.H.Lamb, *Climate, Present, Past and Future*, II (1977), 402, 424-40.
10. H.H.Lamb, *Climate, Present, Past and Future*, I (1972), 236; II, 424, 428.
11. *Ibid.*, II, 427.
12. P.J.Fowler, 'Lowland landscapes: culture, time and *Personality*', in *The Effect of Man on the Landscape: the Lowland Zone*, ed. S.Limbrey and J.G.Evans (CBA Res.Rep.21, 1978), 5; Taylor, *op. cit.*
13. *Britannia*, IX (1978), 406f. A fuller report was delivered by the excavator, Richard White, at the Society of Antiquaries, London, in December 1979 and there is a monograph forthcoming, to be published by the Cambrian Archaeological Association. Doubts have been expressed about the date of the last phase of occupation of this site, since it produces no post-Roman material, and the interpretation of the changes in fossil fauna is controversial. I am most grateful to Mr White for discussing the matter with me. (At Tregaron, on the other hand, there appear to have been centuries of unbroken pastoral use before change to arable in the late twelfth century: J.Turner, 'The anthropogenic factor in vegetational history', *New Phytologist*, LXIII (1964), 73-90.
14. *Canu Llywarch Hen*, 76f.
15. *Ibid.*, 95f.
16. *AC* 1047.
17. *Canu Aneirin*, B4; *V.Cadoci*, ch.44; *V.S.Dauid*, ch.38; *V.Iltuti*, ch.13; *V.S.Dauid*, cc.33, 34.
18. Thomas, *op. cit.*, 59-65; Taylor, *op. cit.*, 14-19. The classic view is that an originally dense post-glacial forest cover — containing oak, alder, birch, elm, pine — was gradually virtually eradicated by the effects of prehistoric agriculture and/or climatic change, while there was subsequently some reversion in the 'dark ages'. (Controversy persists over whether man or climate was more significant in determining vegetational change.) Hence, the great elm decline beginning c.3000 B.C. is the most noted of the changes and generally preceded fluctuation of the other species. Elm decline was accompanied by pine decline, for example, at Tregaron in the Teifi valley; and at an elevation of 1575 feet at Lake Glaslyn north of Pumlumon pollen analysis would indicate relatively open and variably extensive woodland cover,

dominated by oak, alder and hazel — with subsidiary elm, pine, birch and lime. Recent work in Wales, however, has suggested that there may well have been considerable regional variation in original forest cover: hence, there was more alder in the North than in the South-West; and the absence of large tree stumps in the peat may indicate no original forest cover in some areas (A.G.Smith and J.Taylor at the Cardiff meeting of the Society for Landscape Studies, March 1980). These variables, together with the variation in the rates of man's activity, therefore, make it very difficult to generalize about forest clearance in the early medieval period. There is an admirable survey of the range of variables in W.Linnard, 'The history of forests and forestry in Wales up to the formation of the Forestry Commission' (Ph.D. thesis, University of Wales, 1979), 1-55.

19. H.C.Darby and I.S.Maxwell (eds.), *The Domesday Geography of Northern England* (1962), 390.
20. *Journey through Wales*, 187, 194.
21. *Ibid.*, 139.
22. *Ibid.*, 150f.
23. *Armes Prydein*, 1.87; *De Excidio Britanniae*, cc.3, 25.
24. *Canu Llywarch Hen*, 92, 93.
25. *Ibid.*, 92; I.Williams, *The Beginnings of Welsh Poetry*, ed. and trans. R.Bromwich (1972), 101f.; *Canu Taliesin*, II.
26. *V.Tathei*, ch.16; *V.S.Dauid*, ch.35; *V.Iltuti*, cc.4, 6, 13; *V.Cadoci*, cc.12, 24.
27. Darby and Maxwell (eds.), *op. cit.*, 389f.
28. *V.Samsonis*, ch.26.
29. Davies, *Early Welsh Microcosm*, 28-32; *idem, The Llandaff Charters* (1979), 143f.
30. *V.Iltuti*, ch.6; 'Manawydan', 43; *V.Cadoci*, cc.7, 8; *V.Iltuti*, ch.20.
31. *De Excidio Britanniae*, cc.11, 20; cf. *V.Iltuti*, ch.19, and *V.Cadoci*, ch.24.
32. *Canu Llywarch Hen*, 75, 92, 97; *Canu Aneirin*, B39, A3, B36; *V.S.Dauid*, ch.38; *Hist. Brittonum*, prol.; *V.Cadoci*, ch.62; *V.Tathei*, ch.16; *V.Illtuti*, ch.18.
33. *Canu Llywarch Hen*, 92, 93, 94, 96; *Canu Aneirin*, A26, B38, A62, B17; 'Canu Heledd', 79; *V.Cadoci*, ch.8; *V.S.Dauid*, ch.38; 'Math', 68; *Canu Llywarch Hen*, 94, 97; *Canu Aneirin*, A57.
34. W.Linnard, 'Trees in the Law of Hywel': paper delivered at the Welsh Law Colloquium, Bangor, March 1979; cf. Linnard, thesis, 43-51.
35. Davies, *Early Welsh Microcosm*, 30.
36. R.White, 'Cefn Graeanog': lecture delivered to the Society of Antiquaries, London, December 1979.
37. *Canu Llywarch Hen*, 77; *V.Cadoci*, cc.24, 43; *V.S.Dauid*, ch. 38; *V.Cadoci*, ch.21; *Lib. Land.*, xlv; Davies, *Early Welsh Microcosm*, 30.
38. *ECMW, passim* and no.73, p.407; see below, p.217.
39. See below, pp.218f.
40. Davies, *Early Welsh Microcosm*, 32.
41. *Journey through Wales*, 114f.; personal comment from Jeremy Knight.
42. *V.Cadoci*, ch.12; *Canu Llywarch Hen*, 69f.
43. *V.Samsonis*, cc.3, 26.
44. Colloquy, cc. 19, 23.
45. *V.Iltuti*, ch.23.
46. *De Excidio Britanniae*, ch.67.
47. *V.S.Dauid*, ch.44; *V.Cadoci*, cc.22, 24.
48. *Journey through Wales*, 220.
49. *V.Cadoci*, ch.58; Colloquy, ch.15; *Hist. Brittonum*, cc.32, 34; *V.Iltuti*, ch.11; *V. Tathei*, ch.17.
50. See below, p.165f; *Llyfr Blegywryd*, 113; *Journey through Wales*, 236f.
51. *V.Samsonis*, ch.26; *Life of King Alfred*, ch.79; *V.Iltuti*, ch.21; *V.Cadoci*, prol., ch.12.
52. Davies, *Early Welsh Microcosm*, 30f.
53. *V.S.Dauid*, ch.41; *V.Cadoci*, ch.9.
54. *Ibid.*, ch.22; Davies, *Early Welsh Microcosm*, 30.
55. *V.Cadoci*, ch.28 (Giraldus forded the river Taff: *Journey through Wales*, 121); *Journey through Wales*, 182.
56. *V.Cadoci*, ch.44; *Journey through Wales*, 130.
57. *Ibid.*, 196.
58. *Ibid.*, 182; *CBA Group 2 Report*,

xv (1975), 65; Davies, *Early Welsh Microcosm*, 30.

59.   *V.S.Dauid*, cc.37, 39, 45; *V.Cadoci*, cc.10, 27; *V.Iltuti*, ch.24; *V.Gundleii*, ch.12; cf. *Hist. Brittonum*, ch.52.

60.   *V.S.Dauid*, ch.39; *V.Cadoci*, ch.22; *V.Iltuti*, ch.24.

61.   *De Excidio Britanniae*, ch.23 (cf. *Canu Aneirin*, B3); *AC* 1044, 1052; *V.Gundleii*, ch.12.

62.   *Armes Prydein*, l.161.

63.   *V.Cadoci*, ch.10; *V.Iltuti*, ch.22; *De Excidio Britanniae*, ch.19; *V.Kebii*, ch.15.

64.   *Journey through Wales*, 252.

65.   *Canu Llywarch Hen*, 96; *De Excidio Britanniae*, ch.25; *V.Tathei*, ch.3; *V.Gundleii*, ch.12; *V.Cadoci*, ch.22; *V.S.Dauid*, ch.3; M.Lapidge, 'The Welsh-Latin poetry of Sulien's family', *Studia Celtica*, VIII-IX (1973-4), 68-106.

66.   *V.Cadoci*, ch.29; *V.S.Dauid*, cc.37, 39.

67.   E.G.Bowen, *The Settlements of The Celtic Saints in Wales* (2nd edn 1956), 104-17, 125, 128, 131-6; see further below, pp.25f.

68.   L.Alcock, *Dinas Powys* (1963), 26-34, 65f.; *De Excidio Britanniae*, ch.25; W.Davies, 'Roman settlements and post-Roman estates in south-east Wales', in *The End of Roman Britain*, ed. P.J.Casey (BAR 71, 1979), 154; L.Alcock, 'Dark age objects of Irish origin from the Lesser Garth Cave, Glamorgan', *BBCS*, XVIII (1958-60), 221, 226; *idem*, 'Pottery and settlements in Wales and the March, A.D.400-700', in *Culture and Environment*, ed. I.Ll.Foster and L.Alcock (1963), 298f.; A.H.A.Hogg, 'Native settlement in Wales', in *Rural Settlement in Roman Britain*, ed. C.Thomas (1966), 38; *Britannia*, IX (1978), 406f; cf. L.Laing (ed.), *Studies in Celtic Survival* (1977), 57-60; RCAHMW Glamorgan, I pt 1, 15-20.

69.   Davies, 'Roman settlements', 153-61.

70.   *Journey through Wales*, 251f.

71.   'Manawydan', 43; *V.Gundleii*, ch.1; *V.Cadoci*, ch.24; *V.Iltuti*, ch.11.

72.   *V.Gundleii*, ch.15; Davies, *Early Welsh Microcosm*, 123.

73.   Bowen, *Settlements of the Celtic*

Saints, 146-59.

74.   *V.Cadoci*, cc.1, 21, 41.

75.   See below, pp.43-6; G.R.Jones, 'Post-Roman Wales', in *The Agrarian History of England and Wales*, I pt 2, ed. H.P.R.Finberg (1972), 339, 341f.; Professor Jones emphasized his point in a paper read to the Cardiff meeting of the Society for Landscape Studies, March 1980.

76.   C.A.Smith, 'A morphological analysis of late prehistoric and Romano-British settlements in north-west Wales', *PPS*, LX (1974), 157-69.

77.   Cf. the valuable comments of P.Smith in Ucko, Tringham and Dimbleby, *op.cit.*, 409.

78.   *Llyfr Blegywryd*, 77.

79.   *Hist. Brittonum*, ch.34; *V.S.Dauid*, cc.16, 17; *V.Cadoci*, ch.23.

80.   'Branwen'; 'Manawydan', 41; *De Excidio Britanniae*, ch.66; Colloquy, ch.14.

81.   *Hist. Brittonum*, cc.34, 40; cf. Jones, *op.cit.*, 359-64.

82.   *V.Carantoci*, I.4; *V.S.Dauid*, cc.16-17; *AC* 822.

83.   L.Alcock, 'Excavations at Degannwy Castle, Caernarvonshire, 1961-6', *Arch.J.*, CXXIV (1967), 190-201.

84.   'Etmich Dinbych' in Williams, *op. cit.*, 163ff.; ll.11f., 19-21, 33-40, 48-51.

85.   Alcock, *Dinas Powys*; for a more recent view on the provenance of imported wares see C.Thomas, 'Imported Late Roman Mediterranean pottery in Ireland and western Britain: chronologies and implications', *Procs. Royal Irish Academy*, LXXVI, C(1976), 245-55.

86.   *Hist. Brittonum*, ch.42; Alcock, *Dinas Powys*, 65f.

87.   W.Gardner and H.Savory, *Dinorben* (1964), 13f., 99; but cf. Alcock, 'Pottery and settlements', 300.

88.   E.G.Bowen and C.A.Gresham, *History of Merioneth* I (1967), 164f.

89.   *BBCS*, XXVIII (1978-80), 319f.

90.   See Laing (ed.), *op. cit.*, 57-60; Jones, *op. cit.*, 293. Professor Jones has also pointed to the re-use of Roman sites in the late medieval

period as the centres of estates, like the *henllys* of the maerdref of Meliden, which sits above Roman remains; such cases may increase the likelihood of the continuous use of some sites since Roman times, though it clearly does not necessarily imply this: G.R.Jones, 'The pattern of settlement on the Welsh border', *AgHR*, VIII (1960), 66-81.

91. Davies, 'Roman settlements', 154.
92. *Idem, Early Welsh Microcosm*, 136.
93. *V.Cadoci*, ch.35.
94. *Ibid.*, cc.12, 21, 8.
95. R.White, *Early Christian Gwynedd* (1975), 10.
96. H.M.Taylor and J.Taylor, *Anglo-Saxon Architecture* (1965), II, 497-9.
97. See further below, pp.190f; cf. C.Thomas, *The Early Christian Archaeology of North Britain* (1971), 51-68; I am indebted to the Rev. Wyn Evans for many helpful discussions on early Welsh church sites; the observations on the significance of Eglwys Gymyn are essentially his.
98. *Journey through Wales*, 252; see above, p.20.
99. *V.Iltuti*, ch.8; *V.Gundleii*, cc.11, 15.
100. Smith, 'A morphological analysis'; *idem*, 'Late prehistoric and Romano-British enclosed homesteads in north-west Wales', *Arch. Camb.*, CXXVI (1977); Smith refers to his excavated examples by numbers (C828 and C1173) but gives no key — the latter is clearly Cae'rmynydd. See further below, p.36.
101. A.H.A.Hogg, 'Native settlement in Wales', in Thomas (ed.), *Rural Settlement*, 37f.
102. See above, n.13.
103. Bowen and Gresham, *op. cit.*, 146; see above, n.68; RCAHMW *Glamorgan*, I pt 1 (1976), 15-21.
104. J.L.Davies, D.B.Hague and A.H.A.Hogg, 'The hut-settlement on Gateholm, Pembrokeshire', *Arch. Camb.*, CXX (1971), 102-24; *CBA Group 2 Report*, XII (1972), 40f.; see further below, p.143.
105. 'Etmich Dinbych' and the three ninth-century Juvencus *englynion* in Williams, *op. cit.*, 163ff., 90;

Canu Llywarch Hen, 69; *Canu Aneirin*, A15, A52 etc.
106. 'Canu Heledd', 82-4.
107. 'Culhwch', 97f., 110; 'Pwyll', 5f.
108. Colloquy, ch.19.
109. *De Excidio Britanniae*, ch.27; *Hist. Brittonum*, cc.37, 46.
110. 'Culhwch', 111; 'Pwyll', 5f.; *V.Cadoci*, prol., ch.1; *V.Gundleii*, ch.3.
111. *Canu Aneirin*, A36; 'Culhwch', 111, 113, 122; *V.Tathei*, ch.11.
112. 'Preface on Penance', 1; 'Book of David', 11; Colloquy, cc.17, 22; 'Math', 63; cf. *Journey through Wales*, 237.
113. *Canu Llywarch Hen*, 96; 'Marwnad Cynddylan'.
114. 'Culhwch', 108, 109; *V.S.Dauid*, ch.28; 'Pwyll', 5f.; *Canu Aneirin*, A87; *V.Paterni*, ch.25; *V.Cadoci*, cc.17, 1, 34.
115. 'Canu Heledd', 85.
116. *V.Cadoci*, ch.5; 'Culhwch', 110f.; Colloquy, ch.1; 'Pwyll', 5f.; *Journey through Wales*, 235.
117. 'Culhwch', 110, 112, 116, 117; 'Math', 70; Colloquy, ch.19.
118. *Journey through Wales*, 238.

2 Economy

1. 'Math',68; *V.Cadoci*, ch.48.
2. *AC* 537, 547, 682, 989, 994; *De Excidio Britanniae*, ch.22; *Hist. Brittonum*, ch.64; *BT* 987, 989, 994; *V.Cadoci*, ch.7; cf. *V.Cadoci*, ch.11 and *V.Iltuti*, ch.24.
3. *Canu Taliesin*, X; cf. *V.Cadoci*, ch.30 and *De Excidio Britanniae*, ch.16.
4. *Canu Aneirin*, B4; *V.Gundleii*, ch.11.
5. *Canu Taliesin*, I, II; *De Excidio Britanniae*, ch.19.
6. 'Manawydan', 43f.; *V.Cadoci*, ch.21.
7. *Ibid.*, ch.36.
8. E.G. Bowen (ed.), *Wales, A Physical, Historical and Regional Geography* (1957), 112, 113.
9. See above, pp.6-9.
10. See above, p.11.
11. *V.S.Dauid*, ch.18; see above, p.13.
12. S.Limbrey and J.G.Evans (eds), *The Effect of Man on the Landscape: The Lowland Zone* (CBA Res.Rep.21, 1978), 82f.
13. *V.Iltuti*, cc.8-10.

14. 'Culhwch', 104, 118; 'Pwyll', 3; 'Math', 69; 'Manawydan', 42f.; cf. *V.S.Dauid*, ch.2, *V.Kebii*, ch.17, *V.Cadoci*, ch.19.

15. *De Excidio Britanniae*, ch.19; Davies, *Early Welsh Microcosm*, 35f.

16. *Canu Aneirin*, A87.

17. *V.Cadoci*, ch.24; Davies, *Early Welsh Microcosm*, 36; H.C.Darby and I.S.Maxwell (eds.), *The Domesday Geography of Northern England* (1962), 361f., 384, 389; H.C.Darby and I.B.Terrett (eds.), *The Domesday Geography of Midland England* (1954), 141f.

18. *Lib. Land.*, 174b, 183a, 225, 234, 257; Davies, *Early Welsh Microcosm*, 36.

19. *Journey through Wales*, 93, 173, 195, 198; cf. 'Manawydan', 42 and *V.S.Dauid*, ch.2.

20. Colloquy, ch.25; *V.Iltuti*, ch.10.

21. *V.S.Dauid*, cc.2, 39, 43; 'Manawydan', 42.

22. *De Excidio Britanniae*, ch.3; *V.Cadoci*, ch.9; *Journey through Wales*, 93, 102f., 187.

23. *V.Cadoci*, ch.8; *Canu Aneirin*, A40; *V.Iltuti*, cc.9,10.

24. *BT* 1022, 1063; *Armes Prydein*, 1.36; cf. *Llyfr Blegywryd*, 74.

25. 'Manawydan', 54; *Journey through Wales*, 93, 102, 194.

26. 'Preface on Penance', 1; Colloquy, ch.5.

27. L.Alcock, *Dinas Powys* (1963), 34-42.

28. 'Preface on Penance', 1, 22; 'Book of David', 11; *V.Cadoci*, cc.19, 24, 28, 29; see below, p.151.

29. *V.Samsonis*, ch.16.

30. Colloquy, cc.5, 6.

31. *Journey through Wales*, 233, 235, 236f.

32. See above, p.21.

33. A.H.A.Hogg, 'Native settlement in Wales', in *Rural Settlement in Roman Britain*, ed. C. Thomas (1966), 32; N.Johnson, 'Location of pre-medieval fields in Caernarvonshire', in *Early Land Allotment in the British Isles*, ed. H.C.Bowen and P.J.Fowler (BAR 48, 1978), 127-32.

34. C.A.Smith, 'Late prehistoric and Romano-British enclosed homesteads in north-west Wales', *Arch. Camb.*, cxxvi (1977), 38f.

35. *Idem*, 'A morphological analysis of late prehistoric and Romano-British settlements in north-west Wales', *PPS*, lx (1974), 165f.; see above, p.27.

36. Bowen and Fowler (eds.), *op. cit.*, 23-7, 119-25.

37. RCAHMW *Radnor*, 114; *Arch. Camb.*, cxvi (1967), 57-60.

38. *Med. Arch.*, xv (1971), 58-72.

39. 'Culhwch', 114.

40. *Canu Aneirin*, A43; *De Excidio Britanniae*, cc.3, 16; *V.Cadoci*, cc.11, 43, 48; *V.Iltuti*, ch.24; *V.Kebii*, ch.10; Colloquy, ch.5; *Hist. Brittonum*, pref.

41. *V.Cadoci*, ch.64; *V.S.Dauid*, ch.12.

42. Richard White, at the Society of Antiquaries, December 1979.

43. Bromwich, *TYP*, 26; *V.Gundleii*, cc.6, 15; *V.Cadoci*, ch.7; 'Culhwch', 105; *Journey through Wales*, 233.

44. *V.S.Dauid*, 12; *V.Cadoci*, ch.9.

45. 'Preface on Penance', 26; *V.Kebii*, ch.9; *V.S.Dauid*, ch.22. Cf. *Canu Llywarch Hen*, 72, 77; *Canu Aneirin*, A25, B1, B37.

46. W.Stokes, 'The Welsh glosses and verses in the Cambridge Codex of Juvencus,' *Trans. Philological Soc.* (1860-1), 213; *Canu Aneirin*, B37.

47. 'Culhwch', 114; *V.Gundleii*, ch.4; *V.S.Dauid*, cc.12, 22; *V.Cadoci*, ch.12; 'Canu Heledd', 82.

48. *Canu Llywarch Hen*, 76.

49. *V.S.Dauid*, cc.12, 67; Stokes, *op. cit.*, 210; *V.Iltuti*, ch.24; *Hist. Brittonum*, pref.; *V.Cadoci*, cc.7, 11; *V.Paterni*, ch.28.

50. 'Canu Heledd', 82; 'Culhwch', 114.

51. *Canu Llywarch Hen*, 70; *De Excidio Britanniae*, ch.17.

52. Bromwich, *TYP*, 45; *V.S.Dauid*, cc.16, 35, 40; *V.Cadoci*, cc.33, 41, 63.

53. Davies, *Early Welsh Microcosm*, 53f.

54. *V.Kebii*, ch.10; 'Ordinance of the Dunsaete', *passim*; *V.Cadoci*, cc.1, 22, 24, 52, 62, 65; *Canu Taliesin*, I; *V.Iltuti*, ch.20; Bromwich, *TYP*, 46; *Canu Llywarch Hen*, 91, 94; *V.S.Dauid*, ch.16; *Canu Aneirin*, B30, A39; *V.Bernacii*, ch.10; 'Canu Heledd', 85; *BT* 987.

55. Davies, *Early Welsh Microcosm*, 53f.; *V.Cadoci*, ch.22.

56. *Ibid.*, ch.50; *Lib.Land.*, xlv; cf. *De Excidio Britanniae*, cc.16, 19; *V.S.Dauid*, ch.16.

57. *Canu Llywarch Hen*, 69, 70; *Lib. Land.*, xlv; *V.Cadoci*, ch.8; 'Culhwch', 95, 106, 131; Bromwich, *TYP*, 26; 'Math', 56; *V.Tathei*, ch.16; *V.Iltuti*, ch.23.
58. 'Ordinance of the Dunsaete', 7.
59. L.Alcock, *Dinas Powys* (1963), 192; *idem*, 'Dry bones and living documents', in *The Effect of Man on the Landscape: the Highland Zone*, ed. J.G.Evans, S.Limbrey and H.Cleere (CBA Res.Rep. 11, 1975), 117-22.
60. *V.Cadoci*, ch.8; *V.Tathei*, ch.16; *Canu Llywarch Hen*, 70; Darby and Terrett (eds.), *op. cit.*, 158.
61. *De Excidio Britanniae*, ch.3; *V.Bernacii*, cc.10, 11; *V.Cadoci*, cc.12, 30; *V.Iltuti*, ch.20; M.Lapidge, 'The Welsh-Latin poetry of Sulien's family', *Studia Celtica*, VIII-IX (1973-4), 84, ll.61f.
62. The point was made by Richard Kelly at the Society for Landscape Studies Conference, Cardiff, March 1980; see E.Davies, 'Hendre and hafod in Caernarvonshire', *Trans. Caerns. Hist. Soc.*, XL (1979), 17-46; M.Richards, 'Hafod and hafoty in Welsh place-names', *Montgomeryshire Collns*, LVI (1959-61), 13-20.
63. G.R.Jones, 'Post-Roman Wales', in *The Agrarian History of England and Wales*, I pt 2, ed. H.P.R.Finberg (1972), 288, 294f.; see further below, pp.43-7.
64. Limbrey and Evans (eds.), *op. cit.*, 37, 89.
65. *Canu Llywarch Hen*, 94, 96.
66. Alcock, 'Dry bones and living documents'.
67. Colloquy, ch.2; cf. *V.Iltuti*, ch.13.
68. See below, p.46; cf. *V.Gundleii*, ch.15; *Hist. Brittonum*, ch.68.
69. *Canu Llywarch Hen*, 94; I.Williams, *The Beginnings of Welsh Poetry*, ed. and trans. R.Bromwich (1972), 90; *Canu Aneirin*, A60; *Canu Taliesin*, VII.
70. *V.S.Dauid*, ch.43; *V.Paterni*, ch.4; *De Excidio Britanniae*, ch.25; *Canu Llywarch Hen*, 96; *Hist. Brittonum*, ch.30; Stokes, *op. cit.*, 237; *V.Samsonis*, ch.35; *Llyfr Blegywryd*, 63.
71. See above, p.33f.
72. *Armes Prydein*, 1.36; see above, p.34.
73. Colloquy, ch.7.
74. *V.S.Dauid*, cc.22, 41; Darby and Maxwell (eds.), *op. cit.*, 388.
75. Davies, *Early Welsh Microcosm*, 32-50.
76. Jones, 'Post-Roman Wales', 281-382; *idem*, 'Multiple estates and early settlement', in *Medieval Settlement*, ed. P.Sawyer (1976), 15-40.
77. Jones, 'Post-Roman Wales', 312-18.
78. *Ibid.*, 308-11.
79. W.Davies, 'Land and power in early medieval Wales', *Past and Present*, LXXXI (1978), 12-15, 21f.
80. *V.Cadoci*, cc.55, 56, 59, 62; *Lib. Land.*, xlv, 210a; Jones, 'Post-Roman Wales', 300-2, 312; Darby and Terrett (eds.), *op. cit.*, 53-5, 110f., 157; Darby and Maxwell (eds.), *op. cit.*, 389f.
81. A.J.Robertson (ed.), *Anglo-Saxon Charters* (1939), 207, 454; it is, of course, very difficult to establish if the areas compared here are really comparable: one would expect the average *tref* to be of the order of 125 acres and the average hide to be of the order of 120 acres, but massive variations are possible.
82. *ECMW*, nos.116, 255; *V.Carantoci*, I.4, 5; *V.Bernacii*, ch.15; *BT* 1022.
83. *Hist. Brittonum*, ch.32.
84. See below, pp.59f.; *Canu Taliesin*, X.
85. Hist. Brittonum, cc.52, 65; *V.Paterni*, cc.16, 17; *V.Gundleii*, ch.15; *V.Cadoci*, ch.24.
86. *Canu Aneirin*, A73.
87. T.Jones, 'The Black Book of Carmarthen "Stanzas of the Graves"', *Procs. British Academy*, LIII (1967), no.60; *V.Cadoci*, ch.7.
88. *British Numismatic J.*, XXIX (1958-9), 255-8; J.D.A.Thompson, *Inventory of British Coin Hoards, A.D.600-1500* (1956), no.131; and *Archaeology in Wales*, XIX (1979), 36.
89. *Canu Taliesin*, III.
90. *V.S.Dauid*, ch.22; *V.Bernacii*, ch.1; *De Excidio Britanniae*, cc.32, 66.
91. *Canu Llywarch Hen*, stanzas 134, 135 in the translation by P.K.Ford, in Ford, *The Poetry of Llywarch Hen* (Berkeley, Cal., 1974).
92. 'Canu Heledd', 85; *Canu Taliesin*, I, IV, V.

93. *BT* 1022; *Armes Prydein*, l.2.
94. Colloquy, ch.4.
95. *ECMW*, no.33; Lapidge, *op. cit.*, 86, ll.121-3; *Canu Aneirin*, A33; *V.Cadoci*, ch.69; 'Canu Heledd', 85.
96. *Hist. Brittonum*, ch.30; *V.Cadoci*, cc.5, 8, 24, 65.
97. *Canu Aneirin, passim; Hist. Brittonum*, pref.; 'Pwyll', 17; 'Branwen', 31; 'Math', 57; *V.Cadoci*, cc.62, 65; RCAHMW *Caernarvon*, I, lxix.
98. *Hist. Brittonum*, cc.25, 30; cf. *De Excidio Britanniae*, ch.66.
99. *V.S.Dauid*, ch.12.
100. *Lib. Land.*, 151b.
101. Alcock, *Dinas Powys*, 44-7; Richard White, Society of Antiquaries, December 1979.
102. *V.Cadoci*, cc.27, 55; Davies, *Early Welsh Microcosm*, 53f.
103. *Llyfr Blegywryd*, 41, 106.
104. Alcock, *Dinas Powys*, 47-9.
105. *V.Samsonis*, ch.3.
106. *V.Cadoci*, ch.35.
107. *Canu Aneirin*, A18.
108. *V.Cadoci*, ch.35; *Hist. Brittonum*, ch.40.
109. Williams, *op. cit.*, 164; *Canu Llywarch Hen*, 66; Bromwich, *TYP*, 26; *Lib. Land.*, 127a; *Hist. Brittonum*, ch.50; *V.Iltuti*, ch.23;. *V.Cadoci*, ch.8; *V.Tathei*, cc.14, 16.
110. Bromwich, *TYP*, 44; *V.S.Dauid*, ch.37; *V.Paterni*, ch.31; *V.Iltuti*, ch.8; *V.Cadoci*, ch.1.
111. *V.S.Dauid*, ch.38; *V.Cadoci*, cc.24, 43, 58, 62, 65; *V.Iltuti*, ch.24; Stokes, *op. cit.*, 222.
112. *ECMW*, no.149; Bromwich, *TYP*, 44; *V.S.Dauid*, ch.38; Colloquy, ch.5; *De Excidio Britanniae*, ch.19; *V.Samsonis*, ch.16.
113. *V.Cadoci*, ch.1; Colloquy, ch.5.
114. *Canu Taliesin*, I, II.
115. 'Pwyll', 9.
116. *V.Cadoci*, ch.63.
117. *Canu Aneirin*, A73.
118. For example: *Canu Llywarch Hen*, 70; *Canu Aneirin*, B4, B38, A4, A26; *Canu Taliesin*, I, III, V; *Hist. Brittonum*, ch.65.
119. *V.Iltuti*, ch.2.
120. *Canu Taliesin*, IV, VIII; *V.Cadoci*, ch.24.
121. *Ibid.*, ch.63.
122. Williams, *op. cit.*, 164, l.44; *Canu Aneirin*, A31, B13, B34.
123. *Ibid.*, B40.
124. *V.S.Dauid*, cc.2, 22, 33, 48; *Canu Aneirin*, A33; *V.Samsonis*, ch.3.
125. *V.S.Dauid*, ch.5; *V.Samsonis*, ch.9.
126. *Lib. Land.*, 146; *V.Cadoci*, ch.66.
127. *Lib. Land.*, xliii.
128. *V.Cadoci*, cc.56, 59, 60, 61, 62, 64, 65, 66, 67, 68; *Lib. Land.*, xliii, xlv; Davies, *Early Welsh Microcosm*, 50-9.
129. *V.Cadoci*, cc.62, 65.
130. Colloquy, ch.27.
131. *V.Cadoci*, ch.50.
132. *BT* 1088.
133. *V.Cadoci*, ch.36.
134. Colloquy, ch.16.
135. *V.Gundleii*, ch.13; W.M.Hennessy (ed.), *Annals of Loch Cé* (Rolls Series, 54, 2 vols., 1871), 1014.
136. *De Excidio Britanniae*, cc.66, 67.
137. *Canu Aneirin*, A31.
138. *Canu Llywarch Hen*, 94; Davies, *Early Welsh Microcosm*, 51-4; *V. Cadoci*, ch.27; *ECMW*, no.253; 'Manawydan', 44f.
139. *Lib. Land.*, xliii, xlvi; Davies, *Early Welsh Microcosm*, 51-4; *V.Cadoci*, cc.24, 55, 60, 65, 69.
140. 'Culhwch', 97; *V.Cadoci*, ch.69; see below, p.55.
141. 'Ordinance of the Dunsaete', 7.
142. *V.Samsonis*, ch.3; Davies, *Early Welsh Microcosm*, 59-61.
143. *Hist. Brittonum*, cc.25, 30; Colloquy, ch.4.
144. *British Numismatic J.*, XVII (1923-4), 305.
145. Davies, *Early Welsh Microcosm*, 60; R.H.M.Dolley, *The Hiberno-Norse Coins in the British Museum* (1966), no.3, 70, 99, 117, 143, 153; Thompson, *op. cit.*, no.10, 32, 131, 305, 306; *Arch. Camb.*, CXIX (1970), 75-8; H.R.Loyn, *The Vikings in Wales* (1976), 14.
146. Stokes, *op. cit.*, 223.
147. *AC* 989; *BT* 989.
148. *V.Cadoci*, cc.27, 50; *V.S.Dauid*, ch.30; Darby and Terrett (eds.), *op. cit.*, 53-5, 110f., 157.
149. *De Excidio Britanniae*, ch.3; *Hist. Brittonum*, ch.9.
150. *Ibid.*, ch.52.
151. L.Alcock, 'Pottery and settlements in Wales and the March, A.D.400-700', in *Culture and Environment*, ed. I.Ll.Foster and L.Alcock (1963), 297-9; *idem*,

Dinas Powys, 49-54; *Arch. Camb.*, LXXXII (1927), 191f.

152. I.Williams, 'Glosau Rhydychen: mesurau a phwysau', *BBCS*, v (1929-31), 226-48.

153. Bromwich, *TYP*, 37; *V.Bernacii*, ch.3; *V.Iltuti*, cc.13, 15; *V.Cadoci*, ch.10; *V.Gundleii*, ch.13; Davies, *Early Welsh Microcosm*, 61.

154. Loyn, *op. cit.*, 12-15, 17-21; Thompson, *op. cit.*, no.32; see further below, pp.117-20.

155. *Hist. Brittonum*, ch.40; Bromwich, *TYP*, 43; *V.S.Dauid*, ch.41; *V.Cadoci*, ch.24.

156. Colloquy, ch.4.

157. *V.S.Dauid*, ch.12.

158. *V.Cadoci*, ch.59.

159. 'Manawydan', 43ff.

160. *De Excidio Britanniae*, cc.3, 19, 24, 26.

161. Davies, *Early Welsh Microcosm*, 61f.; cf. *V.Cadoci*, ch.1 — Meuthi's *oppidum*. W.Davies, 'The Latin charter tradition in western Britain, Brittany and Ireland in the medieval period', in *Ireland and Europe*, ed. D.Dumville, R.McKitterick and D.Whitelock (1982), 258-80; T.James, *Carmarthen, an Archaeological and Topographical Survey* (1980), 20f.

162. *BT* 1056; *AC* 866; *Hist. Brittonum*, cc.10, 49; *V.Paterni*, ch.28.

163. *CBA Group 2 Report*, XIX (1979), 39; *Med. Arch.*, XVII (1973), 73.

164. *Hist. Brittonum*, ch.25; *V.Cadoci*, cc.21, 41; *V.Gundleii*, ch.15; Davies, *Early Welsh Microcosm*, 62.

165. G.Duby, *The Early Growth of the European Economy* (1973; trans. 1974), 120-54.

3   Social Ties and Social Strata

1. See above, pp.41-7.

2. *De Excidio Britanniae*, ch.66; *V.Samsonis*, ch.30; *V.Cadoci*, prol., ch.14; *V.Tathei*, cc.4, 7; see above, pp.46-9.

3. 'Canu Heledd', 85f.

4. *Hist. Brittonum*, ch.32; *V.Cadoci*, ch.1.

5. *V.S.Dauid*, cc.34, 56; *V.Cadoci*, prol.; *V.Iltuti*, ch.11.

6. *V.Cadoci*, ch.21; 'Pwyll', 14; 'Manawydan', 51; *BT* 1022.

7. *De Excidio Britanniae*, ch.34; *Canu Taliesin*, III; *V.Cadoci*, cc.8,69.

8. See above, pp.51f.

9. See below, pp.164-6.

10. *V.Iltuti*, ch.24; *De Excidio Britanniae*, ch.66, 67.

11. Cf. *Llyfr Blegywryd*, 81, 96; A.W.Wade-Evans, *Welsh Medieval Law* (1909), 204.

12. *Llyfr Blegywryd*, 59; cf. Wade-Evans, *op. cit.*, 246.

13. *V.S.Dauid*, ch.5; *Lib. Land.*, 121; see further below, p.138.

14. *Lib. Land.*, 233.

15. *Hist. Brittonum*, ch.63; Colloquy, ch.24; *V.S.Dauid*, ch.53; M.Lapidge, 'The Welsh-Latin poetry of Sulien's family', *Studia Celtica*, VIII-IX (1973-4), 86,ll.124f.

16. *V.Samsonis*, ch.6; *Hist. Brittonum*, pref.; *AC* 1047.

17. *V.Cadoci*, prol.; 'Pwyll', 20.

18. *V.Cadoci*, ch.13.

19. *V.Gundleii*, ch.1; *V.Paterni*, ch.2; *V.Iltuti*, ch.1; *V.Cadoci*, pref., prol.; *Canu Llywarch Hen*, 73; 'Ordinance of the Dunsaete', 5; Lapidge, *op. cit.*, 84, ll.86f.

20. 'Culhwch', 96; *V.Wenefrede*, ch.10.

21. *V.Samsonis*, ch.6.

22. Davies, *Early Welsh Microcosm*, 108-16; *Lib. Land.*, xliii.

23. *Journey through Wales*, 221.

24. I have benefited from the discussion of these points in Thomas Charles-Edwards's O'Donnell lectures in Oxford, 1979, on concepts of freedom.

25. *Journey through Wales*, 251.

26. H.C.Darby and R.Welldon Finn (eds.), *The Domesday Geography of South-West England* (1967), 317-21, 364-73.

27. *V.Carantoci*, I.4; *V.S.Dauid*, ch.17; *V.Cadoci*, cc.7,33; T.M Charles-Edwards, 'The seven bishop-houses of Dyfed', *BBCS*, XXIV (1970-2), 253f.

28. I.Williams, *The Beginnings of Welsh Poetry*, ed. and trans. R.Bromwich (1972), 164, 1.24; *Armes Prydein*, 1.34.

29. Davies, *Early Welsh Microcosm*, 43, 180f.; *Lib. Land.*, 218.

30. Davies, *Early Welsh Microcosm*, 43.

31. *Lib. Land.*, xlvi.
32. F.L.Attenborough (ed.), *The Laws of the Earliest English Kings* (1922), 84-6, cl.43.
33. *Colloquy*, ch.27.
34. See above, p.55.
35. *V.Cadoci*, ch.1; *V.S.Dauid*, ch.37; *V.Tathei*, ch.16.
36. See G.R.Jones, 'Post-Roman Wales', in *The Agrarian History of England and Wales*, I pt 2, ed. H.P.R.Finberg (1972), 299-308, 320-49, for a useful recent summary of different types of tenure.
37. *V.Cadoci*, ch.7.
38. *Ibid.*, ch.6.
39. *Ibid.*, cc.22, 34.
40. *Canu Aneirin*, B20, B31.
41. *Ibid.*, B26.
42. *Ibid.*, B30, A2, B39, A65, A16; *Canu Taliesin*, IV; 'Canu Heledd', 83f.; Williams, *op. cit.*, 164, ll.34-36.
43. *De Excidio Britanniae*, ch.27; Davies, *Early Welsh Microcosm*, 112-16; *AC* 768; *V.S.Dauid*, cc.16, 19; cf. T.M. Charles-Edwards, 'The date of the four branches of the Mabinogi', *Trans. Hon. Soc. Cymmrodorion* (1970), 276f. on 'submission'.
44. *V.Iltuti*, ch.2; *V.Cadoci*, cc.8, 16, 19, 22, 23.
45. Davies, *Early Welsh Microcosm*, 114.
46. *V.Samsonis*, ch.1; *Canu Taliesin*, VII, VIII; *V.Cadoci*, prol.
47. *Canu Aneirin*, B4.
48. See below, p.127.
49. *Canu Taliesin*, V.
50. *Canu Aneirin*, A28; *Journey through Wales*, 261.
51. *De Excidio Britanniae*, ch.28; *V.Samsonis*, ch.6; *V.Cadoci*, ch.65.
52. 'Canu Heledd', 86.
53. *ECMW*, no.33; *Lib. Land.*, xliii; *V.Cadoci*, cc.26, 27; Davies, *Early Welsh Microcosm*, 111; *V.Gundleii*, ch.1.
54. See, for example, *Llyfr Blegywryd*, 45, 77, 67; Wade-Evans, *op. cit.*, 199, 235-42; D.Jenkins and M.E.Owen (eds.), *The Welsh Law of Women* (1980), 43f.
55. *Colloquy*, ch.14.
56. *BT* 1075, 1078; *V.S.Dauid*, ch.14; W.Stokes, 'The Welsh glosses and verses in the Cambridge Codex of

Juvencus', *Trans. Philological Soc.* (1860-1), 234; *ECMW*, no.229; cf. Davies, *Early Welsh Microcosm*, 111; T.M. Charles-Edwards, 'Some Celtic kinship terms', *BBCS*, xxiv (1970-2), 105-22; *idem*, 'Nei, keifn, and kefynderw', *BBCS*, xxv (1972-4), 386-8; D.Dumville, 'Sub-Roman Britain: history and legend', *History*, lxii (1977), 182.
57. *V.Cadoci*, ch.26; Bromwich, *TYP*, no.81; *V.Iltuti*, ch.1; *Canu Taliesin*, I, VI; 'Canu Heledd', 80, 84; see above, pp.202f.
58. *V.Bernacii*, ch.1; cf. *Journey through Wales*, 251, cited above; see below, p.58.
59. *De Excidio Britanniae*, ch.18; *V.Cadoci*, ch.21; *Hist. Brittonum*, ch.34; see below, p.74.
60. See above, p.73.
61. *Lib. Land.*, 127b.
62. *V.Samsonis*, cc.2, 29; *V.Cadoci*, cc.56, 57, 68; *Lib. Land.*, xlvi; Davies, *Early Welsh Microcosm*, 55.
63. See below, pp.123f.
64. *V.Samsonis*, ch.6; *Hist. Brittonum*, ch.38; 'Canu Heledd', 84; *V.Cadoci*, prol., cc.6, 14, 28.
65. *ECMW*, nos.26, 32, 183, 284, 33.
66. Cf. *Llyfr Blegywryd*, 53, 45, 77, 47; Wade-Evans, *op. cit.*, 185-7, 233f., 199.
67. *V.Cadoci*, cc.69, 70; *Lib. Land.*, xliii; *ECMW*, no.284; Davies, *Early Welsh Microcosm*, 111.
68. *V.Cadoci*, cc.56, 59, 62, 65, for example.
69. *V.Cadoci*, ch.62; hence, *BT* 986, *V.Cadoci*, ch.6; *Lib. Land.*, xliii.
70. Cf. *Llyfr Blegywryd*, 77; Wade-Evans, *op. cit.*, 199.
71. *Armes Prydein*, l.14; *V.Cadoci*, cc.56, 59, 61; Davies, *Early Welsh Microcosm*, 55.
72. *V.Samsonis*, prol., cc.2, 40, 14; *Life of King Alfred*, ch.79; cf. *Journey through Wales*, 253.
73. *V.Cadoci*, pref.; *V.Gundleii*, ch.1; *V.Cadoci*, ch.68.
74. See below, pp.123f.
75. See above, pp.43-6.
76. *Journey through Wales*, 80, 128, 193, 261.
77. *Lib. Land.*, 180b, 274, 152; *V.Cadoci*, cc.15, 57; *Hist. Brittonum*, ch.57.
78. *V.Cadoci*, cc.28, 55, 60, 65, 69; Davies, *Early Welsh Microcosm*,

43-59.

79. 'Manawydan', 41.
80. 'Culhwch', 112; *V.Cadoci*, ch.25; *V.Samsonis*, ch.1.
81. 'Pwyll', 12; *Hist. Brittonum*, ch.37.
82. 'Book of David', 6; *V.Iltuti*, ch.1; *V.Gundleii*, ch.2; 'Culhwch', 112; *Canu Aneirin*, A9; Jenkins and Owen (eds.), *op. cit.*, 69-90.
83. Cf. *Hist. Brittonum*, ch.63; *De Excidio Britanniae*, ch.35.
84. *Journey through Wales*, 263.
85. *De Excidio Britanniae*, cc.28, 35.
86. 'Marwnad Cynddylan'; 'Culhwch', 95; 'Pwyll', 17; *V.Cadoci*, ch.14.
87. Jenkins and Owen (eds.), *op. cit.*, 79-81.
88. *Canu Aneirin*, B11; *De Excidio Britanniae*, ch.32; *V.S.Dauid*, ch.56; cf. Jenkins and Owen (eds.), *op. cit.*, 21.
89. 'Culhwch', 95; *De Excidio Britanniae*, ch.6; *V.Iltuti*, ch.26; *V.Cadoci*, ch.1; *V.Samsonis*, cc.6, 14; *V.S.Dauid*, ch.39; cf. E.Phillips, 'Modrydaf', *BBCS*, xxv (1972-4), 119f.
90. *V.Samsonis*, ch.1; *Hist. Brittonum*, cc.10, 46.
91. Cf. *Llyfr Blegywryd*, 45, 65; Wade-Evans, *op. cit.*, 185f., 192f.; Jenkins and Owen (eds.), *op. cit.*, 57.
92. *Lib. Land.*, 186a, 223, 257.
93. *Ibid.*, 259, 261.
94. Attenborough (ed.), *op. cit.*, 84, cl. 42.
95. *BT* 1078; cf. *AC* 880.
96. 'Manawydan', 44.
97. *Canu Taliesin*, III.
98. *Hist. Brittonum; Armes Prydein; AC* 754, cf. 768, 784, etc.; J.F.Kenney, *Sources for the Early History of Ireland: Ecclesiastical* (Columbia, 1929), 556.
99. *Hist. Brittonum*, prol., cc.42, 62; *V.S.Dauid*, ch.58; *V.Gundleii*, ch.11; *V.Paterni*, ch.2; *V.Cadoci*, ch.27.
100. *De Excidio Britanniae*, cc.4, 14, 19, 25, 26 etc.; *ECMW*, no.103 (it should be noted, however, that the date of this inscription has been seriously questioned: R.B.White, *Arch. Camb.* (forthcoming).
101. Davies, *Early Welsh Microcosm*, 88f.; *Journey through Wales*, 77, 183ff.; *ECMW*, nos. 87, 126; *BT* 848, 934, 984, 1022, 1075;

Williams, *op. cit.*, 166, l.65; *V.S.Dauid*, ch.4; *Canu Aneirin*, A19, A73; *AC* 848, 902; *V.Cadoci*, cc.7, 13, 23, 24, 41, 46, 69; *Canu Taliesin*, I; *Hist. Brittonum*, cc.14, 48, 70, 71, 72, 73, 74; H.C.Darby and I.B.Terrett (eds.), *The Domesday Geography of Midland England* (1954), 157; H.C.Darby and I.S.Maxwell (eds.), *The Domesday Geography of Northern England* (1962), 386f.; *V.Pauli*, ch.1.
102. *Canu Taliesin*, IV; *Canu Aneirin*, B8, B21, A15 etc.
103. *BT* 984, 1047, 1075; Davies, *Early Welsh Microcosm*, 108-10; cf. Charles-Edwards, 'Some Celtic kinship terms', 116-22; M.Richter, *Giraldus Cambrensis. The Growth of the Welsh Nation* (1972), 61-86; idem, 'The political and institutional background to national consciousness in medieval Wales', in *Nationality and the Pursuit of National Independence*, ed. T.W.Moody (1978), 38f.
104. Lapidge, *op. cit.*, 82-4; ll.54, 57, 61-8.
105. Stokes, *op. cit.*, 212.
106. See below, p.132.

4 Secular Politics

1. T.M.Charles-Edwards, 'Native political organisation in Roman Britain and the origin of MW *brenhin*', in *Antiquitates Indogermanicae*, ed. M.Mayrhofer, W.Meid, B.Schlerath and R.Schmitt (Innsbruck, 1974), 40-4; see above, p.62.
2. A.H.M.Jones, *The Later Roman Empire, 284-602* (4 vols., 1964), I, 366-522, III, 382; S.Frere, *Britannia* (1967), 210f.; R.Reece and C.Catling, *Cirencester* (BAR 12, 1975); A. McWhirr (ed.), *The Archaeology and History of Cirencester* (BAR 30, 1976).
3. Frere, *op. cit.*, 210-15.
4. V.E.Nash-Williams, *The Roman Frontier in Wales* (2nd edn 1969, ed. M.Jarrett), 73f.; cf. T.James, *Carmarthen, an Archaeological and Topographical Survey* (1980), 5-12.

5.   G.Simpson, *Britons and the Roman Army* (1964); *idem*, 'Caerleon and the Roman forts in Wales in the second century A.D.', 2 parts: *Arch. Camb*, CXI (1962), 103-66; CXII (1963), 13-76.

6.   Frere, *op. cit.*, 356; Nash-Williams, *op. cit.*, 59-64, 85-8, 70-3, 135-7, 56-9, 22-8; Simpson, *Britons and the Roman Army*, 163-7.

7.   Frere, *op. cit.*, 286; Nash-Williams, *op. cit.*, 63; G.R.Jones, 'Post-Roman Wales', in *The Agrarian History of England and Wales*, I pt 2, ed. H.P.R.Finberg (1972), 313-20.

8.   Frere, *op. cit.*, 361.

9.   W. Davies, 'Roman settlements and post-Roman estates in south-east Wales', in *The End of Roman Britain*, ed. P.J.Casey (BAR 71, 1979), 153-6.

10. L. Alcock, *Dinas Powys* (1963), 61; C.Thomas, 'Irish settlements in post-Roman western Britain', *J. Roy. Institution Cornwall*, VI (1972), 251-74; M.Richards, 'Irish settlements in south-west Wales: a topographical approach', *J. Roy. Soc. Antiquaries Ireland*, XC (1960), 133-62.

11. *ECMW*, no.138; M.Miller, 'Date-guessing and Dyfed', *Studia Celtica*, XII-XIII (1977-8), 36f.

12. A.Hood (ed. and trans.), *St Patrick, His Writings and Muirchu's Life* (1978); P.C.Bartrum (ed.), *Early Welsh Genealogical Tracts* (1966), 4.

13. *Hist. Brittonum*, ch.62.

14. Frere, *op. cit.*, 352; J.Morris, *The Age of Arthur* (1973), 66; L.Alcock, *Arthur's Britain* (1971), 125-9; M.Miller, 'The foundation-legend of Gwynedd in the Latin texts', *BBCS*, XXVII (1976-8), 515-32; cf. alternatively D.Dumville, 'Sub-Roman Britain: history and legend', *History*, LXII (1977), 181f.

15. See above, pp.22-4.

16. K.H.Jackson, *Language and History in Early Britain* (1953), 78-80 esp.

17. *ECMW*, 3-10.

18. *De Excidio Britanniae*, ch.31.

19. *Ibid.*, ch.33.

20. *Hist. Ecclesiastica*, III.1; cf. II.20.

21. *ECMW*, no.13.

22. *Ibid.*, no.138.

23. *V.Samsonis*, cc.1, 6.

24. Davies, *Early Welsh Microcosm*, 77, 93; *Lib. Land.*, 121, 122, 123, 166.

25. Davies, *Early Welsh Microcosm*, 76, 77, 79, 94; *Lib. Land.*, 72a-76b, 151a, 161-164.

26. *AC 613*; *Hist. Ecclesiastica*, II.2.

27. *Canu Taliesin*, I.

28. The genealogy of the Powys kings preserved on the Pillar of Elise (Bartrum, *op. cit.*, 2) does not associate the line with Cadell; it is therefore clear that not all Powys historians of the ninth century wished to classify the family as Cadelling. There are several possible explanations for the omission — variant tradition, desire to avoid the servile origin of the line implied by *Hist. Brittonum*, cc.32-5, alternative interests — but it remains true that descent from Cadell remains the most common attribution in the ninth century and later. Cf. D.Kirby, 'Welsh bards and the border', in *Mercian Studies*, ed. A.Dornier ((1977), 36f.

29. Davies, *Early Welsh Microcosm*, 80, 88; *Lib. Land.*, 146, 154, 167.

30. *Life of King Alfred*, ch.80; *AC 848*, 895.

31. *Hist. Brittonum*, ch.49.

32. Bartrum (ed.), *op. cit.*, 9, 10, 2; cf. Bromwich, *TYP*, lxxxvii, on the Brittonic gods from whom dynasties claimed descent.

33. M.Biddle, 'The development of the Anglo-Saxon town', *Settimane di Studio del Centro italiano di Studi sull 'alto medioevo*, XXI (1974), 205-12.

34. *ASC 577*. The manner of reference does not make it clear whether the kings were kings of the cities or simply involved in the engagement by which the cities were lost.

35. A.W. Wade-Evans (ed.), *Vitae Sanctorum Britanniae et Genealogiae* (1944), 274-8.

36. Bartrum (ed.), *op. cit.*, 4, 9f. (no.2); see Miller, 'Date-guessing and Dyfed'.

37. *Hist. Brittonum*, ch.49.

38. Davies, *Early Welsh Microcosm*, 93-5.

39. *Lib. Land.*, 146, 154, 167; *V.Cadoci*, prol.; 'De Situ Brecheniauc', Bartrum (ed.), *op.*

cit., 14-16.

40. *Lib. Land.*, 77, 125a, 125b, 127a, 127b; *ECMW*, no.138; *Journey through Wales*, 223.

41. *ECMW*, no.13; *Journey through Wales*, 223; M.Miller, *The Saints of Gwynedd* (1979), 1-3.

42. *ECMW*, no.182; *AC* 822; cf. *Journey through Wales*, 223; see above, p.94.

43. See above, p.94.

44. *AC* 816 (MS C); *BT* 816.

45. *V.Cadoci*, cc.41, 44; J.E.Lloyd, *A History of Wales, from the Earliest Times to the Edwardian Conquest* (1911), 281f.; *ECMW*, no.272; Jackson, *op. cit.*, 355.

46. D.Dumville, 'The Anglian collection of royal geneaologies and regnal lists', *Anglo-Saxon England*, v (1976), 30f.

47. *AC* 798.

48. *De Excidio Britanniae*, ch.32; Bartrum (ed.), *op. cit.*, 10.

49. *Canu Llywarch Hen*, 79-86.

50. *Ibid.*, 79, 82, 84, 86.

51. *Ibid.*, 79-86.

52. *Journey through Wales*, 223.

53. 'Marwnad Cynddylan'.

54. Stanza 111 (*Canu Llywarch Hen*, ed. I.Williams, 1935, 48); see W.Davies and H.Vierck, 'The contexts of Tribal Hidage: social aggregates and settlement patterns', *Frühmittelalterliche Studien*, VIII (1974), 236-9, for a brief discussion of Mercia and the Wrekin. Bartrum, *op. cit.*, 12 (no.25); cf. the similar comments of William of Malmesbury, cited by Bartrum (ed.), *op. cit.*, 128. A Morfael and Rhiadaf occur in the later genealogies of 'Bonedd yr Arwyr', Bartrum (ed.), *op. cit.*, 85; while there is a 'Caranfael' in HG no.24, *ibid.*, 12; such occurrences can really have no value as evidence, however.

55. It should not be forgotten that 'Marwnad Cynddylan' does refer to Cynddylan as 'Cadelling'.

56. See below, p.112.

57. See below, p.114.

58. *De Excidio Britanniae*, ch.33.

59. *Hist. Brittonum*, ch.62.

60. See above, p.92.

61. *Hist. Ecclesiastica*, II.20, III.1.

62. *AC* 754.

63. See above, p.82.

64. Wade-Evans (ed.), *op. cit.*, 72-8.

65. *AC* 844; Bartrum (ed.), *op. cit.*, 9 (no.1). There is some disagreement between this and the later genealogies; see Bartrum (ed.), *op. cit.*, 151, for discussion of the problems.

66. *Ibid.*, 46 (no.17).

67. *Ibid.* (nos.17, 18), 151; *AC* 854, 871; W.M.Hennessy (ed.), *Annals of Ulster* (Rolls Series, 2 vols., 1887), 855, 876, 877; *Journey through Wales*, 221f.

68. *Life of King Alfred*, ch.66.

69. *AC* 877, 880, 894; *Life of King Alfred*, ch.80.

70. *AC* 903; Bartrum (ed.), *op. cit.*, 9 (nos.1,2); cf. D.Kirby, 'Hywel Dda: Anglophil?', *Welsh Hist. Rev.*, VIII (1976-7), 1-13.

71. *AC* 986, 999, 1000.

72. *AC* 1039; Bartrum (ed.), *op. cit.*, 47 (no.27).

73. *AC* 1055, 1063; *ASC* 1052/3, 1063; H.C.Darby and I.B.Terrett (eds.), *The Domesday Geography of Midland England* (1954), 142-6.

74. *ASC* 1063; *BT* 1075; see also A.Jones (ed.), *The History of Gruffydd ap Cynan* (1910); D.Simon Evans (ed.), *Historia Gruffudd vab Kenan* (1977) (Welsh edition).

75. *AC* 814; Bartrum (ed.), *op. cit.*, 9 (no.2).

76. Davies, *Early Welsh Microcosm*, 97.

77. *AC* 1018, 1022, 1023; Bartrum (ed.), *op. cit.*, 47 (no.27).

78. *AC* 1033.

79. *AC* 1045, 1046.

80. *AC* 1022, 1023, 1049, 1073 etc.; *BT* 1039, 1044, 1049, 1052 etc.

81. *AC* 1055.

82. Lloyd, *op. cit.*, 400-46.

83. *Ibid.*, 402ff.

84. W.de Gray Birch, *Cartularium Saxonicum* (3 vols., 1885-93), no.702; *ASC* 916.

85. *Lib. Land.*, 237b; Davies, *Early Welsh Microcosm*, 184.

86. Bartrum (ed.), *op. cit.*, 45 (no.8).

87. Lloyd, *op. cit.*, 397, 402.

88. *AC* 760, 778, 784.

89. *Life of King Alfred*, ch.14.

90. C.Fox, *Offa's Dyke* (1955); D.Hill, 'Offa's and Wat's Dykes — some exploratory work on the frontier between Celt and Saxon', in *Anglo-Saxon Settlement and Landscape*, ed. T.Rowley (BAR 6,

1974), 102-7.
91.   *ECMW*, no.182.
92.   Bartrum (ed.), *op. cit.*, 46 (no.18).
93.   W.Davies, 'Land and power in early medieval Wales', *Past and Present*, LXXXI (1978), 3-23.
94.   *BT* 949, 1022, 1063.
95.   Davies, *Early Welsh Microcosm*, 93.
96.   *Hist. Ecclesiastica*, II.20; *Hist. Brittonum*, ch.64.
97.   N.Chadwick, 'The conversion of Northumbria', in N.Chadwick *et al.*, *Celt and Saxon* (1963), 148f.
98.   *AC* 760, 849; *Life of King Alfred*, cc.78, 80; *AC* 798; *BT* 816; *AC* 877; *ASC 830, 853.*
99.   *BT* 823; *AC* 822; Bartrum (ed.), *op. cit.*, 2.
100. *Lib. Land.*, 192.
101. 'Ordinance of the Dunsaete', 6.
102. 'subdiderat imperio...ut dominium et defensionem ab eo pro inimicis suis haberent', *Life of King Alfred*, ch.80.
103. 'regis dominio...subdidit...ut in omnibus regiae uoluntati sic oboediens esset', *ibid.*
104. *ASC* 893.
105. *Life of King Alfred*, ch.7.
106. *ASC* 916, 918, 927.
107. William of Malmesbury, *De Gestis Regum Anglorum*, ed. W.Stubbs (Rolls Series, 90, 2 vols., 1887-9), I.148.
108. Caer Geri: Cirencester; Aber Peryddon: probably near Monmouth; *Armes Prydein*, ll. 69-72.
109. Florence of Worcester, *Chronicon ex Chronicis*, ed. B.Thorpe (2 vols., 1848-9), I.142f.; *ASC* 972, 973.
110. Lloyd, *op. cit.*, 353. Also 'Worgeat' in 928 and 932, presumably 'Gwriad'; this might possibly refer to the Gwriad who was father of Nowy, active in Gwent c.950.
111. *ASC* 1056.
112. *AC* 943, 951, 967, 983, 1011; *BT* 978.
113. *AC* 983, 993, 1056; *ASC* 1046, 1055.
114. *ASC* 1049.
115. W.Davies, *The Llandaff Charters* (1979), 145f.; *idem*, 'The orthography of personal names in the charters of *Liber Landavensis*', *BBCS*, XXVIII (1978-80), 554; *Arch. Camb.*, CXXVII (1978), 124f.

116. *ECMW*, nos.65, 180, 181, 190; *Arch. Camb.*, CVI (1957), 109-16.
117. D.Dumville, *England and the Celtic World in the Ninth and Tenth Centuries* (forthcoming 1982).
118. *AC* 853, 876; Hennessy (ed.), *op. cit.*, 855, 876; *BT* 855, 877; cf. A.P.Smyth, *Scandinavian Kings in the British Isles, 850-880* (1977), 94, 265.
119. *Life of King Alfred*, ch.54; *AC* 895; *ASC* 914; *AC* 902; *BT* 918.
120. *Journey through Wales*, 163.
121. *AC* 989; 972, 979, 982, 987, 988, 999, 1001.
122. *Ibid.*, 1039, 1042, 1044; *ASC* 1049, 1055.
123. *AC* 1071, 1078; *BT* 1091; H.R.Loyn, *The Vikings in Wales* (1976).
124. See above, pp.54f.; Loyn, *Vikings in Wales*, 14.
125. *Idem, The Vikings in Britain* (1977), 53.
126. *Armes Prydein*, ll.9-11.
127. *BT* 992; *ASC* 1055; *AC* 1056.
128. Loyn, *Vikings in Wales*, 8-10.
129. B.G.Charles, *Old Norse Relations with Wales* (1934); *idem*, *Non-Celtic Place-Names in Wales* (1938); Loyn, *Vikings in Wales*; *idem*, *Vikings in Britain*, 149f.; M.Gelling, W.F.H.Nicolaisen, M.Richards, *The Names of Towns and Cities in Britain* (1970), 135, 178.
130. *ECMW*, 27-47; nos.37, 38, 190, 303, 360.

5   Kings, Law and Order

1.   *BT* 1078.
2.   *De Excidio Britanniae*, ch.27.
3.   *Canu Aneirin*, B 14.
4.   *Canu Taliesin*, III, 1.20.
5.   *Canu Taliesin*, VII, ll.9, 10.
6.   *Canu Taliesin*, I, 1.15.
7.   *V.Iltuti*, ch.2; *V.Gundleii*, ch.1.
8.   *Canu Taliesin*, III, 1.26; *De Excidio Britanniae*, ch.34; see further above, p.60.
9.   See above, pp.47f.
10.   *V.Cadoci*, cc.1, 39, 41, 44, 69; *V.Iltuti*, cc.8-10, 17, 25; cf. *Hist. Brittonum*, ch.32.
11.   *De Excidio Britanniae*, ch.34.
12.   *Canu Taliesin*, VII, 1.6.

13.   *V.Gundleii*, ch.1.
14.   *De Excidio Britanniae*, ch.21.
15.   'Branwen', 35; cf. D.Jenkins and M.E.Owen (eds.), *The Welsh Law of Women* (1980), 43.
16.   *Canu Aneirin*, B4; cf. 'Culhwch', 97.
17.   *De Excidio Britanniae*, ch.33.
18.   *Hist. Brittonum*, cc.62, 35.
19.   See above, pp.110f., for references, illustration and text.
20.   *Hist. Brittonum*, ch.29.
21.   *Canu Taliesin*, IX, ll.20-1.
22.   *BT* 1022; *V.Tathei*, ch.1, for example.
23.   See above, pp.104-7.
24.   *V.Cadoci*, pref.
25.   *V.Gundleii*, ch.1.
26.   See above, pp.98f.
27.   Davies, *Early Welsh Microcosm*, 102.
28.   See above; see also D.O'Corráin, 'Irish regnal succession', *Studia Hibernica*, XI (1971), 7-39.
29.   See D.Binchy, *Celtic and Anglo-Saxon Kingship* (1970), 25-30; D.Dumville, 'The aetheling: a study in Anglo-Saxon constitutional history', *Anglo-Saxon England*, VIII (1979), 1-34.
30.   *V.Cadoci*, pref.; *V.Carantoci*, II.4.
31.   'Culhwch', 99.
32.   'Branwen', 30; *V.Cadoci*, ch.22; *Hist. Brittonum*, ch.37.
33.   See above, pp.82f.
34.   See below, pp.132-4.
35.   'Preface on Penance', 23.
36.   *V.S.Dauid*, ch.64.
37.   Davies, *Early Welsh Microcosm*, 133f.; *Lib. Land.*, 237b.
38.   *De Excidio Britanniae*, cc.66-7.
39.   Davies, *Early Welsh Microcosm*, 130f.; *Arch. Camb.*, XIV, 3rd ser. (1868), 336-8; *V.Iltuti*, ch.17.
40.   For example, *De Excidio Britanniae*, ch.33; *Hist. Brittonum*, cc.45, 46; *Canu Taliesin*, IV, ll.17, 18; *V.Cadoci*, cc.8, 22.
41.   *Canu Taliesin*, V, ll.5-8.
42.   *V.Cadoci*, ch.24.
43.   *Hist. Brittonum*, ch.33.
44.   J.E.Lloyd, *A History of Wales, from the Earliest Times to the Edwardian Conquest* (1911), 339.
45.   See above, p.114.
46.   *V.Cadoci*, cc.22, 23, 24, 25, 69; *V.Gundleii*, ch.13.
47.   For example, *V.Iltuti*, ch.8; *V.Kebii*, ch.8; *V.Tathei*, ch.6; *Arch. Camb.*, XIV, 3rd ser. (1868), 336-8; Davies, *Early Welsh Microcosm*, 50f., and *passim*; cf. M.Miller, *The Saints of Gwynedd* (1979), 114f.
48.   *V.Cadoci*, ch.62.
49.   See below, pp.132f., and Davies, *Early Welsh Microcosm*, 103-5.
50.   *Llyfr Blegywryd*, 72-5; A.W.Wade-Evans, *Welsh Medieval Law* (1909), 204-8, for example.
51.   *V.Iltuti*, cc.9, 10, 18.
52.   *Hist. Brittonum*, cc.38, 42, 46.
53.   *De Excidio Britanniae*, ch.27; *Canu Taliesin*, XII, l.21; *V.Cadoci*, ch.22; *V.Iltuti*, ch.17; *V.Gundleii*, ch.14.
54.   *Hist. Brittonum*, cc.21, 30, 57; 'Culhwch', 131. Cf. Bromwich, *TYP*, no.51 — though this is probably a very late Triad based on Geoffrey of Monmouth.
55.   *V.Cadoci*, cc.22-6, 69.
56.   See above, p.116; 'Ordinance of the Dunsaete', 9; *AC* 1087.
57.   *Llyfr Blegywryd*, 72-4; Wade-Evans, *op. cit.*, 204-8, for example; see G.R.Jones, 'Post-Roman Wales', in *The Agrarian History of England and Wales*, I pt 2, ed. H.P.R.Finberg (1972), 299-302; see above, pp.43-7.
58.   *V.Bernacii*, cc.14, 15; *V.Tathei*, ch.9; *V.Paterni*, ch.31; *V.Iltuti*, cc.10, 17.
59.   *V.Cadoci*, cc.55, 62, 64, 68.
60.   Davies, *Early Welsh Microcosm*, 101.
61.   See above, p.55.
62.   *V.Iltuti*, ch.17; *V.Cadoci*, ch.69; *V.Bernacii*, ch.11; 'Math', 55, 60; 'Branwen', 26.
63.   *V.Cadoci*, ch.25; VCH *Hereford*, 311. W.Davies, 'Braint Teilo', *BBCS*, XXVI (1974-6), 123-37.
64.   *V.Samsonis*, ch.6; *Hist. Brittonum*, ch.33; Colloquy, cc.22, 24; Bromwich, *TYP*, 13; 'Pwyll', 4; 'Branwen', 26; *V.Iltuti*, cc.17, 20; *Canu Aneirin*, B29; *Canu Llywarch Hen*, 72; *Armes Prydein*, l.18. See also Jones, *op. cit.*, 373-5; *BBCS*, XXV (1972-4), 14-19.
65.   'Branwen', 32, 33.
66.   Colloquy, ch.24; see fig.1.
67.   *V.Gundleii*, ch.1; *V.Cadoci*, ch.69; 'Branwen', 29, 32.
68.   It is usually considered that the commote had a much later origin than the cantref (see Lloyd, *op.*

cit., 300f.), on grounds of absence of reference to it in sources of pre-1100, and that it was a sub-division of the cantref made for convenience and efficiency in the early Norman period; that cantref and commote had the same essential administrative function, at different periods, but that the cantref had a much earlier non-administrative origin and significance. See above, pp.82f.; *Lib. Land.*, 255; *BT* 1075; *V.Cadoci*, pref., ch.69; *Hist. Brittonum*, ch.14; cf. T.M. Charles-Edwards, 'The seven bishop-houses of Dyfed', *BBCS*, xxiv (1970-2), 251f., for suggestions on the pre-Norman cantrefs of Dyfed.

69. *ECMW*, no.103 (but see above, p.82); *De Excidio Britanniae*, ch.26; this reading of the stone has, however, been seriously questioned — see R.B.White, *Arch. Camb.*, forthcoming.

70. Davies, *Early Welsh Microcosm*, 108-15; *V.Cadoci*, ch.68; VCH *Hereford*, 311.

71. *Lib. Land.*, xliiif.; cf. *Canu Llywarch Hen*, ed. I.Williams (1935), 42, stanza 75.

72. *Hist. Brittonum*, ch.45; Colloquy, ch.24; 'Culhwch', 96; 'Branwen', 34;Bromwich, *TYP*, 1, 92; *V.S.Dauid*, ch.57; *V.Carantoci*, II.4.

73. *De Excidio Britanniae*, cc.26, 27, 33 etc.

74. Davies, *Early Welsh Microcosm*, 112; Bromwich, *TYP*, 54; *Canu Taliesin*, I; 'Branwen', 30; *V.Cadoci*, cc.1, 16, 23, 24, 25, 26, 53, 69; *V.Iltuti*, cc.25, 26; *V.Gundleii*, ch.12.

75. Bromwich, *TYP*, 54, cf.53; *V.Iltuti*, ch.25; *V.Gundleii*, ch.12; *Journey through Wales*, 257.

76. *De Excidio Britanniae*, ch.27; 'Ordinance of the Dunsaete'; T.Jones, 'The Black Book of Carmarthen ''Stanzas of the Graves'''', *Procs. British Academy*, LIII (1967), 128, stanza 59; *V.Cadoci*, cc.1, 8; *V.Paterni*, ch.31; *V.Tathei*, cc.13, 16.

77. *V.Cadoci*, ch.24.

78. 'Ordinance of the Dunsaete', 1.

79. *V.Iltuti*, ch.23.

80. Colloquy, ch.23.

81. 'Preface on Penance', 6; 'Sinodus Aquilonalis Britaniae', in *The Irish Penitentials*, ed. L.Bieler (Dublin, 1963) 66, cl.3; 'Sinodus Luci Victorie', *ibid.*, 68, cl.1.

82. *V.Cadoci*, cc.8, 25.

83. *Hist. Brittonum*, ch.33; 'Manawydan', 51; *V.Cadoci*, ch.33.

84. 'Ordinance of the Dunsaete', 1, 2.

85. *V.Cadoci*, ch.69; 'Stanzas of the Graves', 128.

86. *De Excidio Britanniae*, ch.27; VCH *Hereford*, 310.

87. 'Sinodus Luci Victorie', cl.4; *V.Cadoci*, cc.43, 69; VCH *Hereford*, 310; Davies, *Early Welsh Microcosm*, 111; *Lib. Land.*, 249b, 263.

88. 'Book of David', 7, 11; *V.Paterni*, ch.31; *V.Cadoci*, cc.21, 22.

89. 'Stanzas of the Graves', 130, stanza 62; *V.Cadoci*, ch.22.

90. *Lib. Land.*, 237b, 233; *Armes Prydein*, ll.141-4.

91. 'Ordinance of the Dunsaete', 5; *V.Cadoci*, cc.22, 69; see above, pp.76, 80.

92. *Lib. Land.*, 186a, 223.

93. *Llyfr Blegywryd*, 24f., 29; Wade-Evans, *op. cit.*, 147, 191-3.

94. 'Pwyll', 4.

95. *V.Cadoci*, cc.22, 23, 24, 25, 69; cf.cc. 33, 50.

96. *V.S.Dauid*, ch.57.

97. *Llyfr Blegywryd*, 54; *Journey through Wales*; 254; Davies, 'Braint Teilo', 128.

98. See above, pp.132f.

99. 'Book of David', 7, 11; *V.Cadoci*, ch. 57; Davies, *Early Welsh Microcosm*, 112.

100. 'Sinodus Luci Victorie', 5; *V.Cadoci*, ch.33, 34; Davies, *Early Welsh Microcosm*, 133.

101. Davies, 'Braint Teilo'; *V.Cadoci*, ch.34; cf. ch.16. See D.Stephenson, *Thirteenth-Century Welsh Law Courts* (1980), on thirteenth-century judges.

102. *V.Cadoci*, ch.22.

103. *Lib. Land.*, 218.

104. *V.Cadoci*, ch.37; *V.Gundleii*, ch.16.

105. *V.Cadoci*, cc.33, 34, 53, 54, 69.

106. Davies, *Early Welsh Microcosm*, 109; cf. 'Manawydan', 44, where prisons for those who disturb the peace by fighting are mentioned. *V.Gundleii*, ch.14; *V.Tathei*, cc.8, 17.

107. *V.Cadoci*, ch.69.
108. *Canu Aneirin*, B37, A18, A39; *V.Cadoci*, ch.53; cf. ch.8.
109. See above, p.132.
110. *De Excidio Britanniae*, ch.5; *V.Cadoci*, ch.53; *V.Gundleii*, cc.1, 14.
111. Davies, 'Braint Teilo', *V.Paterni*, ch.26.

6   The Church — Institutions and Authority

1. See further W.Davies, 'The Celtic Church', *J.Religious History*, VIII (1974-5), 406-11.
2. See p.143 for charters.
3. H.M.Taylor and J.Taylor, *Anglo-Saxon Architecture* (1965), 497-9.
4. T.M.Charles-Edwards, 'The seven bishop-houses of Dyfed', *BBCS*, XXIV (1970-2), 251-2, 262; D.Knowles and R.N.Hadcock, *Medieval Religious Houses, England and Wales* (2nd edn 1971), 476, 477; J.E.Lloyd, *A History of Wales, from the Earliest Times to the Edwardian Conquest* (1911), 150; *ECMW*, nos. 326-34, 391-4; J.M.Lewis, 'A survey of the early Christian monuments of Dyfed west of the Taf', in *Welsh Antiquity*, ed. G.C.Boon and J.M. Lewis (1976), 185f.; J.L.Davies, D.B.Hague, and A.H.A.Hogg, 'The hut-settlement on Gateholm, Pembrokeshire', *Arch. Camb.*, CXX (1971), 102-10; D.B.Hague, 'Grassholm', *CBA Group 2 Report*, XII (1972), 40f.; RCAHMW *Anglesey*, 141-4; D.B. Hague, 'Some Welsh evidence', *Scottish Arch. Forum*, V (1973), 17-35; cf. C.Thomas, *The Early Christian Archaeology of North Britain* (1978), 68; C.W.Johns, 'The Celtic monasteries of north Wales', *Trans. Caerns. Hist. Soc.*, XXI (1960), 14-43.
5. See E.G.Bowen, *The Settlements of the Celtic Saints in Wales* (2nd edn 1956), 104-17, 126, 139 etc.
6. Davies, *Early Welsh Microcosm*, 121-4.
7. *Ibid.*, 140f.
8. *Lib. Land.*, 72a, 73a, 161, 162a.
9. See Bowen, *op. cit., passim*, and see further below, pp.162f.
10. Davies, *Early Welsh Microcosm*,

141-3; O.Chadwick, 'The evidence of dedications in the early history of the Welsh church' in N.Chadwick *et al.*, *Studies in Early British History* (1954), 173-88.
11. *V.Gundleii*, ch.8; *V.Paterni*, ch.14.
12. *De Excidio Britanniae*, ch.34; 'Preface on Penance', 1, 2, 3; 'Sinodus Aquilonalis Britanniae', in *The Irish Penitentials*, ed. L.Bieler (Dublin, 1963), 66, cl.1; cf. 'Book of David', 10.
13. See K.Hughes, *The Church in Early Irish Society* (1966), 17-35; N.Chadwick, 'Intellectual contacts between Britain and Gaul in the fifth century', in N.Chadwick *et al.*, *op. cit.*, 254.
14. 'Marwnad Cynddylan'; *Hist. Ecclesiastica*, II.2; *V.Cadoci*, cc.55, 56, 61, 63, 64, 67, 68; *Life of King Alfred*, ch.79.
15. Hughes, *op. cit.*, 39-64.
16. *V.Samsonis*, cc.20, 38, 40-2, 50, 52, 59.
17. *V.Cadoci*, cc.58, 63.
18. *V.Pauli*; Hughes, *op. cit.*, 69-72; *Analecta Bollandiana*, LXXIII (1955), 197-213, 289-322; see W.Davies, 'The Latin charter tradition in western Britain, Brittany and Ireland in the early medieval period', in *Ireland and Europe*, ed. D.Dumville, R.McKitterick and D.Whitelock (forthcoming).
19. See Hughes, *op. cit.*, 29-35, 71-4; K.H.Jackson, *Language and History in Early Britain* (1953), 122-48; D.Greene, 'Some linguistic evidence relating to the British church', in *Christianity in Britain, 300-700*, ed. M.W.Barley and R.P.C.Hanson (1968), 75-86; W.Davies, 'The Latin charter tradition'.
20. Lewis, *op. cit.*; R.B.White, *Early Christian Gwynedd* (1975), 7; Thomas, *op. cit.*, 50f., 67f., 138f.
21. *Life of King Alfred*, ch.79; *Lib. Land.*, xlvi; Davies, *Early Welsh Microcosm*, 135f.
22. *Ibid.*, 125-8.
23. *Journey through Wales*, 262-4, for example.
24. *V.S.Dauid*, ch.20; J.Conway Davies, *Episcopal Acts and Cognate Documents relating to Welsh Dioceses, 1066-1272* (2 vols., 1946-8), 493-537.

25. Davies, *Early Welsh Microcosm*, 155.
26. Charles-Edwards, *op. cit.*, 256, 259.
27. *Hist. Ecclesiastica*, II.2; Bromwich *TYP*, no.90.
28. *V.Gundleii*, ch.8; *V.Wenefrede*, ch.19; *V.Cadoci*, ch.1; *V.Pauli*, ch.7.
29. Davies, *Early Welsh Microcosm*, 125, 128.
30. *De Excidio Britanniae*, cc. 21, 28, 32, 34, 66, 67.
31. 'Preface on Penance', 1.
32. *V.Samsonis*, ch.36.
33. *Ibid.*, ch.16.
34. *Ibid.*, ch.30.
35. *Ibid.*, cc.21, 30.
36. *Ibid.*, cc.7-16.
37. *Ibid.*, cc.20-1, 33, 36.
38. *Ibid.*, cc.40-1.
39. *Hist. Ecclesiastica*, IV.27-30; *Adomnan's Life of Columba*, ed. A.O. and M.Anderson (1961), 109-11; K.Hughes and A.Hamlin, *The Modern Traveller to the Early Irish Church* (1977), 23, 25.
40. *V.Samsonis*, ch.15, 21, 24, 30, 36, 45.
41. *Ibid.*, cc.45.
42. *Journey through Wales*, 96-8.
43. Bromwich, *TYP*, no.90.
44. *V.Carantoci*, II.4; *V.Bernacii*, cc.4, 6, 9; *V.Kebii*, cc.10, 15; *V.Iltuti*, cc.7, 9, 11, 16, 18; *V.Tathei*, cc.1, 12; *V.Paterni*, cc.3, 5; *V.Gundleii*, ch.6.
45. *V.Cadoci*, cc.8, 11, 12, 19, 53.
46. *V.S.Dauid*, cc.12, 14, 20, 21, 28.
47. *Ibid.*, ch.29.
48. *Ibid.*, cc.21-30.
49. *Ibid.*, cc.4, 9, 17, 31, 34, 56.
50. RCAHM *Anglesey*, 141-4; Hague, 'Some Welsh evidence'; *Med. Arch.*, xiv (1970), 171f.; RCAHM *Glamorgan*, I pt 3, 14f.; see above pp.28f.
51. *V.S.Dauid*, ch.24; *V.Tathei*, ch.15; *V.Cadoci*, cc.8, 27, 48, 63.
52. *V.S.Dauid*, ch.20; *V.Bernacii*, ch.6; *V.Wenefrede*, ch.7; *V.Cadoci*, cc.8, 9, 12.
53. *Ibid.*, ch.21, 58, 63; *V.Gundleii*, ch.8; *V.Paterni*, cc.14, 24.
54. *V.Samsonis*, cc.16, 34; *Lib. Land.*, xlvi; *V.Cadoci*, cc.58, 65, 68.
55. Davies, *Early Welsh Microcosm*, 127f.
56. *Colloquy*, ch.5.
57. *V.Cadoci*, cc.12, 33, 49, 50; *V.S.Dauid*, ch.10, 29, 35, 38.
58. *V.Cadoci*, ch.24.
59. *V.Pauli*, ch.4; *V.Iltuti*, ch.14.
60. See below, p.158.
61. Cf. *V.Samsonis*, ch.36; *V.Cadoci*, cc.1, 7, 28.
62. *De Excidio Britanniae*, ch.1; *ECMW*, no.33.
63. *Lib. Land.*, xlvi.
64. *Life of King Alfred*, ch.79.
65. *V.Samsonis*, cc.14, 16, 40.
66. *V.Cadoci*, ch.59.
67. See Conway Davies, *op. cit.*, 493-537.
68. *Journey through Wales*, 262-4.
69. Davies, *Early Welsh Microcosm*, 128-30.
70. *De Excidio Britanniae*, ch.66.
71. *ECMW*, nos.33, 46, 83; *Lib. Land.*, xlv-vi; Davies, *Early Welsh Microcosm*, 125f.; *Colloquy*, ch.5; *V.S.Dauid*, cc.9, 64.
72. Davies, *Early Welsh Microcosm*, 126f. I am grateful to the Rev. Wyn Evans for pointing out to me that *presbiter* and *sacerdos* are glossed by different vernacular terms in the Old Cornish *Vocabularium Cornicum*.
73. *Journey through Wales*, 161-3.
74. See L.Fleuriot, 'Les évêques de la ''Clas Kenedyr'', évêché disparu de la région de Hereford, *Études Celtiques*, xv (1976-7), 225-6; reference to the death of Bishop Cynog (associated with Brecon), *AC* 606, may be a tenth-century acknowledgement of the existence of this bishop's seat.
75. Davies, *Early Welsh Microcosm*, 149-59.
76. *AC* 809; *BT* 944; R.I.Best and H.J.Lawlor (eds.), *The Martyrology of Tallaght* (Henry Bradshaw Soc. 68, 1931), 70.
77. The document recording Maelgwn's grant to Llanelwy is likely to have a pre-Conquest origin; *Arch. Camb.*, xiv, 3rd ser. (1868), 336-8; see Davies, 'The Latin charter tradition', and cf. *AC* 612.
78. *V.Paterni*, ch.20; *V.S.Dauid*, ch.44.
79. Cf.Davies, *Early Welsh Microcosm*, 146-8.
80. See Charles-Edwards, *op. cit.*
81. *Life of King Alfred*, ch.79.
82. *V.S.Dauid*, cc.46, 49, 53; Bromwich, *TYP*, p.229 and no.1;

Davies, *Early Welsh Microcosm*, 149.
83. *V.S.Dauid*, cc.15, 16, 42, 49, 50, 53, 56, 57.
84. See Conway-Davies,*op. cit.*, 190-232; M. Richter, *Giraldus Cambrensis* (1972).
85. Cf. Charles-Edwards, *op. cit.*, 257; see below, pp.200f.
86. *V.Gundleii*, ch.5; *V.Tathei*, ch.6; *V.Iltuti*, ch.7.
87. *V.Paterni*, ch.14; *V.Iltuti*, ch.10; cf. *V.Cadoci*, ch.37.
88. *V.Paterni*, ch.30; *V.Tathei*, ch.6.
89. *V.Paterni*, cc.24, 27.
90. *V.Samsonis*, cc.13, 15, 34, 43, 44.
91. Davies, *Early Welsh Microcosm*, 133f.
92. 'Preface on Penance', 4.
93. *V.Iltuti*, ch.19.
94. *V.Samsonis*, cc.38, 40.
95. *V.Cadoci*, cc.10, 11, 12, 17, 21, 24, 35, 36, 37, 54; see further W. Davies, 'Property rights and property claims in Welsh *Vitae* of the eleventh century', in *Hagiographie, cultures et sociètès*, ed. E.Patlagean and P.Riché (Paris, 1981), 515-33.
96. *V.Cadoci*, ch.58.
97. *V.S.Dauid*, ch.13; *V.Paterni*, ch.27.
98. Davies, *Early Welsh Microcosm*, 139-41.
99. *Ibid.*, 141-6; Davies, 'Property rights'.
100. See G.H. Doble, *The Saints of Cornwall* (1923-44, repr. in 5 vols., 1960-70), *passim*.
101. Bowen, *op. cit.*, 33-103.
102. Davies, *Early Welsh Microcosm*, 150-1.
103. *ECMW*, nos.116, 124.
104. *Lib. Land.*, 164, 169b; *V.Tathei*, ch.6; *V.Iltuti*, ch.25.
105. Davies, *Early Welsh Microcosm*, 37f.; *idem*, 'Unciae: land measurement in the *Liber Landavensis*', *AgHR*, xxi (1973), 111-21.
106. *V.Cadoci*, ch.30; *V.Iltuti*, ch.23; Colloquy, ch.5.
107. *V.Cadoci*, cc.7, 24; *V.Pauli*, ch.4; etc.
108. See above pp.42,67f.; *V.Cadoci*, cc.24, 43, 58; *V.Iltuti*, ch.24.
109. *V.Cadoci*, ch.58; *Lib. Land.*, 264b; Colloquy, ch.5.
110. See above, pp.46f.
111. *V.Cadoci*, cc.23, 43; Davies, *Early Welsh Microcosm*, 128.
112. *V.Iltuti*, ch.12.
113. *V.Cadoci*, cc.48-50, 51.
114. See above, pp.33f.; *V.Cadoci*, ch.24.
115. *V.Cadoci*, ch.22; *V.Iltuti*, ch.15; Davies, *Early Welsh Microcosm*, 61.
116. *Ibid.*, 48-50; *V.Cadoci*, cc.55, 62.
117. See above, p.137.
118. *V.Cadoci*, ch.22; see Davies, 'Property rights', for further discussion.
119. *V.S.Dauid*, ch.57.
120. *Lib. Land.*, 217, 218, 239, 259, 261, 271.
121. *Lib. Land.*, 237b.
122. *De Excidio Britanniae*, ch.21; *V.Gundleii*, ch.14.
123. *V.Cadoci*, cc.7, 16, 23, 24, 30.
124. *V.Kebii*, ch.13; *V.Cadoci*, cc.35, 69; *Hist. Brittonum*, cc.47, 54.
125. *V.S.Dauid*, ch.64; *V.Iltuti*, ch.19.
126. *Life of King Alfred*, ch.79; see above, p.107.

7 Christianity and Spirituality

1. *De Excidio Britanniae*, ch.4.
2. *Hist. Brittonum*, ch.31.
3. *Ibid.*, cc.32, 35, 52.
4. *V.Cadoci*, ch.26; *V.Carantoci*, I.2.
5. *V.S.Dauid*, ch.16.
6. Bromwich,*TYP*, no.37R.
7. S.Frere, *Britannia* (1967), 331-4; P.A.Rahtz, 'Late Roman cemeteries and beyond', in *Burial in the Roman World*, ed. R.Reece (CBA Res.Rep. no.22, 1977), 53-64; J.Myres, 'Pelagius and the end of Roman rule in Britain', *J.Roman Studies*, L (1960), 21-36; C.J.S.Green, 'The significance of plaster burials for the recognition of Christian cemeteries', in Reece (ed.), *op. cit.*, 50-2; W.Liebeschutz, 'Did the Pelagian movement have social aims?', *Historia*, xii (1963), 227-41; J.Morris, 'Pelagian literature', *J.Theological Studies*, n.s. xvi (1965), 25-60.
8. P.Rahtz and L.Watts, 'The end of Roman temples in the west of Britain', in *The End of Roman Britain*, ed. P.J.Casey (BAR 71, 1979), 183-210; N.Chadwick, 'Intellectual contacts between Britain and Gaul in the fifth century', in N.Chadwick *et al.*, *Studies in Early British History*

(1954), 189-263; Rahtz, 'Late Roman cemeteries', 55f.; M.W.Barley and R.P.C.Hanson (eds.), *Christianity in Britain, 300-700* (1968), esp. 75-92; C.Thomas, 'Imported Late Roman Mediterranean pottery in Ireland and western Britain: chronologies and implications', *Procs. Royal Irish Academy*, LXXVI,C (1976), 245-55; 'Marwnad Cynddylan'.

9. *ECMW*, 4-16; C.Thomas, *The Early Christian Archaeology of North Britain* (1971), 10-47.

10. M.Miller, *The Saints of Gwynedd* (1979), 11, 119.

11. See below, pp.180-2.

12. *Canu Aneirin*, A20, A29; *Hist. Brittonum*, ch.33.

13. *V.Gundleii*, ch.2; *V.Paterni*, ch.1; *V.Cadoci*, pref.; *V.Tathei*, ch.1.

14. *V.Cadoci*, cc.26, 39.

15. I.Williams, *The Beginnings of Welsh Poetry*, ed. and trans. R.Bromwich (1972), 101f.

16. *De Excidio Britanniae*, cc.21, 22, 24.

17. *Hist. Brittonum*, ch.45; *Colloquy*, ch.24.

18. *Canu Aneirin*, B5, B6, A18.

19. *De Excidio Britanniae*, cc.28, 66, 67.

20. *Colloquy*, ch.19.

21. *V.S.Dauid*, cc.4, 9, 17, 18, 31, 32, 34 etc; see above, p.154.

22. See above, p.168.

23. *Armes Prydein*, ll.105f.

24. 'Book of David', 10; *De Excidio Britanniae*, ch.35; *ECMW*, no.32; *Lib. Land.*, xliii, xlv; *Armes Prydein*, ll.139f.

25. *Hist. Brittonum*, ch.54; *V.S.Dauid*, ch.17.

26. *V.S.Dauid*, ch.11; *V.Cadoci*, cc.13, 24, 34, 46; *De Excidio Britanniae*, cc.11, 12.

27. Davies, *Early Welsh Microcosm*, 132; A.W.Wade-Evans (ed.), *Vitae Sanctorum Britanniae et Genealogiae* (1944), *passim*.

28. *V.Samsonis*, cc.9, 12, 20, 23, 24; *V.Machutis*, ch.1; *V.Pauli*, ch.3; R.I.Best and H.J.Lawlor (eds.), *The Martyrology of Tallaght* (Henry Bradshaw Soc. 68, 1931), 35, 70.

29. Davies, *Early Welsh Microcosm*, 131f.

30. *ECMW*, no.239; *Arch. Camb.*, XIV, 3rd ser. (1868), 336-8 (see W.Davies, 'The Latin charter tradition in western Britain, Brittany and Ireland in the early medieval period', in *Ireland and Europe*, ed. D.Dumville, R.McKitterick and D.Whitelock (forthcoming); P.C.Bartrum (ed.), *Early Welsh Genealogical Tracts* (1966), 14-16.

31. G.S.M.Walker (ed.), *Sancti Columbani Opera* (Scriptores Latini Hiberniae, Dublin, 1957), 8; Best and Lawlor (eds.), *op. cit.*, 13, 20, 35, 70; W.Stokes (ed.), *The Martyrology of Oengus the Culdee* (Henry Bradshaw Soc. 29, 1905), 38, 80; *Analecta Bollandiana*, LXXIII (1955), 206-11.

32. Davies, *Early Welsh Microcosm*, 132; *AC* 454, 457, 521, 718; *Hist. Brittonum*, cc.16, 32, 48, 50, 55, 65, etc.; Colloquy, cc.15, 16, 19, 23; *V.Cadoci*, cc.10, 26, 27; *Armes Prydein*, l.25; *V.S.Dauid*, cc.3, 35-7, 40.

33. Davies, *Early Welsh Microcosm*, 132; *Hist. Brittonum*, cc.33, 52, 54; *Armes Prydein*, ll.41, 98; *Canu Aneirin*, A29; *V.S.Dauid*, ch.2; *V.Cadoci*, cc.1, 8; *V.Iltuti*, cc.7, 16, 18; *V.Tathei*, ch.6.

34. S.Harris, 'The Kalendar of the Vitae Sanctorum Wallensium', *J.Hist.Soc. Church in Wales*, III (1953), 3-53; see below, p.214.

35. *Armes Prydein*, ll.139, 140; *V.Cadoci*, ch.35; *V.Iltuti*, ch.10; *V.Gundleii*, ch.14; *V.S.Dauid*, ch.57, etc.

36. See above, p.137.

37. *Lib. Land.*, xliii.

38. *Lib. Land.*, 144, 164, 187.

39. *Lib. Land.*, 73a.

40. *Lib. Land.*, 162a.

41. *V.Cadoci*, ch.31; *V.S.Dauid*, ch.1; *V.Gundleii*, ch.11.

42. See above, pp.151-3.

43. *Journey through Wales*, 189.

44. *V.S.Dauid*, cc.41, 43.

45. *V.Cadoci*, cc.7, 29.

46. *Hist. Brittonum*, cc.32-4, 40, 47, 48, 71.

47. *Ibid.*, cc.26, 32.

48. *V.Cadoci*, ch.39.

49. I have confined my examples to the eleventh-century Lives of Cadog and David; there are many comparable examples from the twelfth-century Lives, though there are also noticeable differences in emphasis which

reflect some changing attitudes in that century. See W.Davies, 'Property rights and claims in Welsh *Vitae* of the eleventh century' in *Hagiographie, cultures et sociétés*, ed. E.Patlagean and P.Riché (Paris, 1981), 515-33.

50. *V.S.Dauid*, cc.7, 11, 51; *V.Cadoci*, cc.14, 21, 26; *Hist. Brittonum*, ch.54.

51. *V.Cadoci*, cc.7, 12, 28, 29, 31; *V.S.Dauid*, cc.13, 33, 35.

52. *V.Cadoci*, cc.6, 11, 29; *V.S.Dauid*, ch.33.

53. *Hist. Brittonum*, ch.32.

54. *V.Cadoci*, cc.8, 12, 29, etc.

55. *V.Cadoci*, ch.1; *V.S.Dauid*, ch.8, etc.

56. F.Jones, *The Holy Wells of Wales* (1954), 49f., 142f., 151, 179, 182; RCAHMW *Caernarvon*, 205f.; RCAHMW *Anglesey*, 123; cf. S.Victory, *The Celtic Church in Wales* (1977), 79f., pl.IV.

57. *V.Cadoci*, cc.21, 27, 31, 34; *V.S.Dauid*, ch.48.

58. *V.Paterni*, ch.11; Williams, *op. cit.*, 189, 181ff.; cf. Victory, *op. cit.*, 76-88.

59. *V.Cadoci*, cc.34, 55-69; *Lib. Land.*, xliii-vii.

60. *V.Tathei*, ch.13; *V.S.Dauid*, ch.6.

61. *V.Cadoci*, ch.39.

62. *Ibid.*, cc.39, 40.

63. *Ibid.*, cc.35, 36, 37, 44, 50; *V.S.Dauid*, ch.39.

64. *BT* 1089; *V.Iltuti*, ch.22; *Hist. Brittonum*, ch.71.

65. Victory, *op. cit.*, 81.

66. *V.S.Dauid*, ch.18; *V.Cadoci*, ch.46; Thomas, *Early Christian Archaeology of North Britain*, 89, 137-41, 143f.

67. R.B.White, 'Excavations at Arfryn, Bodedern, long-cist cemeteries and the origins of Christianity in Britain', *Trans. Anglesey Ant. Soc. and Field Club* (1971-2), 19-51; *idem, Early Christian Gwynedd* (1975), 7; *idem*, 'New light on the origins of the kingdom of Gwynedd', in *Astudiaethau ar yr Hengerdd*, ed. R.Bromwich and R.B.Jones (1978), 350-5; Thomas, *Early Christian Archaeology of North Britain*, 64.

68. Rahtz, 'Late Roman cemeteries', 56-9; C.Houlder, 'The henge monuments at Llandegái', *Antiquity*, XLII (1968), 217, 221; cf.

Thomas, *Early Christian Archaeology of North Britain*, 62f.

69. D.B.Hague, 'Whitesands Bay', *CBA Group 2 Report*, x (1970), 27f.; *Arch.J.*, CXIX (1962), 335.

70. *Arch. Camb.*, VII, 6th ser. (1907), 267-76; J.M.Lewis, 'A survey of the early Christian monuments of Dyfed west of the Taf', in *Welsh Antiquity*, ed. G.C.Boon and J.M.Lewis (1976), 192; cf. Thomas, *Early Christian Archaeology of North Britain*, 70f., 73, 168-73, 144; *CBA Group 2 Report*, IX (1969), 30.

71. *V.S.Dauid*, ch.39; *V.Cadoci*, cc.35, 36.

72. 'Sinodus Aquilonalis Britaniae', in *The Irish Penitentials*, ed. L.Bieler (Dublin, 1963), cl.3, 4; 'Sinodus Luci Victorie', *ibid.*, cl.6; cf. T.M.Charles-Edwards, 'The social background to Irish *peregrinatio*', *Celtica*, XI (1975-6), 43-59.

73. *V.Samsonis*, ch.37; J.F.Kenney, *Sources for the Early History of Ireland: Ecclesiastical* (Columbia, 1929), 556; Lewis, *op. cit.*, 181; cf. P.O'Ríain, 'The Irish element in Welsh hagiographical tradition', in *Irish Antiquity*, ed. D.O'Corráin (forthcoming); M.Lapidge, 'The Welsh-Latin poetry of Sulien's family', *Studia Celtica*, VIII-IX (1973-4), 84-7.

74. *AC* 854, 885, 928; *BT* 682, 975.

75. Colloquy, cc.15, 16, 19; *V.Cadoci*, cc.26, 27, 32, 35.

76. *V.S.Dauid*, ch.44; *V.Kebii*, I.3; *V.Paterni*, ch.20; *V.Cadoci*, cc.14, 26, 32.

77. *V.Cadoci*, cc.31, 36, 42; *AC* 1079; *BT* 1081.

78. *AC* 453, 665, 768; *Hist. Brittonum*, ch.63.

79. *V.Cadoci*, pref.; *V.Tathei*, ch.17; *AC* 1047.

80. Harris, *op. cit.*; H.J.Lawlor (ed.), *The Psalter and Martyrology of Ricemarch* (Henry Bradshaw Soc. 47, 1914).

81. *V.Cadoci*, ch.35; *V.S.Dauid*, cc.34, 49; *V.Wenefrede*, ch.29.

82. *De Excidio Britanniae*, ch.25.

83. *ECMW*, no.301; *Canu Taliesin*, X, for example.

84. *Hist. Brittonum*, ch.54; *Armes Prydein*, 1.105; *V.Paterni*, ch.29.

85. *V.S.Dauid*, cc.5, 62; *V.Cadoci*, ch.37.

86. *V.Samsonis*, ch.2; *V.Gundleii*, cc.12, 13; *BT* 1091.
87. *Canu Aneirin*, B40.
88. *V.Samsonis*, ch.22.
89. *Ibid.*, cc.18, 41; *V.S.Dauid*, ch.62.
90. *Canu Taliesin*, III; *Hist. Brittonum*, cc.52-4, 63, 65 (cf.33, 35).
91. 'Culhwch', 95; 'Pwyll', 20; *V.S.Dauid*, ch.7; 'Math', 62f.; *V.Iltuti*, ch.1; *V.Cadoci*, cc.1, 4.
92. 'Pwyll', 20; 'Math', 68; cf. *V.Cadoci*, ch.1; cf. *Hist. Ecclesiastica*, II.2.
93. *Canu Llywarch Hen*, 67, 68; *Canu Aneirin*, B2, B34, A1, A12, A15, A40; *Canu Taliesin*, X; *V.Cadoci*, ch.39; *V.S.Dauid*, ch.65; T.Jones, 'The Black Book of Carmarthen "Stanzas of the Graves"', *Procs. British Academy*, LIII (1967), 97-138.
94. I am grateful to Mr G. Williams of the Dyfed Archaeological Trust for pointing out that some of the long cist burials at Llanwnwr and at Caerau, St Dogmaels, were reputed to have contained ashes.
95. 'Marwnad Cynddylan'.
96. *Hist. Brittonum*, cc.71, 73, 74; Jones, 'Stanzas of the Graves', stanzas 1, 10, 33, 67; cf. 'De Situ Brecheniauc', Bartrum (ed.), 14-16.
97. 'Canu Heledd', 86; Jones, 'Stanzas of the Graves', stanzas 51, 63; *Canu Llywarch Hen*, 68; *Canu Aneirin*, A1, A5; 'Culhwch', 95; cf. *V.Cadoci*, ch.28: 'Carn Tylywai'.
98. *ECMW*, nos. 62, 101, 287.
99. *De Excidio Britanniae*, ch.24; *Hist. Brittonum*, ch.44; *V.Iltuti*, ch.22; *V.Cadoci*, ch.21.
100. *V.Bernacii*, ch.16; *V.Gundleii*, ch.10; *V.Paterni*, ch.28; *V.Tathei*, cc.13, 17; *V.Cadoci*, cc.36, 38.
101. *Ibid.*, cc.28, 53.
102. *Ibid.*, ch.66; *Lib. Land.*, 121, 146; Davies, *Early Welsh Microcosm*, 132.
103. *V.Cadoci*, ch.53.
104. *ECMW*, no.78.
105. See above, p.182; *ECMW*, no.167.
106. *Ibid.*, nos.73, 67a, 159; see L.Alcock, *Arthur's Britain* (1971), 247-8; see above, pp.110f., for Elise's pillar.
107. See Thomas, *Early Christian Archaeology of North Britain*, 50-8, 67f.; *idem*, 'The evidence from North Britain', in Barley and Hanson (eds.), *op. cit.*, 107; *idem*, 'An early Christian cemetery and chapel on Ardwall Isle, Kirkcudbright', *Med. Arch.*, XI (1967), 165-77; see above, pp.19-21.
108. *Arch. Camb.*, VIII, 6th ser. (1908), 242-57; *ibid.*, XVIII, 6th ser. (1918), 174-6; *ECMW*, nos.301, 326-34; Lewis, *op. cit.*, 187.
109. C.A.R.Radford, 'St Justinian's Chapel', *Arch.J.*, CXIX (1962), 335; Hague, *op. cit.*; Lewis, *op. cit.*, 186; J.F.Jones, 'Llanllwni "crouched burial"', *Carmarthen Antiquary*, CXI (1961), 207; D.B.Hague, 'Some Welsh evidence', *Scottish Arch. Forum*, V (1973), 29-34.
110. *Arch. Camb.*, CXXII (1973), 147-53; *CBA Group 2 Report*, XVI (1976), 44; Houlder, *op. cit.*, 221; *CBA Group 2 Report*, XIX (1979), 35; *Arch. Camb.*, CXIX (1970), 68-70; Lewis, *op. cit.*, 187; cf. *Arch. Camb.*, XXI (1847), 30-4; *CBA Group 2 Report*, V (1965), 23; *Arch. Camb.*, CXX (1971), 49.
111. Personal comment from Jeremy Knight; V.Gregory (forthcoming). *CBA Group 2 Report*, XIX (1979), 55; Glamorgan Gwent Archaeological Trust Report, 1978-9, 35f.
112. *Arch. Camb.*, LXXXI (1926), 1-35; Dyfed Archaeological Record, PRN2096-7; F.Lynch, 'Report on the re-excavation of two Bronze Age cairns in Anglesey', *Arch. Camb.*, CXX (1971), 46-9; White, 'Excavations at Arfryn', 25-32.
113. *CBA Group 2 Report*, XIX (1979), 35; Houlder, *op. cit.*, 216, 221.
114. *De Excidio Britanniae*, cc.66, 107.
115. *Canu Aneirin*, A33; *V.Gundleii*, ch.15; *V.S.Dauid*, ch.5.
116. *V.Cadoci*, cc.57, 58, 65; W.Davies, *The Llandaff Charters* (1979), 139.
117. *Lib. Land.*, xliii.
118. 'Sinodus Luci Victorie', Bieler (ed.), *op. cit.*, 68, cl.1-8; 'Book of David', 10.
119. *V.Gundleii*, ch.6; 'Pwyll', 19; *V.Wenefrede*, ch.30.
120. *Lib. Land.*, 180b, 189, 244, 267; Davies, *Early Welsh Microcosm*, 133f.
121. *V.Cadoci*, cc.53, 54, 57, 67.

Appendix — The Source Material

1. See below, p.202.
2. See below, p.213.
3. See below, p.213.
4. See below, p.213.
5. See below, p.217.
6. K.Hughes, 'The Welsh Latin Chronicles: *Annales Cambriae* and related texts', *Procs. British Academy*, LIX (1973), 3-28; M.H.Davies, 'A palaeographical and textual study of the text of the Annales Cambriae in BL Harley MS 3859' (M.A. thesis, University of Wales, 1978), 18, 53.
7. K.Jackson, 'On the northern British section in Nennius', in N.Chadwick *et al.*, *Celt and Saxon* (1963), 20-62; M.Davies, *op. cit.*, 31f., 36, 47.
8. D.Dumville, 'On the north British section of the *Hist. Brittonum*', *Welsh Hist. Rev.*, VIII (1977), 345-54, against this view, is not convincing.
9. W.Davies, 'The Latin charter tradition in western Britain, Brittany and Ireland in the early medieval period', in *Ireland and Europe*, ed. D.Dumville, R.McKitterick and D.Whitelock (forthcoming).
10. W.Davies, *The Llandaff Charters* (1979); *idem*, '*Liber Landavensis*: construction and credibility', *Eng.Hist.Rev.*, LXXXVIII (1973), 335-51, for a summary.
11. Davies, 'The Latin charter tradition'.
12. Printed in *Lib. Land.*, xliii-vii; see Davies, 'The Latin charter tradition', for dating.
13. *National Library of Wales J.*, II (1941-2), 11.
14. J.Leland, *Itinerary* (repr.1964), IV.168.
15. H.Ellis (ed.), *Registrum vulgariter nuncupatum 'The Record of Caernarvon'* (1838), 257.
16. *Arch. Camb.*, XIV, 3rd ser. (1868), 336-8; see Davies, 'The Latin charter tradition', for discussion.
17. See above, pp.200f.
18. P.C.Bartrum (ed.), *Early Welsh Genealogical Tracts* (1966), 9-13.
19. D.Dumville, 'Kingship, genealogies and regnal lists', in *Early Medieval Kingship*, ed.

P.Sawyer and I.Wood (1977), 72-104; see Bartrum (ed.), *op. cit.*, for comprehensive treatment.
20. M.Miller, 'Historicity and the pedigrees of the Northcountrymen', *BBCS*, XXVI (1974-6), 255-80; *idem*, 'Date-guessing and pedigrees', *Studia Celtica*, X-XI (1975-6), 96-109; *idem*, 'Date-guessing and Dyfed', *Studia Celtica*, XII-XIII (1977-8), 33-61; *idem*, 'The foundation-legend of Gwynedd in the Latin texts', *BBCS*, XXVII (1976-8), 515-32.
21. Bartrum (ed.), *op. cit.*, 1-3.
22. A.Owen (ed.), *Ancient Laws and Institutes of Wales* (1841), for the corpus of texts; *Llyfr Iorwerth*, ed. A.R.Wiliam (1960); A.W. Wade-Evans, *Welsh Medieval Law* (1909); *Llyfr Blegywryd*; see J.G.Edwards, 'Studies in the Welsh laws since 1928', *Welsh Hist. Rev.*, special volume (1963), 1-18.
23. H.D.Emanuel, 'The Latin texts of the Welsh laws', *Welsh Hist. Rev.*, special volume (1963), 25-32; *idem*, *The Latin Texts of the Welsh Laws* (1967); D.Huws, *The Medieval Codex* (1980), 14; *idem*, 'Leges Howelda at Canterbury', *National Library of Wales J.*, XIX (1975-6), 341f.
24. See above, p.132; Emanuel, 'The Latin texts', 30, equally shows the immediacy of the thirteenth-century context.
25. T.M.Charles-Edwards, 'The seven bishop-houses of Dyfed', *BBCS*, XXIV (1970-2), 247-62; cf. *idem*, 'The date of the four branches of the Mabinogi', *Trans. Hon. Soc. Cymmrodorion* (1970), 267, on obsolete law in the *Mabinogi*.
26. H.Wasserschleben (ed.), *Die Irische Kanonensammlung* (2nd edn, Leipzig, 1885); K.Hughes, *Early Christian Ireland: Introduction to the Sources* (1972), 67-95.
27. L.Bieler (ed.), *The Irish Penitentials* (Dublin, 1963), 3.
28. See K.Hughes, *The Church in Early Irish Society* (1966), 43f.
29. See above, p.114.
30. D.Dumville, '"Nennius" and the *Hist. Brittonum*', *Studia Celtica*, X-XI (1975-6), 78-95.
31. See above, pp.200-3.

32. We await Dr Dumville's critical edition of *Hist. Brittonum* for a full appreciation of the range of manuscripts and textual history of this work.

33. See D.Dumville, 'Sub-Roman Britain: history and legend', *History*, LXII (1977), 176f.

34. *Idem*, 'Some aspects of the chronology of the *Hist. Brittonum*', *BBCS*, xxv (1972-4), 439-45.

35. Jackson, *op. cit.*, *pace* Dumville, 'On the north British section of the *Historia Brittonum*'.

36. F.Kerlouégan, 'Le Latin du *De Excidio Britanniae* de Gildas', in *Christianity in Britain, 300-700*, ed. M.W.Barley and R.P.C.Hanson (1968), 151-76; K.H.Jackson, *Language and History in Early Britain* (1953), 40; Dumville, 'Sub-Roman Britain', 183f.

37. M.Miller, 'Relative and absolute publication dates of Gildas's *De Excidio* in medieval scholarship', *BBCS*, xxvi (1974-6), 169-74; but see now T.D.O'Sullivan, *The De Excidio of Gildas, its Authenticity and Date* (Leiden, 1978), who dates it some 20 years earlier. The authenticity of the work has been questioned, principally by Wade-Evans and Grosjean among modern scholars, and largely on grounds that *De Excidio* is really two works; these arguments have been amply countered by Kerlouégan and O'Sullivan. See A.W.Wade-Evans, *Welsh Christian Origins* (1934), 291-2; P.Grosjean, 'Remarques sur le *De Excidio* attribué à Gildas', *Archivum Latinitatis Medii Aevi*, xxv (1955), 164-87.

38. Michael Winterbottom's comments on the style of Gildas are very helpful: Gildas, *The Ruin of Britain*, ed. and trans. M.Winterbottom (1978), 5-9; cf. Winterbottom, 'The preface of Gildas' *De Excidio*', *Trans. Hon. Soc. Cymmrodorion* (1974-5), 277-87.

39. See above, pp.177f.

40. See above, pp.205f.

41. See S.Baring-Gould and J.Fisher, *The Lives of the British Saints* (4 vols., 1907-13), for an insight into the range.

42. K.Hughes, 'British Museum MS Cotton Vespasian A.xiv (*'Vitae Sanctorum Wallensium'*): its purpose and provenance', in N.Chadwick *et al.*, *Studies in the Early British Church* (1958), 183-200.

43. W.Davies, 'Property rights and property claims in Welsh *Vitae* of the eleventh century', in *Hagiographie, cultures et sociétés*, ed. E.Patlagean and P.Riché (Paris, 1981), 515-33; H.D.Emanuel, 'An analysis of the composition of the "Vita Cadoci"', *National Library of Wales J.*, VII (1951-2), 217-27; cf.C.N.L.Brooke, 'St Peter of Gloucester and St Cadoc of Llancarfan', in Chadwick *et al.*, *Celt and Saxon*, 258-322, and D.Kirby, 'A note on Rhigyfarch's *Life of David*', *Welsh Hist. Rev.*, IV (1968-9), 292-7.

44. See above, p.202.

45. J.W.James in *V.S.Dauid*, xi; see above, pp.156f.

46. A.W.Wade-Evans (ed.), *Vitae Sanctorum Britanniae et Genealogiae* (1944), xi-xvi.

47. I.Williams, *The Beginnings of Welsh Poetry*, ed. and trans. R.Bromwich (1972), 89-121.

48. H.J.Lawlor (ed.), *The Psalter and Martyrology of Ricemarch* (Henry Bradshaw Soc., 47, 1914), 121-3; Williams, *Beginnings of Welsh Poetry*, 181-9; M.Lapidge, 'The Welsh-Latin poetry of Sulien's family', *Studia Celtica*, VIII-IX (1973-4), 68-106.

49. See also Williams, *Beginnings of Welsh Poetry*, 41-69, 122-54.

50. See K.H.Jackson, *The Gododdin* (1969), 3-67, 86-91.

51. I.Williams, *Lectures on Early Welsh Poetry* (Dublin, 1944); *idem*, *Beginnings of Welsh Poetry*, 41-9; Jackson, *Gododdin*, 86-91; T.M.Charles-Edwards, 'The authenticity of the *Gododdin*: an historian's view', in *Astudiaethau ar yr Hengerdd*, ed. R.Bromwich and R.B.Jones (1978), 44-71. E.P.Hamp, 'On dating and archaism in the *Pedeir Keinc*', *Trans. Hon. Soc. Cymmrodorion* (1972-3), 98, in a different context, is very good on the metrical problems of incorporating archaisms.

52. Williams, *Lectures; idem, Beginnings of Welsh Poetry*, 122-54; A.O.H.Jarman, 'Saga Poetry — the cycle of Llywarch Hen', in *A Guide to Welsh Literature*, I, ed. A.O.H.Jarman and G.R.Hughes (1976), 81-97, is very good on the significance of the shame motif; cf. Charles-Edwards, 'The authenticity of the *Gododdin*', 54-61, on its absence.

53. Jackson, *Gododdin*, 90; Charles-Edwards, 'The authenticity of the *Gododdin*', 66.

54. D.Dumville, 'Palaeographical considerations in the dating of early Welsh verse', *BBCS*, XXVII (1976-8), 246-52; D.Greene, 'Linguistic considerations in the dating of early Welsh verse', *Studia Celtica*, VI (1971), 1-11; cf. K.H.Jackson, 'Some questions in dispute about early Welsh literature', *Studia Celtica*, VIII-IX (1973-4), 1-32.

55. Cf. Jackson, *Gododdin*, 62.

56. Williams, *Beginnings of Welsh Poetry*, 155-72.

57. See above, p.114.

58. Bromwich, *TYP*, 471-2; Bromwich's note in Williams, *Beginnings of Welsh Poetry*, 125; A.O.H.Jarman, 'Early stages in the development of the Myrddin legend', in Bromwich and Jones (eds.), 326-49.

59. *Armes Prydein*, xii-xx.

60. T.M.Charles-Edwards, 'The date of the four branches of the Mabinogi', *Trans. Hon. Soc. Cymmrodorion* (1970), 263-98; Hamp, 'On dating and archaism in the *Pedeir Keinc*', *Trans. Hon. Soc. Cymmrodorion* (1972-3), 95-103; cf. *idem*, 'Mabinogi', *Trans. Hon. Soc. Cymmrodorion*, (1974-5), 243-9, etc.

61. W.J.Gruffydd, *Math vab Mathonwy* (1928); *idem, Rhiannon* (1953); P.Mac Cana, *Branwen, Daughter of Llŷr* (1958); R.Bromwich, 'The character of the early Welsh tradition', in N.Chadwick *et al., Studies in Early British History* (1954), 83-136; R.S.Loomis (ed.), *Arthurian Literature in the Middle Ages* (1959), 31-43; K.H.Jackson, *The International Popular Tale and Early Welsh Tradition* (1961);

Charles-Edwards, 'The date of the four branches of the Mabinogi'; Hamp, 'Mabinogi', etc.

62. Bromwich, *TYP*.

63. W.M.Lindsay, *Early Welsh Script* (1912), 26-9; Dr D.Dumville at the Celtic Congress, Penzance 1975.

64. See Lindsay, *op. cit.*; Jackson, *Language and History in Early Britain*, 42-59; T.A.M.Bishop, 'The Corpus Martianus Capella', *Trans. Cambridge Bibliographical Soc.*, IV (1964-8), 257-9.

65. W. Stokes 'The Welsh glosses and verses in the Cambridge Codex of Juvencus', *Trans. Philological Soc.* (1860-1), 204ff.; Bishop, *op. cit.*, 258.

66. W.Stokes, 'The Old Welsh glosses on Martianus Capella, with some notes on Juvencus-glosses', *Beiträge zur vergleichenden Sprachforschung*, ed. A.Kuhn, VII (1873), 385ff.; Bishop, *op. cit.*

67. Stokes, 'The Welsh glosses and verses in the Cambridge Codex of Juvencus', 234ff.; R.W.Hunt, *St Dunstan's Classbook from Glastonbury: Codex Bibl. Bodl. Oxon. Auct.F. 4.32* (Umbrae Codicum Occidentalium, 1961).

68. Personal comments from Dr M.Parkes and Dr D.Dumville.

69. I.Williams, 'Glosau Rhydychen: mesurau a phwysau', *BBCS*, V (1929-31), 226-48; *idem*, 'Notes on Nennius', *BBCS*, VII (1935), 380-3; Lindsay, *op. cit.*, 7.

70. I.Williams, 'The Computus Fragment', *BBCS*, III (1926-7), 256f.

71. S.Harris, 'The Kalendar of the Vitae Sanctorum Wallensium', *J.Hist. Soc. Church in Wales*, III (1953), 3-53.

72. Hughes, 'British Museum MS Cotton Vespasian A.xiv', 183-7.

73. Lawlor (ed.), *op. cit.*

74. D.Whitelock, *The Genuine Asser* (1968); H.C.Darby and I.S.Maxwell (eds.), *The Domesday Geography of Northern England* (1962); H.C.Darby and I.B.Terrett (eds.), *The Domesday Geography of Midland England* (1954).

75. Hughes, *Early Christian Ireland*, 99-162; A.P.Smyth, 'The earliest Irish annals: their first contemporary entries, and the earliest centres of recording',

Procs. Royal Irish Academy, LXXII, C (1972), 1-48.

76. Wasserschleben (ed.), *op. cit.*; R.I.Best and H.J.Lawlor (eds.), *The Martyrology of Tallaght* (Henry Bradshaw Soc. 68, 1931); W.Stokes (ed.), *The Martyrology of Oengus the Culdee* (Henry Bradshaw Soc. 29, 1905); Hughes, *Early Christian Ireland*, 67-95, 205-9.

77. See above, pp.207f.

78. J-C.Poulin, 'Hagiographie et Politique. La première vie de S.Samson de Dol', *Francia*, v (1977), 1-26.

79. F.Duine, 'La vie de S.Samson, à propos d'un ouvrage récent', *Annales de Bretagne*, XXVIII (1912-13), 332-56.

80. G.O.Pierce, *The Place-Names of Dinas Powys Hundred* (1968); B.G.Charles, *Non-Celtic Place-Names in Wales* (1938), are especially valuable. For detailed references to local studies see *Bibliography of the History of Wales* and *BBCS*, v (1929-31), 249-64.

81. M.Richards, 'Hafod and hafoty in Welsh place-names', *Montgomeryshire Collns*, LVI (1959-61), 13-20; *idem*, 'Irish settlements in south-west Wales: a topographical approach', *J.Royal*

Soc. Antiquaries Ireland, XC (1960), 133-52; *idem*, 'Early Welsh territorial suffixes', *J.Royal Soc. Antiquaries Ireland*, XCV (1965), 205-12; *idem*, 'Ecclesiastical and secular in medieval Welsh settlement', *Studia Celtica*, III (1968), 9-18; *idem*, *Welsh Administrative and Territorial Units* (1969); *idem*, 'Places and persons of the early Welsh church', *Welsh Hist. Rev.*, V (1971), 333-49; M.Gelling, W.F.H.Nicolaisen and M.Richards, *The Names of Towns and Cities in Britain*, ed. W.Nicolaisen (1970).

82. Jackson, *Language and History in Early Britain*; cf. D.Greene, 'Some linguistic evidence relating to the British church', in Barley and Hanson (eds.), *op. cit.*

83. *ECMW*.

84. *Arch. Camb.*, CXIX (1970), 68-74; *ibid.*, CXXVI (1977), 60-73, etc.

85. Williams, *The Beginnings of Welsh Poetry*, 25-40.

86. Sir Cyril Fox, *Offa's Dyke* (1955); D.Hill, 'Offa's and Wat's Dykes —some exploratory work on the frontier between Celt and Saxon', in *Anglo-Saxon Settlement and Landscape*, ed. T.Rowley (BAR 6, 1974), 102-7; *Med. Arch.*, XXI (1977), 219-22.

87. See above, pp.27f., for example.

Bibliography

Alcock, L., 'Dark age objects of Irish origin from the Lesser Garth Cave, Glamorgan', *BBCS*, xviii (1958-60), 221-7
— *Dinas Powys* (1963)
— 'Pottery and settlements in Wales and the March, A.D.400-700', in *Culture and Environment*, ed. I.Ll. Foster and L.Alcock (1963), 281-302
— 'Excavations at Degannwy Castle, Caernarvonshire, 1961-6', *Arch.J.*, cxxiv (1967), 190-201
— *Arthur's Britain* (1971)
— 'Dry bones and living documents', in *The Effect of Man on the Landscape: The Highland Zone*, ed. J.G.Evans, S.Limbrey and H.Cleere (1975), 117-22
Anderson, A.O. and M. (eds.), *Adomnan's Life of Columba* (1961)
Annals of Loch Cé, ed. W.M.Hennessy (Rolls Series, 54, 2 vols., 1871)
Annals of Ulster, ed. W.M.Hennessy (Rolls Series, 2 vols., 1887)
Armes Prydein, ed. I.Williams, trans. R.Bromwich (Dublin, 1972)
The Anglo-Saxon Chronicle, trans. and ed. D.Whitelock with D.C.Douglas and S.I. Tucker (1961)
Attenborough, F.L. (ed.), *The Laws of the Earliest English Kings* (1922)
Baring-Gould, S. and Fisher, J., *The Lives of the British Saints* (4 vols., 1907-13)
Barley, M.W. and Hanson, R.P.C. (eds.), *Christianity in Britain, 300-700* (1968)
Bartrum, P.C. (ed.), *Early Welsh Genealogical Tracts* (1966)
Biddle, M., 'The development of the Anglo-Saxon town', *Settimane di Studio del Centro italiano di Studi sull'alto medioevo*, xxi (1974), 203-30
Bieler, L.(ed.), *The Irish Penitentials* (Dublin, 1963)
Binchy, D., *Celtic and Anglo-Saxon Kingship* (1970)
Birch, W.de Gray, *Cartularium Saxonicum* (3 vols., 1885-93)
Bishop, T.A.M., 'The Corpus Martianus Capella', *Trans. Cambridge Bibliographical Soc.*, iv (1964-8), 257-75
Bowen, E.G., *The Settlements of the Celtic Saints in Wales* (2nd edn 1956)
— (ed.), *Wales, A Physical, Historical and Regional Geography* (1957)
— and Gresham, C.A., *History of Merioneth*, I (1967)
Bowen, H.C. and Fowler, P.J. (eds.), *Early Land Allotment in the British Isles* (BAR 48, 1978)
'Branwen', *Mabinogion*, 25-40; and *Branwen Uerch Lyr*, ed. D.S.Thomson (Dublin, 1961)
Bromwich, R., 'The character of the early Welsh tradition', in N.Chadwick *et al.*, *Studies in Early British History* (1954), 83-136
— *Trioedd Ynys Prydein* (1961)
Brooke, C.N.L., 'St Peter of Gloucester and St Cadoc of Llancarfarn', in N.Chadwick *et al.*, *Celt and Saxon* (1963), 258-322
Brut y Tywysogyon, Red Book of Hergest Version, ed. and trans. T.Jones (1955); *Brut y Tywysogyon, Peniarth MS 20*, ed. T.Jones (1941); *Brut y Tywysogyon, Peniarth MS 20 Version*, trans. T.Jones (1952)
Canu Aneirin, ed. I.Williams (1938); trans. K.Jackson, *The Gododdin* (1969)
'Canu Heledd', *Canu Llywarch Hen*, 33-48; trans. J.Clancy, *The Earliest Welsh Poetry* (1970), 79-86
Canu Llywarch Hen, ed. I.Williams (1935); trans. J.Clancy, *The Earliest Welsh Poetry* (1970), 65-78, 92-7, and P.K.Ford, *The Poetry of Llywarch Hen* (Berkeley, Cal., 1974)
Canu Taliesin, ed. I.Williams (1960); edition (but not poems) trans. J.Caerwyn Williams (Dublin, 1968); poems translated partly by J.Clancy, *The Earliest Welsh Poetry* (1970), 23-32, and no.I by I.Ll.Foster, *Prehistoric and Early Wales*, ed. I.Ll.Foster and G.Daniel (1965), 229-30
Casey, P.J. (ed.), *The End of Roman Britain* (BAR 71, 1979)

Chadwick, O., 'The evidence of dedications in the early history of the Welsh church', in N.Chadwick *et al.*, *Studies in Early British History* (1954), 173-88

Chadwick, N., 'Intellectual contacts between Britain and Gaul in the fifth century', in N.Chadwick *et al.*, *Studies in Early British History* (1954), 189-263

— 'The conversion of Northumbria', in N.Chadwick *et al.*, *Celt and Saxon* (1963), 138-66

Charles, B.G., *Old Norse Relations with Wales* (1934)

— *Non-Celtic Place-Names in Wales* (1938)

Charles-Edwards, T.M., 'The date of the four branches of the Mabinogi', *Trans. Hon. Soc. Cymmrodorion* (1970), 263-98

— 'Some Celtic kinship terms', *BBCS*, xxiv (1970-2), 105-22

— 'The seven bishop-houses of Dyfed', *BBCS*, xxiv (1970-2), 247-62

— 'Native political organization in Roman Britain and the origin of MW *brenhin*', in *Antiquitates Indogermanicae*, ed. M.Mayrhofer, W.Meid, B.Schlerath, R.Schmitt (Innsbruck, 1974), 35-45

— 'Nei, Keifn, and Kefynderw', *BBCS*, xxv (1972-4), 386-8

— 'The social background to Irish *peregrinatio*', *Celtica*, xi (1975-6), 43-59

— 'The authenticity of the *Gododdin*: an historian's view', in *Astudiaethau ar yr Hengerdd*, ed. R.Bromwich and R.B.Jones (1978), 44-71

Chronicon ex Chronicis. Florence of Worcester, *Chronicon ex Chronicis*, ed. B.Thorpe (2 vols., 1848-9)

Clancy, J., *The Earliest Welsh Poetry* (1970)

Conway Davies, J., *Episcopal Acts and Cognate Documents relating to Welsh Dioceses, 1066-1272* (2 vols., 1946-8)

'Culhwch', *Mabinogion*, 95-136; J.R.Evans (ed.), *The White Book Mabinogion* (1907), 226-54

Darby, H.C. and Maxwell, I.S. (eds.), *The Domesday Geography of Northern England* (1962)

Darby, H.C. and Terrett, I.B. (eds.), *The Domesday Geography of Midland England* (1954)

Darby, H.C. and Welldon Finn, R. (eds.), *The Domesday Geography of South-West England* (1967)

Davies, E., 'Hendre and hafod in Caernarvonshire', *Trans. Caerns. Hist. Soc.*, xl (1979), 17-46

Davies, J.L., Hague, D.B. and Hogg, A.H.A., 'The hut settlement on Gateholm, Pembrokeshire', *Arch. Camb.*, cxx (1971), 102-10

Davies, M.H., 'A palaeographical and textual study of the text of the Annales Cambriae in BL Harley MS 3859' (M.A. thesis, University of Wales, 1978)

Davies, W., *Liber Landavensis*: construction and credibility', *English Hist. Rev.*, lxxxviii (1973), 335-51

— '*Unciae*: land measurement in the *Liber Landavensis*', *AgHR*, xxi (1973), 111-21

— 'The Celtic Church', *J.Religious History*, viii (1974-5), 406-11

— 'Braint Teilo', *BBCS*, xxvi (1974-6), 123-37

— *An Early Welsh Microcosm* (1978)

— 'Land and power in early medieval Wales', *Past and Present*, lxxxi (1978), 3-23

— *The Llandaff Charters* (1979)

— 'Roman settlements and post-Roman estates in south-east Wales', in *The End of Roman Britain*, ed. P.J.Casey (BAR 71, 1979), 153-73

— 'The orthography of personal names in the charters of *Liber Landavensis*', *BBCS*, xxviii (1978-80), 553-7

— 'The Latin charter tradition in western Britain, Brittany and Ireland in the early medieval period', in *Ireland in Medieval Europe*, ed. D.Whitelock, R.McKitterick and D.Dumville (1982), 258-80.

— 'Property rights and property claims in Welsh *Vitae* of the eleventh century', in *Hagiographie, cultures et sociétés*, ed. E.Patlagean and P.Riché (Paris, 1981), 515-33

— and Vierck, H., 'The contexts of Tribal Hidage: social aggregates and settlement patterns', *Frühmittelalterliche Studien*, viii (1974), 223-93

De Excidio Britanniae. Gildas, *The Ruin of Britain*, ed. and trans. M.Winterbottom (1978); and in *Chronica Minora Saec. IV.V.VI.VII*, III, ed. T.Mommsen (MGH AA xiii, Berlin, 1898), 1-110

De Gestis Regum Anglorum. William of Malmesbury, *De Gestis Regum Anglorum*, ed. W.Stubbs (Rolls Series, 90, 2 vols., 1887-9)

'De Raris Fabulis', Oxford Bodleian MS 572, in *Early Scholastic Colloquies*, ed. W.H.Stevenson (1929), 1-11

'De Situ Brecheniauc', *Early Welsh Genealogical Tracts*, ed. P.C. Bartrum (1966), 14-16

Doble, G.H., *The Saints of Cornwall* (1923-44, repr. in 5 vols., 1960-70)

Dolley, R.H.M., *The Hiberno-Norse Coins in the British Museum* (1966)

Domesday Book, seu liber censualis, ed. A.Farley (1783)

Duby, G., *The Early Growth of the European Economy* (1973; trans. 1974)

Duine, F., 'La Vie de S.Samson, à propos d'un ouvrage récent', *Annales de Bretagne*, xxviii (1912-13), 332-56

Dumville, D., 'Some aspects of the chronology of the *Historia Brittonum*', *BBCS*, xxv (1972-4), 439-45

— '"Nennius" and the *Historia Brittonum*', *Studia Celtica*, x-xi (1975-6), 78-95

— 'The Anglian collection of royal genealogies and regnal lists', *Anglo-Saxon England*, v (1976), 23-50

— 'On the north British section of the *Historia Brittonum*', *Welsh Hist. Rev.*, viii (1977), 345-54

— 'Sub-Roman Britain: history and legend', *History*, lxii (1977), 173-92

— 'Palaeographical considerations in the dating of early Welsh verse', *BBCS*, xxvii (1976-8), 246-52

— 'Kingship, genealogies and regnal lists', in *Early Medieval Kingship*, ed. P. Sawyer and I.Wood (1977), 72-104

— 'The aetheling: a study in Anglo-Saxon constitutional history', *Anglo-Saxon England*, viii (1979), 1-34

Edwards, J.G., 'Studies in the Welsh laws since 1928', *Welsh Hist. Rev.*, special vol. (1963), 1-18

Emanuel, H.D., 'An analysis of the composition of the "Vita Cadoci"', *NLW J*, vii (1951-2), 217-27

— 'The Latin texts of the Welsh laws', *Welsh Hist. Rev.*, special vol. (1963), 25-32

— *The Latin Texts of the Welsh Laws* (1967)

Evans, J.G. (ed.), *The White Book Mabinogion* (1907)

Evans, J.G., Limbrey S. and Cleere, H. (eds.), *The Effect of Man on the Landscape: The Highland Zone* (CBA Res. Rep.11, 1975)

'Excerpta Quedam de Libro Dauidis', in *The Irish Penitentials*, ed. L.Bieler (Dublin, 1963), 70-3

Fleuriot, L., 'Les évêques de la "Clas Kenedyr", évêché disparu de la région de Hereford', *Études Celtiques*, xv (1976-7), 225-6

Ford, P.K., *The Poetry of Llywarch Hen* (Berkeley, Cal., 1974)

Foster, I.Ll. and Daniel, G. (eds.), *Prehistoric and Early Wales* (1965)

Fowler, P.J., 'Lowland landscapes: culture, time and *Personality*', in *The Effect of Man on the Landscape: The Lowland Zone*, ed. S.Limbrey and J.G.Evans (CBA Res. Rep.21, 1978), 1-12

Fox, Sir Cyril, *Offa's Dyke* (1955)

Frere, S., *Britannia* (1967)

Gardner, W. and Savory, H., *Dinorben* (1964)

Gelling, M., Nicolaisen, W.F.H. and Richards, M., *The Names of Towns and Cities in Britain*, ed. W.Nicolaisen (1970)

Gesta Regum. See *De Gestis Regum*.

Die Gesetze der Angelsachsen, ed. F.Liebermann (3 vols., Halle, 1903-16).

Green, C.J.S., 'The significance of plaster burials for the recognition of Christian cemeteries', in *Burial in the Roman World*, ed. R.Reece (CBA Res. Rep.22, 1977), 46-53

Greene, D., 'Some linguistic evidence relating to the British church', in *Christianity in Britain, 300-700*, ed. M.Barley and R.Hanson (1968), 75-86

— 'Linguistic considerations in the dating of early Welsh verse', *Studia Celtica*, vi (1971), 1-11

Grosjean, P., 'Remarques sur le *De Excidio* attribué à Gildas', *Archivum Latinitatis*

Medii Aevi, xxv (1955), 155-87

Gruffydd, W.J., *Math vab Mathonwy* (1928)

— *Rhiannon* (1953)

Hague, D.B., 'Whitesands Bay', *CBA Group 2 Report*, x (1970), 27f.

— 'Grassholm', *CBA Group 2 Report*, xii (1972), 40f.

— 'Some Welsh evidence', *Scottish Arch. Forum*, v (1973), 17-35

Hamp, E.P., 'On dating and archaism in the *Pedeir Keinc*', *Trans. Hon. Soc. Cymmrodorion* (1972-3), 95-103

— 'Mabinogi', *Trans. Hon. Soc. Cymmrodorion* (1974-5), 243-9

Harris, S., 'The Kalendar of the *Vitae Sanctorum. Wallensium*', *J.Hist. Soc. Church in Wales*, iii (1953), 3-53

Hill, D., 'Offa's and Wat's Dykes — some exploratory work on the frontier between Celt and Saxon', in *Anglo-Saxon Settlement and Landscape*, ed. T.Rowley (BAR 6, 1974), 102-7

Historia Brittonum. Chronica Minora Saec.IV.V.VI.VII, III, ed. T.Mommsen (MGH AA xiii, Berlin, 1898), 111-222; trans. A.W Wade-Evans, *Nennius's 'History of the Britons'* (1938), 35-84, 114-21

Historia Ecclesiastica Gentis Anglorum, ed. C.Plummer (1896); *Bede's Ecclesiastical History of the English People*, ed. and trans. B.Colgrave and R.A.B.Mynors (1969)

The History of Gruffydd ap Cynan, ed. A.Jones (1910); there is a more recent Welsh edition and commentary: *Historia Gruffud vab Kenan*, ed. D.Simon Evans (1977)

Hogg, A.H.A., 'Native settlement in Wales', in *Rural Settlement in Roman Britain*, ed. C.Thomas (1966), 28-38

Houlder, C., 'The henge monuments at Llandegái', *Antiquity*, xlii (1968), 216-21

Hughes, K., 'British Museum MS Cotton Vespasian A.xiv (''*Vitae Sanctorum Wallensium*''): its purpose and provenance', in N.Chadwick *et al.*, *Studies in the Early British Church* (1958), 183-200

— *The Church in Early Irish Society* (1966)

— *Early Christian Ireland: Introduction to the Sources* (1972)

— 'The Welsh Latin Chronicles: *Annales Cambriae* and related texts', *Procs. British Academy*, lix (1973), 3-28

— and Hamlin, A., *The Modern Traveller to the Early Irish Church* (1977)

Hunt, R.W., *St Dunstan's Classbook from Glastonbury: Codex Bibl. Bodl. Oxon. Auct.F. 4.32* (Umbrae Codicum Occidentalium, 1961)

Huws, D., 'Leges Howelda at Canterbury', *NLW J*, xix (1975-6), 340-4

— *The Medieval Codex* (1980)

Jackson, K.H., *Language and History in Early Britain* (1953)

— *The International Popular Tale and Early Welsh Tradition* (1961)

— 'On the northern British section in Nennius', in N.Chadwick *et al.*, *Celt and Saxon* (1963), 20-62

— *The Gododdin* (1969)

— 'Some questions in dispute about early Welsh literature', *Studia Celtica*, viii-ix (1973-4), 1-32

James, T., *Carmarthen, an Archaeological and Topographical Survey* (1980)

Jarman, A.O.H., 'Saga Poetry — the cycle of Llywarch Hen', in *A Guide to Welsh Literature*, I, ed. A.O.H.Jarman and G.R.Hughes (1976), 81-97

— 'Early stages in the development of the Myrddin legend', *Astudiaethau ar yr Hengerdd*, ed. R.Bromwich and R.B.Jones (1978), 326-49

Jenkins, D. and Owen, M.E. (eds.), *The Welsh Law of Women* (1980)

Johns, C.W., 'The Celtic monasteries of north Wales', *Trans. Caerns. Hist. Soc.*,xxi (1960), 14-43

Johnson, N., 'Location of pre-medieval fields in Caernarvonshire', in *Early Land Allotment in the British Isles*, ed. H.C.Bowen and P.J.Fowler (BAR 48, 1978), 127-32

Jones, A.H.M., *The Later Roman Empire, 284-602* (4 vols., 1964)

Jones, F., *The Holy Wells of Wales* (1954)

Jones, G.R., 'The pattern of settlement on the Welsh border', *AgHR*, viii (1960), 66-81

— 'Post-Roman Wales', in *The Agrarian History of England and Wales*, I pt 2, ed. H.P.R.Finberg (1972), 283-382

— 'Multiple estates and early settlement', in *Medieval Settlement*, ed. P.H. Sawyer (1976), 15-40

Jones, J.F., 'Llanllwni ''crouched burial''', *Carmarthen Antiquary*, CXI (1961), 207

Jones, T., 'The Black Book of Carmarthen ''Stanzas of the Graves''', *Procs. British Academy*, LIII (1967), 97-138

The Journey through Wales. Gerald of Wales, *The Journey through Wales, The Description of Wales*, trans. L.Thorpe (1978); and *Giraldi Cambrensis Opera*, VI, ed. J.F.Dimock (Rolls Series, 1868)

Kenney, J.F., *Sources for the Early History of Ireland: Ecclesiastical* (Columbia, 1929)

Kerlouégan, F., 'Le Latin du *De Excidio Britanniae* de Gildas', in *Christianity in Britain, 300-700*, ed. M.Barley and R.Hanson (1968), 151-76

Kirby, D., 'A note on Rhigyfarch's *Life of David*', *Welsh Hist. Rev.*, IV (1968-9), 292-7

— 'Hywel Dda: Anglophil?', *Welsh Hist. Rev.*, VII (1976-7), 1-13

— 'Welsh bards and the border', in *Mercian Studies*, ed. A.Dornier (1977), 31-42

Knowles, D. and Hadcock, R.N., *Medieval Religious Houses, England and Wales* (2nd edn 1971)

L.Laing (ed.), *Studies in Celtic Survival* (1977)

Lamb, H.H., *Climate, Present, Past and Future* (2 vols., 1972, 1977)

Lapidge, M., 'The Welsh-Latin poetry of Sulien's family', *Studia Celtica*, VIII-IX (1973-4), 68-106

Le Roy Ladurie, E., *Times of Feast, Times of Famine: a History of Climate since the year 1000* (trans. 1972)

Lewis, J.M., 'A survey of the early Christian monuments of Dyfed west of the Taf', in *Welsh Antiquity*, ed. G.C.Boon and J.M.Lewis (1976), 177-92

Liber Landavensis. The Text of the Book of Llan Dâv, ed. J.G.Evans with J.Rhys (1893)

Liebeschutz, W., 'Did the Pelagian movement have social aims?', *Historia*, XII (1963), 227-41

Limbrey, S. and Evans, J.G. (eds.), *The Effect of Man on the Landscape: The Lowland Zone* (CBA Res. Rep. 21, 1978)

Lindsay, W.M., *Early Welsh Script* (1912)

Linnard, W., 'The history of forests and forestry in Wales up to the formation of the Forestry Commission' (Ph.D. thesis, University of Wales, 1979)

Lloyd, J.E., *A History of Wales from the Earliest Times to the Edwardian Conquest* (1911)

Llyfr Blegywryd. Cyfreithiau Hywel Dda yn ôl Llyfr Blegywryd, ed. S.J.Williams and J.E.Powell (1942); *The Laws of Hywel Dda (The Book of Blegywryd)*, trans. M. Richards (1954)

Llyfr Cyfnerth. Ancient Laws and Institutes of Wales, ed. A.Owen (1841); one text is translated by A.W. Wade-Evans, *Welsh Medieval Law* (1909)

Llyfr Iorwerth, ed. A.R.Wiliam (1960)

Loomis, R.S. (ed.), *Arthurian Literature in the Middle Ages* (1959)

Loyn, H.R., *The Vikings in Wales* (1976)

— *The Vikings in Britain* (1977)

Lynch, F., 'Report on the re-excavation of two bronze age cairns in Anglesey', *Arch. Camb.*, CXX (1971), 11-18

The Mabinogion, trans. G. and T.Jones (1949); and *Pedeir Keinc y Mabinogi*, ed. I.Williams (1951)

Mac Cana, P., *Branwen, Daughter of Llŷr* (1958)

'Manawydan', *Mabinogion*, 41-54

The Martyrology of Oengus the Culdee, ed. W.Stokes (Henry Bradshaw Soc. 29, 1905)

The Martyrology of Tallaght, ed. R.I.Best and H.J.Lawlor (Henry Bradshaw Soc. 68, 1931)

'Marwnad Cynddylan', in *Canu Llywarch Hen*, 50-2; trans. J.Clancy, *The Earliest Welsh Poetry* (1970), 87-9

'Math', *Mabinogion*, 55-75

McWhirr, A. (ed.), *The Archaeology and History of Cirencester* (BAR 30, 1976)

Miller, M., 'Relative and absolute publication dates of Gildas's *De Excidio* in medieval scholarship', *BBCS*, xxvi (1974-6), 169-74
— 'Historicity and the pedigrees of the Northcountrymen', *BBCS*, xxvi (1974-6), 255-80
— 'Date-guessing and pedigrees', *Studia Celtica*, x-xi (1975-6), 96-109
— 'Date-guessing and Dyfed', *Studia Celtica*, xii-xiii (1977-8), 33-61
— 'The foundation-legend of Gwynedd in the Latin texts', *BBCS*, xxvii (1976-8), 515-32
— *The Saints of Gwynedd* (1979)
Morris, J., 'Pelagian literature', *J.Theological Studies*, n.s.xvi (1965), 25-60
— *The Age of Arthur* (1973)
Myres, J., 'Pelagius and the end of Roman rule in Britain', *J.Roman Studies*, L (1960), 21-36
Nash-Williams, V.E., *The Early Christian Monuments of Wales* (1950)
— *The Roman Frontier in Wales* (2nd edn, ed. M.Jarrett, 1969)
O'Corráin, D., 'Irish regnal succession', *Studia Hibernica*, xi (1971), 7-39
O'Riain, P., 'The Irish element in Welsh hagiographical tradition', in *Irish Antiquity*, ed. D.O'Corráin (forthcoming)
O'Sullivan, T.D., *The De Excidio of Gildas, its Authenticity and Date* (Leiden, 1978)
Owen, A. (ed.), *Ancient Laws and Institutes of Wales* (1841)
Page, W. (ed.), *Victoria History of the County of Hereford*, I (1908)
Phillimore, E., 'The *Annales Cambriae* and Old Welsh genealogies', *Y Cymmrodor*, ix (1888), 152-9.
Phillips, E., 'Modrydaf', *BBCS*, xxv (1972-4), 119f.
Pierce, G.O., *The Place-Names of Dinas Powys Hundred* (1968)
Poulin, J-C., 'Hagiographie et Politique. La première vie de S.Samson de Dol', *Francia*, v (1977), 1-26
'Praefatio Gildae de Poenitentia', in *The Irish Penitentials*, ed. L.Bieler (Dublin, 1963), 60-5
The Psalter and Martyrology of Ricemarch, ed. H.J.Lawlor (Henry Bradshaw Soc., 47, 1914)
'Pwyll', *Mabinogion*, 3-24
Radford, C.A.R., 'St Justinian's Chapel', *Arch.J.*, cxix (1962), 335
Rahtz, P.A., 'Late Roman cemeteries and beyond', in *Burial in the Roman World*, ed. R.Reece (CBA Res. Rep. 22, 1977), 53-64
— and Watts, L., 'The end of Roman temples in the west of Britain', in *The End of Roman Britain*, ed. P.J.Casey (BAR 71, 1979), 183-201
RCAHMW, *Inventory of Ancient Monuments in Wales and Monmouthshire, Anglesey* (1937)
RCAHMW, *Inventory of Ancient Monuments in Wales and Monmouthshire, Caernarvonshire* (3 vols., 1956-64)
RCAHMW, *Inventory of Ancient Monuments in Wales and Monmouthshire, Glamorgan*, I, pts 1 and 3 (1976)
RCAHMW, *Inventory of Ancient Monuments in Wales and Monmouthshire, Radnor* (1913)
Reece, R. and Catling, C., *Cirencester* (BAR 12, 1975)
Registrum vulgariter nuncupatum 'The Record of Caernarvon', ed. H.Ellis (1838)
M.Richards, 'Hafod and hafoty in Welsh place-names', *Montgomeryshire Collns*, LVI (1959-61), 13-20
— 'Irish settlements in south-west Wales: a topographical approach', *J.Royal Soc. Antiquaries Ireland*, xc (1960), 133-62
— 'Norse place-names in Wales', *Procs. Int. Congress Celtic Studies* (Dublin, 1962), 51-60
— 'Early Welsh territorial suffixes', *J.Royal Soc. Antiquaries Ireland*, xcv (1965), 205-12
— 'Ecclesiastical and secular in medieval Welsh settlement', *Studia Celtica*, iii (1968), 9-18
— *Welsh Administrative and Territorial Units* (1969)
— 'Places and persons of the early Welsh church', *Welsh Hist. Rev.*, v (1971), 333-49
Richter, M., *Giraldus Cambrensis. The Growth of the Welsh Nation* (1972)

—'The political and institutional background to national consciousness in medieval Wales', in *Nationality and the Pursuit of National Independence*, ed. T.W.Moody (1978), 37-55.

Robertson, A.J. (ed), *Anglo-Saxon Charters* (1939)

St Patrick, His Writings and Muirchu's Life, ed. and trans. A.Hood (1978)

Sancti Columbani Opera, ed. G.S.M.Walker (Scriptores Latini Hiberniae, Dublin, 1957)

Simpson, G., 'Caerleon and the Roman forts in Wales in the second century A.D.', 2 pts, *Arch. Camb.*, CXI (1962), 103-66; CXII (1963), 13-76

—*Britons and the Roman Army* (1964)

'Sinodus Aquilonalis Britaniae', in *The Irish Penitentials*, ed. L.Bieler (Dublin, 1963), 66

'Sinodus Luci Victorie', in *The Irish Penitentials*, ed. L.Bieler (Dublin, 1963), 68

Smith, C.A., 'A morphological analysis of late prehistoric and Romano-British settlements in north-west Wales', *PPS*, XL (1974), 157-69

—'Late prehistoric and Romano-British enclosed homesteads in north-west Wales', *Arch. Camb.*, CXXVI (1977), 38-52

Smyth, A.P., 'The earliest Irish annals: their first contemporary entries, and the earliest centres of recording', *Procs. Royal Irish Academy*, LXXII, C (1972), 1-48

—*Scandinavian Kings in the British Isles, 850-880* (1977)

Stephenson, D., *Thirteenth-Century Welsh Law Courts* (1980)

Stevenson, W.H. (ed.), *Asser's Life of King Alfred* (1904)

Stokes, W., 'The Welsh glosses and verses in the Cambridge Codex of Juvencus, The Old-Welsh glosses at Oxford', *Trans.Philological Soc.* (1860-1), 204-49, 288-93

—'The Old-Welsh glosses on Martianus Capella, with some notes on Juvencus-Glosses', *Beiträge zur vegleichenden Sprachforschung*, ed. A.Kuhn, VII (1873), 385-416

Taylor, J., 'The role of climatic factors in environmental and cultural changes in prehistoric times', in *The Effect of Man on the Landscape: the Highland Zone*, ed. J.G.Evans, S.Limbrey and H.Cleere (CBA Res. Rep.11, 1975), 6-19

Taylor, H.M. and Taylor, J., *Anglo-Saxon Architecture* (1965)

Thomas, C. (ed.), *Rural Settlement in Roman Britain* (1966)

—'An early Christian cemetery and chapel on Ardwall Isle, Kirkcudbright', *Med. Arch.*, XI (1967), 127-88

—'The evidence from North Britain', in *Christianity in Britain, 300-700*, ed. M.Barley and R.Hanson (1968), 93-121

—*The Early Christian Archaeology of North Britain* (1971)

—'Irish settlements in post-Roman western Britain', *J.Royal Inst. Cornwall*, VI (1972), 4, 251-74

—'Imported Late Roman Mediterranean pottery in Ireland and western Britain: chronologies and implications', *Procs. Royal Irish Academy*, LXXVI, C (1976), 245-55

Thomas, D. (ed.), *Wales, A New Study* (1977)

Thompson, J.D.A., *Inventory of British Coin Hoards, A.D.600-1500* (1956)

Thomson, D.S. (ed.), *Branwen Uerch Lyr* (Dublin, 1961)

Ucko, P.J., Tringham, R. and Dimbleby, G.W. (eds.), *Man, Settlement and Urbanism* (1972)

Victory, S., *The Celtic Church in Wales* (1977)

Vita Bernacii, Vitae Sanctorum Britanniae 2-14

Vita Cadoci, Vitae Sanctorum Britanniae, 24-140

Vita Carantoci, Vitae Sanctorum Britanniae, 142-8

Vita Gundleii, Vitae Sanctorum Britanniae, 172-92

Vita Iltuti, Vitae Sanctorum Britanniae, 194-232

Vita Kebii, Vitae Sanctorum Britanniae, 234-50

Vita Machutis, 'La plus ancienne vie de S.Malo', in F.Lot, *Mélanges d'histoire Bretonne* (Paris, 1907), 294-329

Vita Paterni, Vitae Sanctorum Britanniae, 252-68

Vita Pauli, 'Vie de S.Paul de Léon en Bretagne', ed. C.Cuissard, *Revue Celtique*, V (1881-3), 413-60

254 Wales in the Early Middle Ages

Vita Samsonis, La Vie de S.Samson, ed. R.Fawtier (Paris, 1912); trans. T.Taylor,
   The Life of St Samson of Dol (1925)
Vitae Sanctorum Britanniae et Genealogiae, ed. A.W.Wade-Evans (1944)
Vita S. Dauid. Rhigyfarch's Life of St David, ed. J.W.James (1967); trans.
   A.W.Wade-Evans, Y Cymmrodor, xxiv (1913), 1-73
Vita Tathei, Vitae Sanctorum Britanniae, 270-86
Vita Wenefrede, Vitae Sanctorum Britanniae, 288-308
Wade-Evans, A.W., Welsh Medieval Law (1909)
— Welsh Christian Origins (1934)
— Nennius's 'History of the Britons' (1938)
Wasserschleben, H. (ed.), Die Irische Kanonensammlung (2nd edn, Leipzig, 1885)
White, R.B., 'Excavations at Arfryn, Bodedern, long-cist cemeteries and the origins
   of Christianity in Britain', Trans. Anglesey Antiq. Soc. and Field Club (1971-2),
   19-51
— Early Christian Gwynedd (1975)
— 'New light on the origins of the kingdom of Gwynedd', in Astudiaethau ar yr
   Hengerdd, ed. R.Bromwich and R.B.Jones (1978)
Whitelock, D., The Genuine Asser (1968)
Williams, I., 'The Computus Fragment', BBCS, iii (1926-7), 245-72
— 'Glosau Rhydychen: mesurau a phwysau', BBCS, v (1929-31), 226-48
— 'Notes on Nennius', BBCS, vii (1933-5), 380-9
— Lectures on Early Welsh Poetry (Dublin, 1944)
— The Beginnings of Welsh Poetry, ed. and trans. R.Bromwich (1972)
Winterbottom, M., 'The preface of Gildas' de Excidio', Trans. Hon. Soc.
   Cymmrodorion (1974-5), 277-87

Index

For ease of reference by non-Welsh readers this index is arranged in English alphabetical order; Welsh dd, ll, rh are each therefore treated as two separate letters. Pre-1974 county names have been used for identification throughout.